BAD B*TCH IN THE KITCH

CASSIE YEUNG
BAD B*TCH

Clarkson Potter/Publishers
New York
Photographs by Jenny Huang

IN THE KITCH

Craveable Asian Recipes to Ditch the Takeout

Introduction   8

GET IN, BESTIES, WE'RE GOING SHOPPING   12

DON'T TRIP, GET EQUIPPED   24

FIRST BITE, BESTIES   28

NOODZ   70

SKIP THE TAKEOUT   98

Acknowledgments 264
Index 267

TASTE OF SINGAPORE
130

YUM TONG
160

EAT YOUR VEGGIES
182

NOT TOO SWEET
210

WHOLE LOTTA BASICS
236

INTRODUCTION

Whenever I'm asked about my journey with cooking, content creation, or entrepreneurship, my first instinct is to steal a line from The Queen. I'm talking about the OG baddie herself, Britney Spears—*this is a story about a girl named Lucky*. It all started with a passion for cooking, a cheap ring light, and a dream. I truly believe I got lucky and grew my following by posting what was (and still is) authentic to me, like a hangover ramen or beef and broccoli after a long nap. Millions of online besties later, I like to think of myself as a chef for the people—no professional culinary training or commercial restaurant experience here, just a girl who followed her mom around the kitchen and really loves to cook (and eat, duh). Lucky for me, this is very relatable. And I quickly realized it's one of the reasons people enjoy learning recipes from a home cook, someone not so different from who they are.

Before I was a social media chef, I spent my entire life thinking I was going to be a professional dancer. I *lived*, *breathed*, and *ate* dance like nothing else existed. I started competing at the young age of five, then continued all the way through college at Rutgers University. I gained some independence when I went off to college, but my parents were nearby and my mom's home-cooked meals were always calling me on speed-dial. I wasn't raised on takeout—my mom cooked every single night and I shadowed her around the kitchen. She was born and raised in Singapore, where she helped take care of her eight siblings (I know, right, nine kids). One of her jobs was to feed the family, and she cooked almost every meal. And watching her in our family kitchen, I fell in love with cooking.

Once I graduated in 2016, I auditioned and earned a spot on the esteemed NBA Brooklynettes. This made me fall in love with everything Brooklyn had to offer, but I'm a Jersey girl at heart. I commuted from my family home in NJ and didn't leave the nest until I moved to California at twenty-three to be with an awful excuse of a boyfriend (yuck, we won't even get into that). Living across the country was the first time I really experienced freedom, and this was where my love for cooking began to skyrocket. My mom was no longer there to make my favorite meals, so I started reimagining them and crushing every craving from my own kitchen.

While I was there, I still wanted to be a dancer, but you know how things go—while my heart was on the stage, my butt landed in a full-time desk job as an IT finance budget analyst (who was she?) *and* a part-time job as an indoor cycling and group fitness instructor. I started finding joy in teaching fitness. I also began making my own sourdough bread, and I would bring the hard-earned results to my fitness clients (will do squats for bread!).

I discovered my independence in California, and it taught me that if I wanted something bad enough, I had to *really* go after it. Eventually I realized my future didn't reside there or in either of the fields I was working in.

Right before my sister was married, I moved back to the East Coast to be closer to my family. This meant moving in with my parents and I felt a little lost. The one thing that I was consistently passionate about and that had always brought me joy was *cooking*. I had already started to play around with editing and posting videos in California, and that's what gave me the idea to become a content creator. I was ready to jump in, so I had the dreaded conversation with my traditional Asian parents, who always wanted me to take the established route of going to school, earning a degree, and getting a high-paying job. They (surprisingly) took the idea very well—and they also gave me a three-month timeline to prove to them that this could work. If it didn't?

I'd have to get a full-time "conventional" job. That was enough for me to put all of my energy into this idea so I could prove to myself and to them that it was more than a dream (and let's be real—it was also an incentive to move out!).

So, I made a TikTok account and got right to it. Instead of trying to replicate other content using ASMR, aesthetic overhead shots, and voiceovers, I found my style: speaking to my audience like we were besties on FaceTime. Just by being authentically myself, a hundred followers quickly turned into five hundred, then into one thousand when I started to post recipes. But it was a video of me cooking ramen with a hangover the day after my sister's wedding that took things to the next level. When it went viral, it clicked for me that people craved real content and that I didn't need to try to be anything or anyone but myself. I started posting more instructional videos and recipes that were far from polished—I made mistakes (like missing the pot entirely when pouring in a sauce or forgetting ingredients), I used unconventional techniques (like using a chopstick to check the temperature of frying oil and warming butter in my bra!), and I cooked with long-ass stiletto nails (you have a problem with that?). Instead of trying to fit the mold of what people *thought* a chef should look and act like, I showed people that you can be a *bad b*tch in the kitch*.

Not long after, I heard from an agent who said they were casting for a Gordon Ramsay TV show. Naturally, I thought it was spam because why would Gordon Ramsay want me?? Shortly after, I received an email, and before I knew it, I was selected as a contestant for season two of Fox's *Next Level Chef*. I had all but a few days to prepare and pack my bags for London, where filming took place. I won't spoil it for you, but most important, I gained so much knowledge from three amazing mentors and my fellow contestants. I like to think it was an accelerated culinary school. And if I did one thing right, it was represent my heritage well and that was the biggest win. Oh! And they let me say "You can't keep a bad b*tch down too long" on national television, which is huge since those are words I abide by.

I might not be a "professional," but I believe cooking shouldn't be intimidating or so strict. When you cook in your own kitchen you can make your own rules, and I believe rule number one is to have fun! Why can't you yell "behind!" in your own kitchen or show off your baddie nails as you pleat dumplings *like a boss*? The best food sometimes comes from letting loose and cooking the way you want to, and the way that feels good to YOU.

When I cook, it's usually Asian food, because that's what feels good to me—it's what I crave, what I grew up with, and it's just damn delicious, too! So many people know and love Asian cuisine but don't always know how easy it can be to re-create their favorite dishes at home. So let me be your Asian bad b*tch auntie—I'll share some of my favorite Asian recipes, many of them that originated from my family, and with high hopes of making them less intimidating for you to make for your besties and fam. We'll be covering the basics, making some apps, getting into noodles, doing a deep dive into takeout dishes, learning about Singaporean recipes that influenced my mom, and of course dishing out soups, veggies, and desserts along the way.

From one baddie to another, let's do this!

For all my visual learners, I thought it'd be helpful to include videos from my channels where it all began. Some recipes include specific techniques that could be better explained with a walk-through. Use a smartphone to scan the QR code associated with a specific recipe, and I'll guide you through it!

GET IN, BESTIES,

WE'RE GOING SHOPPING

PANTRY STAPLES

The question I'm asked the most is *"What Asian pantry basics do I need?!"* So let's start off with the absolute must-haves so you can take a trip to the Asian market and be set up for success. The following ingredients are my most frequently used. Having these on hand will make so many meals possible in a pinch.

Light soy sauce
Pretty predictable and self-explanatory. If there's one thing you *absolutely* need, it's a good soy sauce. My personal fave is Lee Kum Kee's Premium Soy Sauce. Don't be afraid of getting the big-boy 64-ounce size—we'll be using it up!

Dark soy sauce
While it's not *absolutely* make-or-break if you replace dark soy with light soy sauce for a recipe, I find it's the special ingredient in many dishes that make them Instagram worthy. We eat with our eyes first, and dark soy adds a deep color to dishes that make them extra desirable. The flavor is similar to light soy sauce but actually is less salty. My favorites come from the Lee Kum Kee brand, Premium Dark Soy Sauce and Mushroom Flavored Dark Soy Sauce.

Kecap manis
Also known as sweet soy sauce, kecap manis has a much thicker and syrupy consistency than regular light and dark soy sauces. It's popular in Indonesian and other Southeast Asian dishes, so we'll be using it a lot in the chapter of Singaporean recipes! You can find this at most Asian markets or order it online.

Fish sauce
Don't be alarmed by the smell straight from the bottle—fish sauce is the salty, pungent addition that *makes* so many Thai and Vietnamese dishes. The Three Crabs brand is my go-to.

Oyster sauce
This is a thick, dark brown sauce used in many stir-fries and marinades. I use oyster sauce just as much as I use soy sauce, and that says *a lot*. Go for the Lee Kum Kee brand oyster sauce *or* Lee Kum Kee's vegan oyster flavored sauce.

Shaoxing wine
This is the secret to getting that true Chinese takeout flavor—it's a Chinese rose wine that adds a nice deep complexity and punch to stir-fries. You may not be able to distinguish it, but including it in recipes gives them that extra *oomph*. I use the Blooming brand (red label). Note that if you prefer to leave dishes alcohol-free, this can easily be omitted and replaced with chicken or veggie broth.

Rice vinegar
The perfect *twang* as I like to call it. Acidity completes a lot of dishes, and rice vinegar has a mild level of acidity for dressings and sauces compared with white distilled vinegar. I like the Marukan brand.

Mirin
A subtly sweet Japanese rice wine that I like to use in Soy-Marinated Eggs (page 63) and Basic Udon Noodle Soup (page 88). If needed, you can substitute with rice vinegar and a bit of granulated sugar in a pinch.

Curry blocks
These come in clutch when it's time for a quick Chicken Katsu Curry (page 120). The Golden Curry brand in the medium-hot and hot spice levels are my favorite. One package includes two separate curry blocks, each split into four cubes. They're portioned into perforated packs, making them easy to keep on hand. You can find them in any Asian market or order them online.

Toasted sesame oil
The nutty, aromatic finish to any dish. Toasted sesame oil is quite strong, so a little goes a long way. I like Kadoya's sesame oil.

Chili crunch
There are so many chili oils on the market, and while I've tried many, my favorite has remained Laoganma Spicy Chili Crisp. If you love spice and texture, you can add this as the razzle-dazzle to complete any dish.

Gochugaru
So many of my favorite recipes use Korean chili flakes. They are far less spicy than typical red pepper flakes, so they add a subtly sweet and vibrant spice without scorching your palate. I don't have a favorite brand, but I also opt for coarse gochugaru over the fine powder.

Dried chilies
Seems pretty vague, right? But the Chinese dried chili peppers that I use in General Tso's Chicken (page 107) are labeled and sold with the name "Dried Chili," so that's what I'm calling for! These shiny, dried whole red chilies can be fried in oil for that extra spice in dishes or rehydrated in water and pureed to be used in sauces.

Sriracha
I wish I was being dramatic when I say I put sriracha on *everything*. Sriracha doesn't bring a lot of spice, in my opinion, but more of an acidic spicy *flavor*. The OG Rooster (Huy Fong) brand is the best; when you find it, *stock up*.

Tamarind paste
Tamarind paste can easily be mistaken with tamarind concentrate. If using concentrate, make sure to dilute with water according to the package's instructions, and then use the called-for amount after it has been diluted. If you can't find tamarind paste or are in a pinch, you can substitute with 2 tablespoons tomato paste mixed with 1 tablespoon distilled white vinegar.

Palm sugar
Commonly used in Thai recipes, this resembles the flavor of brown sugar (easy sub!). Palm sugar can come in tub/paste form, disks, or cubes. If in a solid form, grate it with a Microplane or shave thin slices using a sharp knife.

Rock sugar
Also known as lump sugar, this adds a subtle amount of sweetness to my 45-Minute Phở Gà (page 92), Oxtail Phở (page 96), and Auntie's Whole Braised Duck (page 152). It can easily be found in Asian markets or online but can be subbed with granulated sugar in a pinch.

Kosher salt
There's so many different types of salt, but Diamond Crystal Kosher Salt is my favorite to use in every recipe. The grains are coarse, aren't overpowering, and have a clean salt flavor.

Chicken bouillon powder
One of my favorite cooking secrets is using chicken bouillon powder as a flavor enhancer in sauces, stir-fries, and soup. My favorite is Lee Kum Kee Chicken Bouillon Powder. I also love their Mushroom Bouillon Powder for a vegetarian option!

Neutral oil
My favorite neutral-flavored oil to cook with is avocado oil—it has the highest smoke point out of all of the oils so it's not likely to burn. This makes it the perfect oil for deep-frying. We love versatility.

SEND NOODZ (and Wrappers!)

When you walk into the noodle section of an Asian market, it's very easy to get overwhelmed by the wide variety. Noodles come in all sizes, shapes, and forms—from egg noodles to rice noodles, wide noodles to extra-thin ones, dried versus fresh, just to name a *few*. You'll also find different types of dumpling and wonton wrappers, spring roll and summer roll wrappers galore, so I'll take you through my favorites. Let's go over my most frequently used and what you'll need for these recipes.

Fresh wide rice noodles (ho fun)
Rice noodles are the main character of some of my favorite dishes, and using fresh noodles truly makes them all that much better. These slippery steamed noodles are amazing for stir-fries like Beef Chow Fun (page 79), Pad See Ew (page 84), and Char Kway Teow (page 142), but they can also be used in soups like my beloved Wonton Soup (page 166). Most Asian markets will have fresh batches in stock in the morning with limited quantities, and yes, they often sell out (and yes, they're really *that* good). They are extremely easy to make homemade (for real—see page 251), and the extra time is worth it.

Pad Thai noodles/rice sticks
When it comes to pad Thai, some stores will offer noodles specifically marked as *Pad Thai Noodles*, but they are simply rice noodles, also called rice sticks. They come in many sizes, but I personally prefer the medium because the small ones are a bit too thin for my liking, while the large (if I'm being honest) don't satisfy my aesthetic needs. Rice noodles are dried and will need to be cooked before stir-frying.

Pho noodles
Pho noodles are thin, fresh rice noodles—they require only a dunk in boiling water and a quick rinse before drinking up that amazing pho broth. Look for the pink packaging for my favorite Sincere Orient Food pho noodles. Dried rice sticks can also be used here.

Lo mein noodles/egg noodles/yellow noodles
Lo mein noodles are thick and sturdy yellow egg noodles. My favorite is the Twin Marquis brand, but if you can't find them, you can use fresh yellow or egg noodles. It's important to note that some noodles are pre-boiled while others are uncooked. Pre-boiled are ready to go—all you need to do is rinse them in hot water to loosen before stir-frying. Uncooked lo mein noodles will need to be boiled for five minutes prior to stir-frying. While they're named lo mein noodles, they can also be used in Hokkien Prawn Mee (page 140) in place of mee hoon noodles.

White noodles
White noodles are doughy, wheat-based Shanghai-style noodles that are beautifully chewy in a soup or stir-fry. They come in thin and thick styles, but I prefer thick. I love using these in Scallion Oil Noodles (page 76), but they can also be used in Hokkien Prawn Mee (page 140) in place of bee hoon noodles. My favorite brand is Twin Marquis Thick Shanghai Style Plain Noodle. These come raw, so you will need to boil them for five minutes before preparing your dish.

Udon
Udon looks very similar to white noodles and can be used interchangeably with them, but udon has more of a bouncy texture that sets it apart. Dried udon is available, but I typically buy it pre-boiled. The noodles can be rinsed under hot water to loosen and ready them to be prepared. Use Twin Marquis Udon Noodle in Basic Udon Noodle Soup (page 88)!

Rice vermicelli
These thin angel-hair-like vermicelli-style rice noodles are fragile, differentiating them from regular rice sticks. They are packaged in dry bundles and cook quickly in boiling water. They're great in stir-fries and broth, but my favorite way to use them is in the filling for Shrimp & Pork Summer Rolls (page 50).

Mung bean vermicelli
These dry noodles come in bundles and look very similar to rice vermicelli, but don't mistake the two—these bad boys turn clear when they're cooked. I love using these in my Fried Pork Spring Rolls (page 49) and Not Boring Vegetarian Dumplings (page 198) because they soak up any sauce like a sponge.

Spring roll wrappers
If you've ever wondered what the difference is between spring rolls and egg rolls, it's all in the wrapper. Egg roll skins are thick and will bubble up when fried, while spring roll wrappers are thin and delicate pastry sheets that fry up flat and crispy. My favorite is Spring Home's TYJ Spring Roll Pastry.

Summer roll wrappers
Fresh summer rolls require a round rice-paper sheet. These come dry and soften when they're dunked in water. Some packages will instruct you to dunk the sheets in hot water, but I prefer to use cool water so that they don't soften too quickly (and risk tearing). Once they're soft and pliable, you fill them with fixings (page 50) and roll. Some brands may label these as spring roll wrappers. Just make sure to look for clear, round rice paper sheets and not pastry sheets!

Dumpling wrappers
I've included a recipe for homemade dumpling wrappers (page 247) but let's be honest, everyone loves a shortcut. Store-bought wrappers come in handy when making large batches of dumplings and save you from rolling out a wrapper for every individual dumpling. I prefer a thicker dumpling skin, so my favorite is Twin Marquis Shanghai Style Dumpling Wrapper.

Wonton wrappers
These are square and thinner than dumpling wrappers, which are round. Homemade ones are very doable (page 248), but Twin Marquis Wonton Wrappers are a great option for Shrimp Wontons (page 44) and Siu Mai (Steamed Pork & Shrimp Dumplings) (page 54).

Cooking rice noodles can be tricky sometimes—boiling can cook the noodles unevenly, leaving the outsides soft while the insides remain uncooked. To circumvent this, I soak them in cool water for thirty minutes prior to using them, then boil for just two to three minutes. Strain and rinse the noodles under cool water to stop them from cooking further, then enjoy in soups or add to a stir-fry.

DON'T TRIP,

GET EQUIPPED

Wok it like you talk it

The number one most-used item in my kitchen is my wok. Woks are designed for high heat and rapid cooking. Traditionally, woks have a rounded bottom and are used over a high open flame, which would require a wok ring for gas stoves. That said, I like to use one that has a flat base at home, which I think is optimal for either a gas range or an induction stovetop. Look for one that heats evenly, is nonstick, and is light, which makes aggressive sautéing nice and easy.

Pots

A heavy-bottomed, deep pot is essential for making stocks, boiling noodles, and deep-frying. An 8-quart pot is versatile and gets the job done in my kitchen!

Saucepans

A 2- to 4-quart saucepan will be your favorite tool for making soups, boiling wontons, heating up sauces, and much more. Look for one in a durable material—I like stainless-steel or hybrid cookware.

Skillets

A flat-bottomed pan with slightly raised edges is my best friend when it comes to achieving a beautiful sear on meats and dumplings but it is also a good base for a bamboo steamer basket. Look for one in a durable material—I like stainless-steel or hybrid cookware. I find a 10-inch skillet to be the most versatile, but I also love my 8-inch skillet for frying eggs and 12-inch one for bigger batches.

Microplane

Say hello to one of my biggest secret weapons in the kitchen—I love using grated garlic and ginger in marinades and sauces—even if it means putting my nails at risk (!). The finer you work these aromatics, the more oils they release, ultimately making the flavor they contribute to a dish more potent. Plus, I love how the texture is effortlessly uniform and mixes evenly into dishes.

Knife sets

Baddies use sharp knives! A great knife (or three) is the most essential tool for any cook. My favorite knife set is from Hedley & Bennett. Their Chef's Knife Set comes with a paring knife, chef's knife, and bread knife, which are all you really need. Bonus if you get the Cassie Yeung × H&B knife collab!

Sheet pans

Stainless-steel sheet pans are an absolute must in my kitchen. I ordered my 9×7-inch rimmed sheet pans on Amazon, and aside from baking with them, I use them to steam the perfect Homemade Flat Rice Noodles (page 251), as a cooling rack for deep-fried goodies, to store dough when we're practicing *love her, leave her alone*, and for so much more.

Bamboo steamer basket

Steaming is a gentle cooking technique perfect for dumplings, vegetables, fish, and more. A bamboo basket has a perforated bottom that sits on top of simmering water from which steam rises and gently cooks the food. I prefer to use my wok as the base, but you can choose any pan that the basket snugly fits within (I find a 10-inch frying pan works well).

Wire steaming rack

If you don't have a bamboo steamer basket, a wire steaming rack is another great option (it can also double as a cooling rack). Instead of sitting within a wok or pan, a wire steaming rack fits inside a wok or large pot in the water and elevates a plate so the food cooks in the steam.

Plate tongs

This is the tool that you never knew you needed. Plate tongs can grasp opposite sides of a plate or bowl, distributing the weight and keeping it steady, making it *so* easy to lift it in and out of a steamer. I ordered mine on Amazon!

FIRST
BESTIES
BITE

BITE BESTIES FIRST

RECIPE LIST

Har Gow (Crystal Shrimp Dumplings)
34

Pork Dumplings
40

Shrimp Wontons
44

Fried Pork Spring Rolls
49

Shrimp & Pork Summer Rolls
50

Crab Rangoons
53

Siu Mai (Steamed Pork & Shrimp Dumplings)
54

Scallion Pancakes
59

Soy-Marinated Eggs
63

Takeout-Style Chicken Wings
64

Crispy Pork Belly
67

Air Fryer Char Siu (Chinese BBQ Pork)
68

What better way to start the fun than with a few appetizers and dim sum dishes?

Taking your first bite of food is often the best bite (which is why I always share my first bite on social with you all). We'll be covering my favorites, from a variety of dumplings (pan-fried pork dumplings, deep-fried shrimp wontons, and soup dumplings, too) to the iconic Chinese American crispy-skin takeout chicken wings. Dim sum translates to *touch the heart* in Chinese and that's exactly what these small plates do—each is made with love and will be a showstopper whether served as a prelude or the main event.

HAR GOW (Crystal Shrimp Dumplings)

MAKES 18 DUMPLINGS

1 cup wheat starch

¾ cup sifted tapioca flour, plus more for dusting

¾ cup boiling water

1 tablespoon lard (see Note)

Neutral oil (I use avocado oil), for the bowl

½ pound jumbo shrimp (about 25/pound), peeled and deveined (see page 46)

¼ cup drained canned water chestnuts, finely chopped

1 teaspoon light soy sauce

1 teaspoon oyster sauce

1 teaspoon toasted sesame oil

½ teaspoon chicken bouillon powder

¼ teaspoon ground white pepper

½-inch knob of ginger, peeled

1 large garlic clove

Of all the dumplings, har gow is the one I think of as the hot, rich auntie of the group because of their chic transparent cloak, aka the skin. What makes them stand out are their clear dumpling skins, which is where they get the name "crystal shrimp dumplings." I adore clear rice noodles, so shape-shifting them into tender shrimp dumplings is my dream. The dumpling skin is very delicate so it can be intimidating to make, but with the exact right measurements (sorry, we don't abide by *"no measurements, just vibes"* for this one) and some patience, you'll pull them together like a pro. I like to hand-mince the prawns so that the filling still has some texture to it and add in water chestnuts for an extra bite. As always, dumplings are amazing to make ahead of time and freeze for when you're craving a little dim sum!

Make the dough: In a medium bowl, mix the wheat starch and tapioca flour. Using a rubber spatula, mix aggressively as you slowly pour in the boiling water until the water is fully absorbed and the dough starts to come together, about 2 minutes. Transfer to a clean work surface and smear the lard over the dough. The dough should cool off quickly as you work with it. Knead until the dough is completely smooth and is just slightly tacky, about 10 minutes. If the dough is at all sticky, dust lightly with more tapioca flour and knead it in. Continue to knead just until the dough no longer sticks. Put the dough in a lightly oiled bowl, cover with plastic wrap, and rest for 15 minutes.

Prepare the filling: Using a food processor, or a knife to chop by hand, pulse the shrimp into a paste that's a little chunky (you can also process or chop it into a finer paste). Transfer to a medium bowl, then add the water chestnuts, soy sauce, oyster sauce, sesame oil, chicken bouillon powder, and white pepper. Grate the ginger and garlic into the bowl (baddies, watch your nails). Using a fork, mix aggressively until well combined, then whip the mixture to make it really light; this should take about 2 minutes.

Assemble the dumplings: Split the dough into 3 equal pieces and roll each piece into a rope about ¾-inch thick. Dampen a lint-free tea towel with very hot water to cover the dough and keep it warm and moist. Remove 1 rope and cut it into 6 equal pieces. Use the palm of your hand to press and flatten out one piece to a round, 3-inch wrapper. The dough should be very soft and easy to work with.

Place the dumpling wrapper in the palm of your hand and spoon 1 heaping teaspoon of the filling into the middle. Don't be tempted to add more or it will make folding difficult! Fold one edge of the dumpling wrapper over and pinch just the center of the halves together so they stick.

Starting on one side of the pinched area, use your pointer finger and thumb to grab the front half of the wrapper and pleat it toward the center. Repeat two more times until you are left with a gap at the end. Push the gap inward to create two small flaps on the end and pinch them shut. Repeat on the other side, pleating toward the center. Put the dumpling on a sheet pan, cover it with plastic wrap or a tea towel, and repeat the process of rolling out the wrapper, adding filling, pleating, and covering.

To cook immediately: In a wok or large pot, bring 2 inches of water to a boil over medium heat. Set up a bamboo steamer or wire steamer rack (see page 27).

If using a bamboo steamer, line it with perforated parchment paper and add half of the har gow, giving each a little personal space so they're not touching. Cover and steam over medium heat until the wrappers turn translucent, about 5 minutes. Remove the har gow and transfer to a clean plate. Repeat with the second batch (or freeze it). Enjoy immediately.

If using a steamer rack, add half the har gow, making sure they're not crowded and touching, onto a heat-safe plate lined with parchment paper, cover, and steam over medium heat until the wrappers turn translucent, about 5 minutes. Remove and transfer to a clean plate and enjoy!

To freeze: Line a sheet pan with parchment paper. Lay the dumplings flat side down in one layer, making sure they aren't touching on the pan, and transfer to the freezer. Once completely frozen, after about 4 hours, transfer the dumplings to a resealable bag or container and freeze for up to 4 months. Cook from frozen following the same instructions if you were to enjoy immediately.

> **NOTE**
>
> Lard is a cooking fat similar to butter or shortening that will help improve the texture and make this a smooth and tender dough. Lard can be found in the refrigerated section near the butter in most supermarkets—you can substitute with oil if needed.

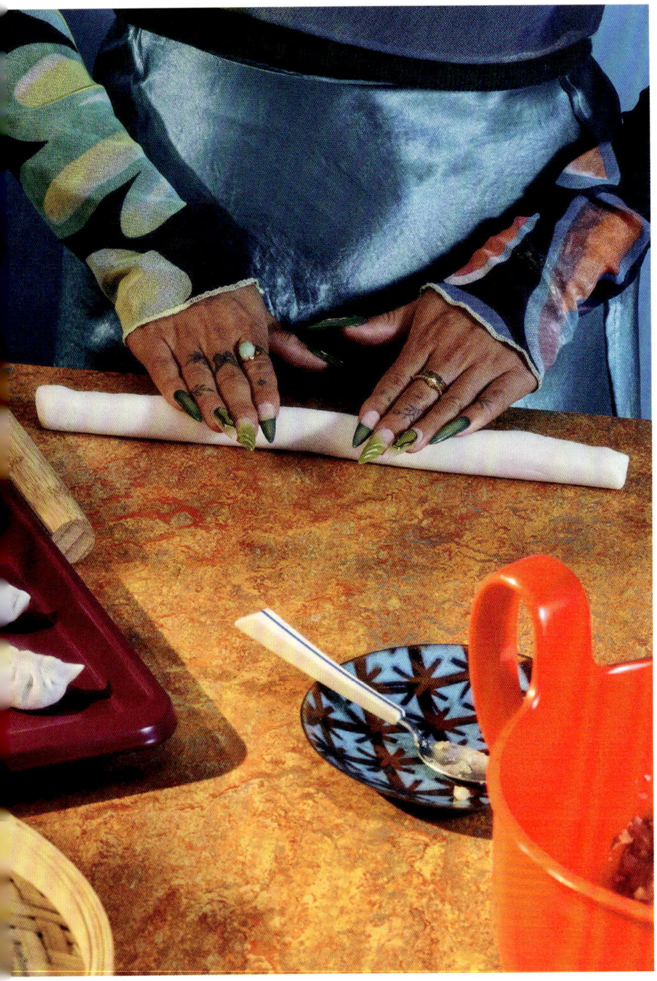

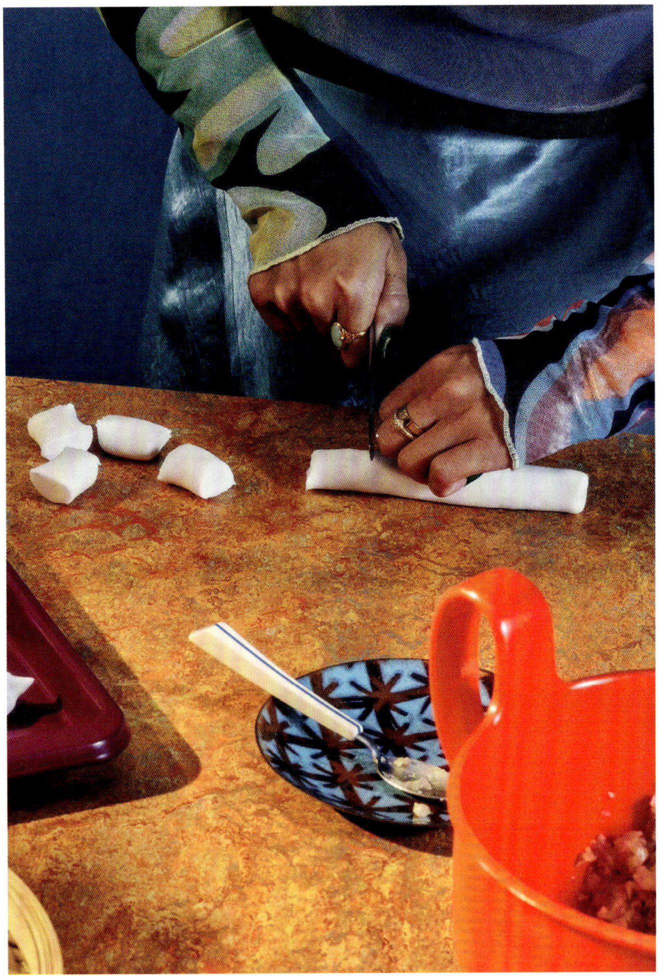

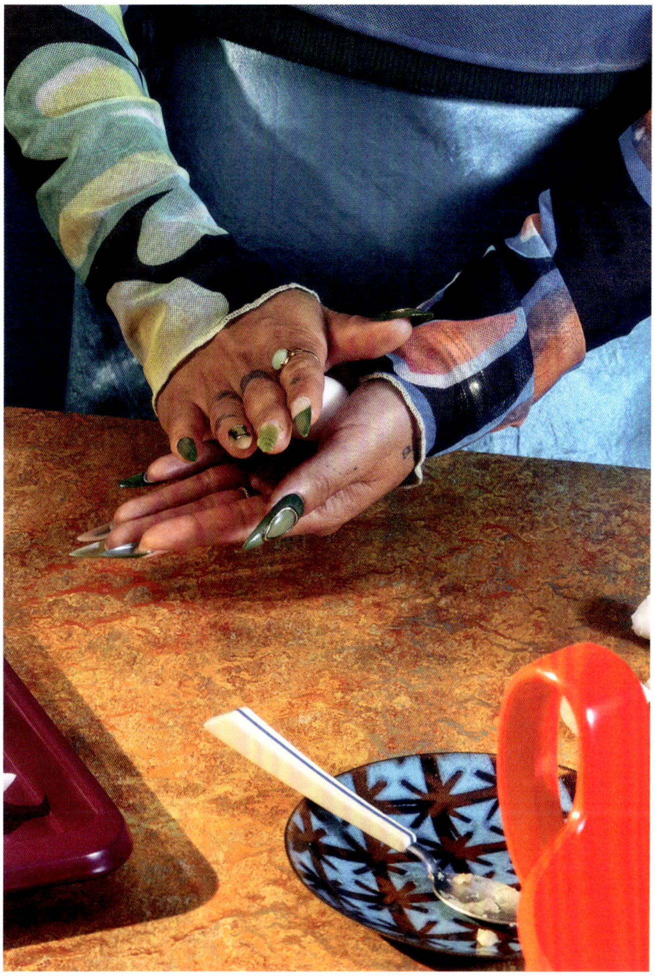
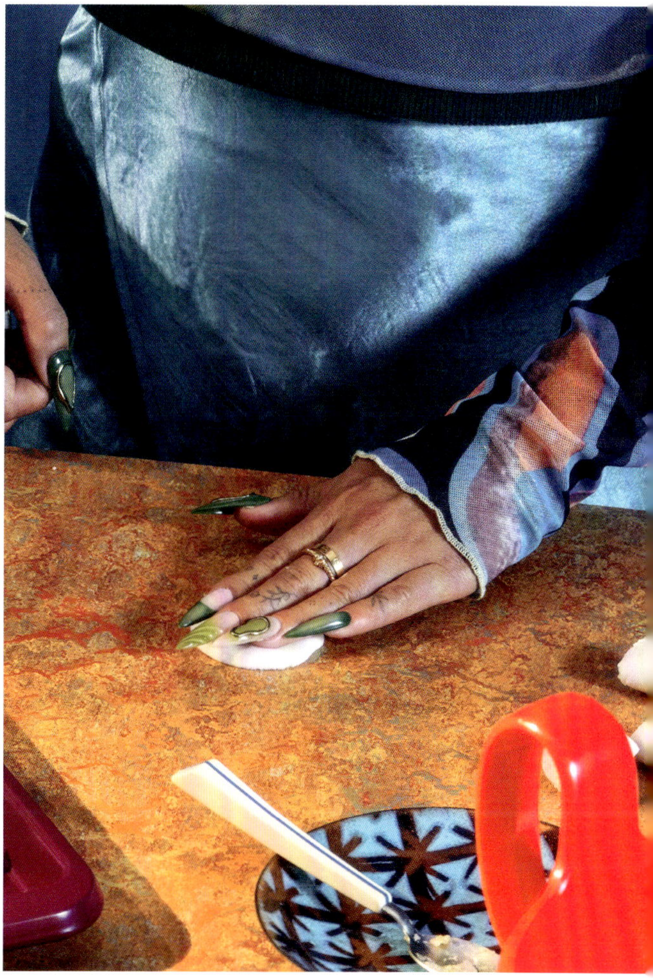

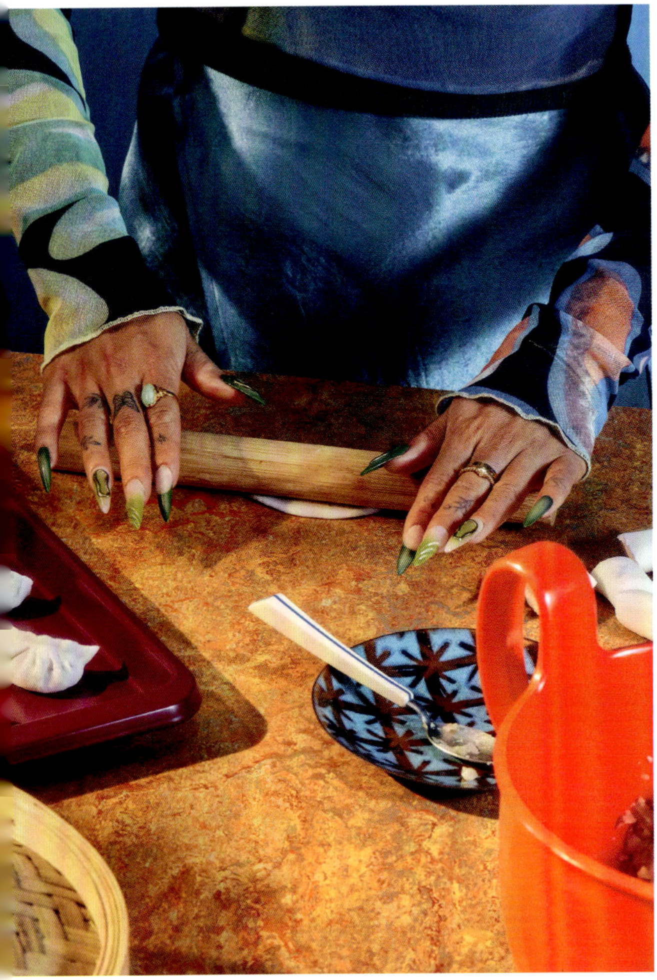

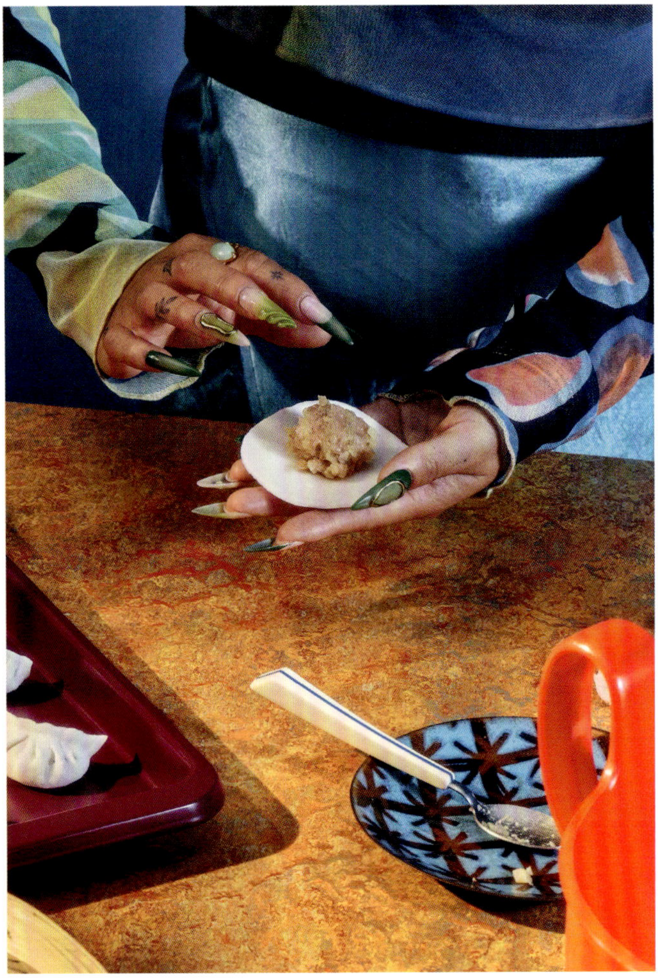

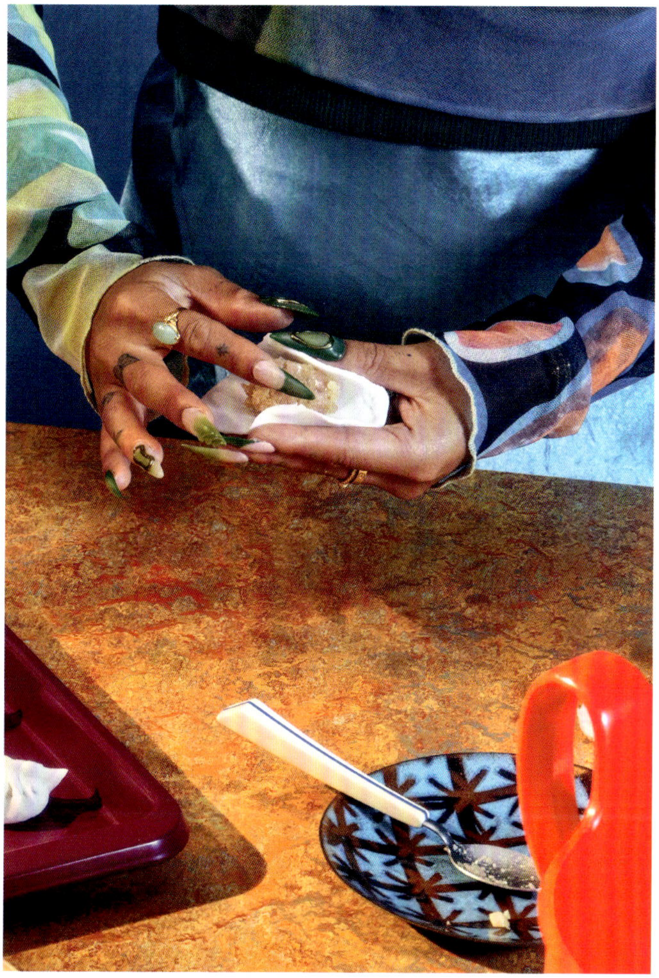

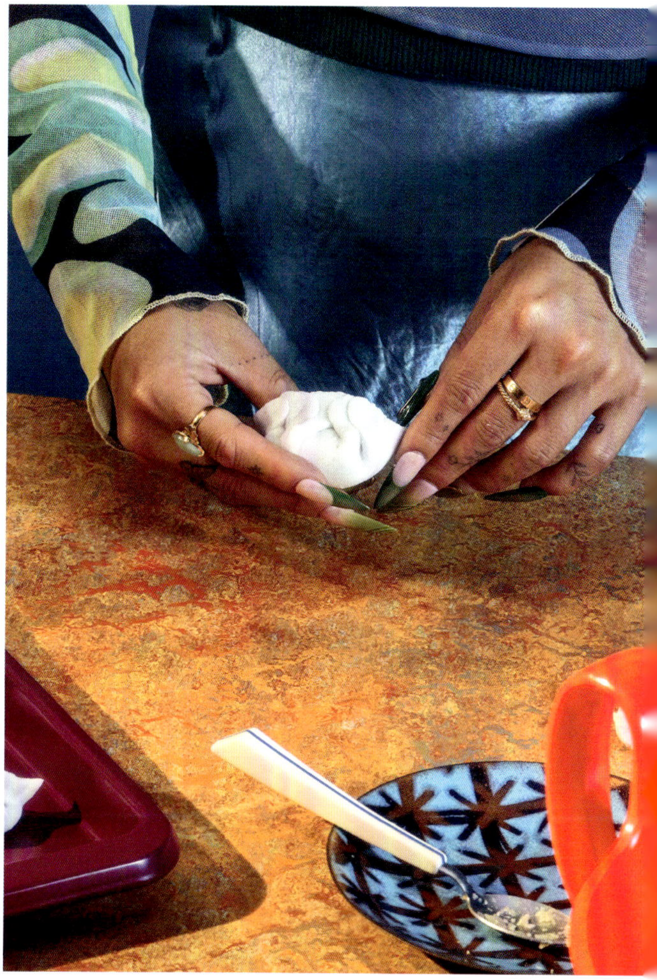

PORK DUMPLINGS

MAKES ABOUT 100 DUMPLINGS (trust—you'll be happy you have a giant batch in your freezer!)

- ½ small head of napa cabbage (about 1 pound)
- 3 tablespoons plus ½ teaspoon kosher salt
- 1 pound fatty ground pork
- ¼ cup stemmed and finely chopped fresh shiitake mushrooms (about 2)
- 1 green onion, green top only, finely chopped
- ¼ cup finely chopped fresh cilantro (see Note)
- 1-inch knob of ginger, peeled
- 3 large garlic cloves
- 2 tablespoons light soy sauce
- 1 tablespoon rice vinegar
- 1 tablespoon oyster sauce
- 1 tablespoon cornstarch
- 1 teaspoon chicken bouillon powder
- 1 teaspoon ground white pepper
- 1 teaspoon sugar
- 1 teaspoon toasted sesame oil
- 2 (10-ounce) packages dumpling wrappers or 3 batches Homemade Dumpling Wrappers (page 247)

In my glory days, I was a member of my college dance team and cheered on the sidelines at every football game. This meant my mother, being the number one dance mom, not only attended each football game but provided food for every tailgate as well. While it would've been expected to bring typical tailgate foods like cold-cut sandwiches or wings, my mom wasn't typical—she was better. She brought trays on trays of juicy and so, so good pan-fried pork dumplings. This caused a huge frenzy among my teammates, their family and friends, and just about anybody who would walk by and get a whiff of "Betty's dumplings."

My mother is notorious for keeping a stash of dumplings in the freezer for a quick snack or meal or to fry up for any social gathering. Once I moved out on my own, I made sure to do the same. Homemade dumplings are a labor of love, yes, but the process can actually be a great way to bring people together and have fun with your friends (dumpling party!). Plus they're just so satisfying to eat and really do make the perfect little host gifts to bring to a dinner party instead of wine or flowers. I love making a big batch to eat right away and freeze so I can have some anytime. Steamed, deep-fried, or pan-seared, they are simply delicious in any form.

Prepare the filling: Chop the cabbage extra fine (just like you), then transfer it to a large bowl, massage well with 3 tablespoons salt, and set aside, allowing it to release excess moisture. After the cabbage has shrunk down, 5 to 10 minutes later, rinse off all of the salt, strain, and squeeze out all of the water.

In a large bowl, mix together the cabbage, ground pork, mushrooms, green onion, and cilantro. Now get out your grater and grate the ginger and garlic into the bowl (baddies, watch your nails). Add the soy sauce, rice vinegar, oyster sauce, cornstarch, chicken bouillon powder, white pepper, sugar, sesame oil, and the remaining ½ teaspoon salt and stir to combine with a spoon or chopsticks, being sure not to overmix—stop stirring just when everything is evenly combined or else you'll have tough dumplings.

Assemble the dumplings: Fill a small bowl with water and keep it close by. Place a dumpling wrapper in the palm of your hand and add 1 level teaspoon of the mixture to the middle. Don't be tempted to add more (you'll want to add more . . . don't do it!), or it will make folding difficult. Dip your finger into the water and wet the edge of half of the dumpling wrapper.

Fold over the wet edge of the dumpling wrapper and pinch just the center of the halves together. The dumpling should look like a half moon. Starting on one side of the pinched area, use your pointer finger and thumb to grab the front half of the wrapper and pleat it toward the center. Repeat two more times until you are left with a gap at the end. Push the gap inward to create two small flaps on the end and pinch them shut. Repeat on the other side, pleating toward the center. Put the dumpling on a sheet pan and repeat with the remaining wrappers until you run out of filling (if you have any extra wrappers, you can freeze them).

FOR SERVING

Neutral oil (I use avocado oil), as needed

1 teaspoon toasted sesame seeds, for razzle-dazzle

Green tops from 2 (or more!) green onions, finely chopped, for razzle-dazzle

Wet-Wet Sauce (see page 255)

To pan-fry the dumplings: Heat a medium skillet on medium-high. When the pan is hot, add 3 tablespoons water. Reduce the heat to low, then add however many dumplings you like (or can fit) to the skillet, making sure not to crowd them together (no sticking!). Cover and steam for 5 minutes. Remove the lid and raise the heat to medium for another minute or until the remaining water has evaporated.

Drizzle in 2 tablespoons neutral-flavored oil and sear until the bottoms are crispy, 3 to 5 minutes. Once they are done cooking, the dumplings will easily lift off the pan (if they don't, they aren't ready and need another few seconds). Transfer to a platter and garnish with a pinch of sesame seeds and the green tops of 1 to 2 green onions per batch. Best enjoyed with Wet-Wet Sauce (page 255)!

To deep-fry: In a wok or large pot, heat 2 inches of neutral oil to 350°F (if you don't have a thermometer, do the wooden chopstick test on page 47). Fit a wire rack into a sheet pan or line a plate or sheet pan with paper towels. Carefully drop in a few of the dumplings, taking care not to crowd the pan and cool the oil, and fry, stirring occasionally, until the skin is golden brown, 3 to 5 minutes. Use a spider or slotted spoon to remove the dumplings to the rack to drain and cool a bit. Repeat with more dumplings, if desired. Transfer to a serving dish and serve.

To freeze: Line a sheet pan with parchment paper. Lay the dumplings flat side down on the pan in a single layer so they're not touching and transfer to the freezer. Once completely frozen, transfer the dumplings to a resealable bag or container and freeze for up to 4 months. Cook from frozen following the same pan-frying instructions as above, adding an additional tablespoon of water to the steaming step (4 tablespoons water total) and an additional minute or until all of the water has evaporated, or deep-fry them using the instructions, adding an additional minute.

> **NOTE**
>
> You don't need to drive yourself crazy picking cilantro leaves from the stems, just cut off the thickest stems and you're good to go. The tender stems have great flavor and texture.

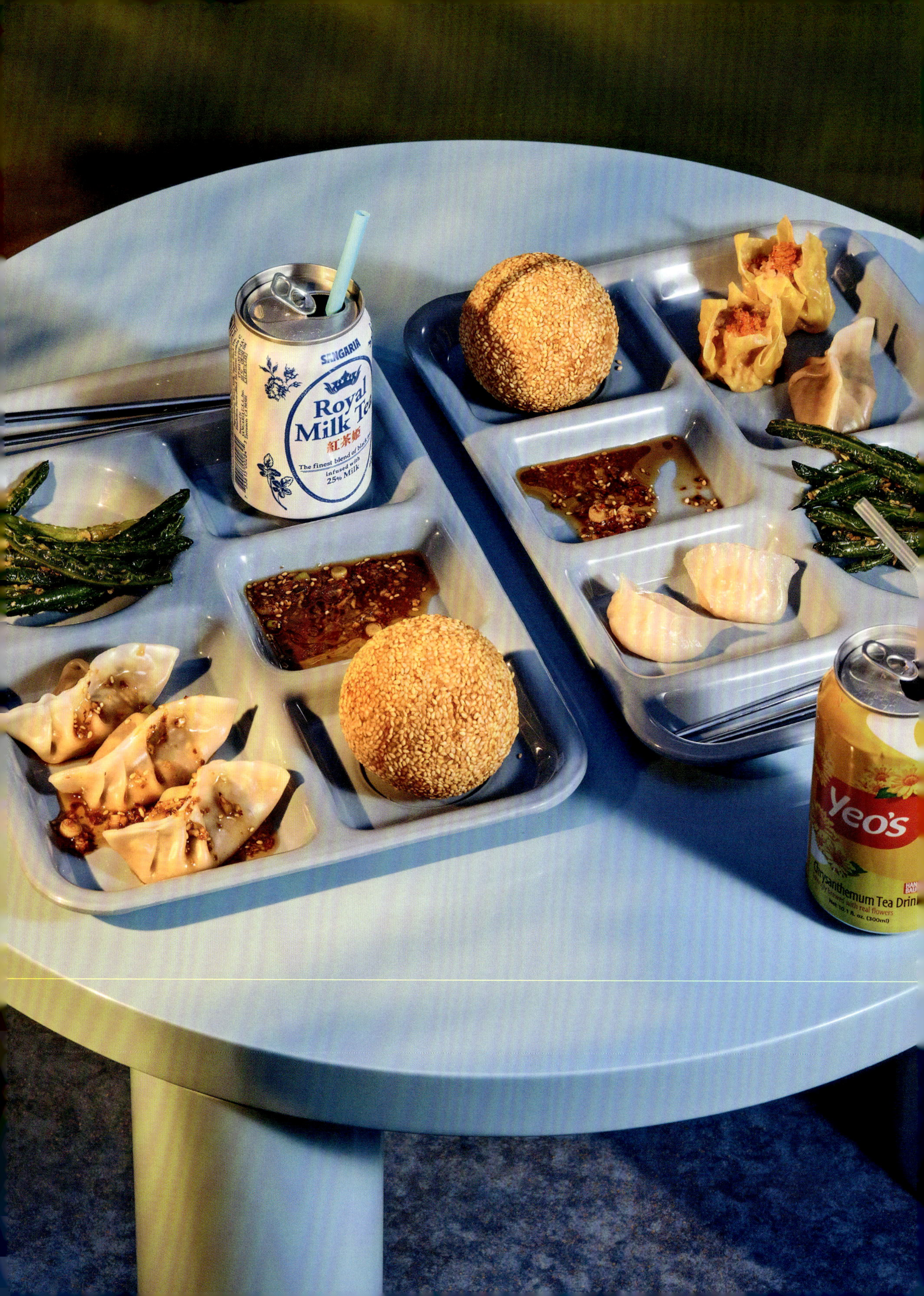
SANGARIA
Royal
Milk Tea
infused with
25% Milk
Yeo's

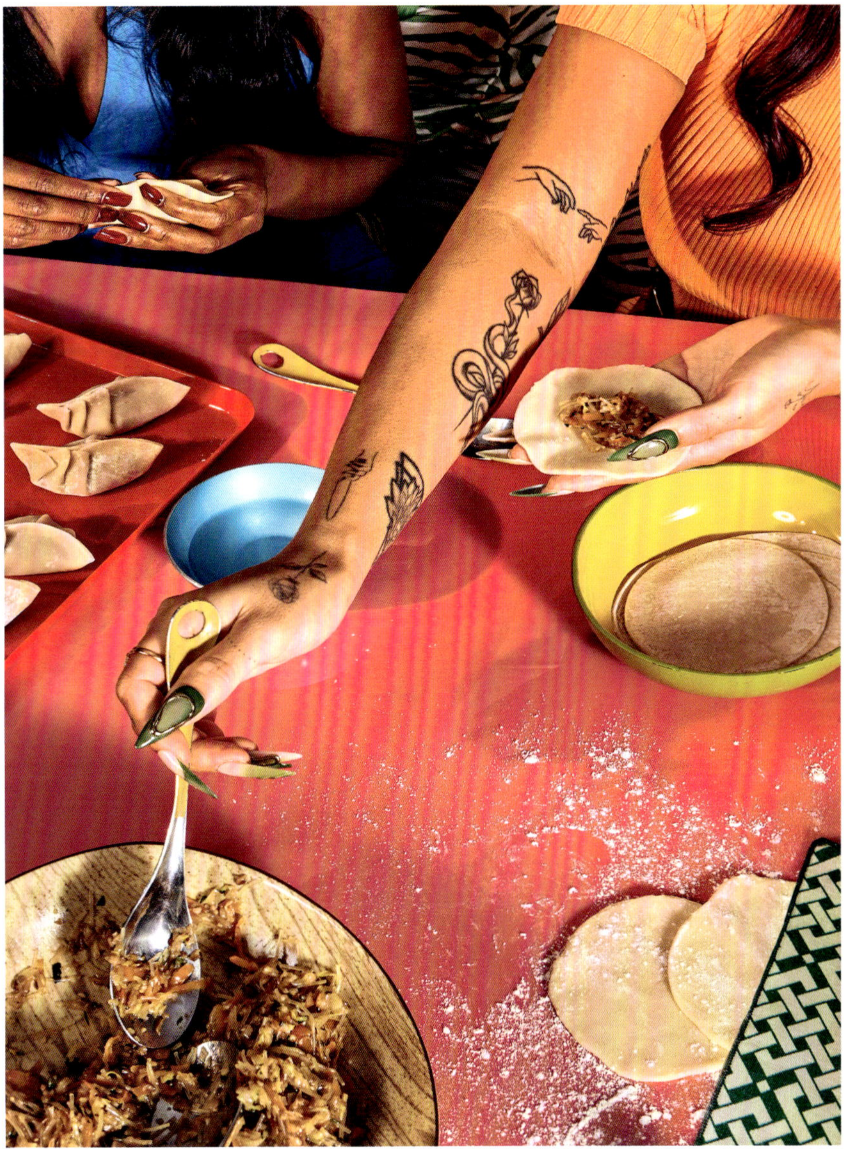

SHRIMP WONTONS

MAKES ABOUT 60 WONTONS

1 pound jumbo shrimp (around 25/pound), peeled and deveined (see Note)

¼ cup stemmed and finely chopped fresh shiitake mushrooms (about 2)

2 green onions, white and green parts, finely chopped

¼ cup fresh cilantro, roughly chopped

1-inch knob of ginger, peeled

4 large garlic cloves

2 tablespoons light soy sauce

1 tablespoon rice vinegar

1 tablespoon oyster sauce

1 tablespoon cornstarch

1 teaspoon toasted sesame oil

1 teaspoon chicken bouillon powder

1 teaspoon sugar

1 teaspoon ground white pepper

¼ teaspoon kosher salt, plus more for cooking

1 (1-pound) package Twin Marquis Hong Kong Style Wonton Wrapper

Wet-Wet Sauce (page 255), for serving

When you have guests over, whether you planned on it or not, let me tell you, there's nothing quite as impressive as whipping up a quick bowl of spicy wontons, wonton noodle soup, or fried wontons to serve them. And if you have some tucked away in your freezer, it's so easy. Homemade wontons—and any dumplings for that matter—are always better than store-bought because you can control not only the flavor but the consistency of the filling. I prefer my wontons to have some texture, so I chop my shrimp by hand (rather than grind in a food processor) so that I get a few bigger bites of shrimp in each wonton.

I have a special connection to these wontons because I find myself using this as an activity to connect with my friends and loved ones. Creating the simple filling and then having everyone get in on the fun of folding them is so satisfying (especially with a cocktail in hand). Enjoy them immediately or freeze them to have ready for whenever. My favorite way to serve them is swimming in Wet-Wet Sauce or in a steaming-hot bowl of Wonton Soup (page 166).

Prepare the filling: Chop up the shrimp into a paste of desired consistency (I like mine a little chunky, but if you like it smoother, use a food processor). Transfer to a medium bowl, then add the shiitake mushrooms, green onions, and cilantro. Now get out your grater and grate the ginger and garlic into the bowl (baddies, watch your nails). Add the soy sauce, rice vinegar, oyster sauce, cornstarch, sesame oil, chicken bouillon powder, sugar, white pepper, and salt. Using a pair of chopsticks or a spoon, mix until well combined and be careful not to overmix.

Fold the wontons: Fill a small bowl with water and keep it close by. Place a wonton skin on a clean work surface and, using a spoon, add 1 level teaspoon of the filling to the center. Using your finger or a pastry brush, lightly brush the edges of the wonton skin with water. Take one corner of the wonton skin and fold over to meet the opposite corner to create a triangle, with the point facing away from you. Use your fingers to seal the edges while making sure to pinch out any air inside. Then, take the two ends of the triangle and fold downward while pushing your fingers in to overlap at the bottom and press to seal to create a "diamond-shape" wonton. Put the dumpling on a sheet pan and repeat with the remaining filling (if you have a few wrappers left over, you can freeze them).

(recipe continues)

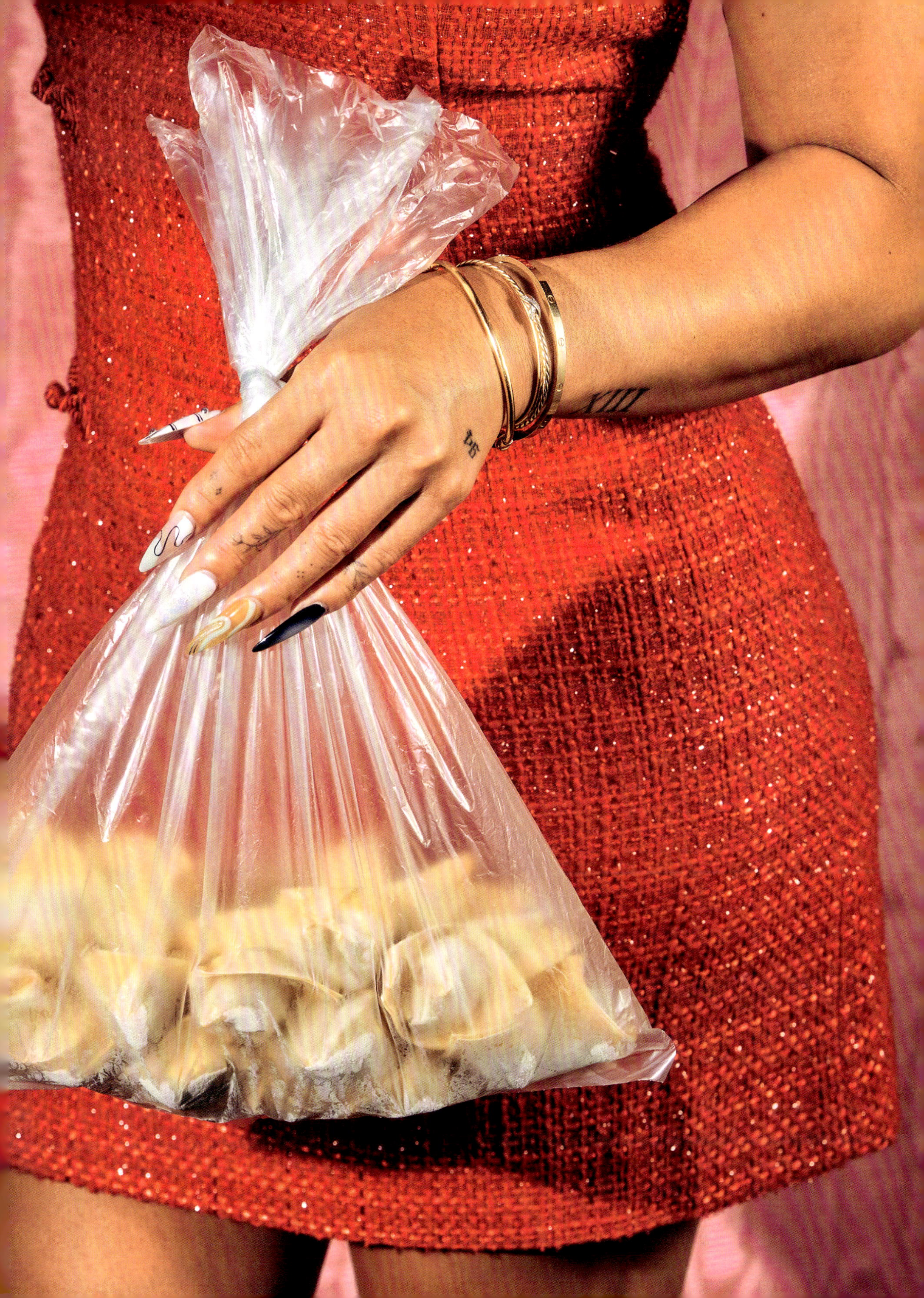

To boil the wontons: Bring a medium pot of salted water to a boil over medium-high heat—make sure it's salty like pasta water, or as salty as you felt about the ending of your last situationship! Use a slotted spoon to carefully lower a few wontons in at a time—don't add too many or you will overcrowd the pot and increase the chance of them sticking to one another. Stir gently to make sure none stick. Boil until the wontons float to the surface of the water, 3 to 5 minutes. Use a slotted spoon or mesh strainer to remove to a clean plate. Repeat with more wontons, if you like, and serve immediately with a good amount of Wet-Wet Sauce.

To deep-fry: Fill a medium pot with 3 inches (or up to halfway) of neutral oil and heat to 375°F (if you don't have a thermometer, do the wooden chopstick test, page 47). Fit a cooling rack over a sheet pan or line a plate with paper towels. Using a slotted spoon, carefully lower a few wontons into the oil, making sure not to overcrowd the pot and drop the oil temperature. Fry and occasionally stir gently, until they are golden brown, 2 to 3 minutes. Use a mesh strainer or slotted spoon to transfer them to the cooling rack or paper towel–lined plate. Repeat with more wontons, if you like, and serve immediately.

To freeze: Add the wontons to a parchment-lined sheet pan, leaving space around each to avoid sticking. Lightly cover the pan with plastic wrap and freeze for 8 hours or until solid. Once they're frozen, they will no longer stick and can be transferred to a resealable bag or container and frozen for up to 4 months. Cook from frozen following the same instructions for boiling or deep-frying as above, adding a minute or two if needed.

> **NOTE**
>
> We want to make sure we remove the "vein" or, rather, digestive tract from the shrimp (we love shrimp but not the ick!). The vein runs along the back of the shrimp—it's usually visible as a dark line. To devein, use a chef's knife to make a long, shallow slit running alongside the vein, then use the tip of the knife to pull it out.

CHOPSTICK TEST FOR DEEP-FRYING

When it comes to deep-frying, it's very important to heat the oil to the right temperature. If the oil is too cold, whatever it is you're trying to fry will absorb the oil rather than develop a crispy or crunchy exterior. But if the oil is too hot, you risk scorching the outside too quickly while leaving the inside raw.

So how do you know when the oil is just right? If I'm being completely honest, and I always want to be honest with you, I never take the temperature of the oil when I'm deep-frying. We didn't even have a thermometer when I was growing up! But we still fried the crispiest Crab Rangoons (page 53) and crunchiest Fried Pork Spring Rolls (page 49).

The secret? A good old wooden chopstick (we love women in STEM).

Fill a heavy-bottomed pot with a high-smoke-point oil (never more than halfway full) and set over medium heat. After about 5 minutes, dip a wooden chopstick or the handle of a wooden spoon into the oil. If barely any bubbles form around the wooden chopstick, it means the oil isn't quite hot enough. Keep heating and repeat the chopstick test until the oil steadily and evenly bubbles around the chopstick, meaning it's the perfect temperature (between 350° and 375° Fahrenheit) and ready for deep-frying.

If the oil bubbles quickly and vigorously around the chopstick, the oil could be too hot. An easy solution to cool it down is to add in more room temperature oil and slightly reduce the heat.

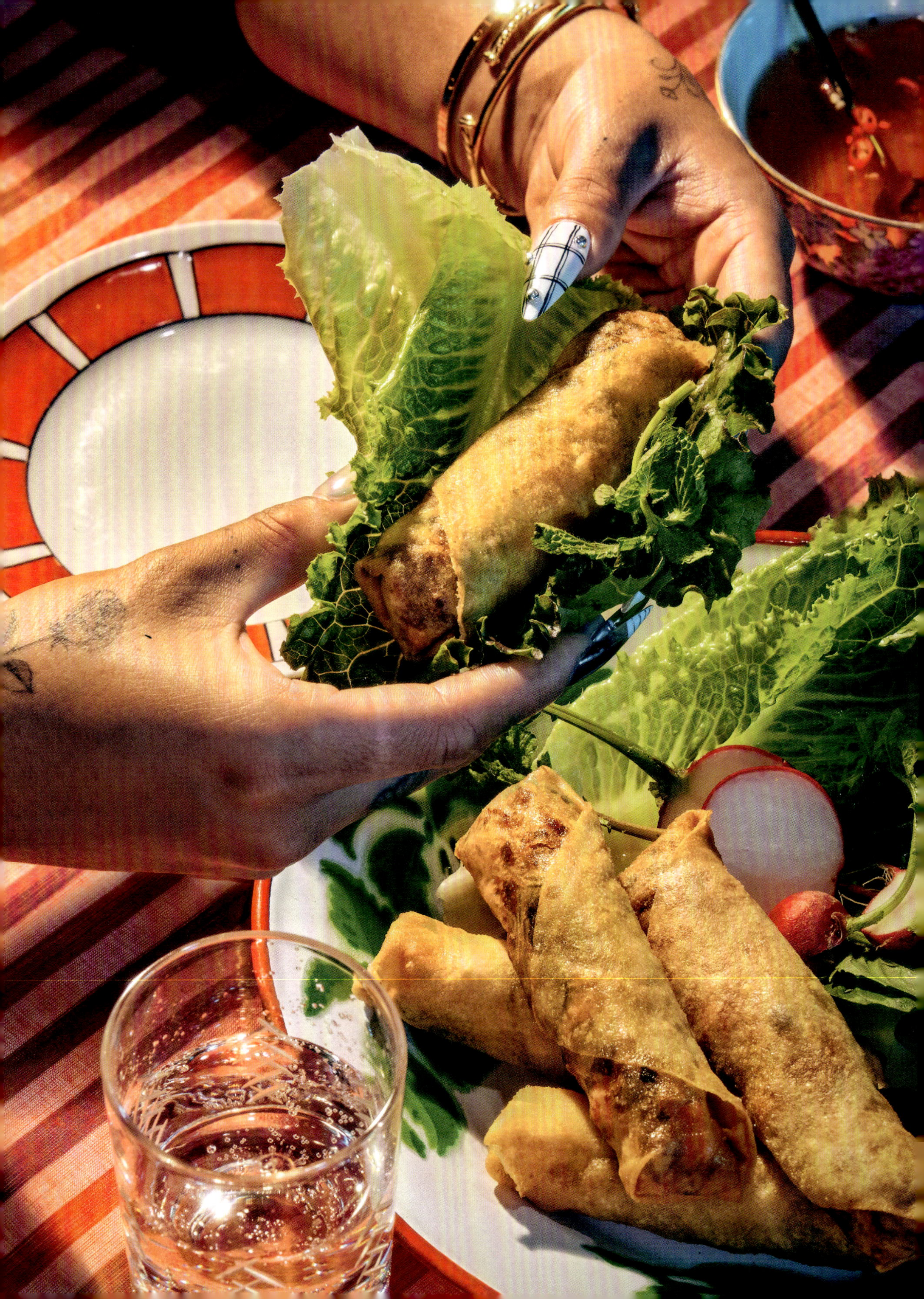

FRIED PORK SPRING ROLLS

MAKES ABOUT 20 SPRING ROLLS

2 cups finely chopped napa cabbage (about ½ a small head)

2 tablespoons kosher salt

5 ounces bean vermicelli noodles

Hot water

2 tablespoons light soy sauce

1 tablespoon rice vinegar

1 tablespoon oyster sauce

1 tablespoon cornstarch

1 teaspoon chicken bouillon powder

1 teaspoon ground white pepper

1 teaspoon sugar

1 tablespoon neutral oil (I use avocado oil), plus more for frying

½ pound fatty ground pork

1 cup stemmed and finely chopped fresh shiitake mushrooms (4 to 6)

2 medium carrots, diced (about 1 cup)

2 green onions, white and green parts, thinly sliced

½-inch knob of ginger, peeled and grated

1 large garlic clove, grated

¼ cup fresh cilantro, finely chopped

1 teaspoon toasted sesame oil

1 large egg

20 square pastry spring roll wrappers (see page 22; from 1 [12-ounce] package)

Sweet chili sauce, store-bought or homemade (see page 259)

These were another one of my mom's usuals to bring to tailgates and special events, and I strongly believe they can pass the test of any picky eater. The filling can be customized with whatever ground protein, or just veggies if you prefer, but I think the most important part of the filling are the bean vermicelli noodles. These guys look similar to rice vermicelli noodles, but instead of turning opaque and starchy when cooked, they turn translucent and slippery. They act as a sponge so they soak up any sauce and flavor from the veggies, which helps the wrapper stay nice and crispy.

Prepare the filling: In a large bowl, massage the napa cabbage with the salt. Set aside for at least 10 minutes and up to 60 minutes to release its moisture. Rinse the cabbage well and squeeze out the remaining water. Return to the bowl.

In a medium bowl, soak the bean vermicelli noodles in enough hot tap water to cover until they are pliable, about 10 minutes. Drain and return to the bowl. Using kitchen shears, roughly cut up the noodles into bite-size pieces.

In a small bowl, mix together the soy sauce, rice vinegar, oyster sauce, cornstarch, chicken bouillon powder, white pepper, and sugar, and set aside.

Heat a wok or large skillet with the neutral oil over medium-high heat. When the oil is hot and shimmering, add the ground pork. Using a spatula, break the pork up and cook, stirring occasionally, until it's mostly browned, about 3 minutes. Add in the mushrooms, carrots, green onions, ginger, and garlic. Stir constantly for 2 minutes, then add in the soy sauce mixture. Mix just to combine and remove from the heat.

To the cabbage, add the drained vermicelli noodles along with the sautéed pork and vegetables and any juices in the pan. Add the cilantro and sesame oil and mix well.

In a small bowl, whisk together the egg with 2 tablespoons water to make an egg wash and set it by your work surface.

Assemble the spring rolls: Lay a spring roll wrapper on your work surface facing you like a diamond. Add ¼ cup of filling in a horizontal log shape close to the bottom corner. Roll the bottom corner up over the filling and tuck in to squeeze out the air. Continue to roll until you can fold in the two side corners. Continue rolling, then using your fingers or a pastry brush, brush the edges with the egg wash and finish rolling until it is sealed. Put the spring roll on a sheet pan, seam side down, and finish with the remaining wrappers and filling.

To serve immediately: Fill a medium pot with 3 inches of neutral oil or just up to halfway, and heat to 375°F (if you don't have a thermometer, do the wooden chopstick test on page 47). Fit a cooling rack over a sheet pan or line a plate with paper towels.

Fry the spring rolls in batches, taking care not to crowd the pot, and flip occasionally using a pair of tongs, until golden brown all over, about 5 minutes total. Remove to the cooling rack. Cool for 5 minutes before serving with the sweet chili sauce.

FIRST BITE, BESTIES

SHRIMP & PORK SUMMER ROLLS

MAKES 18 TO 20 SUMMER ROLLS

Kosher salt

1 pound skinless pork belly

1 medium shallot, halved

Ice water

1 pound jumbo shrimp (around 25/pound), peeled and deveined (see page 46)

8 ounces rice vermicelli noodles

1 (12-ounce) package round rice paper wrappers (they're usually labeled in cm; you want 22 cm)

1 head of green leaf lettuce

1 English cucumber, cut into thin, 2-inch-long matchsticks

2 medium carrots, cut into thin, 2-inch-long matchsticks

1 bunch fresh cilantro, thick stems removed

1 bunch fresh mint, leaves picked

4 green onions, white and green parts, cut into 2-inch lengths then thinly sliced lengthwise

Peanut Dipping Sauce (page 263), for serving

These rolls are exactly how they sound, the epitome of summer (they're like salad but so much more fun!). You can put anything in a rice paper sheet and it'll be delicious, so feel free to switch up the shrimp and pork filling with what you're craving. There's nothing better than pairing these bright, refreshing rolls with an easy, creamy peanut dipping sauce. While these are best fresh, you can totally make them up to three days ahead of time.

Bring a medium pot of salted water to a boil over medium-high heat—make sure it's salty like pasta water, or as salty as your ex after fumbling you! When it comes to a boil, reduce the heat to medium-low and add the pork belly and the shallot. Poach, uncovered, until the pork belly's juices run clear when pierced, 20 to 25 minutes (test by removing the pork belly from the water and piercing the thickest part with the tip of a knife). Remove to a clean plate and cool for at least 10 minutes before slicing crosswise (against the grain) into $1/8$-inch-thick strips.

Bring a small pot of water to a boil over medium-high heat. Fill a small bowl with ice water. Add the shrimp to the boiling water and cook until the shrimp is just opaque and curled into a C shape, 3 minutes. Use tongs or a spider to immediately remove the shrimp to the ice bath (leave the water at a boil). Cool the shrimp for 5 minutes, then drain and cut the shrimp in half lengthwise.

While the shrimp chill, add the rice vermicelli noodles to the boiling water and cook for 2 minutes, stirring constantly so that the noodles don't get gummy. Strain and rinse under cool water, then set aside to drain.

Fill a shallow dish with warm water. Add a rice paper wrapper and flip and swish for 10 seconds or until the wrapper *just* becomes pliable. Be careful not to *over*soak it, or else you might risk tearing the wrapper. (Don't worry if it does not seem completely soft—it will continue to soften on the work surface.) Lay the wrapper flat on a work surface and add a lettuce leaf 2 inches from the bottom. Add about ¼ cup of vermicelli noodles directly over the lettuce, then add about 4 cucumber matchsticks, 4 carrot matchsticks, 2 sprigs of cilantro, and 4 mint leaves above the lettuce on the wrapper. Then above the mint leaves, lay 3 shrimp halves presentation side (outside) down on the wrapper and 3 slices of pork belly directly on top.

Starting from the bottom of the wrapper, fold the edge over the noodles and vegetables and gently pull down to pinch out any excess air. Continue to roll over the pork and shrimp, then fold in the right and left sides of the wrapper. Once there are 2 inches of space from the top, add about 4 green onion slices, allowing some of them to poke out of one end. Tightly roll the rest of the wrapper. Set the summer roll aside seam side down, and continue with the remaining wrappers and fillings. Serve with the peanut dipping sauce.

To store: Individually wrap each summer roll in plastic wrap or if storing on a sheet pan, weave a sheet of plastic wrap under and over alternating rolls and cover with a damp paper towel. They'll keep in the fridge for up to 3 days.

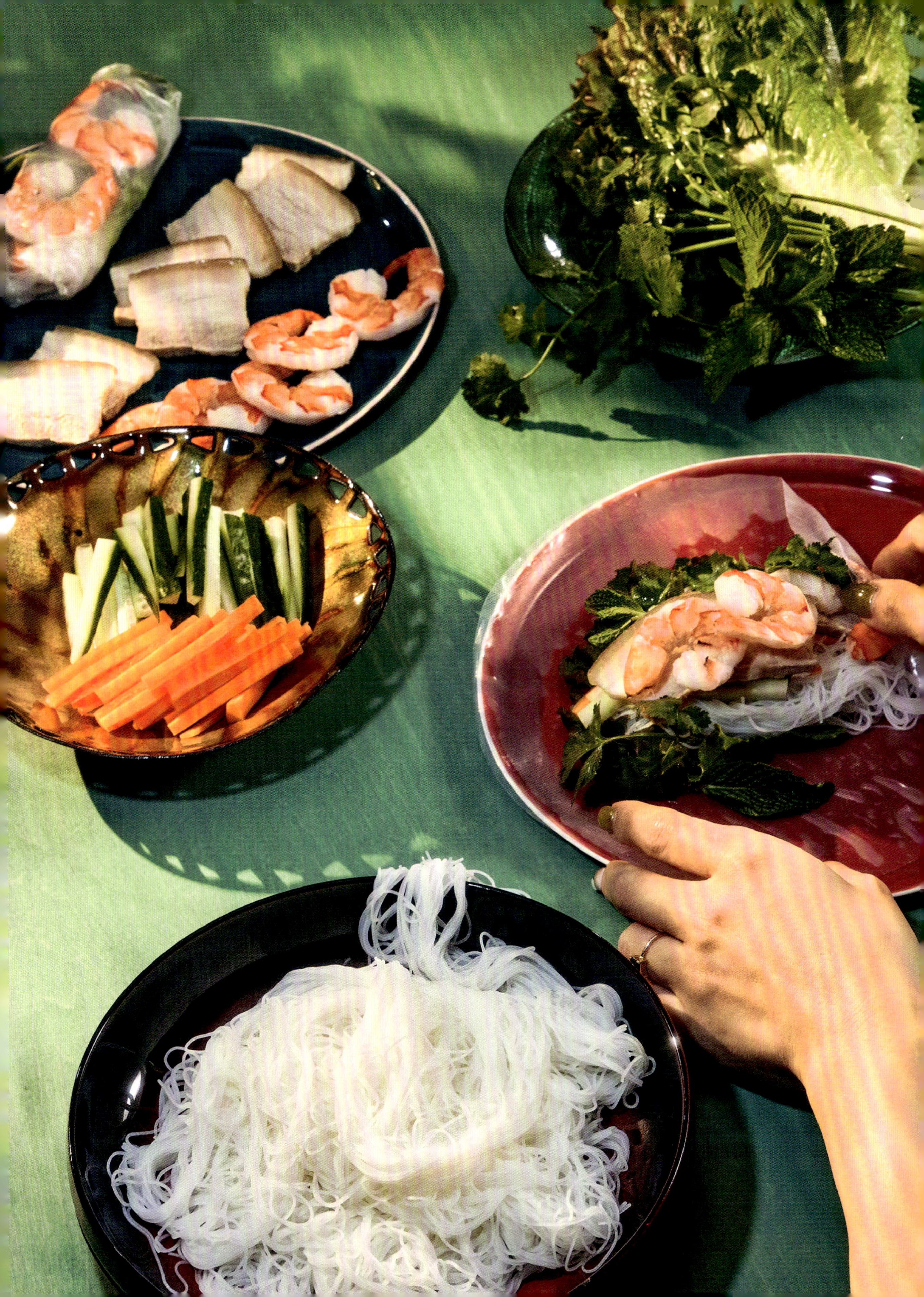

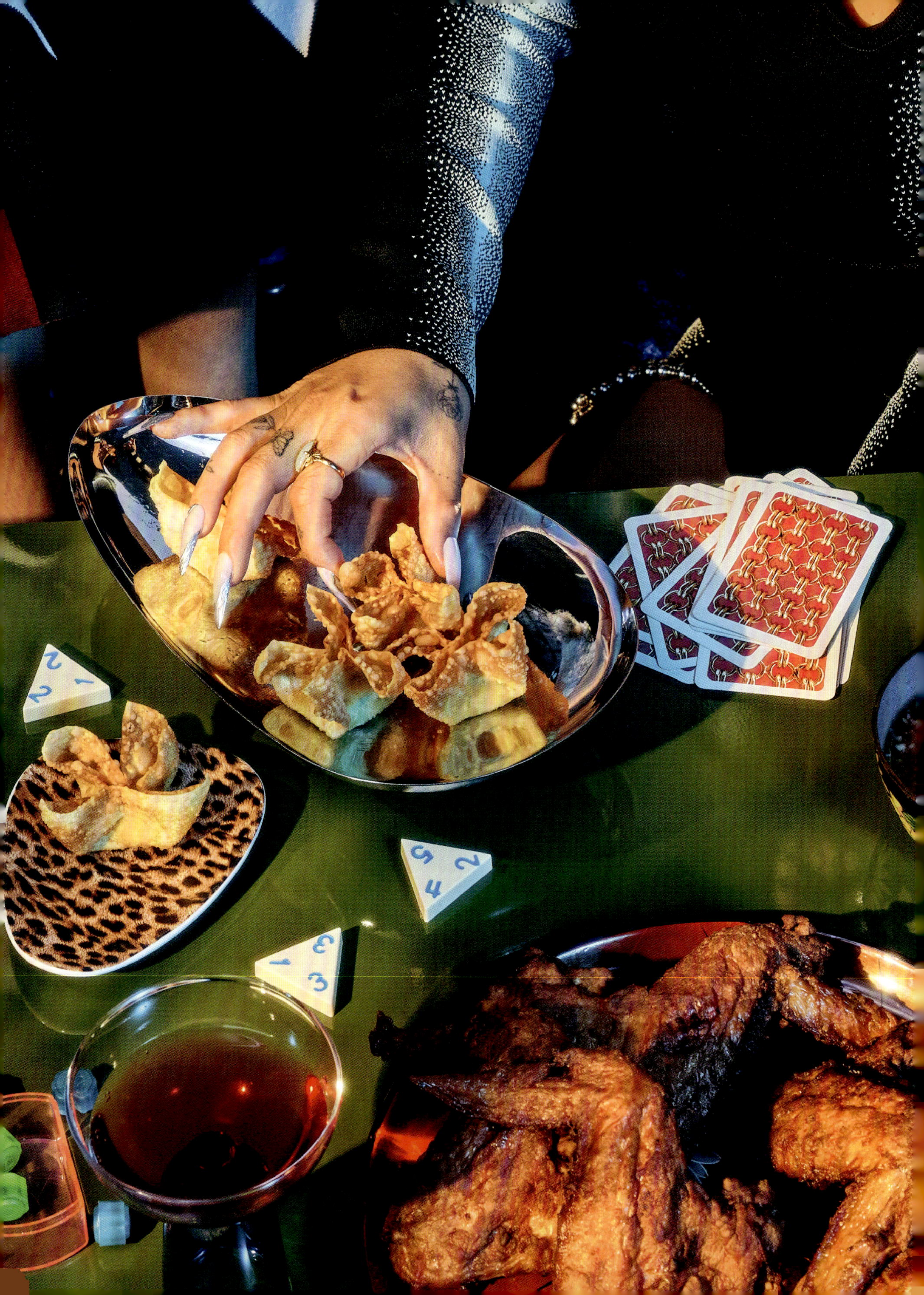

CRAB RANGOONS

**MAKES ABOUT
40 RANGOONS**

8 ounces cream cheese, at room temperature

1 green onion, white and green parts, finely chopped

1 tablespoon light soy sauce

1 teaspoon Worcestershire sauce

1 teaspoon toasted sesame oil

½ teaspoon ground white pepper

1 large garlic clove

8 ounces fresh lump crab meat

40 wonton wrappers, store-bought or homemade (see page 22)

Neutral oil (I use avocado oil), for frying

Sweet chili sauce, store-bought or homemade (see page 259), for serving

Crab rangoons took TikTok by storm with many viral mukbangs, and now the oh-so-catchy tune *"crab rangooooons"* lives rent free in my head (thanks to TikTok brainrot). The first bite of a crispy fried wonton stuffed with crab and cream cheese isn't easy to forget either. I admittingly didn't have my first crab rangoon until I was older since I was a victim of my mom tricking me into thinking I didn't like cheese. She simply hates cheese, and therefore never cooked with it and convinced my sister and me that we didn't like it either. When I did finally try it, it was love at first bite, and I knew I needed to develop my own recipe.

These are such a crowd-pleaser and are extremely simple to make. This recipe calls for fresh crab meat, usually found in the refrigerated section near the seafood in the grocery store, but can be made with imitation crab as well. Be prepared to be addicted, and to fight the desire to keep popping them in your mouth one after the other. Dipped in a sweet chili sauce, these creamy, crispy rangoons are perfect.

Prepare the filling: In a medium bowl, use a rubber spatula to press and work the cream cheese until it's soft enough to mix in the other ingredients easily. Add the green onions, soy sauce, Worcestershire sauce, sesame oil, and white pepper. Now get out your grater and grate the garlic into the bowl (baddies, watch your nails). Mix until well combined. Gently fold in the crab meat, being careful not to overwork the meat or break it up into tiny pieces.

Assemble the rangoons: Fill a small bowl with water and keep it close by. Place a wonton wrapper on a work surface and add 1 level tablespoon of filling into the center of the wrapper. Using your finger, moisten the sides of the wrapper with water. Pick up two opposite corners of the wonton wrapper and pinch the corners at the top to make a triangle. Pick up the other corners and use your fingers to seal the sides to make a purse shape while trying to pinch all of the air out. Set the rangoon aside and cover loosely with plastic wrap, then repeat with the remaining wrappers and filling. (If you have any extra wrappers, you can freeze them.)

To serve immediately: Fill a medium pot with 2 inches of neutral oil or halfway (but don't fill it more than halfway), and heat to 375°F (if you don't have a thermometer, do the wooden chopstick test on page 47). Fit a cooling rack over a sheet pan or line a plate with paper towels.

Cook the crab rangoons in two batches, making sure not to overcrowd the pan. Fry, gently stirring or flipping frequently, until they are golden brown all over, 3 to 5 minutes. Use a slotted spoon to remove to the cooling rack. Cool for 5 to 10 minutes before serving with the sweet chili sauce.

To freeze: On a parchment paper–lined sheet pan, arrange the crab rangoons in a flat layer, making sure they aren't touching, and freeze until solid, about 8 hours. Once frozen, transfer to a resealable bag or container and freeze for up to 4 months. Fry straight from frozen for 7 minutes or until golden brown.

SIU MAI (Steamed Pork & Shrimp Dumplings)

MAKES ABOUT 45 DUMPLINGS

- ½ pound jumbo shrimp (around 25/pound), peeled and deveined (see page 46)
- ½ pound fatty ground pork
- 1 tablespoon light soy sauce
- 2 teaspoons cornstarch
- 1 teaspoon toasted sesame oil
- 1 teaspoon sugar
- 1 teaspoon chicken bouillon powder
- 1 teaspoon ground white pepper
- ½ teaspoon baking soda
- 1½ cups stemmed and finely chopped fresh shiitake mushrooms (about 6)
- 2 green onions, white parts only, thinly sliced
- 1 (1-pound) package of Twin Marquis Hong Kong Style Wonton Wrapper
- Orange tobiko (flying fish roe), for razzle-dazzle

This is another one of my dim sum favorites, and when my family is at dim sum, we can't help grabbing multiple containers off the cart. Siu mai is a Cantonese steamed dumpling. It's made from a thin and delicate Hong Kong–style wrapper that gathers around an exposed pork and prawn filling. There's no special technique to enclose them, so if you struggle with pleating dumplings, this is a great starter dim sum for you—in fact, I love the imperfections in siu mai. Your focus is drawn to the decadent, exposed protein rather than the dumpling wrapper. Top them with a little fish roe razzle-dazzle to give them an extra pop of color.

Prepare the filling: Using a sharp chef's knife, finely chop the shrimp until it becomes a paste (I personally like to leave some chunks in there, but you do you). Transfer to a large bowl and mix in the ground pork, soy sauce, cornstarch, sesame oil, sugar, chicken bouillon powder, white pepper, and baking soda with a pair of chopsticks, being careful not to overwork the mixture. Gently fold in the shiitake mushrooms and green onions.

Assemble the dumplings: Fill a small bowl with water and keep it close by. Make an O shape using your pointer finger and thumb and lay a dumpling wrapper on top of the O. Using a teaspoon, scoop 2 level spoonfuls of filling into the center of the dumpling wrapper, pushing it down to form the siu mai. Use the back of the spoon to flatten the top. Using your fingers, wet the outside of the wrapper and fold down any excess wrapper so the top is flat. Repeat with the remaining wrappers and filling (if you have any extra wrappers, you can freeze them).

To serve immediately: In a wok or large pot, bring 2 inches of water to a boil over medium heat. Set up a bamboo steamer or wire steamer rack (see page 27).

If using a bamboo steamer, line it with a perforated parchment paper (see page 250) and add the siu mai, leaving about 1 inch around each (you'll need to cook them in batches). Cover and steam over medium heat until the pork is no longer pink, 7 to 10 minutes. Remove to a clean plate. Repeat with as many batches as you like.

If using a steamer rack, place the siu mai 1-inch apart onto a parchment-lined heat-safe plate (you'll need to cook them in batches). Cover and steam over medium heat until the pork is no longer pink, about 10 minutes. Remove to a clean plate.

Garnish each piece with a little spoonful of fish roe and enjoy while they're steaming hot (just like you)!

To freeze: Line a sheet pan with parchment paper. Set the siu mai on the pan, making sure they aren't touching, and transfer to the freezer. Once completely frozen, after about 4 hours, transfer the dumplings to a resealable bag or container and freeze for up to 4 months. Freeze and cook from frozen following the same instructions as if you were to enjoy them immediately.

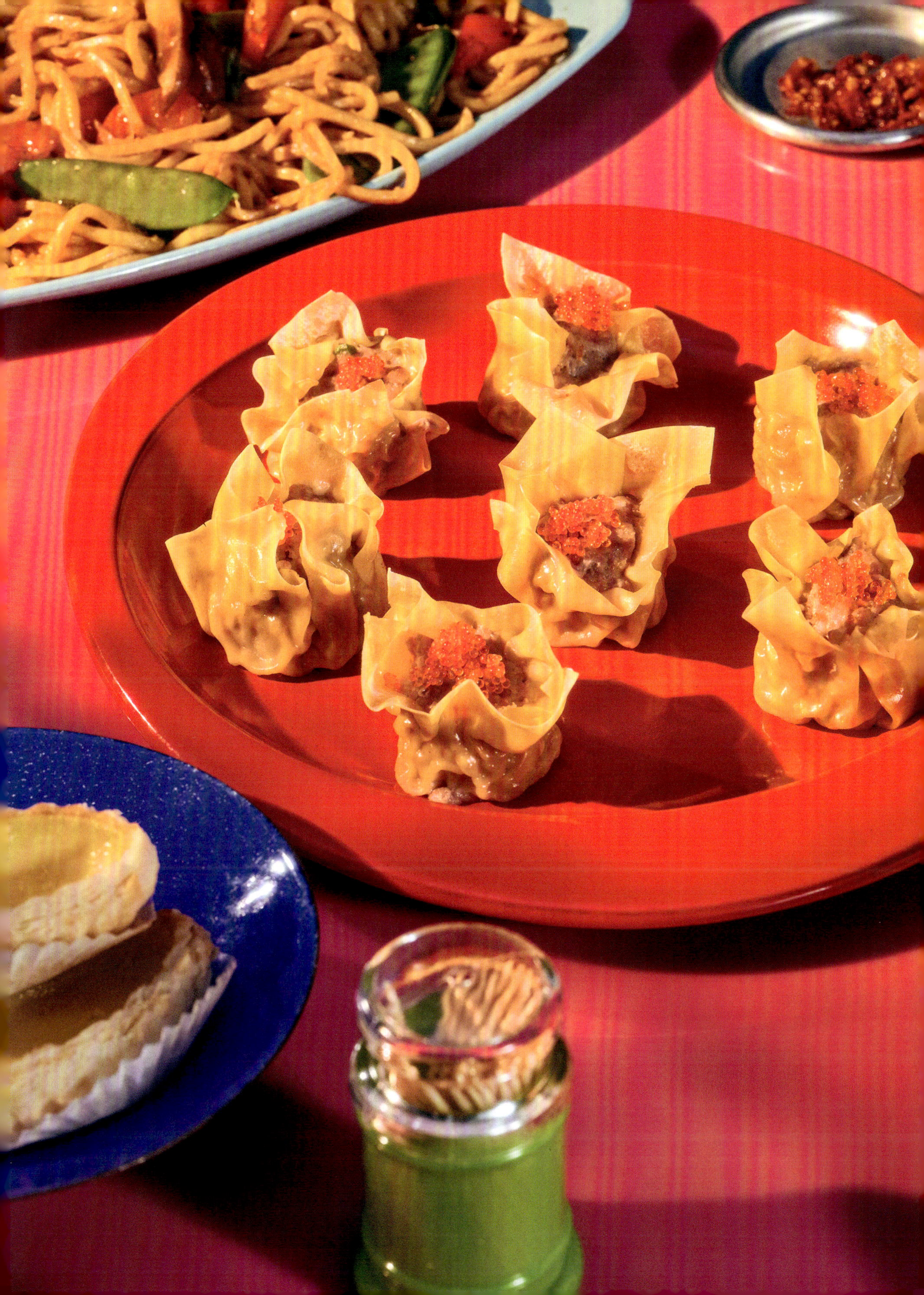

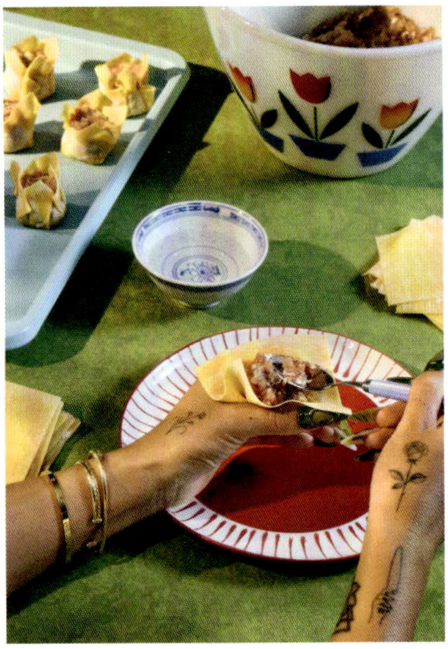

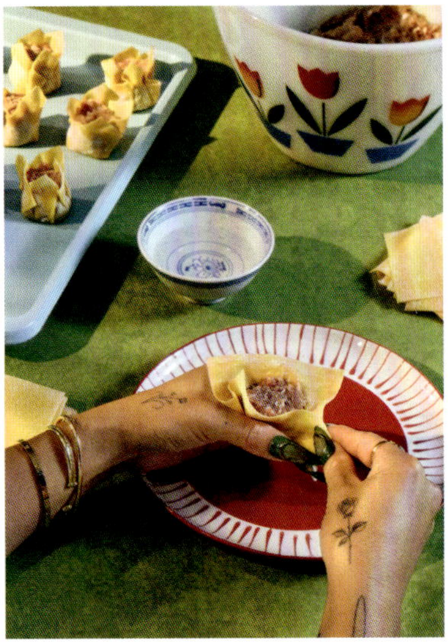

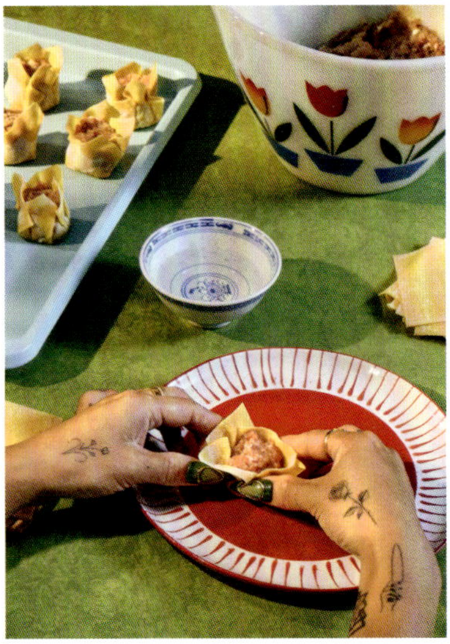

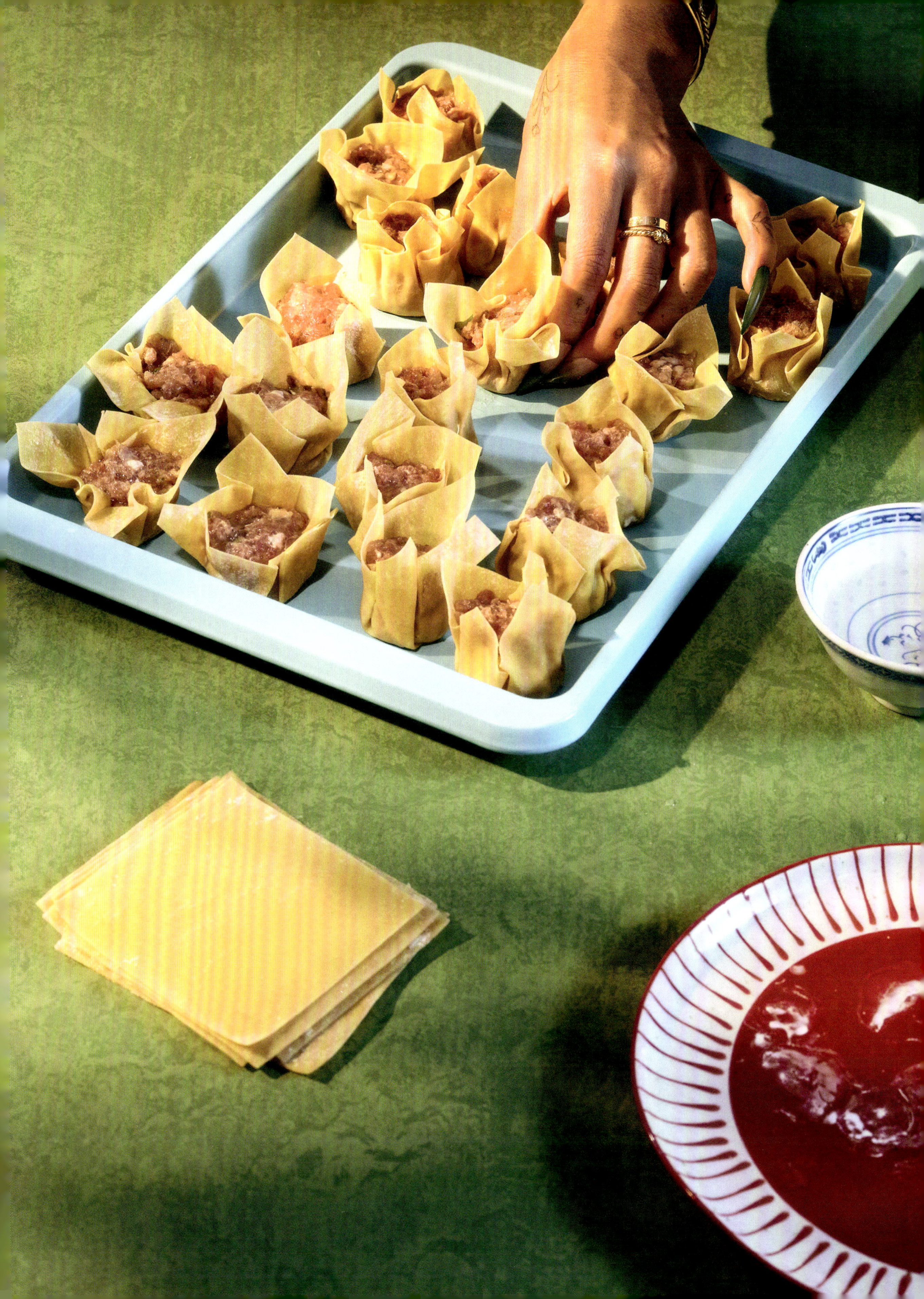

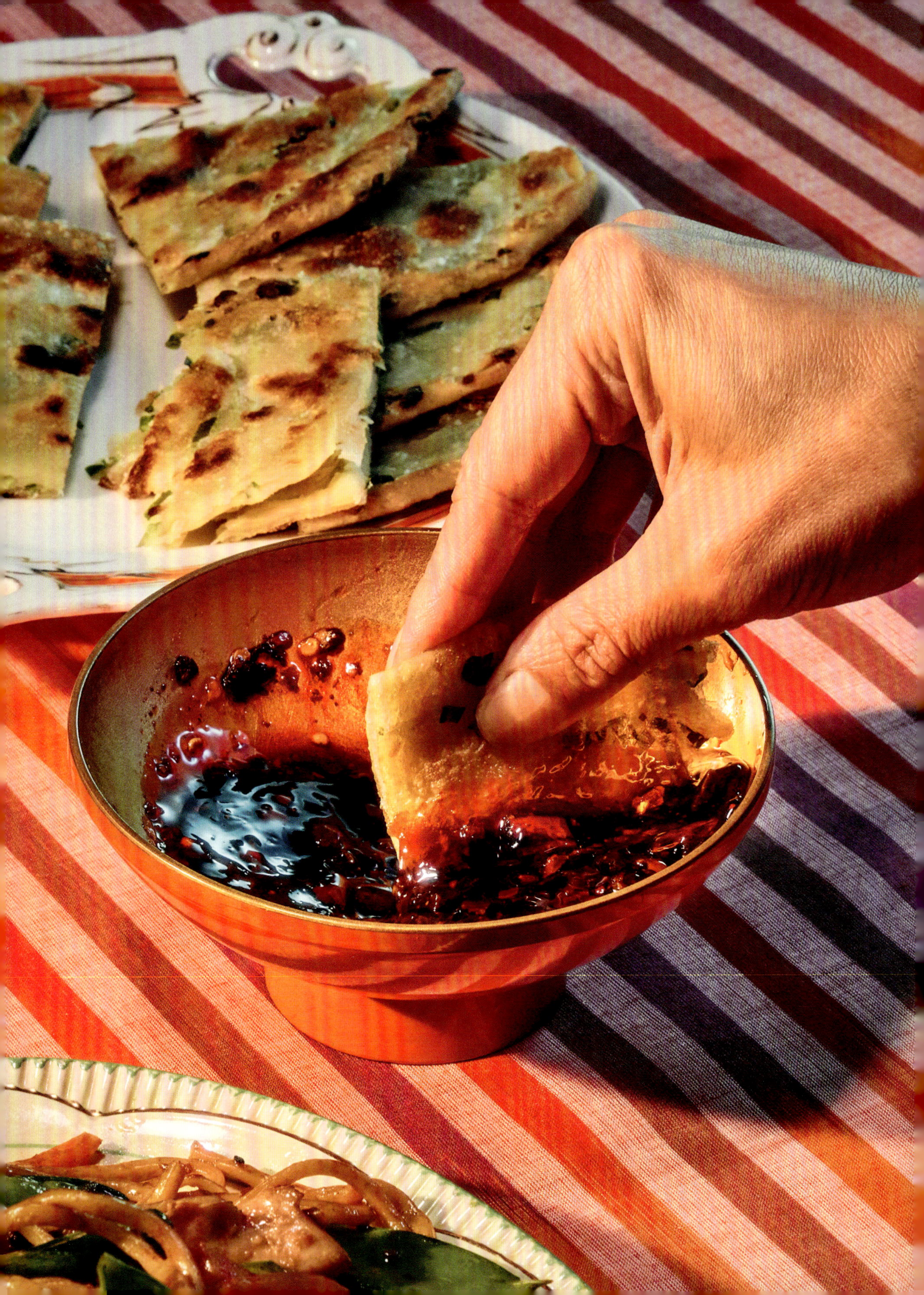

SCALLION PANCAKES

MAKES 4 PANCAKES

DOUGH

2 cups all-purpose flour, plus more for dusting

½ teaspoon kosher salt

1 teaspoon neutral oil (I use avocado oil)

¾ cup boiling water

SCALLION OIL AND FILLING

¼ cup neutral oil (I use avocado oil)

2 tablespoons toasted sesame oil

6 green onions, white and green parts, thinly sliced and separated

2 tablespoons all-purpose flour

½ teaspoon kosher salt

FOR SERVING

Chili oil

Black vinegar

Whether you call them green onions or scallions, they're my not-so-secret way to add some razzle-dazzle to nearly everything. I like my scallion pancakes thick and doughy *and* extra flaky on the outside. First, a simple dough is prepared then brushed with a scallion-infused oil that truly gives the dough a beautiful aroma. If that were not enough, thinly sliced scallions are dispersed and spread into the dough, too. Deep, flaky layers are created by rolling the dough into a rope, twisting the rope into a coil, flattening it, and then pan-frying. These are so fun to pull apart and devour! They're dynamite plain, but who doesn't love a little black vinegar and chili oil for dipping on the side?

Make the dough: In a medium bowl, mix the flour and salt. Using your hands or a wooden spoon, create a well in the center of the dry ingredients. Drizzle the oil in the well along with half of the boiling water. Using a wooden spoon, begin mixing the dough by slowly incorporating the flour in with the wet ingredients. Once everything is combined, add in the remaining water and continue mixing until the dough is shaggy.

Transfer the dough to a clean work surface and knead with your hands until it is smooth, slightly tacky, and bounces back when you poke it gently with your finger, about 10 minutes. If the dough is at all sticky, lightly dust it with more flour and knead it in. Repeat just until the dough no longer sticks. Cover with plastic wrap or a lint-free tea towel and rest at room temp for 20 minutes.

Meanwhile, make the scallion oil and filling: In a small saucepan, heat the neutral oil and sesame oil to 325°F (if you don't have a thermometer, do the wooden chopstick test on page 47). Put the chopped green onion whites in a medium heat-safe bowl. Pour the hot oil onto the onions and use a spoon to mix, then stir in the flour and salt until there are no lumps. It will look like a loose paste.

Roll out the dough: Using a bench scraper or knife, split the rested dough into four equal pieces. Set one piece on a lightly floured work surface and cover the remaining three pieces. Lightly flour your rolling pin and roll the dough out to a ⅛-inch-thick rectangle, about 12 inches by 18 inches. Scoop one-quarter of the scallion oil filling onto the dough and brush from edge to edge. Sprinkle with one-quarter of the green onion greens.

Roll the dough into a tight cylinder along one of the long edges and gently pinch the seam to seal. Starting from one end of the cylinder, roll it into a coil. Using your hands, flatten the coil, then gently roll it out with the rolling pin until it's ¼-inch thick and about 6 inches across (there may be some air bubbles as you roll, but that's fine). The outside should have a nice sheen of oil, which will help with frying. Set aside, cover, and repeat with the remaining dough.

Cook the pancakes: Heat a medium nonstick skillet over medium heat. When the pan is hot, lay one scallion pancake in the pan, pressing lightly with a spatula. Cook until lightly golden, about 4 minutes per side. Transfer to a plate and repeat with all the pancakes.

To serve: Slice each pancake into wedges and enjoy with chili oil and black vinegar for dipping.

razzle

dazzle

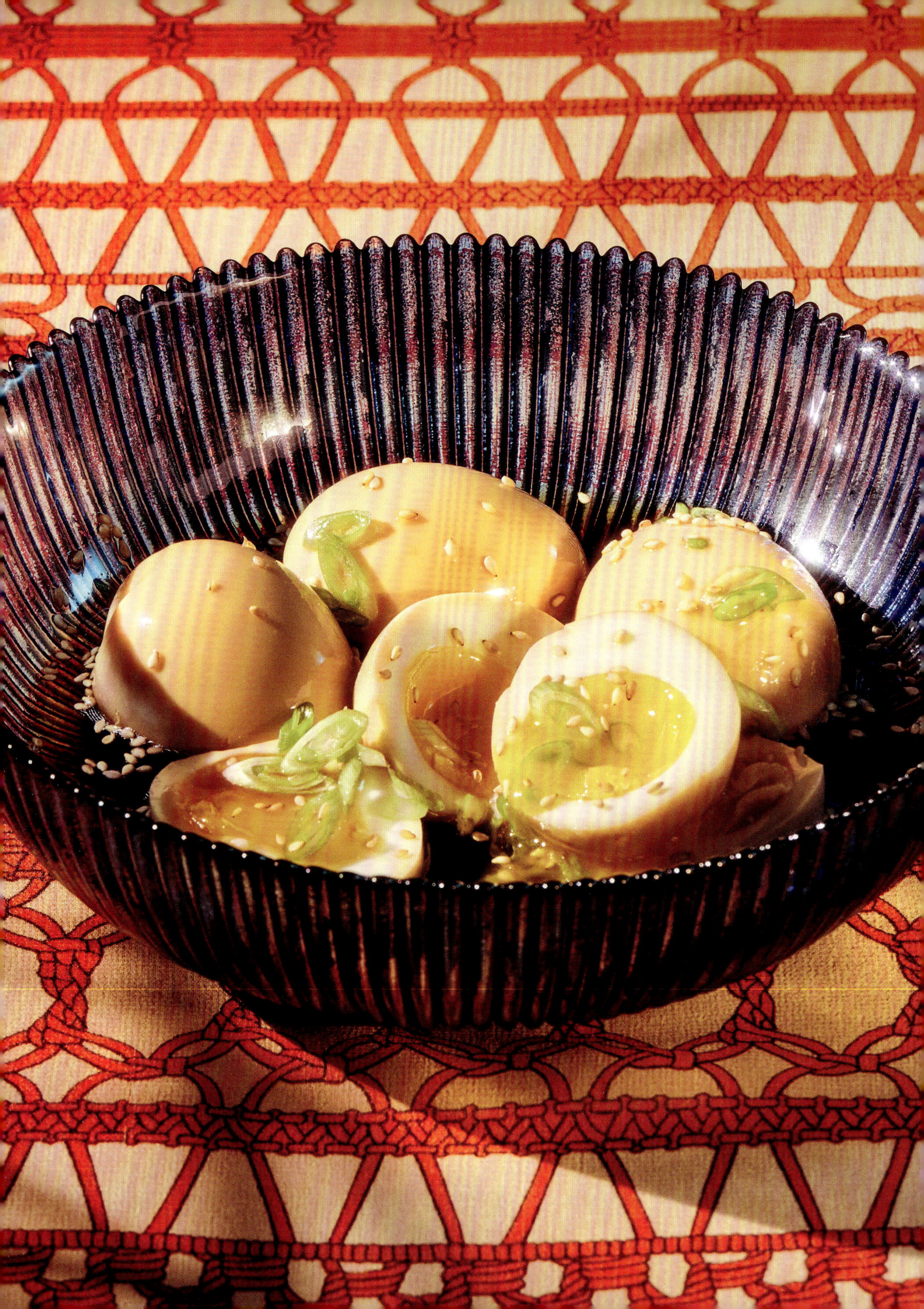

SOY-MARINATED EGGS

MAKES 4 TO 6 EGGS

Ice water

4 to 6 large eggs

½ cup light soy sauce

½ cup store-bought low-sodium chicken broth or vegetable broth

¼ cup mirin

Sometimes, all you need to perk up a dish is a stunning soy-marinated egg. Just when you think there can't be anything better than a jammy egg, you marinate it in a pool of deep umami flavors and you get a picture-perfect hard-boiled egg yolk in the center of an egg white that's been beautifully stained by a simple yet mighty sauce made from soy sauce, mirin, and chicken broth (or veg broth for vegetarians!). I love to prepare these overnight so that I have the perfect accessory to any dish at my fingertips. They can be eaten alone over some rice, but my favorite way is adding them to a big bowl of ramen (see page 91—side note: These immediately elevate instant ramen into an Instagram-worthy meal). These are best eaten within a few days, but they honestly never make it that long, even in my single-person household!

Fill a medium bowl with ice water and set aside. Bring a small pot of water to a boil over medium-high heat. When the water boils, use a slotted spoon to gently lower the eggs in one at a time. Using the spoon, continue rolling the eggs around gently for a minute so that the egg yolk remains in the center. Boil for 6 minutes for a runny yolk or 7 minutes for a jammy one. Use your spoon to transfer the eggs straight to the ice bath and cool for 7 minutes before peeling.

In a quart-size deli container or deep bowl, mix the soy sauce, chicken broth, and mirin. Add the peeled boiled eggs and place a paper towel on the surface of the liquid to keep all of the eggs completely submerged, then cover. Marinate in the fridge for at least 2 hours before serving, or store in the marinade for up to 5 days. When you're ready to serve, remove from the marinade, gently pat dry, and slice in half.

FIRST BITE, BESTIES • 63

TAKEOUT-STYLE CHICKEN WINGS

MAKES ABOUT 12 WINGS

½-inch knob of ginger, peeled

2 large garlic cloves

1 large egg

2 tablespoons all-purpose flour, plus more as needed

1 tablespoon cornstarch

1 tablespoon light soy sauce

1 tablespoon Shaoxing wine

2 teaspoons granulated garlic

2 teaspoons sweet paprika

1 teaspoon toasted sesame oil

1 teaspoon kosher salt

1 teaspoon sugar

Sriracha or red pepper flakes, to taste (optional but highly recommended)

3 pounds whole chicken wings (about 12)

Neutral oil (I use avocado oil), for frying

You're either already very familiar or completely unaware that some of the BEST fried wings come from your local Chinese takeout spot. They're golden and crispy from head to toe—or wing-tip if you will—and completely penetrated with salty, savory flavor. I first became addicted to these when I was in college. Wings were something I craved often, but I always wanted them from the Chinese restaurant. It became an ongoing discussion among my friends that they were the best, and after a few studies of ordering and feasting on late-night wings from various places, I think I won that argument. These are marinated and coated in a wet batter, which limits the mess and allows you to prep the wings overnight. The longer they marinate with the deep umami soy marinade, the more those flavors penetrate to the very bone. Double-frying is key for that extra crispness!

Grate the ginger and garlic into a large bowl (baddies, watch your nails); grating lets the flavor really penetrate the chicken. Add the egg, flour, cornstarch, soy sauce, Shaoxing wine, granulated garlic, paprika, sesame oil, salt, sugar, and sriracha (if using; no measurements here, just spicy vibes). Whisk until well combined and smooth.

Pat the chicken dry with paper towels so that it's thirsty for that marinade and mix thoroughly in the batter. Cover and marinate the chicken in the fridge for at least 2 hours, or up to overnight for the best results.

Take the chicken out of the fridge 30 minutes before frying to let it come to room temperature. Mix in more flour 1 tablespoon at a time until the batter coats the chicken and is the consistency of a runny pancake batter (I usually need 2 to 3 tablespoons).

Fill a large, deep pot with 6 inches of neutral oil or halfway (but don't fill it more than halfway), and heat to 350°F. Fit a cooling rack over a sheet pan or line a plate with paper towels.

Fry the wings in small batches for 5 minutes just to parcook them, then remove to the cooling rack.

Raise the heat of the oil to 400°F. Then add all of the pieces back in at once (or in two batches if they won't all fit) and double-fry until they reach your desired color—I like mine dark, like a good Jersey tan—about 3 minutes. Remove to the cooling rack to drain for a minute or two, and then enjoy immediately.

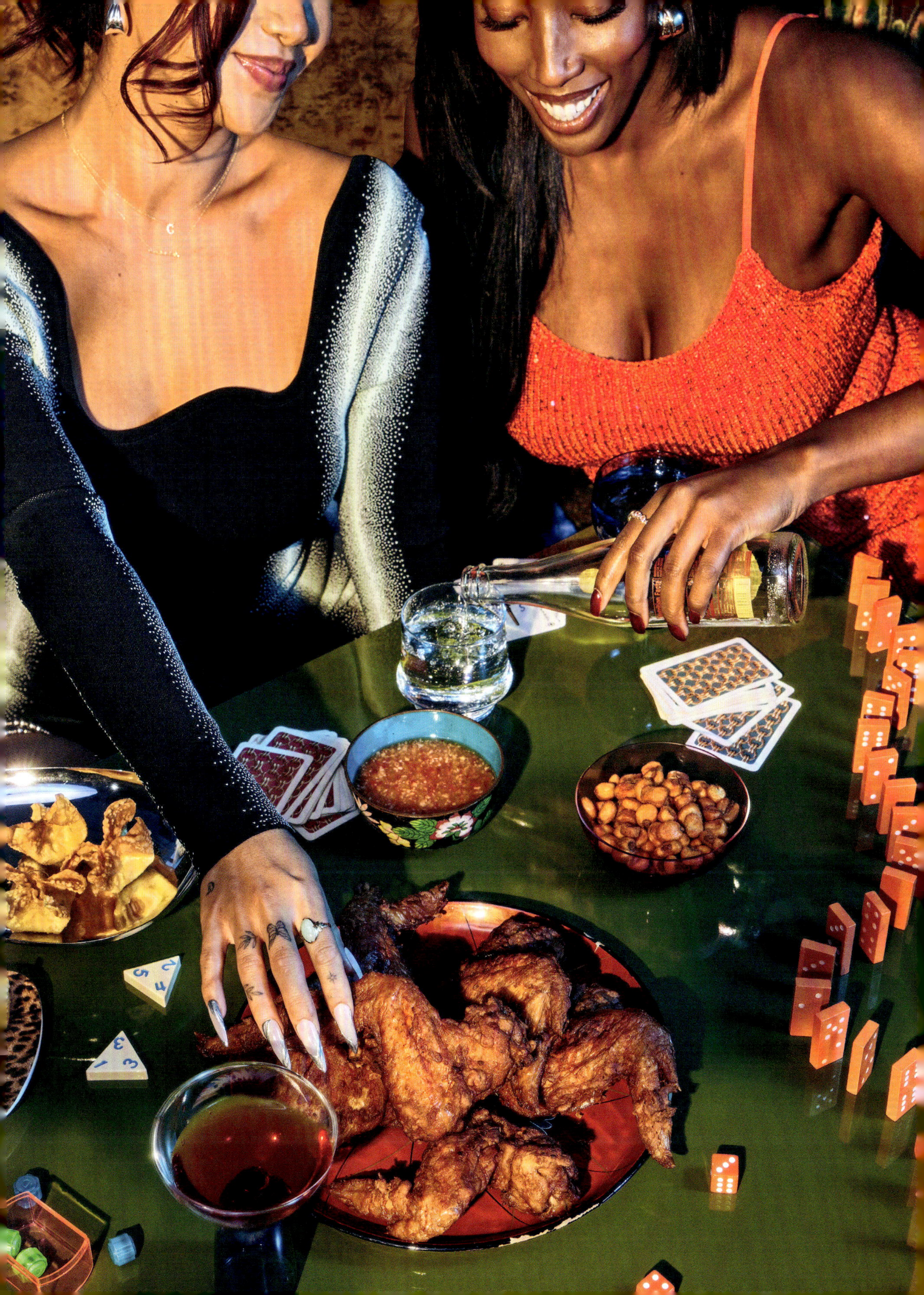

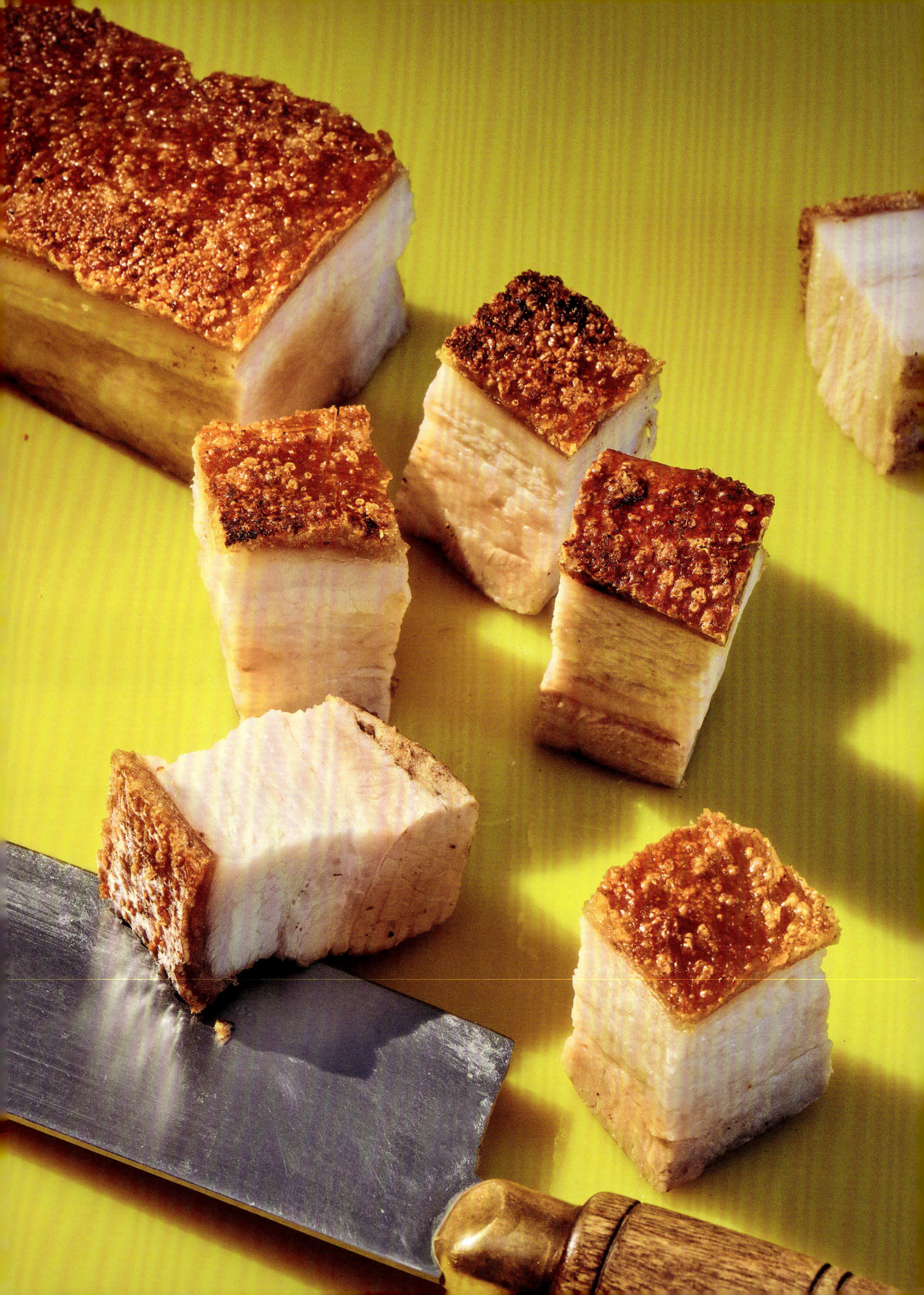

CRISPY PORK BELLY

SERVES 6 TO 8

Ice water

¼ cup kosher salt, plus more for poaching the pork belly

3 pounds skin-on pork belly (choose a piece with more meat than fat and no wrinkles on the skin)

2 tablespoons Shaoxing wine

2 teaspoons sugar

½ teaspoon Chinese five-spice powder

Get your mukbang on and prepare for the best ASMR—crispy pork belly that has a *serious* crunch unlike anything else! My mom has always been the cook of our family, but this recipe actually comes from my dad. There aren't many dishes that he cooks, but he takes a high interest in making crispy pork belly because he loves it *that* much. The signature crackling pork skin is salty, savory, and crunchy like a chicharron, and it's simply addicting. If that wasn't enough, right beneath that crispy crunch is the juicy Chinese five-spice-powder-infused belly meat, its flavor heightened with a little sugar and Shaoxing wine. To create that desirable bubbly skin, pierce the pork skin aggressively and leave the skin exposed in the fridge to dry out. The meat on the other hand is massaged and pampered with the seasoning to penetrate overnight. My dad is rather particular, so I always think that goes to show how good this crispy pork belly really is.

Bring a large pot of water to a boil over high heat. Fill a large bowl with ice water and set aside. Salt the boiling water—make sure it's salty like pasta water, or as salty as you are when all of the items you left in your cart sell out. Use a pair of tongs to add the pork belly skin side down and cook until the water comes back up to a boil, 7 to 8 minutes. Remove from the heat and transfer the pork belly to the ice bath and chill for 2 minutes, then remove to a clean plate and pat dry with paper towels.

Using a fondue fork, skewer, or sharp paring knife, poke the pork skin (not through to the meat) all over to create the cracked, crispy skin when it bakes.

In a small bowl, use a spoon to mix the ¼ cup of salt, Shaoxing wine, sugar, and five-spice powder to create a loose paste. Using your hands or a pastry brush, rub the sides and the bottom of the meat with the marinade, leaving the skin bare. Place the pork belly onto a sheet of aluminum foil skin side up and fold the sides up to cover the spice-rubbed meat, leaving the skin exposed. Refrigerate overnight to dry the skin and marinate the meat.

Preheat the oven to 400°F (convection mode; 425°F if using a regular oven). Discard the aluminum foil and transfer the pork belly to a wire rack set over a sheet pan. Bake until the skin is so blistered and crispy you could shatter it, about 1 hour. Rest for 10 minutes before slicing however you prefer (I usually go for bite-size pieces) and serving.

AIR FRYER CHAR SIU (Chinese BBQ Pork)

SERVES 4 TO 6

PORK BUTT

2 pounds boneless, skinless pork butt

2 red bean curd cubes plus 2 teaspoons red bean curd juice

3 tablespoons light soy sauce

2 tablespoons hoisin sauce

2 tablespoons light brown sugar

1 tablespoon Shaoxing wine

3 tablespoons honey

1 teaspoon toasted sesame oil

1 teaspoon Chinese five-spice powder

2 large garlic cloves

2 to 4 drops red food coloring (optional)

FOR SERVING

6 stalks gai lan (Chinese broccoli)

The Perfect Steamed Rice (page 242)

After a day of running errands with my dad when I was young, we'd always stop for a takeout order of char siu. I distinctly remember getting the classic order of char siu with Chinese broccoli over a bed of white rice. Fast forward to my adolescence and my dad started to make it at home: The smell would radiate through the house. It's incredibly easy to cook, and using an air fryer further cuts the time down by half. You can use different cuts of pork for this recipe, but I love using pork butt for its fat content. This also requires a bit of a unique ingredient, red fermented bean curd, which not only adds to the flavor but gives the char siu its signature red color (it comes in cubes—you can find it in a small jar in the sauce aisle of an Asian market). You'll be surprised how simple this is to make—and how good Chinese barbecue is!

Marinate the pork: Slice the pork in half lengthwise to make 2 strips about 2-inches wide and add to a large resealable bag or bowl. In a small bowl, use a fork to mash the red bean curd cubes. Whisk in the red bean curd juice, soy sauce, hoisin sauce, brown sugar, Shaoxing wine, 1 tablespoon of the honey, the sesame oil, and five-spice powder. Now get your grater and grate the garlic into the mixture (baddies, watch your nails). Whisk in the red food coloring (if using) one drop at a time until it's the color you desire (I usually use 2 or 3 drops). Pour the marinade on top of the pork, seal the bag, and mix well or mix by hand in a bowl (wear a glove if using the food coloring). Transfer to the fridge and marinate at least 5 hours or up to overnight for best results.

Preheat your air fryer to 400°F. Remove the pork butt pieces from the bag or bowl and let the marinade drip off the pork (reserving the rest of the marinade for later), then put the pieces in the air fryer basket, leaving about an inch between them, or cook in batches if both pieces don't fit. Air-fry for 7 minutes.

Meanwhile, in a small saucepan, pour the remaining marinade plus the remaining 2 tablespoons honey and stir and bring to a boil over medium-high heat, stirring frequently. Cook until slightly reduced, about 5 minutes, adjusting the heat if the marinade starts to bubble up. Remove from the heat and set aside.

After 7 minutes, use a pair of tongs to flip the pork and baste with the reduced marinade on all sides using a pastry brush. Air-fry for another 7 to 10 minutes or until there is a nice char on the pork and the juices run clear when you poke it in the thickest part. If you like, you can baste it once more now. Remove the cooked pork to a clean plate and rest for 10 minutes.

To serve: Set up a bamboo steamer (see page 27) in a wok or large pot filled with 3 inches of water. Put the pot over medium-high heat, and when the water starts to boil and create steam, add the gai lan to the steamer and reduce to medium heat. Cover and steam until the gai lan is bright green and the stalks are easily pierced with a knife, about 5 minutes. Remove the basket from the steamer and remove the gai lan to a clean plate.

Slice the char siu to desired thickness (I prefer mine about ¼-inch thick) and serve over steamed white rice and the gai lan.

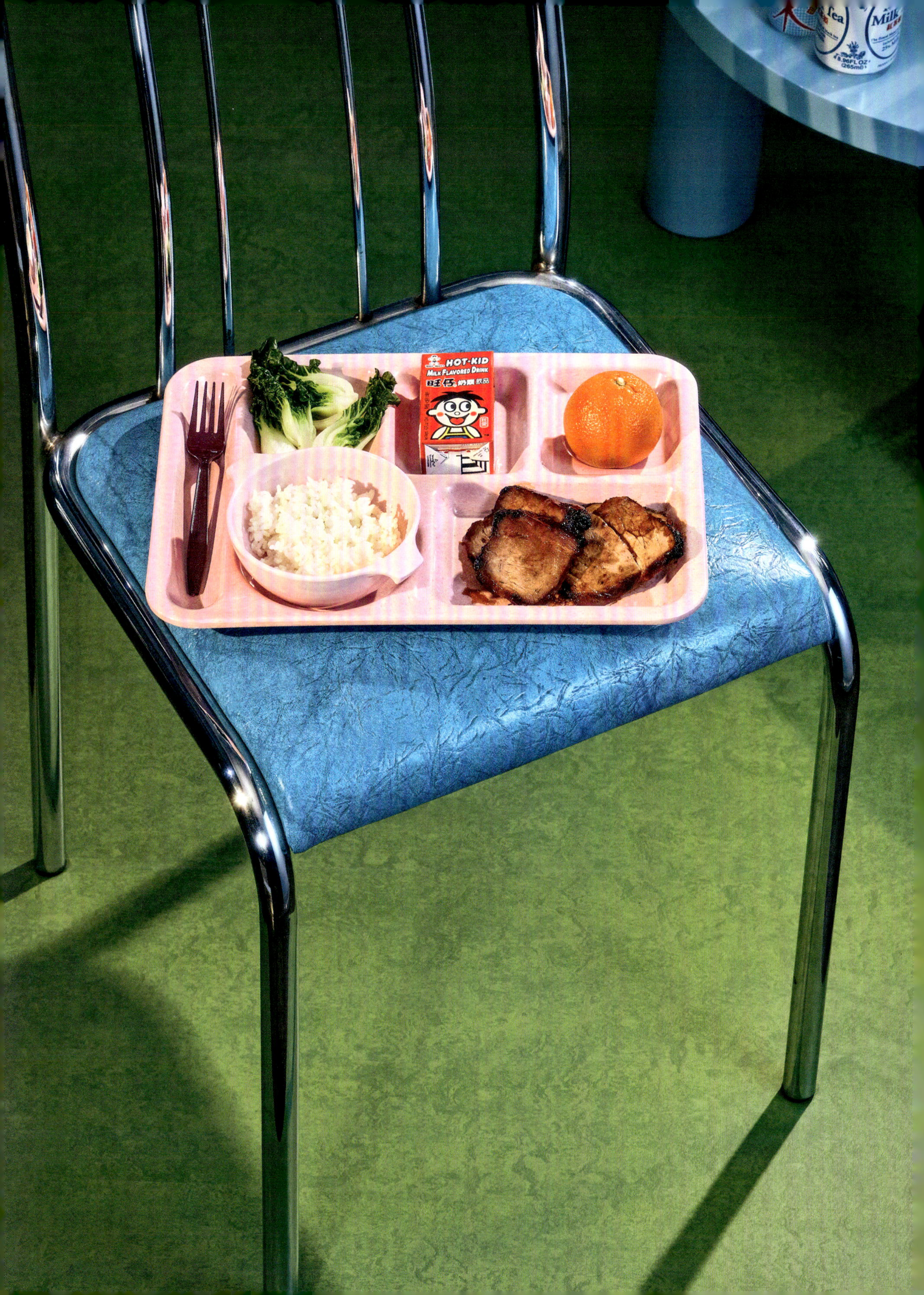
HOT-KID
MILK FLAVORED DRINK

NOODZ

DDZ NOODZ

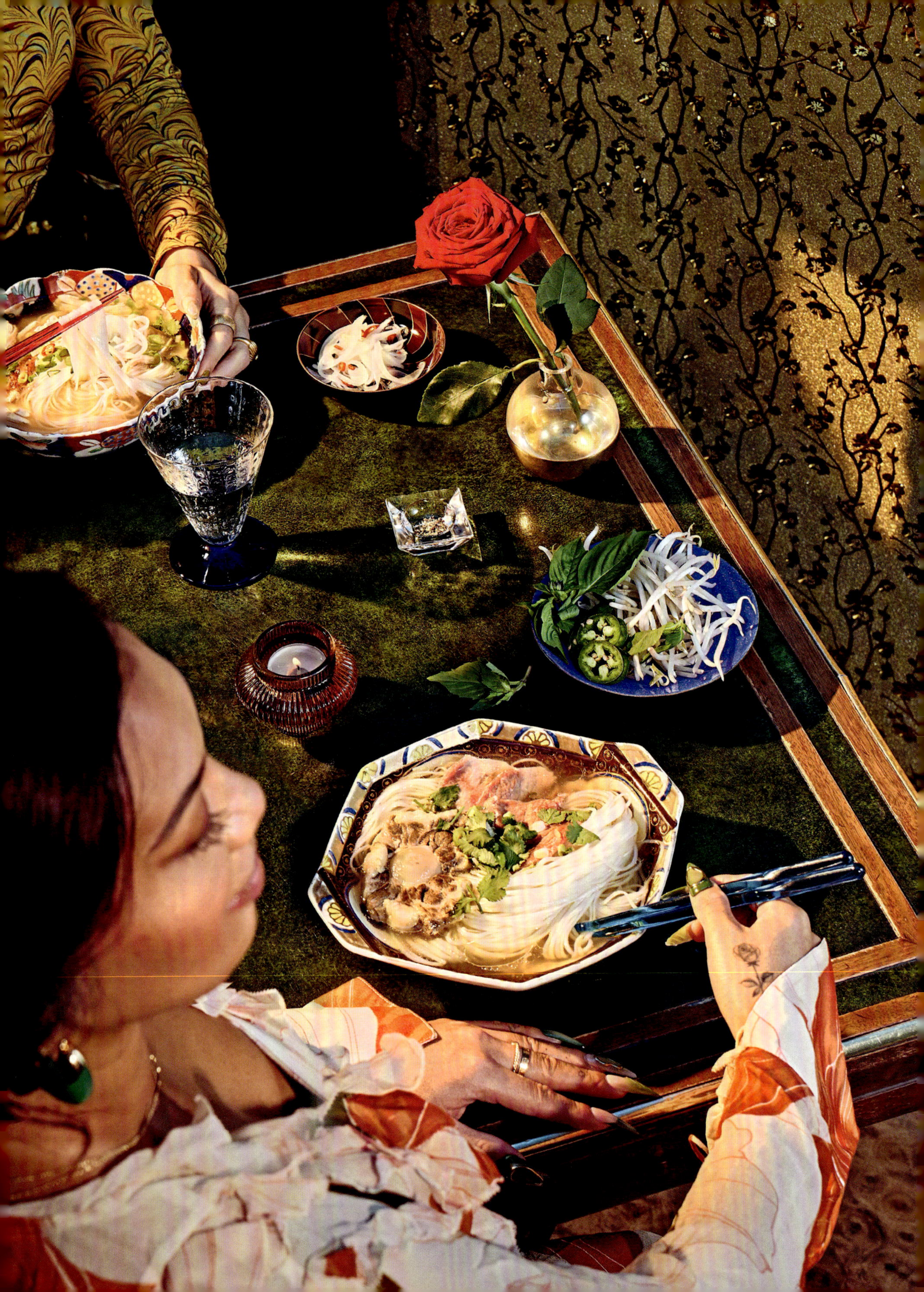

RECIPE LIST

Scallion Oil Noodles
76

Beef Chow Fun (Ho Fun)
79

Chicken Lo Mein
80

Pad Thai
83

Pad See Ew
84

Drunken Noodles (Pad Kee Mao)
87

Basic Udon Noodle Soup
88

Spicy Miso Instant Ramen
91

45-Minute Phở Gà (Chicken Pho)
92

Taiwanese Beef Noodles
95

Oxtail Phở
96

Welcome to what is quite possibly my favorite food group: noodles.

All shapes and sizes are welcome here, from thick, chewy, and flat rice noodles to thin and delicate ramen noodles. Whether drowned in a slowly simmered soup or stir-fried in a mouthwatering umami sauce, I am equally obsessed with all of them. When I can't decide what I want to eat, noodles hit every time. These are my favorites, and they never let me down. Happy slurping!

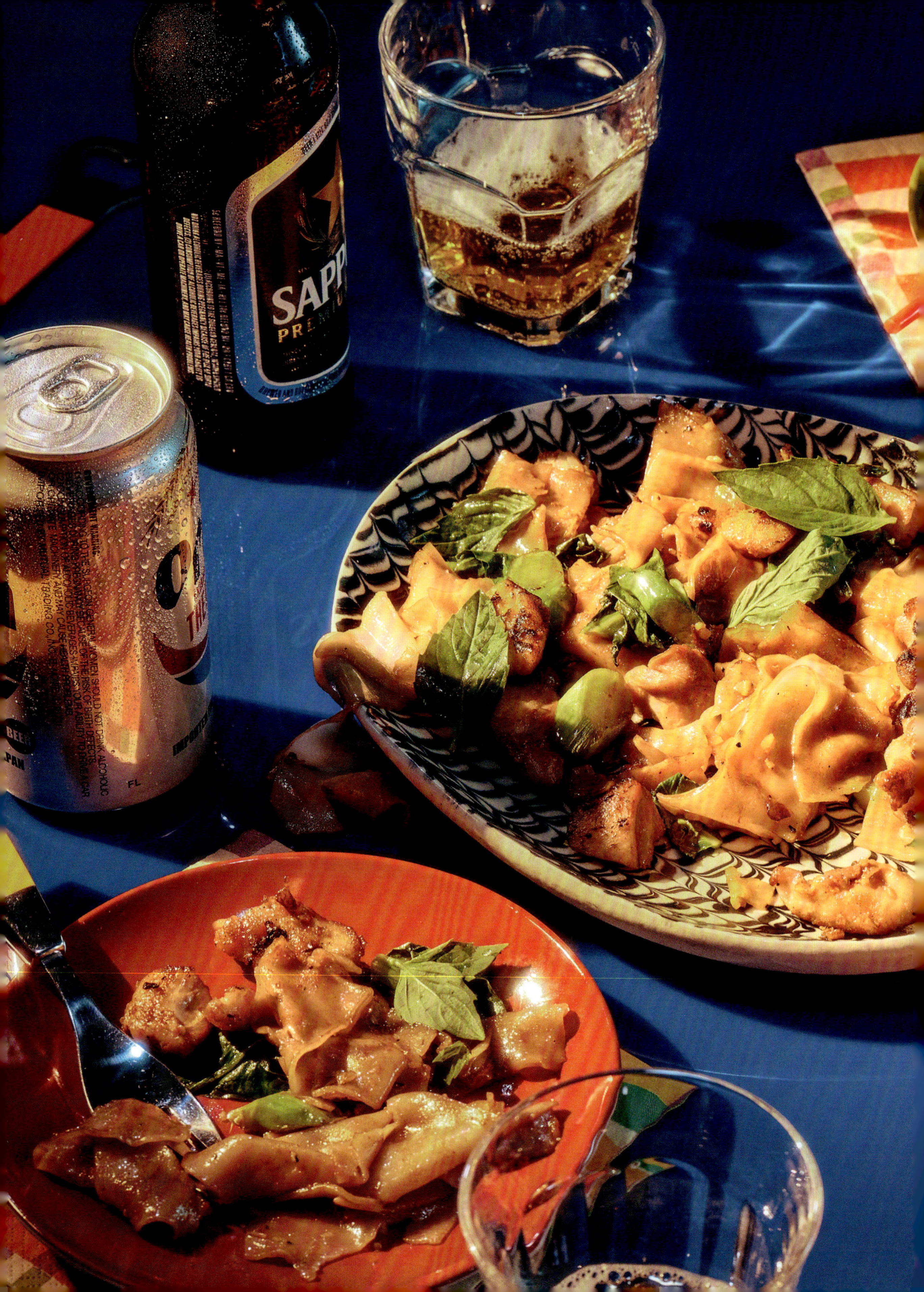

Orion
OKINAWA'S CRAFT
THE DRAFT
IMPORTED BY MUTUAL TRADING CO., INC. EL MONTE, CA 91731

SCALLION OIL NOODLES

SERVES 4 ON THEIR OWN, OR MORE AS PART OF A SPREAD

Kosher salt

1 pound any fresh wheat noodle (I like Twin Marquis Thin Shanghai Style Plain Noodle)

1 cup neutral oil (I use avocado oil)

10 green onions, white and green parts, separated and cut into 2-inch pieces

¼ cup light soy sauce

2 tablespoons dark soy sauce

2 tablespoons oyster sauce

1 tablespoon sugar

2 green onions, green tops only, thinly sliced, for razzle-dazzle

Please meet my favorite pull-together struggle meal that I make when I don't feel like putting much effort into a dish. Ready in less than thirty minutes, it's also highly customizable with whatever protein and veggies I might have in the fridge. This recipe calls for thin Shanghai-style plain noodles, but the beauty of fragrant, light onion-flavored scallion oil is that it tastes delicious on whatever noodle you desire (or have lying around). Bonus if you fry an egg and slide it on top—and don't forget the final touch of green onion razzle-dazzle!

Bring a medium pot of salted water to a boil—make sure it's salty like pasta water, or as salty as you are when your best friend denies your FaceTime call. Add the noodles and cook as the package instructs until they are tender. Drain and set aside.

While the noodles boil, make the scallion oil: In a wok or medium pot off the heat, add the oil and the green onion whites. Put over a medium-low heat and bring to a gentle simmer. Slowly cook for 10 minutes without stirring, until the green onion whites begin to turn golden brown. Add the green onion greens, stir once to combine, and fry uninterrupted over medium-low heat, being careful not to let them burn, until they've collapsed and are starting to brown, another 5 minutes. Use a slotted spoon or tongs to remove and discard the green onions. Remove from the heat and let the oil cool in the wok for 5 minutes.

In a small bowl, stir together the light soy sauce, dark soy sauce, oyster sauce, and sugar until well combined. Pour the sauce into the oil and mix until all of the sugar is dissolved. In a large bowl, combine the noodles and as much of the sauce as you like and toss to coat. Transfer the noodles to a serving dish and garnish with the green onion tops. (Any extra sauce can be stored in an airtight container in the fridge for 1 week.)

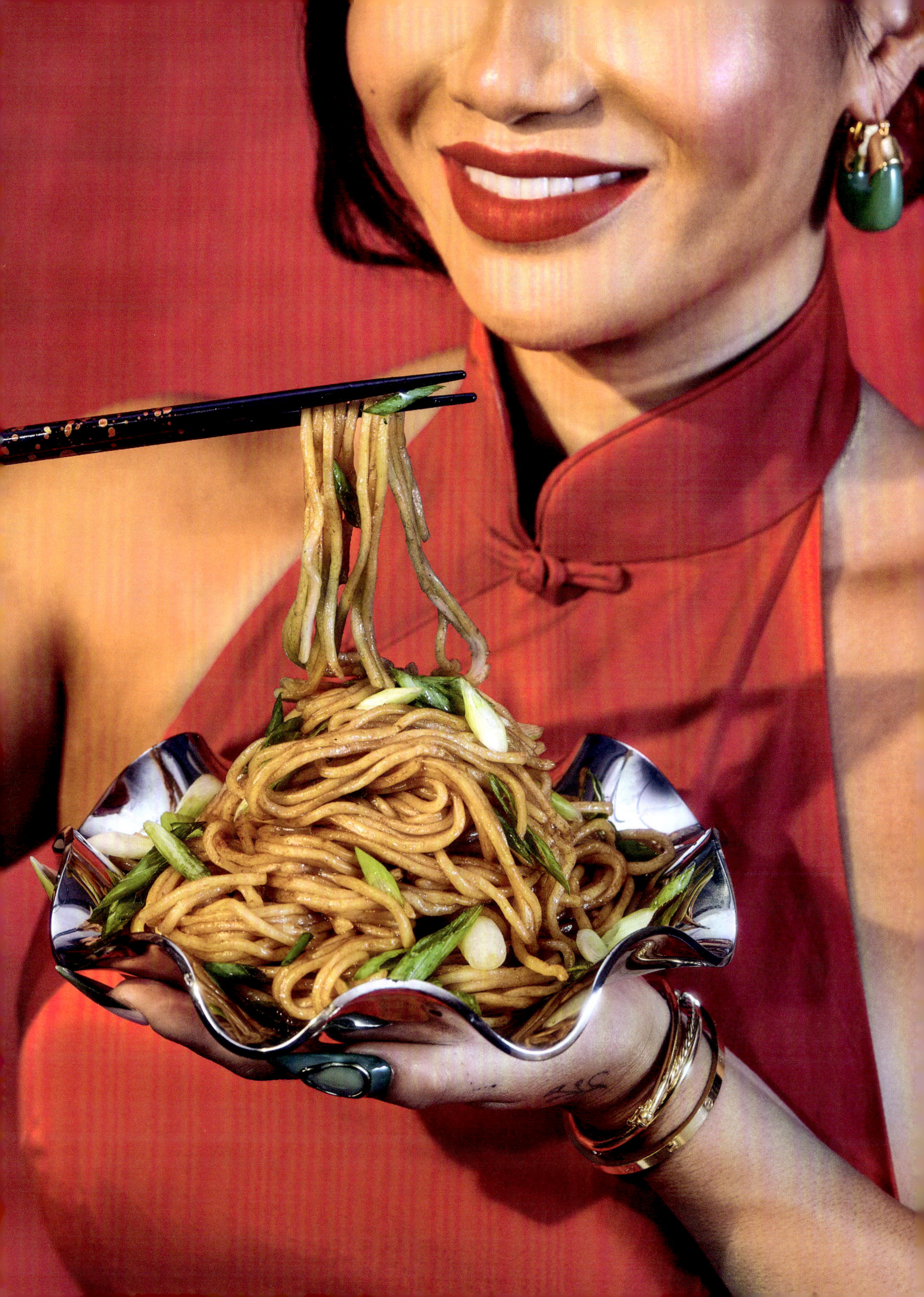

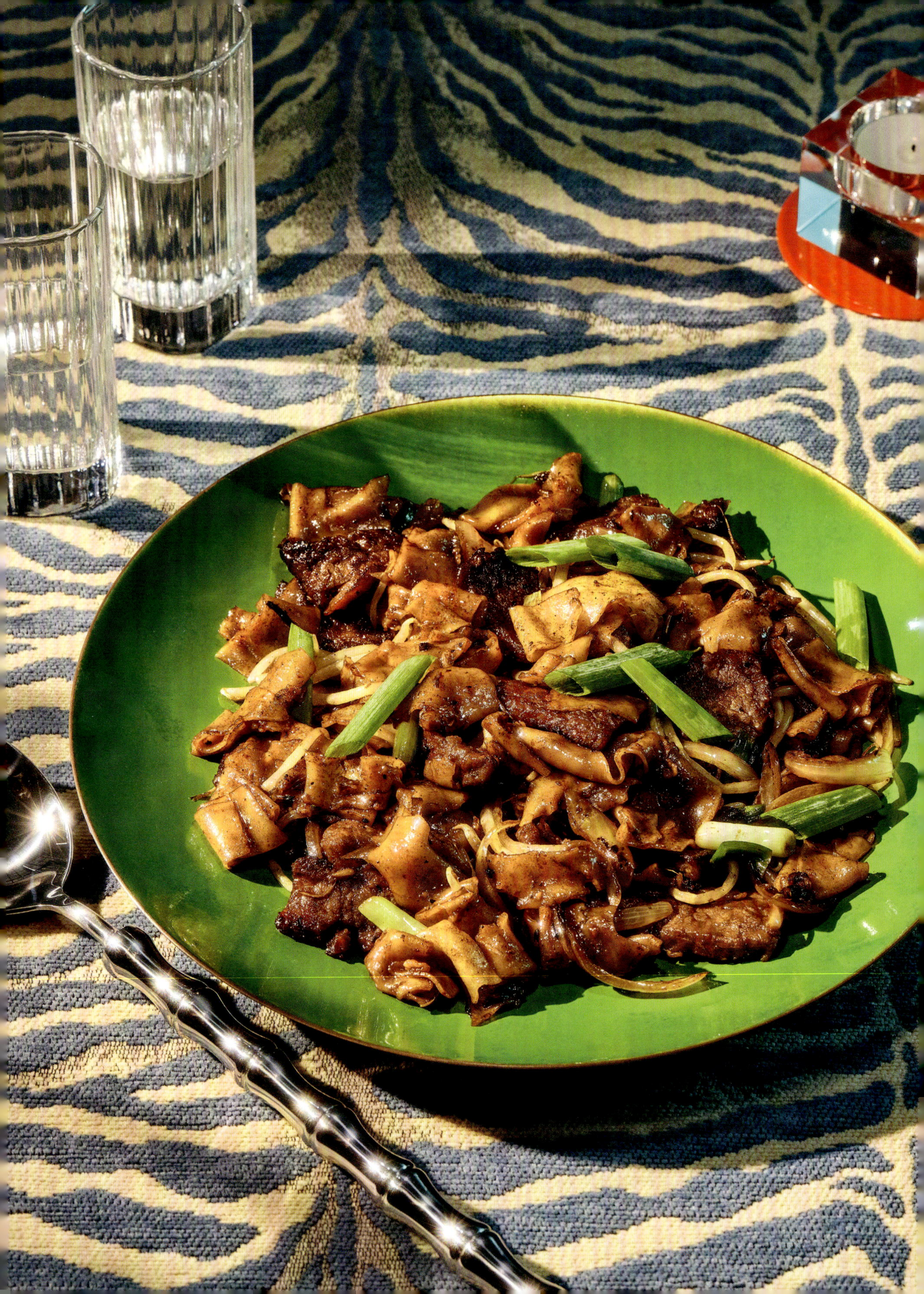

BEEF CHOW FUN (Ho Fun)

SERVES 2 ON THEIR OWN, 4 AS PART OF A SPREAD

BEEF AND MARINADE

- 1 pound flank steak
- 2 large garlic cloves
- 1-inch knob of ginger
- 1 teaspoon cornstarch
- 2 tablespoons plus 1 teaspoon neutral oil (I use avocado oil)
- 1 teaspoon light soy sauce
- ½ teaspoon baking soda

HO FUN SAUCE

- 3 tablespoons light soy sauce
- 2 tablespoons dark soy sauce
- 2 tablespoons Shaoxing wine
- 1 teaspoon toasted sesame oil
- 1 teaspoon ground white pepper
- ½ teaspoon sugar

NOODLES

- ½ medium yellow onion, thinly sliced
- 1 teaspoon kosher salt
- 1 pound fresh wide rice noodles, store-bought or homemade (see page 251)
- 3 green onions, white and green parts, cut into 1-inch pieces
- 1 cup fresh bean sprouts
- Toasted sesame oil, for serving
- 2 green onions, green tops only, thinly sliced, for razzle-dazzle

For as long as I can remember, my mom has always cooked every night of the week—except on occasional Fridays when she and my dad hosted friends to play mahjong. That was the only time we would *ever* order takeout, and I loved it (no offense, Mom) because it meant I could order beef chow fun, one of my absolute favorite noodle dishes. Now instead of ordering them, I make the noodles myself because, as we know, everything tastes better homemade. I marinate flank steak with cornstarch, baking soda, garlic, ginger, and soy sauce, which makes it so succulent and flavorful. And the flat, wide rice noodles perfectly soak up the slightly sweetened soy sauce and also take on a smoky char when they're tossed around in the wok. Simple bean sprouts and green onions are all you need to finish the dish. You can totally pull this together in under one hour—plus these noodles in particular reheat super well, making for excellent leftovers.

Marinate the beef: Slice the flank steak in half with the grain (lengthwise), then slice against the grain (crosswise) and at an angle to create ⅛-inch-thick strips and add them to a medium bowl. On a clean cutting board, mince the garlic and then the ginger. Add half of each to the beef (reserve the other half for the noodles). Mix in the cornstarch, 1 teaspoon of the neutral oil, the soy sauce, and baking soda, and set the meat aside to marinate for at least 30 minutes or up to 24 hours, covered, in the fridge.

Make the ho fun sauce: In a small bowl, mix together the light soy sauce, dark soy sauce, Shaoxing wine, sesame oil, white pepper, and sugar until combined.

Brown the meat: Heat a wok or large skillet with the remaining 2 tablespoons neutral oil over medium-high heat. When the oil is hot and shimmering, add the meat. Using a spatula, spread the meat flat into a single layer and don't stir (love her, leave her alone). Once the pieces begin to brown around the edges, 2 to 3 minutes, sauté—we're stirring aggressively here—for 30 seconds until the meat is no longer pink. Transfer to a clean plate.

Make the noodles: Add the yellow onion and reserved garlic and ginger to the wok, season with the salt, and cook, stirring constantly, until the onion begins to soften, about 1 minute. Add the noodles and sauce followed by the green onions and bean sprouts. Stir to coat the noodles with sauce, then love her and leave her alone so the noodles can char. After about 2 minutes, give the noodles a stir, then leave her alone for another 2 minutes or until they are charred all over. Add the beef back in and mix to combine. Finish with a drizzle of sesame oil and the green onion tops, and enjoy right away!

CHICKEN LO MEIN

SERVES 2 ON THEIR OWN, 4 AS PART OF A SPREAD

CHICKEN AND MARINADE

1 pound boneless, skinless chicken thighs

1 tablespoon light soy sauce

1 teaspoon oyster sauce

1 teaspoon plus 1 tablespoon neutral oil (I use avocado oil)

1 teaspoon cornstarch

½ teaspoon baking soda

2 small garlic cloves

1-inch knob of ginger, peeled

SAUCE AND NOODLES

3 tablespoons light soy sauce

2 tablespoons oyster sauce

2 tablespoons store-bought low-sodium chicken broth or water

2 teaspoons dark soy sauce

1 teaspoon toasted sesame oil

1 teaspoon sugar

Ground white pepper

Kosher salt

1 pound thick fresh egg noodles

Neutral oil, as needed

2 garlic cloves, minced

1-inch knob of ginger, peeled and minced

2 tablespoons Shaoxing wine

1 red bell pepper, halved, cored, and thinly sliced (about ½ cup)

3 or 4 green onions, white and green parts, separated and cut into 1-inch pieces

1½ cups stemmed and thinly sliced fresh shiitake mushrooms (about 7)

½ cup snow peas

I attended college before delivery services like Uber Eats and DoorDash were available (can you imagine?), so my options for takeout at Rutgers University were limited. The one thing that was always accessible was Chinese food, and the first thing I always ordered to test out a new spot was lo mein. I'm very particular about my lo mein, so I spent my college years ordering from all the restaurants and chasing the most perfect version. Here's where I landed: tender and moist chicken thigh (in this case marinated in oyster sauce with garlic and ginger; also feel free to sub in shrimp or steak) entangled in egg noodles slicked with the right amount of sauce, and paired with veggies that are just cooked enough so each presents a full-bodied bite.

Prepare and marinate the chicken: Slice the chicken crosswise into 1/4-inch-thick strips. Put the chicken in a medium bowl. Add the soy sauce, oyster sauce, 1 teaspoon neutral oil, the cornstarch, and baking soda. Now get out your grater and grate the garlic and ginger into the bowl (baddies, watch your nails). Massage the marinade into the chicken, and set aside to marinate for at least 30 minutes or up to overnight, covered, in the fridge.

Make the sauce: In a small bowl, mix together the light soy sauce, oyster sauce, chicken broth, dark soy sauce, sesame oil, and sugar, and season with white pepper to taste—no measurements, just vibes for the pepper. Set aside.

Cook the noodles: Bring a medium pot of salted water to a boil—make sure it's salty like pasta water, or as salty as we all are when it's time to go home from vacation! Add the noodles and cook as the package instructs until they are tender. Drain and set aside.

Sauté the chicken: Heat a wok or large skillet with the remaining 1 tablespoon neutral oil over medium-high heat. When the oil is hot and shimmering, let the marinade drip off the chicken (and discard the marinade) and add the chicken to the wok. Use a spatula or wooden spoon to flatten the chicken to create a single layer. Now let's exercise some patience and don't touch her until the meat is browned around the edges, 2 to 3 minutes. Shake the pan to move and flip the chicken, spread it back out into a single layer to cook until golden brown on the other side and cooked through, about another minute. Transfer the meat to a clean plate and set aside.

Finish the noodles: Add more oil to the wok if the wok is dry, followed by the garlic and ginger. Cook, stirring often, until fragrant and lightly brown, about 1 minute. Add the Shaoxing wine and deglaze the wok, stirring and scraping up all the browned goodness from the bottom, for about 1 minute or until the liquid reduces by half. Add in the harder veggies—the bell pepper and green onion whites—and cook for about a minute, stirring occasionally, until they are tender.

Add the shiitake mushrooms, snow peas, and green onion greens, and sauté (we're stirring aggressively here) until the snow peas are bright green, another minute. Return the chicken to the wok along with the noodles and pour in the sauce. Mix well to combine until the sauce coats everything evenly. Enjoy hot!

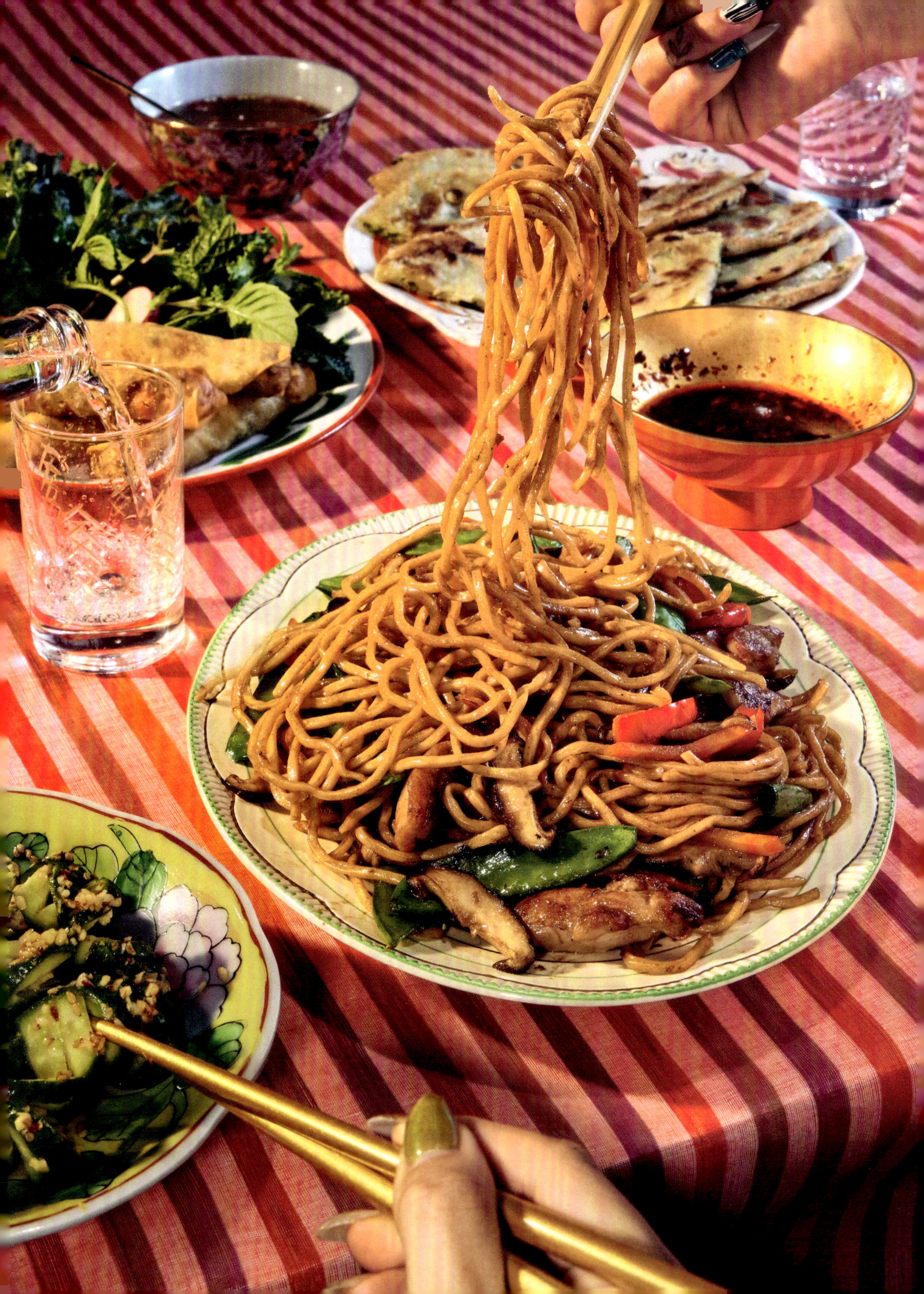

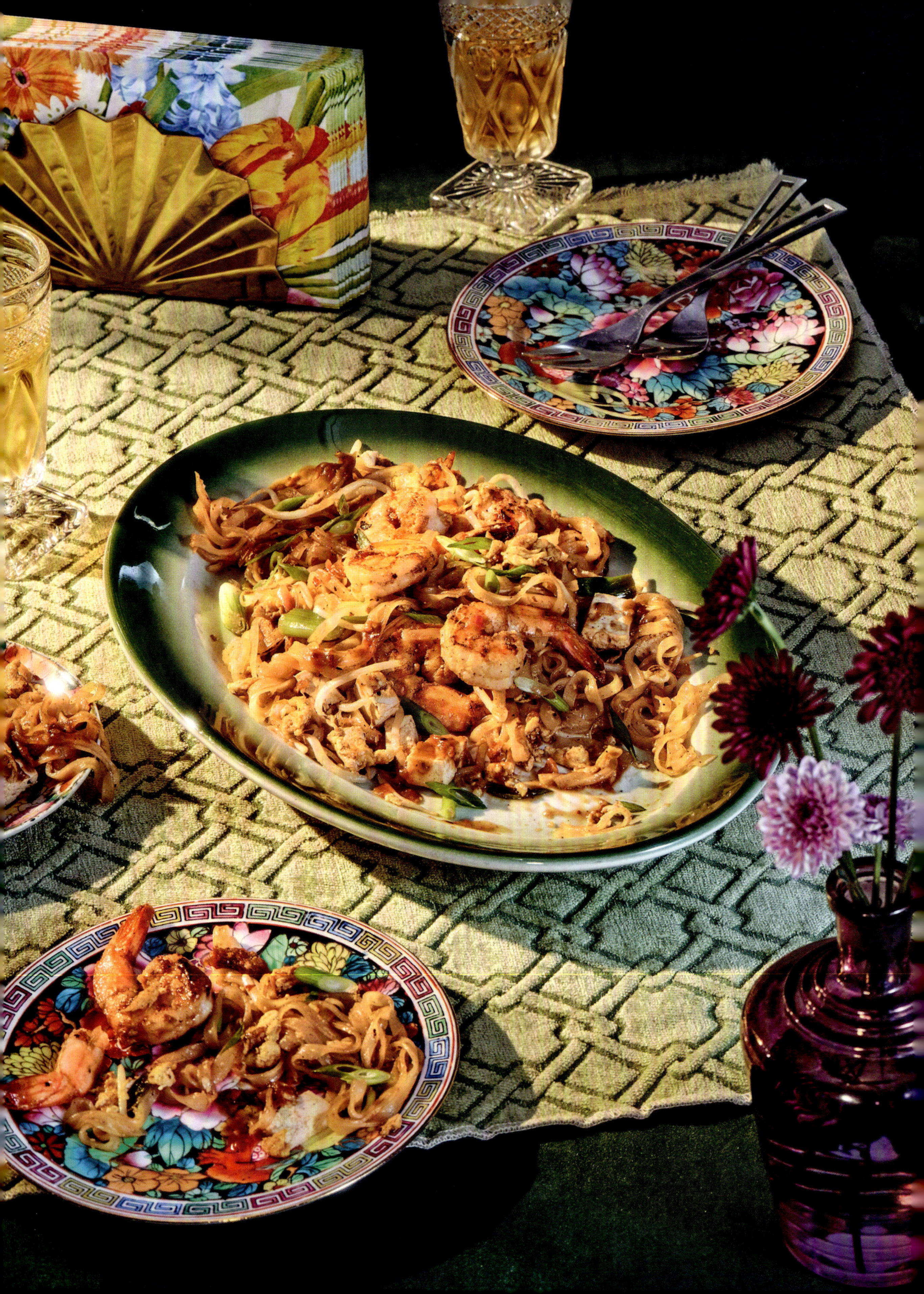

PAD THAI

SERVES 2 ON ITS OWN, 4 AS PART OF A SPREAD

8 ounces dried pad Thai or medium-width flat rice noodles (see page 21)

1 pound jumbo shrimp (around 25/pound), peeled and deveined (see page 46)

1 teaspoon garlic powder

1 teaspoon ground white pepper

¼ cup tamarind paste

¼ cup fish sauce

1 teaspoon chicken bouillon powder

1 to 2 teaspoons dried red pepper flakes, to taste (optional)

2 tablespoons neutral oil (I use avocado oil), plus more as needed

1 medium shallot, diced

4 large garlic cloves, minced

2 tablespoons palm sugar (see page 16) or light brown sugar

8 ounces firm tofu, drained and cut into ¼-inch cubes

2 large eggs, lightly beaten

3 green onions, white and green parts, cut into 1-inch pieces

1 cup fresh bean sprouts

FOR SERVING

Crushed plain roasted peanuts

2 green onions, green tops only, thinly sliced, for razzle-dazzle

1 teaspoon dried red pepper flakes

1 lime, cut into wedges

Pad Thai has always been my go-to order at any Thai restaurant because the noodles are tangy, savory, and chewy, but sometimes I wished its flavors would be more consistent—not too sweet or dry. So I started experimenting with my own recipe at home. When I traveled to Bangkok, I jumped at the chance to take a cooking class with the end goal of learning the techniques and flavors behind a good pad Thai. The chef-instructor kept stressing the word *balance* and how important it is for pad Thai to be the perfect balance of sweet, sour, and spicy. It clicked for me that these are exactly the things I crave when I think of pad Thai: sweet and sour from the tamarind, balanced by the saltiness of the fish sauce and the spice of the bird's-eye chilies. There should be enough sauce so the noodles are textured, far from dry, and not mushy.

What I love about this recipe is that you can make the sauce ahead of time, and even double it to have pad Thai sauce ready to go in your fridge.

In a medium bowl, cover the rice noodles with room temperature water and soak until they are pliable, for at least 30 minutes or up to 1 hour.

Add the shrimp to a small bowl and pat dry with paper towels. Toss to coat with the garlic powder and white pepper. Set aside.

In a small bowl, whisk together the tamarind paste, fish sauce, chicken bouillon powder, and red pepper flakes (if using).

Heat a wok or large skillet with the oil over medium-high heat. When the oil is hot and shimmering, add the shallot and cook, stirring constantly, until it's golden brown, 2 to 3 minutes. Add the garlic and continue stirring constantly until it is also golden brown, about 1 minute. Next, add the sugar and cook, stirring constantly, until melted (for the palm sugar) or caramelized (for the brown sugar), 2 minutes. Pour in the sauce and heat, stirring occasionally, until just combined, just a few seconds. Transfer to a small heat-safe bowl or container and set aside.

Add more oil to the wok if it's dry. Using tongs or a spatula, place the shrimp in the wok in a flat layer and cook without touching until they turn pink around the edges, about 1 minute. Flip the shrimp over and cook on the other side until they're just starting to turn pink, not fully cooked yet, about another 30 seconds, before transferring to a clean plate. If the pan is dry again, add more oil, then add the tofu to the wok and cook, tossing occasionally, until golden, 3 to 5 minutes.

Meanwhile, bring a kettle of water to a boil. Strain the rice noodles, return to the bowl, and pour over enough boiling water to cover. Soak for just 30 seconds, then strain and add straight to the wok with the tofu. Pour in the sauce, mix well to coat, and let the noodles simmer and soak up the sauce for 1 minute.

Using a spatula, push the noodles to the side and scramble the eggs in the empty space until almost fully cooked, about 30 seconds, then toss with the noodles. Return the shrimp to the wok along with the green onions and bean sprouts and sauté (we're stirring aggressively here) until the shrimp is pink and curled into a C shape, about 1 minute.

Divide the noodles among the plates and top with the crushed roasted peanuts, garnish with the green onion tops and red pepper flakes, and serve with a lime wedge.

PAD SEE EW

**SERVES 2 ON ITS OWN,
4 AS PART OF A SPREAD**

- 1 pound jumbo shrimp (around 25/pound), peeled and deveined (see page 46)
- 1 teaspoon garlic powder
- 1½ teaspoons ground white pepper
- 3 tablespoons light soy sauce
- 2 tablespoons distilled white vinegar
- 1 tablespoon dark soy sauce
- 1 tablespoon oyster sauce
- 2 teaspoons fish sauce
- 2 teaspoons sugar
- ½ teaspoon chicken bouillon powder
- 8 ounces dried wide rice noodles
- 1 tablespoon neutral oil (I use avocado oil), plus more as needed
- 5 stalks gai lan (Chinese broccoli), cut into 2-inch pieces, stalks and leaves separated
- 3 large garlic cloves, minced
- 2 large eggs, lightly beaten
- Toasted sesame oil, for drizzling
- 2 green onions, green tops only, thinly sliced, for razzle-dazzle

Whether to order pad Thai versus pad see ew is an ongoing argument since they're two of the most popular Thai noodle dishes. Pad Thai is tangy and nutty while pad see ew has more salty, charred flavors. When it comes to cooking these dishes at home, pad see ew is the first dish I'd recommend to anyone just starting to dabble in Thai food because it doesn't require a lot of prep work—let's face it, sometimes we just don't feel like chopping 20 ingredients (though my Pad Thai on page 83 is worth it!). I started playing around with my own recipe for pad see ew when one of my friends (might I mention she's a very picky eater at that) told me she tried it and liked it. She's always asking me to cook for her, and since her taste buds are difficult to please, I wanted to develop my perfect version of pad see ew. It's a dish mostly made from pantry ingredients with a rough chop of Chinese broccoli and some fresh garlic, too. Chinese broccoli resembles broccolini with its long and lean shape (which you can easily substitute if needed) but instead of florets it has big leaves with a wonderful earthy taste. The stems, when cooked, become a tender yet crunchy addition to the noodles.

In a small bowl, season the shrimp with the garlic powder and 1 teaspoon white pepper, and toss to coat.

In a separate small bowl, whisk together the light soy sauce, white vinegar, dark soy sauce, oyster sauce, fish sauce, sugar, chicken bouillon powder, and the remaining ½ teaspoon white pepper until combined.

Make the rice noodles: Bring a kettle of water to a boil. Add the noodles to a large bowl, cover with the boiling water, and set aside until they're pliable, 6 to 8 minutes, then drain and rinse under cold water.

Heat a wok or large skillet with the neutral oil over medium heat. When the oil is hot and shimmering, add the shrimp, spreading them into one layer using a spatula, and cook without disturbing until the edges begin to turn pink, 1 minute. Flip them over and cook until pink and curled into a C shape, about another 30 seconds, then transfer to a clean plate right away so they don't overcook.

Add more oil if the wok is dry, then add the gai lan stems and cook, stirring frequently, until they have a nice char, 3 to 5 minutes. Add the garlic and cook, stirring and shaking the wok often, until lightly golden and fragrant, about 30 seconds.

Raise the heat to medium-high and add the noodles followed by the sauce. Stir to coat the noodles with sauce, then love her and leave her alone so the noodles can char. After about 2 minutes, give the noodles a stir, then leave her alone for another 2 minutes or until they are charred all over. Using a spatula, push the noodles to the side and scramble the eggs in the empty space until set and just barely cooked, about 1 minute. Return the shrimp to the wok and add the gai lan leaves. Shake the wok violently (or at least with big noodle energy) until well combined and the leaves are wilted, another minute. Turn out onto a platter and finish with the sesame oil, garnish with the green onions, and serve!

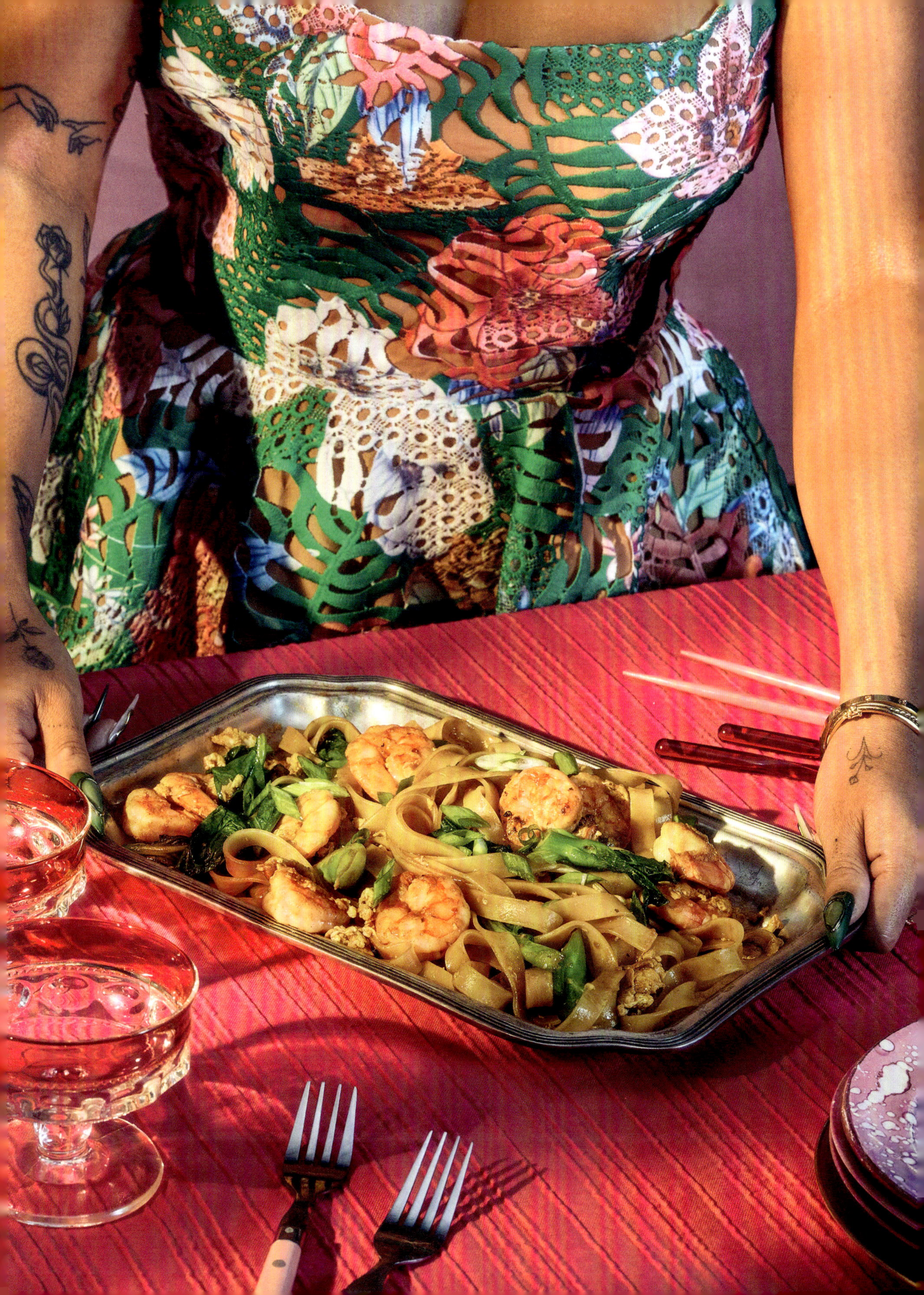

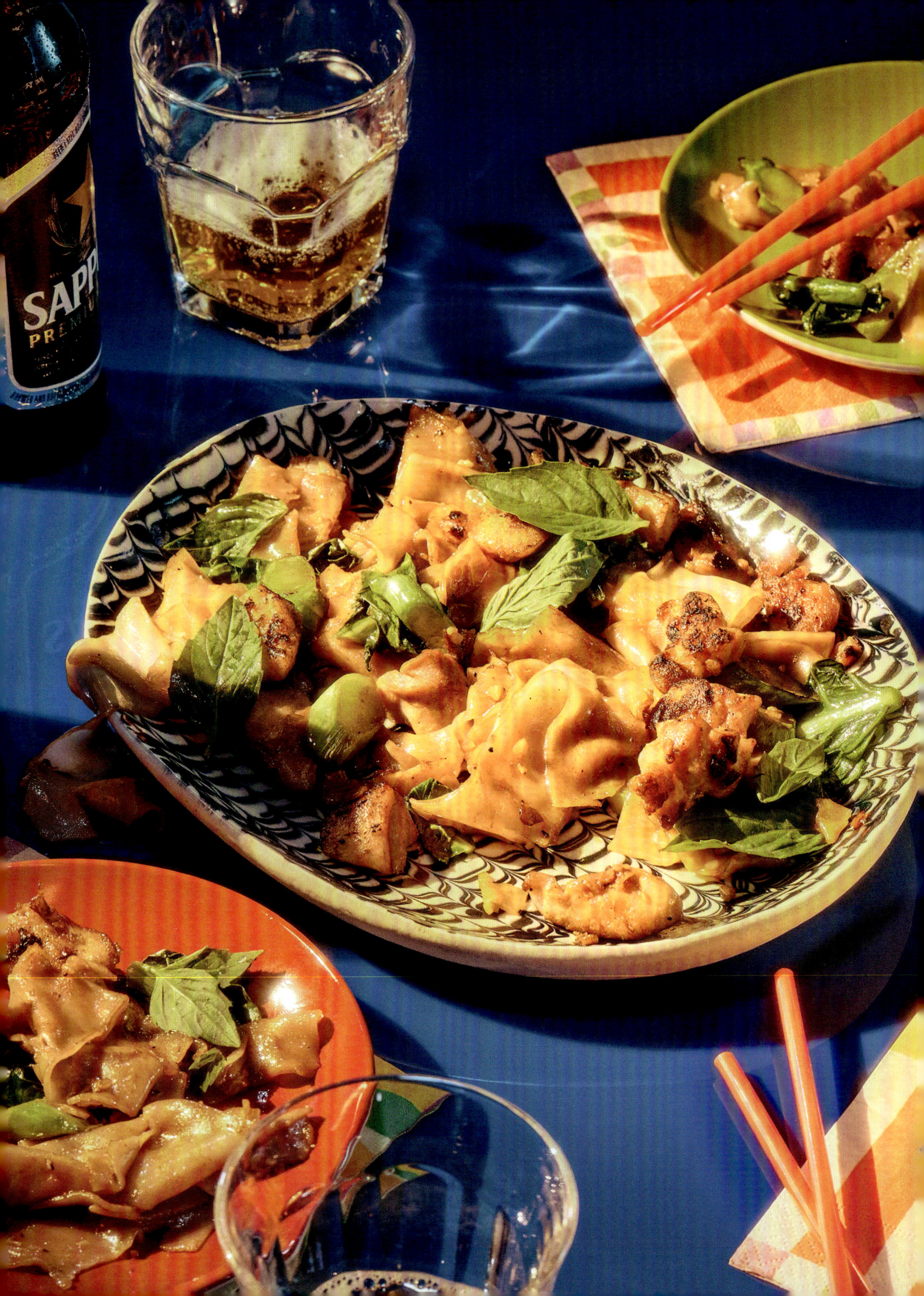

DRUNKEN NOODLES (Pad Kee Mao)

SERVES 2 ON ITS OWN, 4 AS PART OF A SPREAD

- 1 pound boneless, skinless chicken thighs, sliced crosswise into ⅛-inch thick strips
- 4 tablespoons light soy sauce
- 1 teaspoon plus 2 tablespoons neutral oil (I use avocado oil)
- 1 teaspoon cornstarch
- ½ teaspoon baking soda
- 4 large garlic cloves
- 2 or 3 fresh bird's-eye chilies, stems removed, to taste
- 2 tablespoons oyster sauce
- 1 tablespoon dark soy sauce
- 1 tablespoon fish sauce
- 1 tablespoon Shaoxing wine
- 1 tablespoon palm sugar or light brown sugar (see page 16)
- Kosher salt
- 1 pound fresh wide rice noodles, store-bought or homemade (see page 251)
- 3 stalks gai lan (Chinese broccoli), cut into 1-inch pieces, stems and leaves separated
- 1½ cups loosely packed fresh Thai basil, roughly torn, plus extra for razzle-dazzle
- 2 green onions, green tops only, thinly sliced, for razzle-dazzle

My natural instinct when eating a noodle dish is to load it up with sriracha or chili oil. Spice just makes everything better! Drunken noodles, however, need no additional sauce. They're perfect as is, flavor-packed with just the right amount of spice from the bird's-eye chilies in the sauce. It's rumored that this dish was named "drunken noodles" because it is perfect to enjoy after drinking (perhaps too much) alcohol. Spicy noodles that soak up booze? Now that's a dish for me. I'll never stop raving about wide rice noodles, but this particular recipe truly highlights them by hitting every aspect I desire: the perfect heat, the umami flavor from the soy and fish sauces, and the slightly charred texture thanks to the wok-fry.

Place the chicken in a medium bowl. Add 1 tablespoon light soy sauce, 1 teaspoon neutral oil, the cornstarch, and baking soda, and toss to coat all the pieces on both sides.

In a mortar and pestle or using a food processor, pound or pulse together the garlic and chilies into a slightly chunky mix. Add 1 teaspoon of the mixture to the chicken and stir to coat, then set the rest aside.

In a small bowl, whisk together the remaining 3 tablespoons light soy sauce, the oyster sauce, dark soy sauce, fish sauce, Shaoxing wine, and palm sugar until the sugar is dissolved.

Bring a medium pot of salted water to a boil—make sure it's salty like pasta water, or as salty as we all are when the weekend's over and Monday rolls around. Add the noodles and cook as the package instructs until they are tender. Drain and set aside. Or rinse the noodles under hot water to loosen if using homemade, drain, and set aside.

Meanwhile, heat a wok or large skillet with the remaining 2 tablespoons neutral oil over medium-high heat. When the oil is hot and shimmering, add the chicken and use a spatula to spread the meat into a flat, even layer. Cook without messing with it until the meat begins browning around the edges, 2 to 3 minutes. Flip the chicken over and cook until browned and cooked through, about another minute, before transferring to a clean plate.

To the wok, add the remaining garlic and chili mixture, being careful not to inhale—I repeat, *do not inhale*—as those chilies can be dangerous to your nose and eyes. Add in the stems of the gai lan and cook, stirring occasionally, until they begin to char, 2 to 3 minutes. Add the cooked noodles followed by the sauce. Stir to coat the noodles with sauce, then love her and leave her alone so the noodles can char. After about 2 minutes, give the noodles a stir, then leave her alone for another 2 minutes or until they are charred all over.

Return the chicken to the wok followed by the gai lan leaves and the Thai basil. Stir until combined and the leaves wilt, 1 to 2 minutes. Garnish with the green onions and more Thai basil and enjoy right away.

BASIC UDON NOODLE SOUP

SERVES 2 ON ITS OWN, 4 AS PART OF A SPREAD

2 tablespoons light soy sauce

1 tablespoon mirin

4 teaspoons HonDashi stock powder

1 teaspoon dark soy sauce

1 teaspoon sugar

1 cup stemmed and thinly sliced fresh shiitake mushrooms (about 5)

1 cup roughly chopped Chinese spinach leaves (sub with regular spinach or another leafy green)

8 ounces fresh or frozen udon noodles

1 cup Japanese fish cakes, thinly sliced (see Note)

2 green onions, white and green parts, thinly sliced, for razzle-dazzle

The perfectly doughy, bouncy udon noodle has a special place in my heart. I used to get so excited every time my mom would go to the Asian market because it meant she would have packs of udon waiting for me in the fridge. I grew up in an "ingredient household" instead of a ready-to-eat and snack house and anytime there was udon in the fridge, I felt like I was set up for a successful meal because it's so easy to throw together. A basic udon noodle soup is as simple as boiling a few ingredients like dashi powder, soy sauce, and mirin to make a flavorful broth, then boiling the noodles and adding whatever garnishes you have on hand. I often add an egg and any leftovers from the fridge (like shredded chicken or grilled steak) to create a one-of-a-kind combo in less than twenty minutes. This recipe calls for dashi stock but is equally as delicious with chicken, beef, or veggie broth.

In a large pot, combine 8 cups of water, the light soy sauce, mirin, dashi, dark soy sauce, and sugar. Set over medium-high heat and cook, stirring occasionally, until the sugar is dissolved, 5 minutes. When the broth is steaming, add the sliced mushrooms and spinach and cook, stirring occasionally, until the vegetables have softened and wilted, 2 to 3 minutes.

Meanwhile, in a separate medium pot, boil the udon noodles according to the package instructions or just until the noodles separate (they usually come pressed together in a block). Use a spider to remove the noodles (leaving the pot on the heat) and divide among the serving bowls. Add the fish cakes to the pot and boil until they are heated through, about 1 minute. Use the spider to transfer the fish cakes to each bowl. Use the spider to divide the mushrooms and spinach among the bowls, then ladle over the broth. Serve garnished with the green onions.

> **NOTE**
>
> Japanese fish cakes, or kamaboko, are made from a puree of fish, flavorings, and binding agents, then pressed and steamed into round loaves. They are already fully cooked but will need to be sliced and reheated before serving.

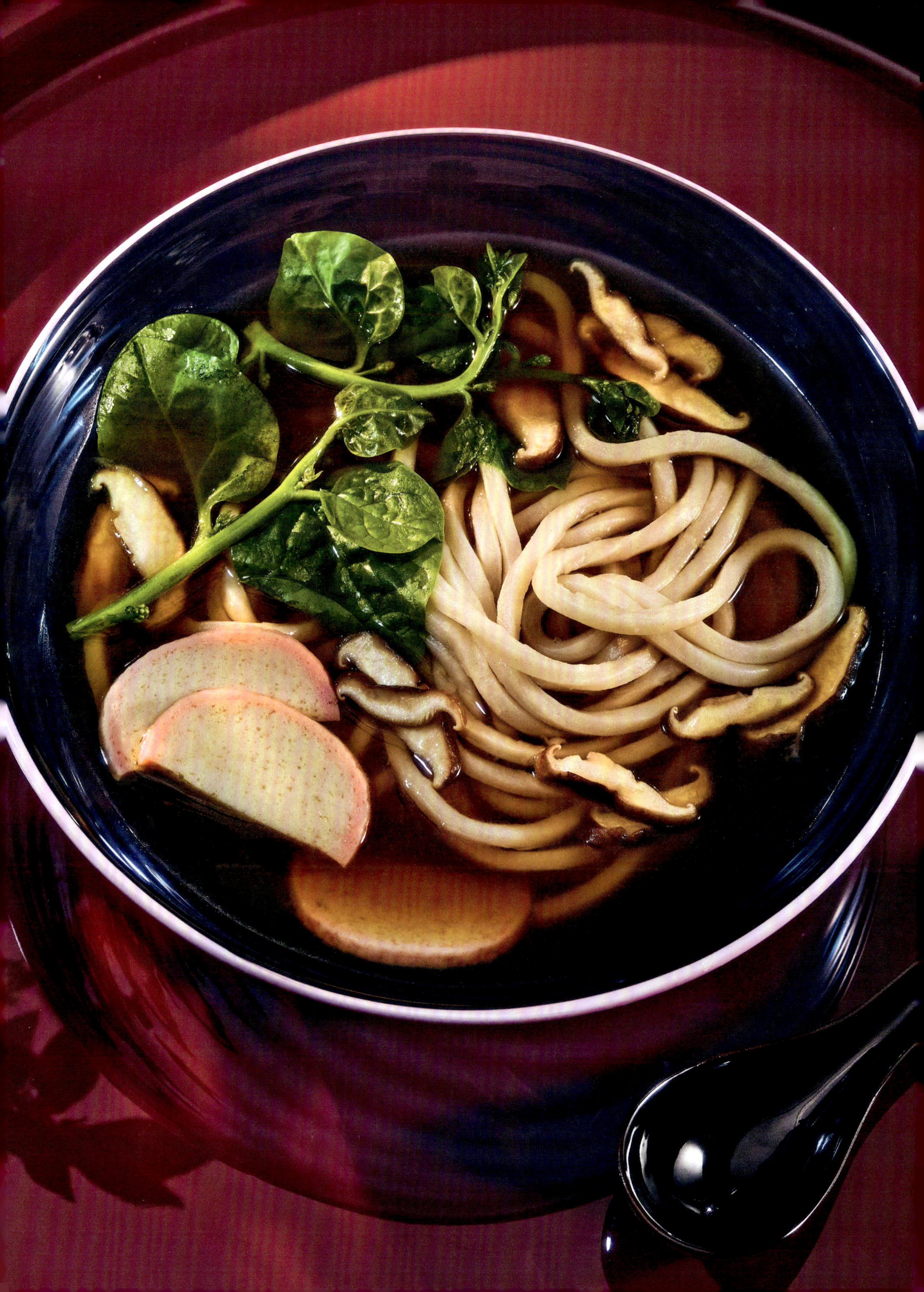

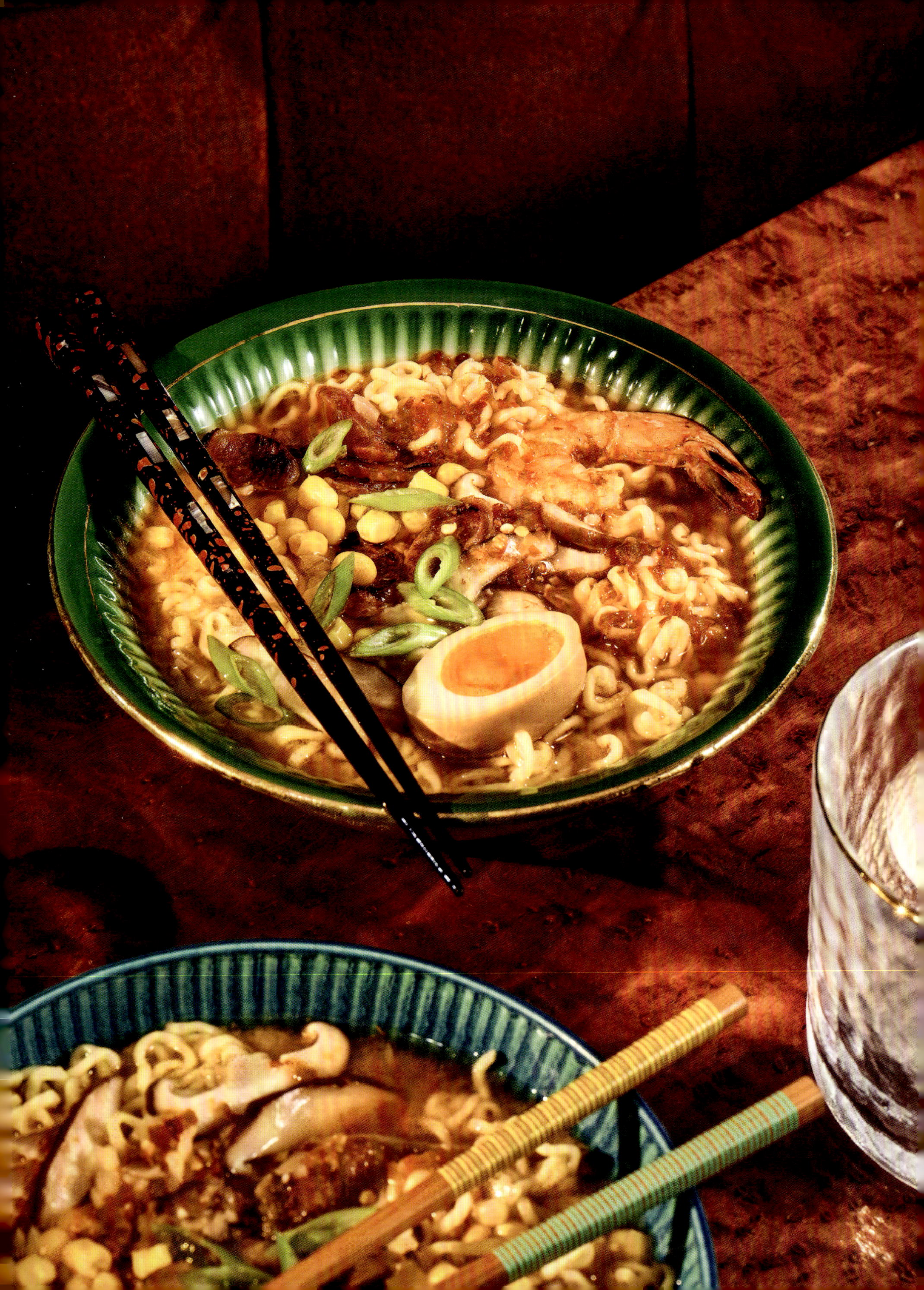

SPICY MISO INSTANT RAMEN

SERVES 2

1 tablespoon neutral oil (I use avocado oil)

½ small white onion, minced (about ¼ cup)

Kosher salt

1½ cups stemmed and thinly sliced fresh shiitake mushrooms (about 7)

4 small garlic cloves, minced

1-inch knob of ginger, peeled and minced

8 cups store-bought low-sodium chicken broth or bone broth

2 tablespoons light soy sauce

1 to 2 tablespoons sambal oelek chili paste or chili garlic sauce, to taste

3 tablespoons white miso paste

2 (4.2-ounce) instant ramen packets, seasoning packets discarded

FOR SERVING

2 Soy-Marinated Eggs (page 63)

1 cup fresh sweet corn, thawed if frozen or drained if canned

Any leftover cooked protein (like chicken, shrimp, or beef; optional)

2 green onions, green tops only, thinly sliced, for razzle-dazzle

I wholeheartedly *love* instant ramen, and at one point as a teenager I was highly fixated on the spicy instant noodle iteration. To spice things up even more, I'd often take the noodles, omit the seasoning packet, and make my own broth—thus, homemade spicy miso ramen was born. The glamorized packaged ramen that I made on TikTok when I was hungover the day after my sister's wedding was actually one of my first recipes to go viral, getting millions of views overnight. It basically kicked off my journey on social media. I think instant ramen is something everybody should have on hand, and switching out the seasoning packet with some other pantry ingredients to make a quick homemade broth can make this "gourmet." Instant ramen gets the job done, but let's add a little razzle-dazzle and make it great.

Heat the neutral oil in a medium pot over medium heat. When it's hot and shimmering, add the onion and season with salt to taste—no measurements, just vibes for the salt. Using a wooden spoon, cook, stirring frequently, until the onion begins to turn translucent, 3 to 5 minutes. Add the mushrooms and cook, continuing to stir frequently, until tender, another 3 to 5 minutes. Stir in the garlic and ginger and cook, stirring constantly, until fragrant, 1 minute.

Pour in the chicken broth and bring to a boil. Reduce the heat to medium-low, stir in the soy sauce and sambal oelek, and simmer until combined and fragrant, about 5 minutes. Remove the pot from the heat. In a small bowl, mix the miso paste with 3 tablespoons of water until smooth and stir into the broth off the heat. Cover and keep warm but don't boil—you lose the nutritional benefits when miso paste is boiled.

Bring a medium pot of salted water to a boil—make sure it's salty like pasta water, or as salty as you are when someone hits you with a Draw 4 in Uno. Add the noodles and cook as the package instructs until they are tender. Drain and divide among 2 big bowls.

Ladle as much of the broth as you like over the noodles and evenly divide the eggs, corn, and any leftover protein you might have (bonus here, not necessary). Garnish with the green onions and enjoy! (I usually have extra broth and I like to save it for sipping!)

45-MINUTE PHỞ GA (Chicken Pho)

SERVES 4 TO 6

PHO

1 medium yellow onion, halved and skin-on

3-inch knob of ginger, skin-on and sliced

½ (1.5-ounce) package pho spice mix (about ¼ cup; see Note)

1 (3-pound) rotisserie chicken, meat shredded and set aside, carcass reserved

¼ cup fish sauce

1 to 2 tablespoons chicken bouillon powder, to taste

1-inch piece rock sugar or 2 teaspoons granulated sugar

Kosher salt

1 pound fresh pho noodles (see page 21)

FOR SERVING

(choose just the noodles or go wild with the toppings!)

Quick Chili-Vinegar Onions (optional; page 202)

Fresh bean sprouts

1 medium jalapeño, sliced into rings

Fresh cilantro leaves, roughly chopped, for razzle-dazzle

Fresh Thai basil leaves, for even more razzle-dazzle

1 lime, cut into wedges

The best thing about pho? The broth! I've made traditional-style pho broth from oxtails as well as from chicken, and it can take up to a full day. So I created this quick recipe that takes forty-five minutes to make. The trick? Rather than braising the meat, use a rotisserie chicken, which is easy to get your hands on and is packed with flavor. Also char the aromatics under a broiler to really enhance the natural sweetness of the onion and ginger. I love to have prepackaged Old Man Que Huong pho spice mix in my pantry at all times so that I can whip this up whenever the craving calls (it's available at Asian markets or online). The spice mix consists of star anise, cinnamon, cloves, coriander seeds, fennel seeds, and fructus amomi (aka a type of cardamom). I also love to take this to the next level by making quick and spicy pickled onions to pair with every bite. This recipe is foolproof and has saved me so many times from my violent cravings!

Make the pho: Preheat the broiler with the oven rack at the top. Line a sheet pan with aluminum foil. Place the onion and ginger on the pan and roast, without turning, until they are slightly charred, 10 to 15 minutes. Cool completely and then peel the skins off.

In a small skillet set over medium heat, toast the pho spices, shaking the pan often, until the spices are fragrant and have some color, 3 to 5 minutes. Add them to a spice bag or to the center of a square of cheesecloth and use kitchen twine to tie the bag or cheesecloth closed.

To a large pot, add the chicken carcass, charred onion and ginger, spice bag, fish sauce, chicken bouillon powder, rock sugar, and enough water to cover (usually about 1 gallon or 16 cups). Bring to a boil over high heat, then immediately reduce the heat to low so the broth simmers gently and cook, covered, until the broth is flavorful, about 45 minutes.

To serve: Bring a medium pot of salted water to a boil—make sure it's salty like pasta water, or as salty as you are when you get invited somewhere exciting but you have work. Cook the rice noodles according to the package instructions. Drain and divide among the bowls.

Strain the broth, discard the solids, and ladle over the rice noodles. I enjoy my pho with some shredded chicken, Chili-Vinegar Onions, bean sprouts, jalapeño slices, cilantro, Thai basil, and a squeeze of fresh lime juice.

> **NOTE**
>
> My favorite brand of pho spice mix is Old Man Que Huong Pho Bac Spice Seasoning. The spice mix is made for a larger serving size, so I use half (about ¼ cup) to make the pho ga, then save the rest for another time, like the Oxtail Phở on page 96.

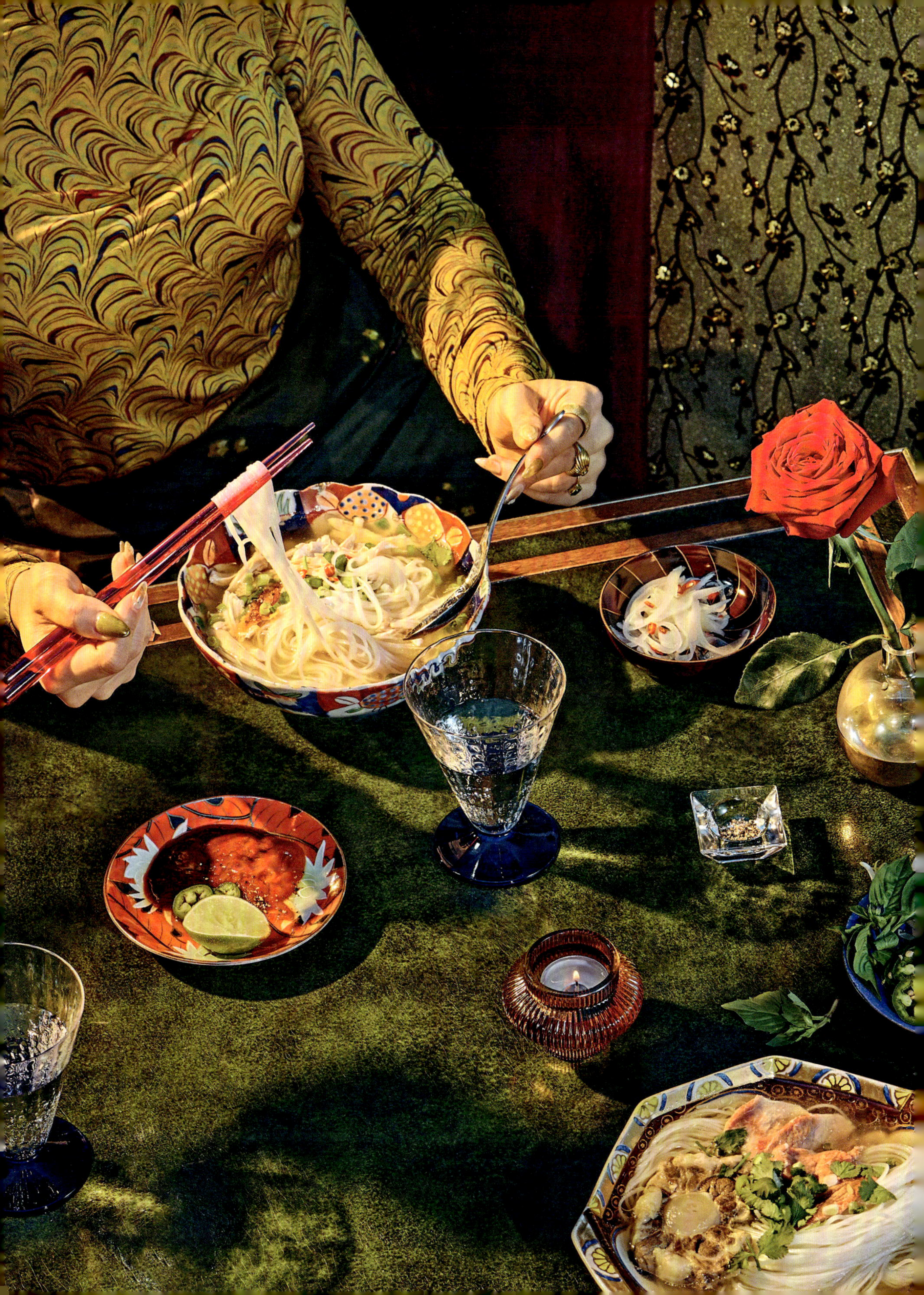

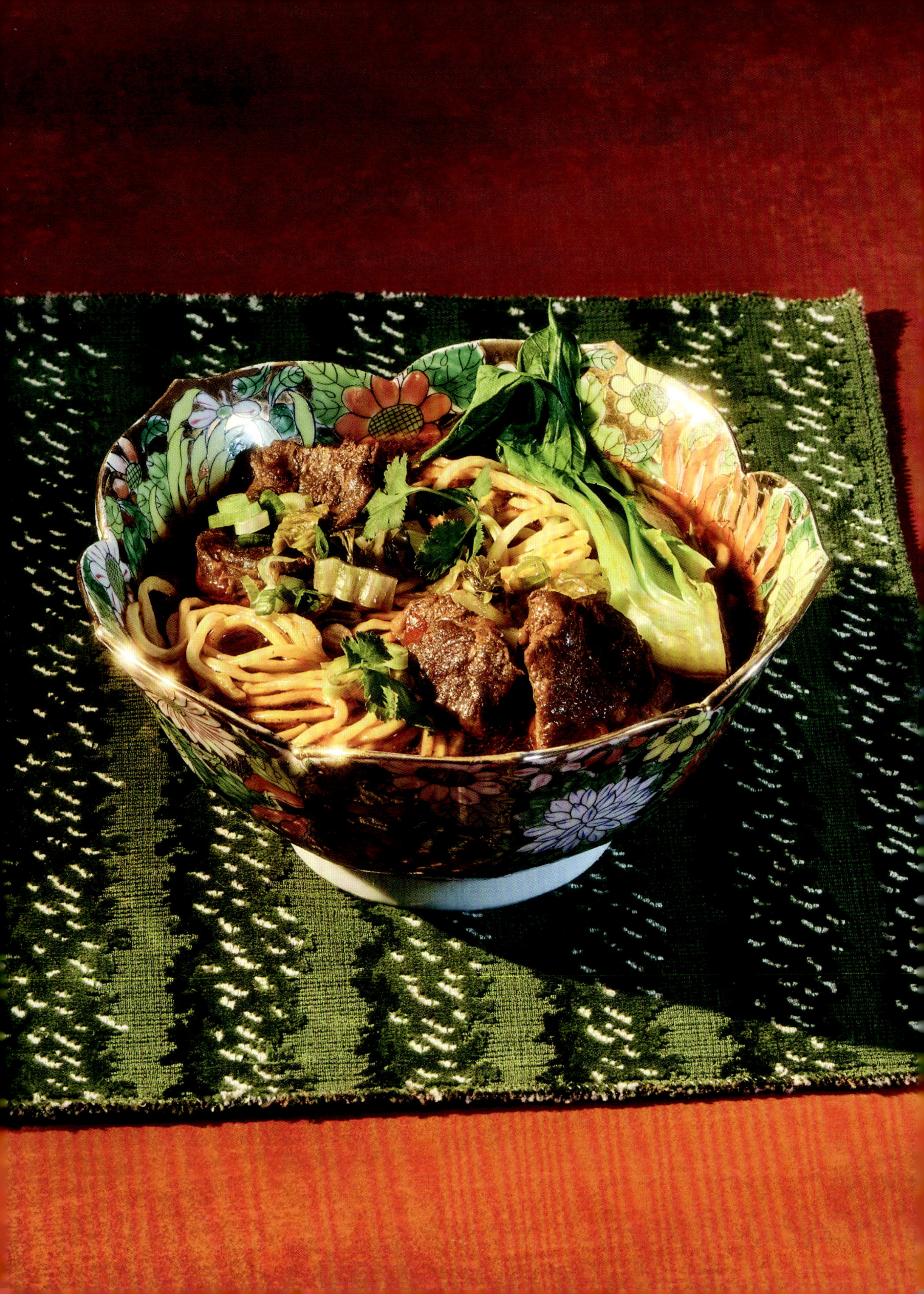

TAIWANESE BEEF NOODLES

SERVES 8

½ cup Shaoxing wine

½ cup light soy sauce

¼ cup dark soy sauce

¼ cup chili bean paste (doubanjiang)

2½ pounds boneless beef shank, cut into 3-inch cubes

2 tablespoons neutral oil

1 large yellow onion, halved and sliced into ¾-inch wedges

1 large beefsteak tomato, halved and sliced into ¾-inch wedges

1-inch knob of ginger, peeled and thinly sliced

6 large garlic cloves, lightly smashed

5 green onions, white and green parts, cut into 1-inch pieces

3 dried bay leaves

1 cinnamon stick

3 whole star anise

1-inch piece rock sugar or 2 teaspoons granulated sugar

8 cups store-bought low-sodium beef broth or bone broth

Kosher salt

2 pounds fresh egg noodles (I like Twin Marquis precooked yellow noodles)

4 heads baby bok choy, core intact and quartered lengthwise

FOR SERVING

Store-bought pickled mustard greens

2 green onions, green tops only, thinly sliced, for razzle-dazzle

Roughly chopped fresh cilantro, for razzle-dazzle

There are many noodles that have become "mainstream," such as ramen and pho, but I strongly believe Taiwanese beef noodles deserve much more attention. This recipe calls for beef shank, an affordable braising meat that becomes so tender in this rich, spicy broth that it convincingly could be mistaken for a more expensive cut. The soup is made rich-rich from simmering beef shank in an aromatic chili broth and is balanced by bright-tasting tomatoes and sweet onion, all of which gets soaked up by thick, doughy noodles. Because patience is not one of my virtues, I use a pressure cooker to cut the cooking time in half, but this can easily be slow-cooked on the stove. Bonus: Your house will smell *amazing*.

In a small bowl, mix together the Shaoxing wine, light soy sauce, dark soy sauce, and chili bean paste until smooth. Set aside.

Pat the beef dry with paper towels. Heat a wok or large skillet with the neutral oil over medium heat. When it's hot and shimmering, sear the beef cubes until they are well browned, 2 to 3 minutes on each side. Add the onion, tomato, ginger, garlic, and green onions and cook, stirring occasionally, until the tomatoes soften, about 5 minutes.

To a spice bag or large square of cheesecloth, add the bay leaves, cinnamon stick, and star anise. Tighten to close the bag or tie with kitchen twine to enclose.

If using a pressure cooker: To an 8-quart pressure cooker or multicooker, transfer the seared beef mixture and the sauce along with the spice bag, rock sugar, and then the beef broth. Cover, seal, and cook on high for 40 minutes, until the beef is tender but still has some bite to it. Turn off the heat and move the pressure knob to manually release the pressure, according to the manufacturer's instructions. Transfer the meat to a plate and set to the side. Strain the broth through a colander or sieve and discard the solids.

If cooking on the stovetop: To a large heavy-bottomed pot, add the seared beef mixture and the sauce along with the spice bag, rock sugar, and then the beef broth. Bring to a boil over high heat, then reduce the heat to low or medium-low so the broth maintains a gentle simmer, cover, and cook until the meat is tender but still has some bite to it, about 3 hours. Transfer the meat to a plate and set to the side. Strain the broth through a colander or sieve and discard the solids.

Bring a medium pot of salted water to a boil—make sure it's salty like pasta water, or as salty as you are when you lose something that was just in your hand. Add the noodles and cook as the package instructs until they are tender. Use tongs or a spider to remove the noodles to a strainer and leave the pot on the stove. Let the noodles drain. Add the bok choy and boil until vibrant and tender, about 2 minutes. Transfer the bok choy to the strainer to drain.

To serve: Divide the egg noodles among the bowls. Add some broth, beef cubes, and bok choy to each serving, then top with the mustard greens and garnish with the green onion tops and cilantro.

OXTAIL PHỞ

SERVES 6

1 large yellow onion, quartered and skin-on

2-inch knob of ginger, skin-on

2 pounds oxtails

2 pounds boneless beef shank

½ (1.5-ounce) packaged pho spice mix (about ¼ cup; see Note on page 92)

½ cup fish sauce

2 (1-inch) pieces of rock sugar or 1 tablespoon granulated sugar

Kosher salt

1½ pounds fresh pho noodles (see page 21)

FOR SERVING

(choose just the meat and lime or make the toppings rain!)

12 to 18 very thin slices raw beef eye round (many stores will sell pre-sliced meat; about 10 ounces total)

Fresh bean sprouts

1 jalapeño, sliced into rings

Fresh cilantro leaves, roughly chopped

Fresh Thai basil leaves, roughly chopped

2 green onions, green tops only, thinly sliced

Quick Chili-Vinegar Onions (page 202; optional)

1 lime, cut into wedges

Hoisin sauce (optional)

Sriracha (optional)

I am obsessed with braised oxtail—it's so fatty, tender, and rich. The oxtail meat and the broth go hand in hand here and are the stars of this dish; slowly simmering the oxtails with charred aromatics and dry spices creates an insanely rich, flavorful broth and also yields oxtail meat that's fall-off-the-bone tender. Truly the hardest part of this process is the torture you endure from the amazing aroma while you wait to enjoy the soup (less torturous if you use a pressure cooker, and more so if you braise on the stovetop since it just takes three times as long!). I promise you, though, the wait—no matter how long—is worth it.

Preheat the broiler with the oven rack at the top. Line a sheet pan with aluminum foil. Place the quartered onion skin side up and ginger on the pan. Broil, without turning, until the onion skins are completely charred and black and the ginger is fragrant, 10 to 15 minutes. Cool completely, then peel the skins off.

In a large pot, add the oxtails and beef shank and cover with cool water until completely submerged. Bring the water to a rigorous boil over high heat and then cook the meat for 5 to 10 minutes to ensure a clear pho broth (parboiling the meat cleans it, so boil until all of the scum rises to the top of the water). Strain the meat into a colander and rinse well under cool water.

As the meat is parboiling, in a small skillet set over medium heat, toast the pho spices, shaking the pan often, until the spices are fragrant and have some color, 3 to 5 minutes. Add them to a spice bag or to the center of a square of cheesecloth and use kitchen twine to tie the bag or cheesecloth closed.

If using a pressure cooker: To an 8-quart pressure cooker or multicooker, add the parboiled meat, spice bag, peeled onion and ginger, fish sauce, and rock sugar. Cover with 1 gallon (16 cups) of water, or enough to reach the max fill line. Cover, seal, and cook on high for 1 hour. Remove from the heat and move the pressure knob to manually release the pressure, according to the manufacturer's instructions. Transfer the meat to a plate (discard the bones) and set aside. Strain the broth through a colander or sieve and discard the solids.

If cooking on the stovetop: To a large pot, add the parboiled meat, spice bag, peeled onion and ginger, fish sauce, and rock sugar. Cover with 16 cups of water and bring to a boil over high heat. Reduce the heat to low so the broth maintains a gentle simmer, cover, and cook until the meat is tender, about 3 hours. Transfer the meat to a plate (discard the bones) and set to the side. Strain the broth through a colander or sieve and discard the solids.

To serve, bring a medium pot of salted water to a boil—make sure it's salty like pasta water. Boil the noodles according to the package instructions and drain.

To serve: Divide the noodles among serving bowls. Put an oxtail in each serving, and if you like, thinly slice the shank and add some slices to each bowl (I usually don't, but you do you). Add 2 or 3 raw meat slices and as many fresh bean sprouts, sliced jalapeño, cilantro, Thai basil, and green onions as you want, plus the Chili-Vinegar Onions (if using), and then ladle the boiling broth over the noodles. Serve with a lime wedge. This also tastes great with a spoonful of hoisin sauce and sriracha, but the broth is more than perfect on its own!

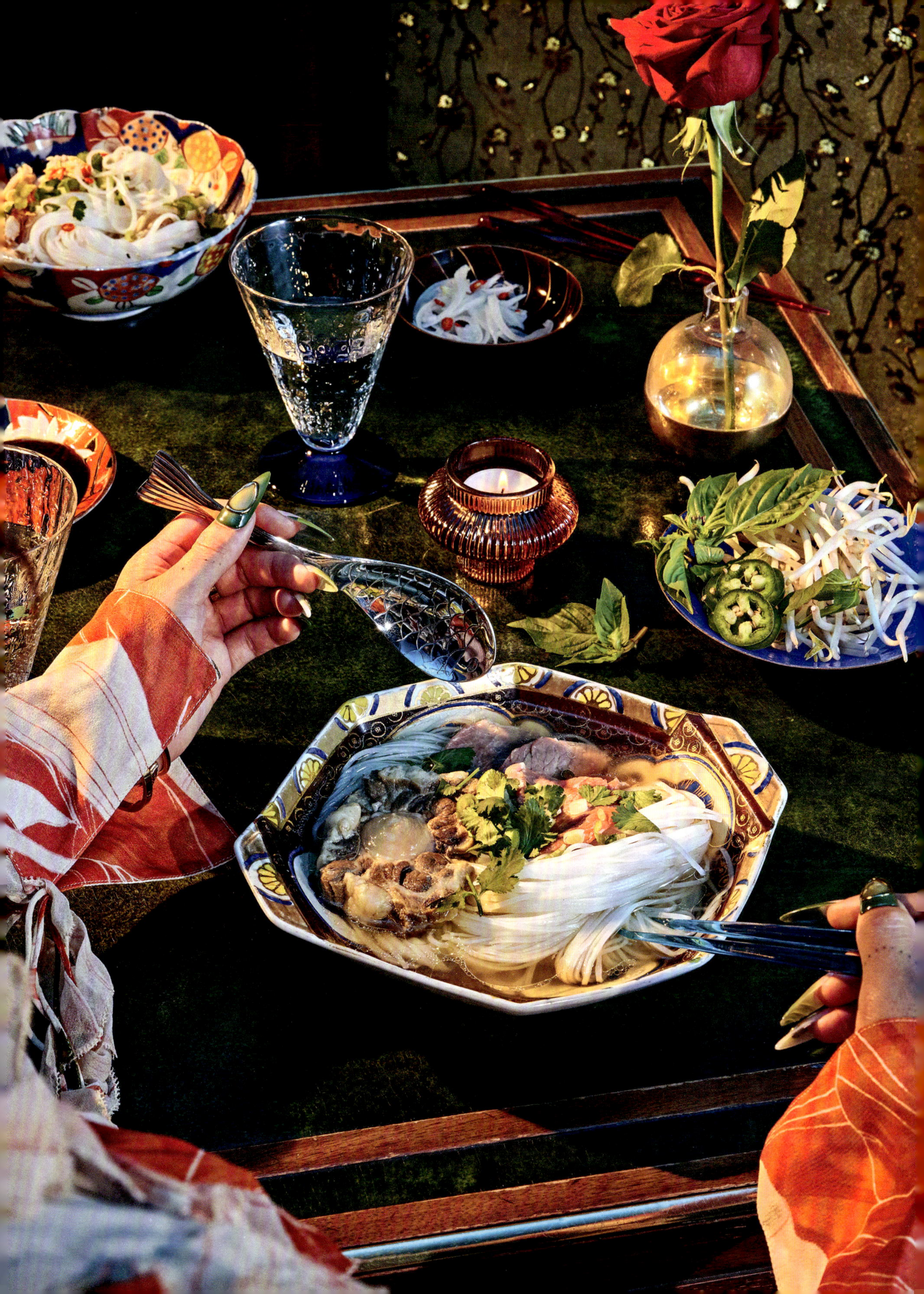

SKIP
TAKEOUT
THE

THE TAKEOUT SKIP

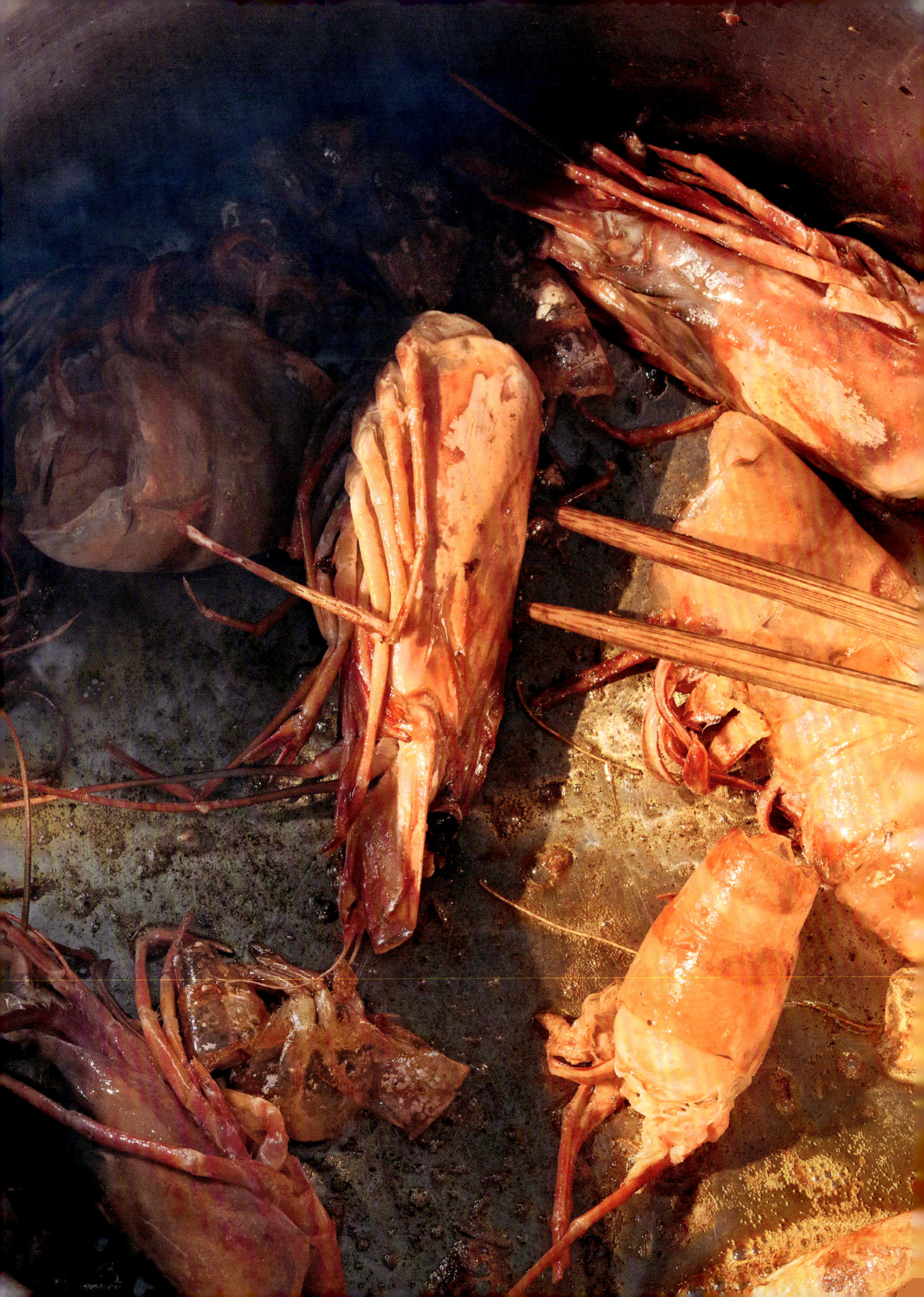

RECIPE LIST

Orange Chicken
104

General Tso's Chicken
107

30-Minute Beef & Broccoli
108

Sweet & Sour Pork
111

Shrimp Fried Rice
112

Walnut Shrimp
115

Ground Beef Bulgogi
116

Shrimp & Pineapple Thai Curry
119

Chicken Katsu Curry
120

Cantonese Steamed Fish
123

Soy Sauce Chicken
127

Shaking Beef
128

Takeout who, bestie?!

Remaking takeout dishes is one of the most rewarding feelings, and I promise you'll be having many "I *did* that" moments, particularly after this chapter. Many people think their favorite takeout dishes are something they can only order. No more getting catfished by takeout—you can control everything that goes into your dish—and it'll be a hit *every* time.

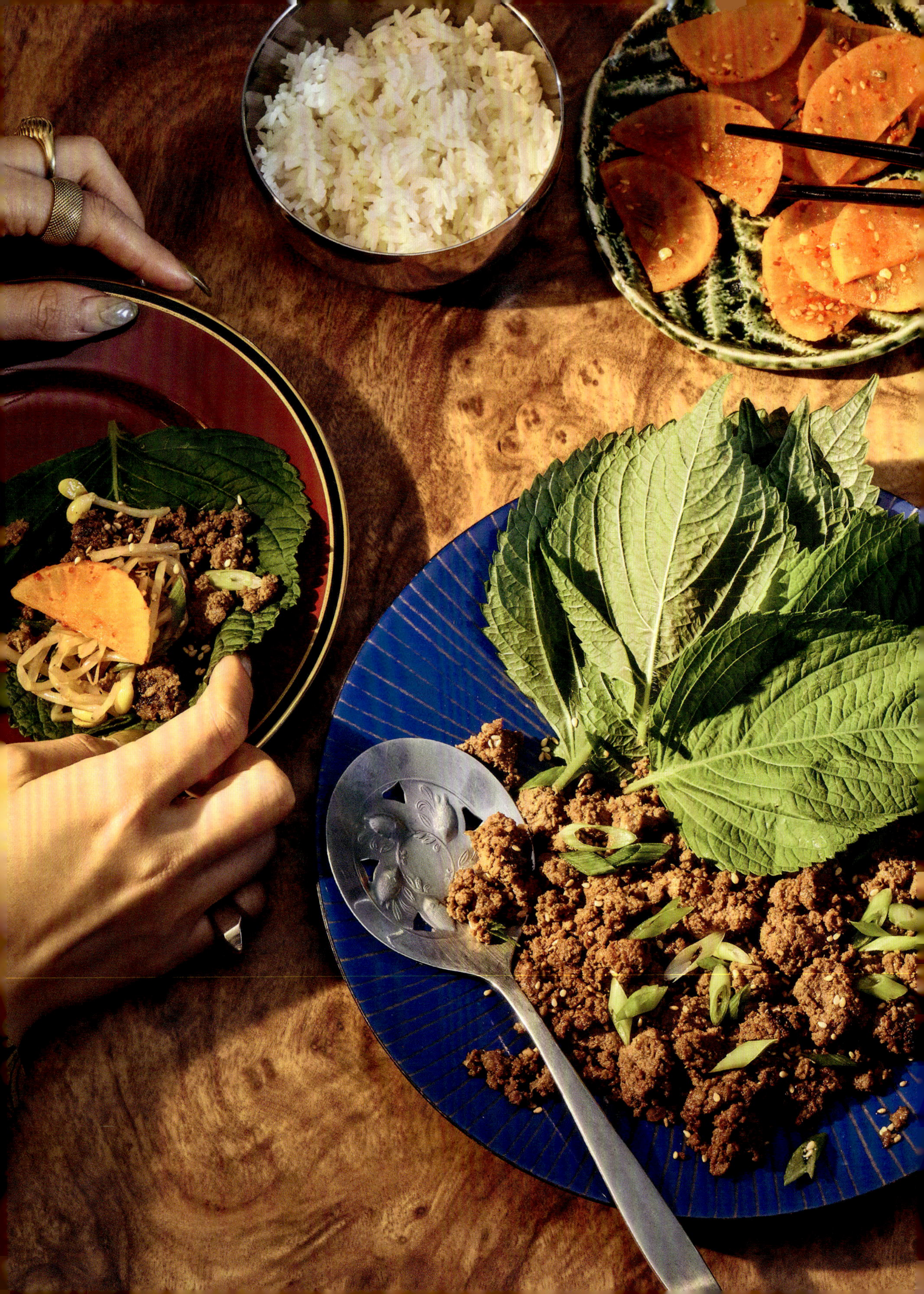

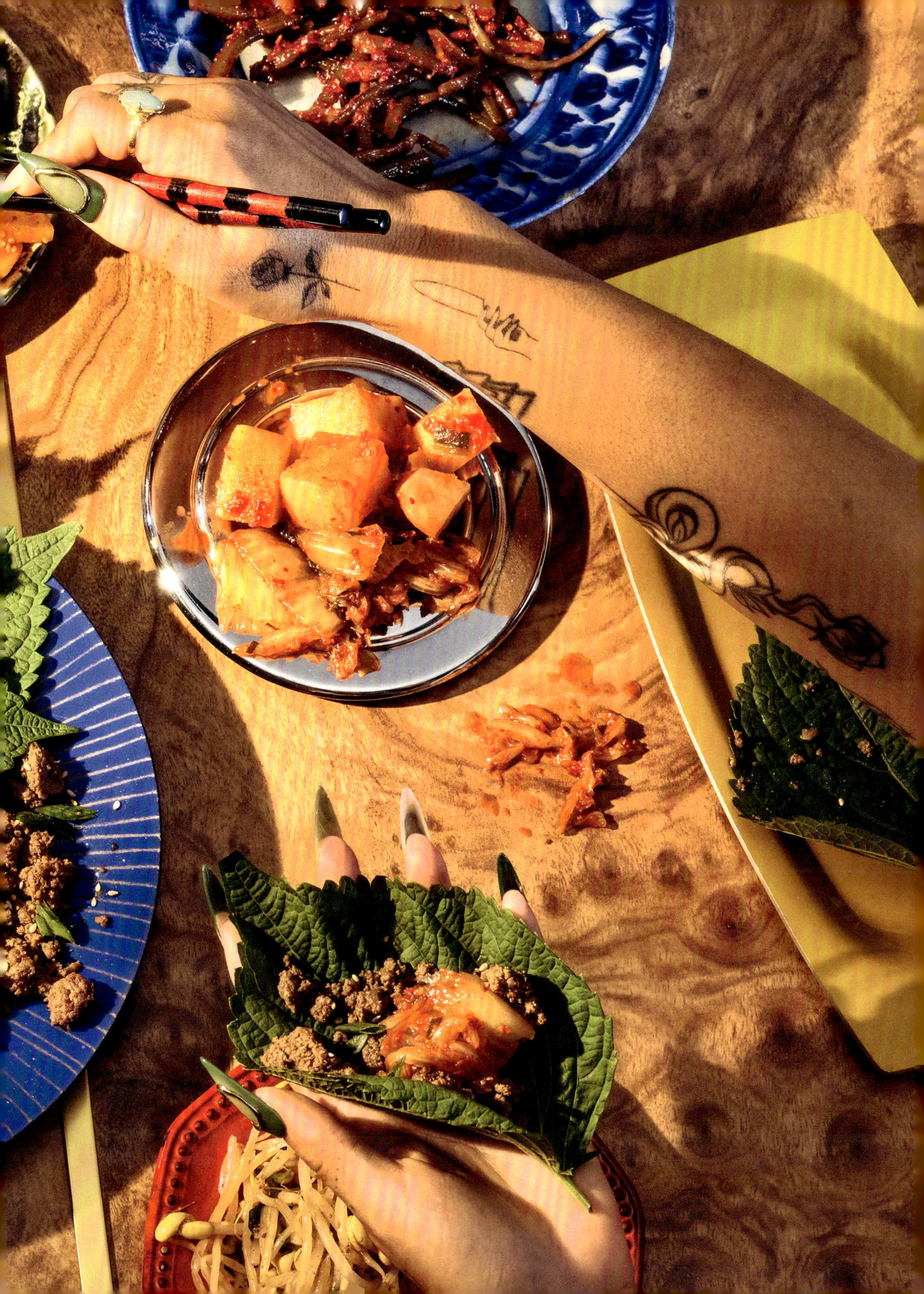

ORANGE CHICKEN

SERVES 2 TO 4

CHICKEN

1 pound boneless, skinless chicken thighs

1 large egg, lightly beaten

1 teaspoon light soy sauce

1 teaspoon neutral oil (I use avocado oil), plus more for frying

1-inch knob of ginger, peeled

1 large garlic clove

3 tablespoons all-purpose flour, plus more as needed

1 tablespoon cornstarch, plus more as needed

1 teaspoon baking powder

1 teaspoon ground white pepper

½ teaspoon kosher salt

SAUCE

¾ cup store-bought low-sodium chicken broth or bone broth

Zest and juice of 1 medium orange (about ¼ cup juice)

2 tablespoons light soy sauce

2 tablespoons rice vinegar

2 tablespoons Shaoxing wine

2 tablespoons light brown sugar

1-inch knob of ginger, peeled

1 tablespoon cornstarch

1 teaspoon toasted sesame oil

FOR SERVING

The Perfect Steamed Rice (page 242)

Toasted sesame seeds, for razzle-dazzle

2 green onions, green tops only, thinly sliced, for razzle-dazzle

No matter how much I was spoiled by my mom's home-cooked meals, there was always something that made Chinese takeout feel like a treat. Orange chicken with a side of white rice and an orange soda was my go-to, especially from Panda Express. I mean, what's not to love about these bite-size, crispy pieces of chicken (thighs are juicier, but breasts are fine if you prefer) coated in a sweet and tangy sauce? I use orange zest and freshly squeezed orange juice to really underscore the citrusy flavor here—the sweet OJ balances so well with the tanginess of the rice vinegar, the sweetness of the brown sugar, and the umami-saltiness of the soy sauce. We will also be double-frying for the ultimate crispiness before coating in the sticky glaze—and don't be shy with that glaze—whatever drips off the chicken can get soaked up by the rice.

Prepare the chicken: Pat the chicken dry with paper towels and cut into 1-inch pieces. In a medium bowl, add the chicken and toss with the egg, soy sauce, and neutral oil. Now get out your grater and grate the ginger and garlic into the bowl (baddies, watch your nails). Then mix in the flour, cornstarch, baking powder, white pepper, and salt. The batter should be smooth and lightly coat each piece; if not, add a little more flour and cornstarch at a time, in the same 3:1 ratio.

Mix the sauce: In a small bowl, combine the chicken broth, orange zest, orange juice, soy sauce, rice vinegar, Shaoxing wine, and brown sugar. Get the grater back out and grate in the ginger and whisk to combine. In a small bowl, prepare the cornstarch slurry by mixing the cornstarch and 2 tablespoons cold water until smooth—no lumps! Set both aside.

Fry the chicken: Fill a large pot with 4 inches of neutral oil or halfway (but don't fill more than halfway) and heat to 350°F over medium (if you don't have a thermometer, do the wooden chopstick test on page 47). Fit a cooling rack over a sheet pan or line a plate with paper towels.

Using a pair of chopsticks or tongs, gently drop in half the chicken, one at a time and making sure not to overcrowd the pot. Fry until lightly golden, stirring frequently, just to avoid any sticking, 2 to 4 minutes, then use a spider to remove them to the cooling rack. Finish frying the rest of the chicken.

Raise the heat to medium-high and bring the oil to 400°F (if you don't have a thermometer, test one piece of chicken in the oil—it should bubble aggressively). Double-fry the chicken all at once, stirring frequently for even browning, another 2 minutes or until the pieces are golden and cooked through. Remove the pieces back to the cooling rack.

In a wok or clean large pot, pour in the sauce and bring it to a boil over medium-high heat. Using a wooden spoon or spatula, mix in the cornstarch slurry, then reduce the heat to medium-low and simmer, stirring occasionally, until the glaze is bubbling and has thickened enough to coat the back of your spoon, about 5 minutes.

Add the fried chicken and toss in the sauce. Once all of the pieces are coated, remove from the heat and mix in the sesame oil. Spoon the chicken over the white rice and garnish with the sesame seeds and green onions.

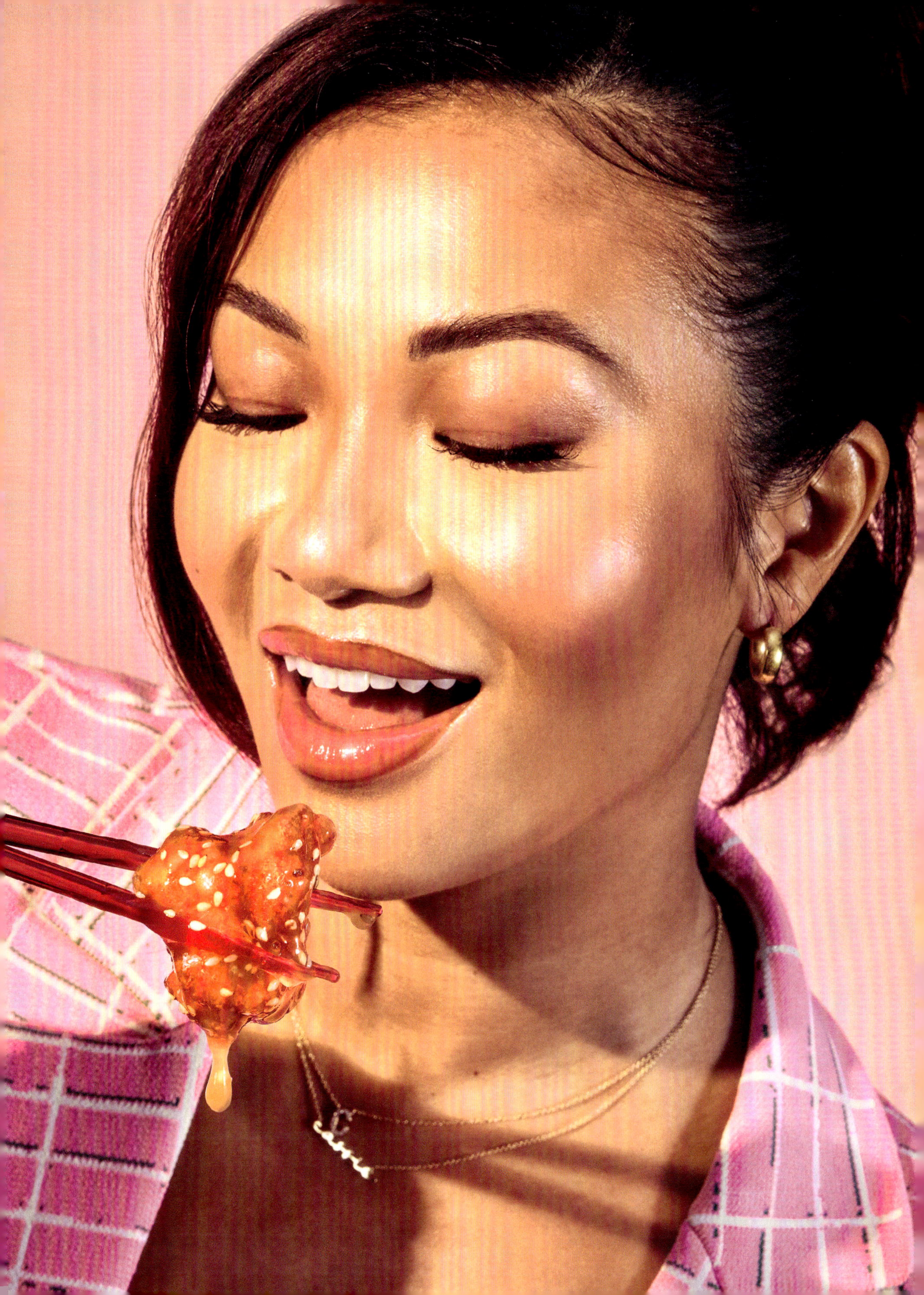

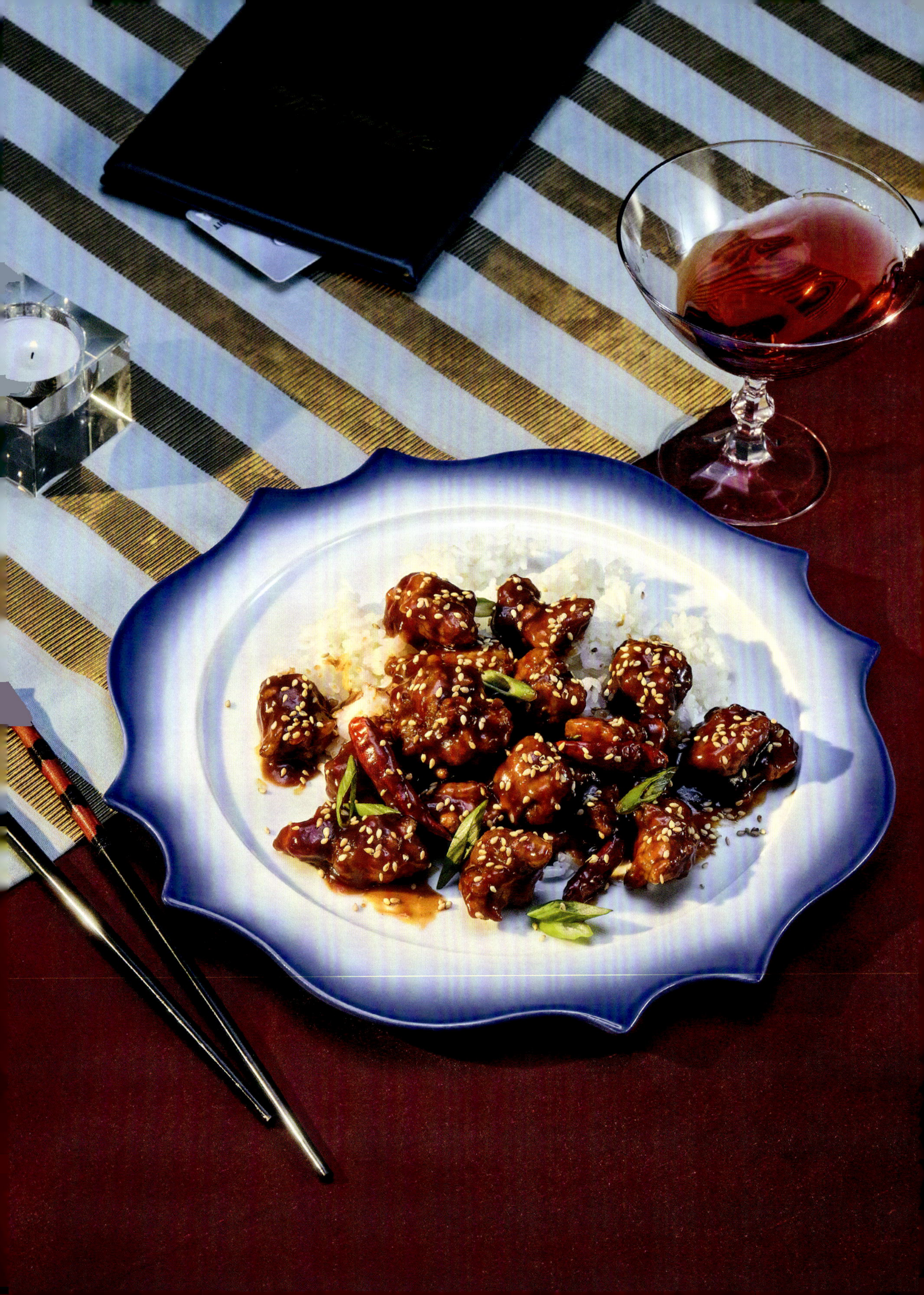

GENERAL TSO'S CHICKEN

SERVES 2 TO 4

CHICKEN

1 pound boneless, skinless chicken thighs

1 large egg, lightly beaten

1 teaspoon light soy sauce

1 teaspoon neutral oil (I use avocado oil), plus more for frying

1-inch knob of fresh ginger, peeled

1 large garlic clove

3 tablespoons all-purpose flour

1 tablespoon cornstarch

1 teaspoon baking powder

1 teaspoon ground white pepper

½ teaspoon kosher salt

SAUCE

½ cup store-bought low-sodium chicken broth or bone broth

¼ cup light soy sauce

¼ cup ketchup

2 tablespoons Shaoxing wine

1 tablespoon light brown sugar

1 tablespoon rice vinegar

2 teaspoons dark soy sauce

1 teaspoon ground white pepper

1-inch knob of fresh ginger, peeled

1 large garlic clove

1 tablespoon cornstarch

1 teaspoon neutral oil

3 to 4 dried red chilies (see page 16)

1 teaspoon toasted sesame oil

FOR SERVING

The Perfect Steamed Rice (page 242)

Toasted sesame seeds

2 green onions, tops sliced

As I got older, my love for orange chicken remained the same, but I sort of graduated into spicy General Tso's chicken territory. While these two legendary dishes have their similarities, it's the sauce that makes each of them unique. General Tso's hits all of the sweet, savory, and tangy notes you crave but with that extra punch of spice. I love using dried chilies in this recipe for an extra pungent kick—they're also very handy to keep in the pantry. You may be surprised to find ketchup in this recipe, but it adds a fantastic sweet and acidic flavor that balances the spice. As always, I'm a saucy girl, so you'll find extra sauce in this recipe to accompany the mandatory scoop of white rice.

Prepare the chicken: Pat the chicken dry with paper towels and cut into 1-inch pieces. In a medium bowl, mix the chicken, egg, soy sauce, and neutral oil. Now get out your grater and grate the ginger and garlic into the bowl (baddies, watch your nails). Then mix in the flour, cornstarch, baking powder, white pepper, and salt. The batter should be smooth and lightly coat each piece; if not, add a little more flour and cornstarch at a time, in the same 3:1 ratio.

Mix the sauce: In a small bowl, whisk the chicken broth, light soy sauce, ketchup, Shaoxing wine, brown sugar, rice vinegar, dark soy sauce, and white pepper. Get the grater back out and grate in the ginger and garlic and whisk to combine. In a small bowl, prepare the cornstarch slurry by mixing the cornstarch and 2 tablespoons cold water until smooth—no lumps! Set both aside.

Fry the chicken: Fill a large pot with 4 inches of neutral oil or fill halfway (but don't fill more than halfway) and heat to 350°F over medium (if you don't have a thermometer, do the wooden chopstick test on page 47). Fit a cooling rack over a sheet pan or line a plate with paper towels.

Using a pair of chopsticks or tongs, gently drop in half the chicken, one piece at a time, making sure not to overcrowd the pot. Fry until lightly golden brown, stirring frequently, just to avoid any sticking, 2 to 4 minutes, then use a spider to transfer to the cooling rack. Finish frying the remaining chicken.

Raise the heat to medium-high and bring the oil to 400°F (if you don't have a thermometer, test one piece of chicken in the oil—it should bubble aggressively). Double-fry the chicken all together, stirring frequently for even browning, another 2 minutes or until the pieces are golden and cooked through. Remove back to the cooling rack.

Make the glaze: Heat a wok or clean large pot with the neutral oil over medium heat. When the oil is hot and shimmering, add the dried chilies and toast, stirring constantly, until fragrant, 1 to 2 minutes. Raise the heat to high, pour in the sauce and bring to a boil. Whisk in the cornstarch slurry, then reduce the heat to medium-low and simmer, stirring frequently, until the sauce thickens to a glaze that will coat the back of your spoon, about 1 minute.

Using a spatula, add the cooked chicken back in and toss in the glaze until each piece is coated. Remove from the heat and mix in the sesame oil. Spoon the chicken over the white rice and garnish with the sesame seeds and green onions.

SKIP THE TAKEOUT • 107

30-MINUTE BEEF & BROCCOLI

SERVES 2 TO 4

BEEF AND MARINADE

1 pound flank steak

1 tablespoon cornstarch

1 tablespoon oyster sauce

1 teaspoon light soy sauce

1 teaspoon neutral oil (I use avocado oil), plus extra for the pan

½ teaspoon baking soda

1-inch knob of ginger, peeled

1 large garlic clove

SAUCE AND BROCCOLI

1 cup store-bought low-sodium chicken broth or beef broth

2 tablespoons light soy sauce

2 tablespoons light brown sugar

1 tablespoon oyster sauce

1 teaspoon dark soy sauce

1 teaspoon toasted sesame oil

Ground white pepper

2 tablespoons of neutral oil

1-inch knob of ginger, peeled and minced

1 large garlic clove, minced

2 tablespoons Shaoxing wine

1 medium head of broccoli, cut into bite-size florets

2 tablespoons cornstarch

FOR SERVING

The Perfect Steamed Rice (page 242)

Toasted sesame seeds

2 green onions, green tops only, thinly sliced, for razzle-dazzle

I whipped up this beefy broccoli one day after waking up from a deliciously long nap with a violent craving for it. I posted the video of my quick dinner (it took thirty minutes, no joke!), and the recipe went on to become one of my most viral videos on TikTok *and* a feature on *Good Morning America*! I always keep flank steak in my freezer. It's one of my favorite cuts of meat to work with because it is easy to find, affordable, and defrosts nicely. The other ingredients are things I always have on hand in the pantry or the fridge, making this a great weeknight option that's quick on time with no sacrifice on flavor.

Prepare and marinate the beef: Cut the flank steak in half with the grain (lengthwise), then slice against the grain (meaning you're cutting crosswise and perpendicular to the direction the muscle fibers run) and at an angle to create ⅛-inch-thick strips.

To a medium bowl, add the cornstarch, oyster sauce, soy sauce, neutral oil, and baking soda. Now get out your grater and grate the ginger and garlic into the bowl (baddies, watch your nails). Mix well, add the sliced flank, toss to coat, and set aside to marinate for at least 20 minutes or up to overnight, covered, in the fridge.

Make the sauce: In a separate small bowl, combine the broth, light soy sauce, brown sugar, oyster sauce, dark soy sauce, and sesame oil and season with white pepper to taste—no measurements, just vibes for the pepper. Mix until smooth and set aside.

Sauté the beef: Coat the bottom of a wok or large skillet with neutral oil (1 to 2 tablespoons) and heat over medium-high heat. When the oil is hot and shimmering, add the meat and the marinade. Use a spatula to flatten the pieces out into an even layer and leave them to cook, untouched and unbothered, to achieve a nice sear. Once you see the meat browning around the edges, about 3 minutes, cook, stirring constantly, until it's no longer pink, another minute. Remove the meat to a clean plate and set aside.

Prepare the broccoli: Add 1 tablespoon of the neutral oil to the wok followed by the ginger and garlic and cook, stirring constantly, until they begin to become fragrant and lightly brown, about 1 minute. Pour in the Shaoxing wine to deglaze the wok—so you're stirring and scrapping up all the browned goodness from the bottom of the wok—and cook for 1 minute, stirring occasionally. Add the broccoli and cook, stirring constantly, until the florets are well combined with the ginger and garlic, about 1 minute. Cover the pan to steam the broccoli for 1 minute, or until the broccoli becomes bright green.

Uncover, add the sauce, and let it come to a boil. In a small bowl, prepare the cornstarch slurry by mixing the cornstarch and 2 tablespoons cold water until smooth—no lumps! Add it to the broccoli mixture. Allow the sauce to simmer, stirring occasionally, until thickened enough to coat the back of a spoon, about 5 minutes, then return the meat to the wok. Let everything cook together, stirring constantly, until the sauce coats the meat evenly, about 2 minutes. Spoon the beef and broccoli over the white rice and garnish with the sesame seeds and green onions.

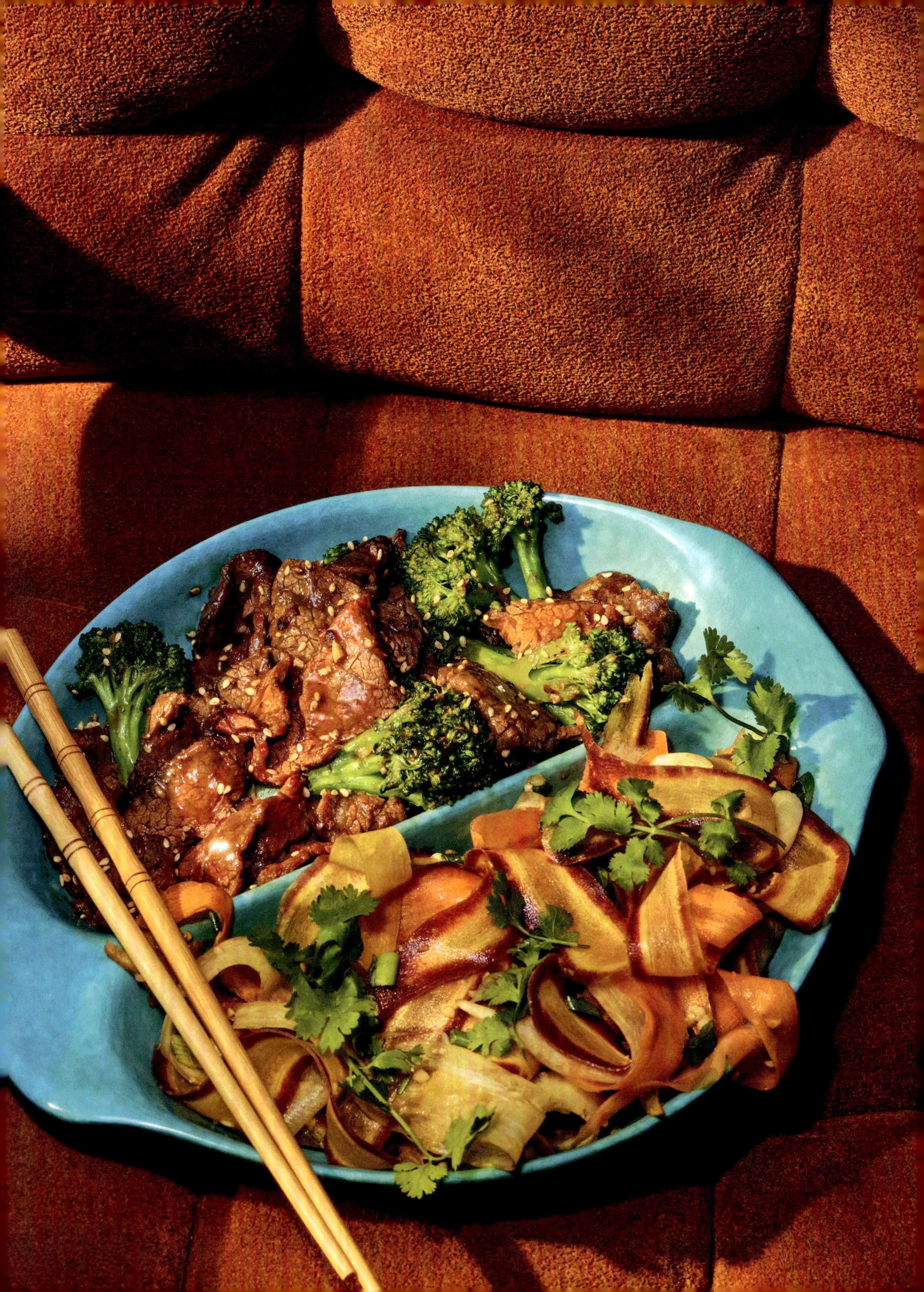

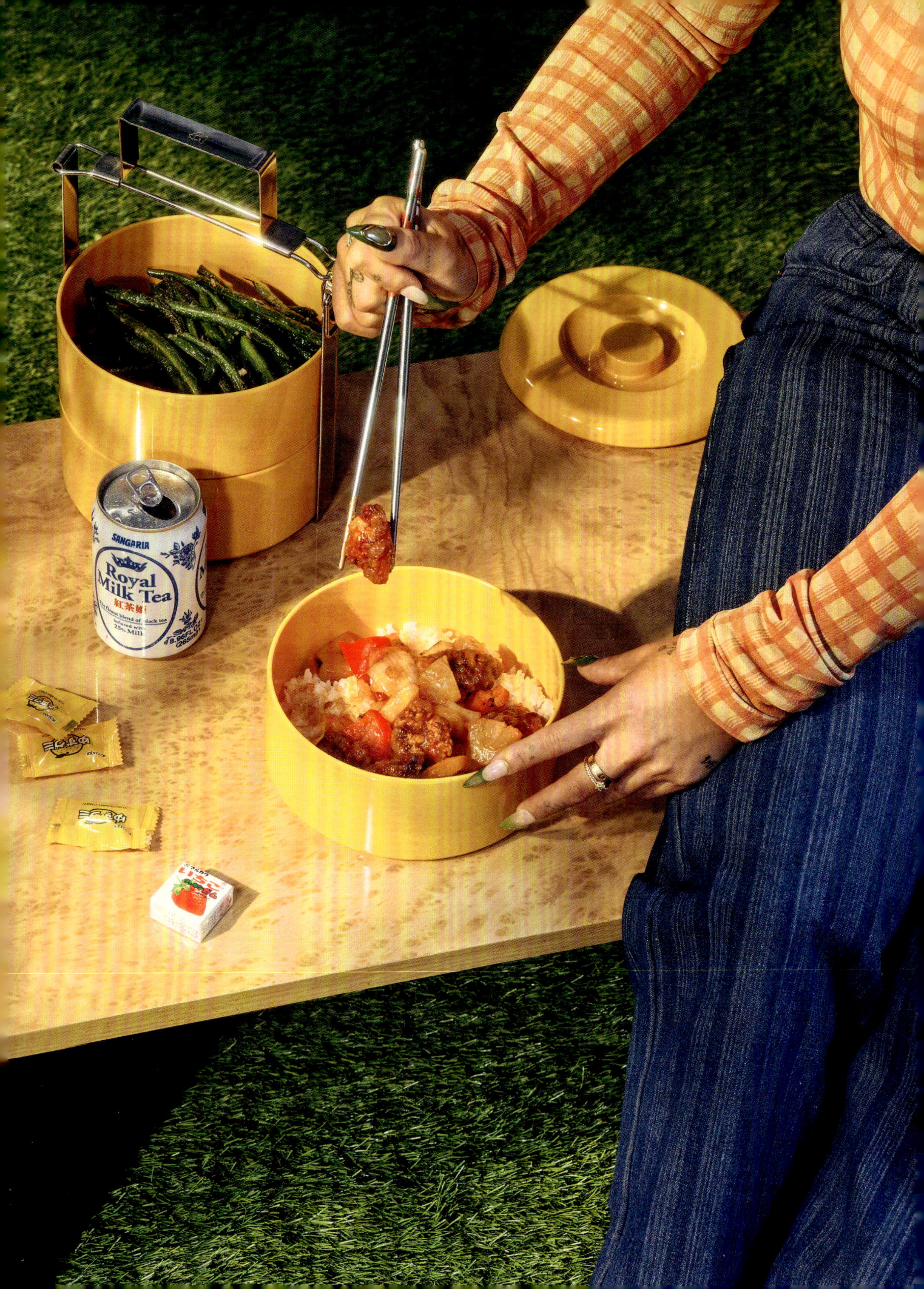
SANGARIA
Royal Milk Tea
紅茶
25% Milk

SWEET & SOUR PORK

SERVES 2 TO 4

PORK AND VEGETABLES

1 pound boneless pork shoulder, patted dry and cut into 1-inch cubes

1 large egg, lightly beaten

1 cup plus 3 tablespoons cornstarch, plus more for the dredge

2 tablespoons all-purpose flour

1 tablespoon light soy sauce

2 large garlic cloves

1 teaspoon neutral oil (I use avocado oil), plus more for frying

½ medium red bell pepper, cut into 1-inch pieces

½ medium orange bell pepper, cut into 1-inch pieces

½ medium yellow onion, cut into 1-inch pieces

1¼ cups (10 ounces) canned or fresh pineapple chunks, strained

SAUCE

¼ cup ketchup

¼ cup light brown sugar

3 tablespoons distilled white vinegar

2 tablespoons light soy sauce

1 teaspoon oyster sauce

2 large garlic cloves

1 tablespoon cornstarch

FOR SERVING

The Perfect Steamed Rice (page 242)

Aside from sweet and sour pork satisfying my eternal craving for that vinegar-forward flavor profile, I love the addition of juicy pineapple that hits my palate. We all know the argument of whether pineapple belongs on pizza or not, but can we discuss pineapple in sweet and sour pork? I say yes! The tangy sauce mixes with the crispy bites of salty pork, sweet peppers, onions, and fresh bursts of pineapple for a match made in heaven. I've found the best ASMR results in the combo of a wet batter for the pork and an additional dry dredge through cornstarch for a crackling crust that becomes the ideal magnet and surface area for the sticky glaze.

Prepare the pork: In a small bowl, mix together the pork, egg, the 3 tablespoons cornstarch, the flour, and soy sauce. Now get out your grater and grate the garlic into the bowl (baddies, watch your nails). Mix to thoroughly combine and coat the pork. In a separate medium bowl, add the remaining 1 cup cornstarch and dredge each piece of pork in it, then transfer to a sheet pan.

Mix the sauce: In a small bowl, whisk together the ketchup, brown sugar, distilled white vinegar, soy sauce, and oyster sauce. Use the grater to grate the garlic into the bowl and whisk. In a small bowl, prepare the cornstarch slurry by mixing the cornstarch and 2 tablespoons cold water until smooth—no lumps!

Fry the pork: Fill a large pot with 4 inches of neutral oil or fill halfway (but don't fill more than halfway) and heat to 350°F over medium (if you don't have a thermometer, do the wooden chopstick test on page 47). Fit a cooling rack over a tray or line a plate with paper towels.

Using a pair of chopsticks or tongs, gently drop in half the pork, one piece at a time, making sure not to overcrowd the pot. Fry until lightly golden brown, stirring frequently, just to avoid any sticking, 2 to 4 minutes, then use a spider to remove to the cooling rack. Finish frying the remaining pork.

Raise the heat to medium-high and bring the oil to 400°F (if you don't have a thermometer, test one piece of pork in the oil—it should bubble aggressively). Double-fry the pork all together, stirring frequently for even browning, another 2 minutes or until the pieces are golden and just cooked through. Remove back to the cooling rack.

Cook the vegetables and bring it all together: Heat a wok or clean large pot with the neutral oil over high heat. When the oil is hot and shimmering, add the red and orange peppers and the onion and cook—we're stirring occasionally but aggressively here—until they are slightly charred, 2 to 3 minutes. Add in the pineapple chunks and keep stirring until they're golden brown, about another minute. Reduce the heat to medium-low and pour in the sauce and stir, then bring to a boil. Immediately stir in the cornstarch slurry and simmer, stirring frequently, until the sauce bubbles and thickens to a glaze that will coat the back of your spoon, about 2 minutes.

Add the cooked pork and cook, stirring constantly, until all of the pieces are well coated and mixed in with the vegetables, about 1 minute. Serve immediately over the white rice.

SHRIMP FRIED RICE

**SERVES 2 ON ITS OWN,
4 AS PART OF A SPREAD**

- ½ pound jumbo shrimp (around 25/pound), peeled and deveined (see page 46)
- ½ teaspoon baking soda
- ½ teaspoon toasted sesame oil
- ¼ teaspoon kosher salt
- ¼ teaspoon ground white pepper
- 1 tablespoon neutral oil (I use avocado oil), plus more if needed
- 2 large eggs, lightly beaten
- ½ medium yellow onion, diced
- 2 green onions, white and green parts, thinly sliced and separated
- 2 large garlic cloves, minced
- ½ cup frozen mixed vegetables (or fresh vegetables of your choice, finely diced)
- 2 cups leftover cold white rice (see page 242)
- 2 tablespoons light soy sauce
- 1 tablespoon oyster sauce
- 1 teaspoon toasted sesame oil

Shrimp fried rice checks all the boxes—it's best made from day-old rice (which is awesome since I always have leftover rice in my fridge), can be made with fresh or frozen veggies (so accessible!), and is humble enough to be a sidekick to a main, but delicious enough to also be the star of the show. If you ever wondered how the shrimp at Chinese restaurants come out so juicy and springy, the secret is marinating with baking soda. This simple addition will make the shrimp plump up, almost resembling lobster!

In a small bowl, mix together the shrimp, baking soda, sesame oil, salt, and white pepper. Set aside to marinate for 30 minutes.

Heat a wok or large skillet with the neutral oil over medium-high heat. When the oil is hot and shimmering, add the shrimp, spreading them flat with a spatula. Cook—resisting the urge to mess with them—until the edges begin to turn pink, about 1 minute. Start stirring and shaking the wok aggressively and continue to cook until they're fully pink and have curled into a C shape, about another minute, then remove to a clean plate.

If the wok looks dry, add more neutral oil and heat until it's hot and shimmering. Crack the eggs into the wok and scramble using the spatula until they are set and just barely cooked, about 1 minute, then push them to the side of the wok. Add in the yellow onion, green onion whites, and garlic. Cook, stirring constantly, for 3 minutes, just until the onion begins to turn translucent, then add in the frozen vegetables and mix everything in with the eggs.

Using your hands or a fork, break up the rice as you add it in the wok. Mix well with everything else, then pour in the soy sauce and oyster sauce. Stir until the sauce is evenly mixed in with the grains of rice and everything is heated through, 3 to 5 minutes. Return the cooked shrimp and add in the sesame oil and give the rice a final mix, 1 minute. Garnish with the green onion greens and serve hot.

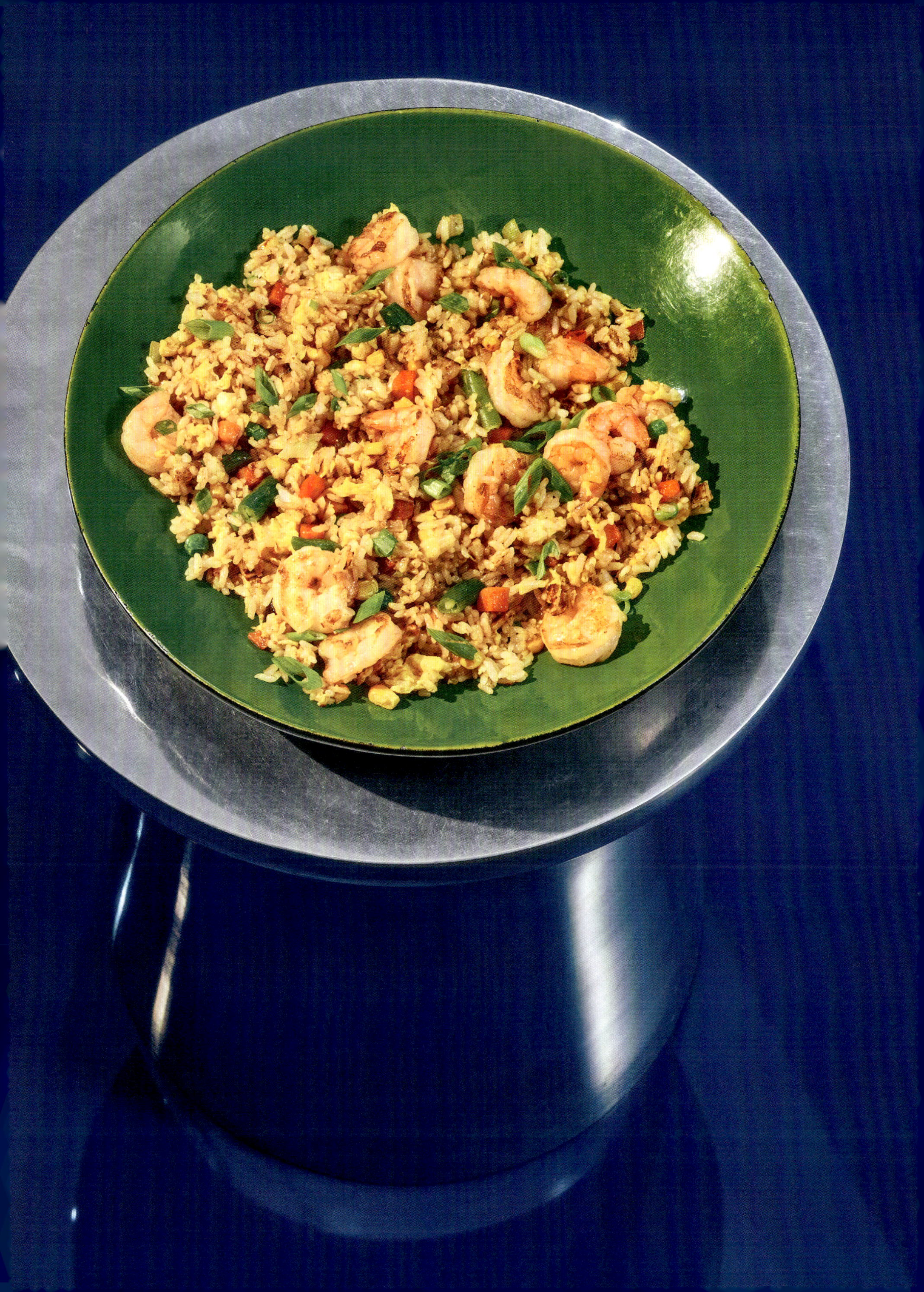

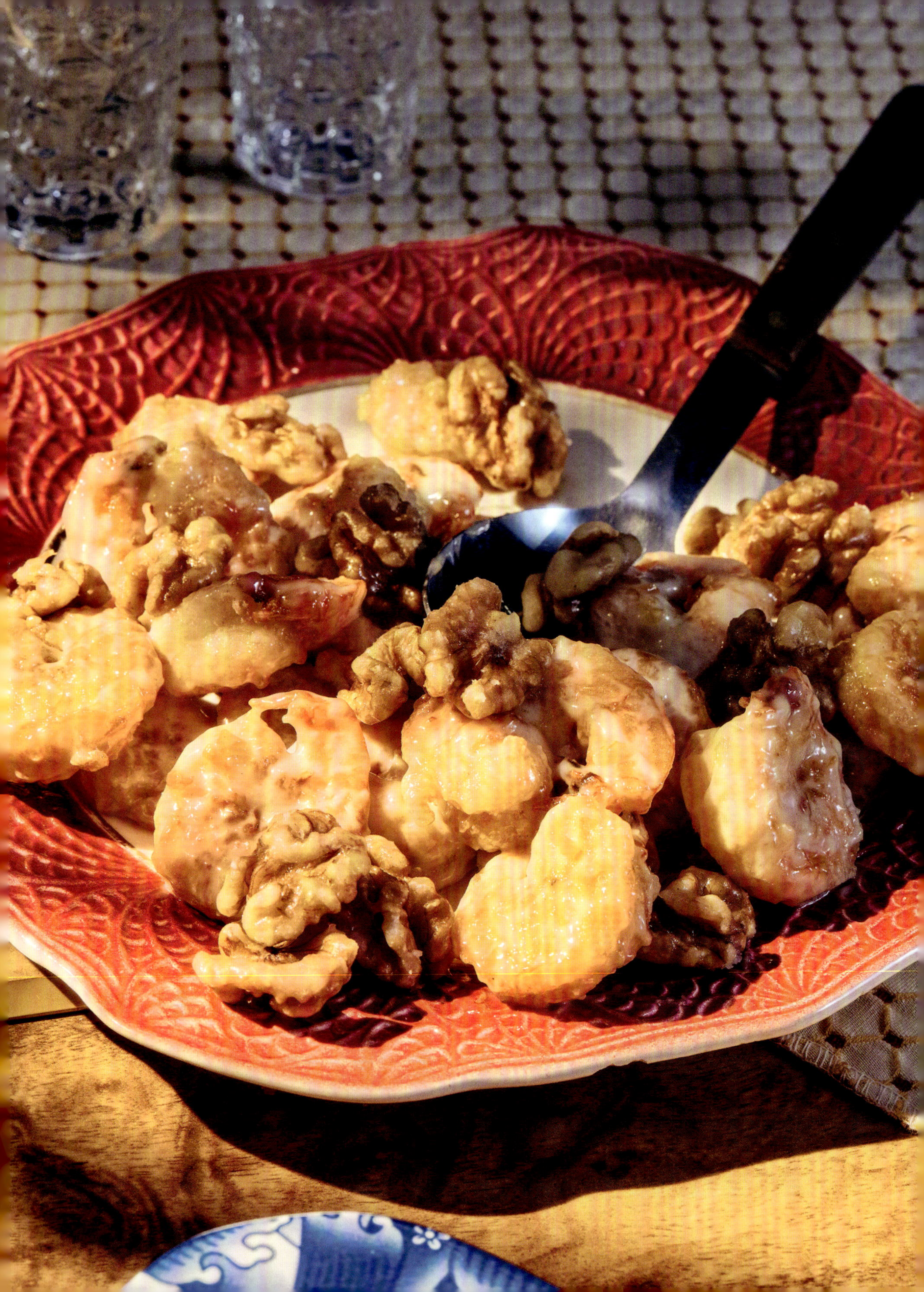

WALNUT SHRIMP

SERVES 2 TO 4

SHRIMP

1 pound jumbo shrimp (around 25/pound), peeled and deveined (see page 46)

1½ teaspoons ground white pepper

½ teaspoon kosher salt

¼ teaspoon baking soda

½ cup cornstarch

Neutral oil (I use avocado oil), for frying

CANDIED WALNUTS

2 tablespoons sugar

25 walnut halves

¼ teaspoon kosher salt

SAUCE

¼ cup mayonnaise

3 tablespoons sweetened condensed milk

2 teaspoons fresh lemon juice

I admittingly am not the biggest fan of mayonnaise. In fact, I kind of have an irrational fear of mayo (well, in large amounts). Walnut shrimp, however, is an easy exception to my rule. There's something special about the way mayo transforms condensed milk and fresh lemon juice into a light, subtly sweet sauce. The light breading on the shrimp soaks it up while the airy coating still stays crisp. Each bite of shrimp is elevated even more with a crunchy candied walnut, made with an easy coat of simple syrup.

Marinate the shrimp: In a medium bowl, mix together the shrimp, ½ teaspoon white pepper, ¼ teaspoon salt, and the baking soda until the shrimp is evenly coated. Set aside to marinate for 30 minutes.

In a small bowl, mix the cornstarch, the remaining 1 teaspoon white pepper, and the remaining ¼ teaspoon salt. Coat each piece of shrimp evenly in the dredge and set aside on a clean plate.

Make the candied walnuts: Line a sheet pan with parchment paper. In a wok or large skillet, make the simple syrup by whisking the sugar and 2 tablespoons water until all of the sugar dissolves. Now put that whisk down and leave the simple syrup alone so she doesn't form crystals. Bring to a simmer over medium heat. Using a spatula, toss in the walnuts and salt, then keep tossing aggressively until each piece is coated in the syrup. Remove to the prepared pan and spread in a flat layer to cool while you finish the shrimp; the walnuts will still be syrupy, and that's what we want.

Make the sauce: In a small bowl, mix together the mayonnaise, sweetened condensed milk, and lemon juice until combined. Set aside.

Fry the shrimp: Fill a medium pot with 3 inches of neutral oil or halfway (but don't fill it more than halfway) and heat to 375°F (if you don't have a thermometer, do the wooden chopstick test on page 47). Fit a cooling rack over a sheet pan or line a plate with paper towels.

Using a pair of chopsticks or tongs, gently drop in half the shrimp, one at a time, making sure not to overcrowd the pot. Fry the shrimp, stirring gently to prevent sticking, until lightly golden brown, 2 to 3 minutes, then remove with a spider to a cooling rack. Finish frying the remaining shrimp.

Add the shrimp to a large bowl, add the sauce to taste, and toss until each shrimp is lightly coated. To serve, sprinkle the candied walnuts over the cooked shrimp and enjoy immediately.

GROUND BEEF BULGOGI

SERVES 4 TO 6

¼ medium yellow onion, roughly chopped

¼ large Asian pear (or sub with an apple, pear, or whole peeled kiwi), cored and roughly chopped

4 medium garlic cloves

2 tablespoons light soy sauce

1 tablespoon mirin

1 tablespoon gochujang (Korean chili paste)

1 tablespoon light brown sugar

1 pound 93% lean ground beef

2 green onions, white and green parts, thinly sliced and separated

½ teaspoon kosher salt

½ teaspoon freshly ground black pepper

2 tablespoons neutral oil (I use avocado oil)

1 teaspoon toasted sesame seeds

1 teaspoon pure toasted sesame oil

FOR SERVING

The Perfect Steamed Rice (page 242)

Easy Kimchi (page 196)

Banchan-Style Korean Bean Sprouts (page 195)

Green leaf lettuce, leaves separated

Toasted sesame seeds, for razzle-dazzle

I went through a big fitness and meal-prep phase where I was trying to eat my healthiest but meals became, for lack of a better word, *boring*. I got so sick of eating ground beef, rice, and broccoli and knew I needed to switch it up—and the answer is right here. This is my *favorite* recipe to prep for the week because it's as easy as adding aromatics and seasoning to a blender, mixing it in with the ground beef, and stir-frying it. Asian pear is our star ingredient, not only adding a subtle sweetness but also doubling to tenderize the beef. If you can't get your hands on an Asian pear, you can substitute with an apple, a pear, or even a kiwi! We're really going to practice *love her, leave her alone* here: The secret to that charred, crispy beef is allowing it to cook uninterrupted. As tempted as you may be to sauté aggressively, refrain for the sake of that coveted Korean barbecue flavor. I love serving this with jasmine rice, kimchi, a bean sprout salad, and green leaf lettuce for lettuce wraps. Bulgogi is the perfect way to make healthy eating fun.

In a blender, combine the yellow onion, Asian pear, garlic, soy sauce, mirin, gochujang, and brown sugar, and blend into a smooth paste. Transfer the mixture to a large bowl, then stir in the ground beef, green onion whites, salt, and black pepper until evenly combined. Don't be alarmed if the mixture looks wet; that's what we want.

Heat a wok or large skillet with the oil over high heat. When the oil is hot and shimmering, add the meat mixture and use a spatula to spread and press gently into a flat, thin layer. Allow the meat to cook WITHOUT stirring—we are truly loving her and leaving her alone here—until the excess juices have cooked off and evaporated, 5 to 8 minutes. As the juices cook off, the marinade may start to burn in spots on the wok, but that's also what we want: It adds flavor! When you no longer see any juice, start stirring the meat aggressively (avoiding scraping the burned bits on the wok into the meat) and use the spatula to break the meat up into small pieces. Cook for another minute or until the meat is brown and charred. Remove the wok from the heat and sprinkle with the sesame seeds and sesame oil. Stir to combine, then transfer the meat to a clean plate.

Enjoy with the steamed rice, kimchi, bean sprout salad, and lettuce for DIYing your own wraps. Garnish with the sesame seeds and green onion greens.

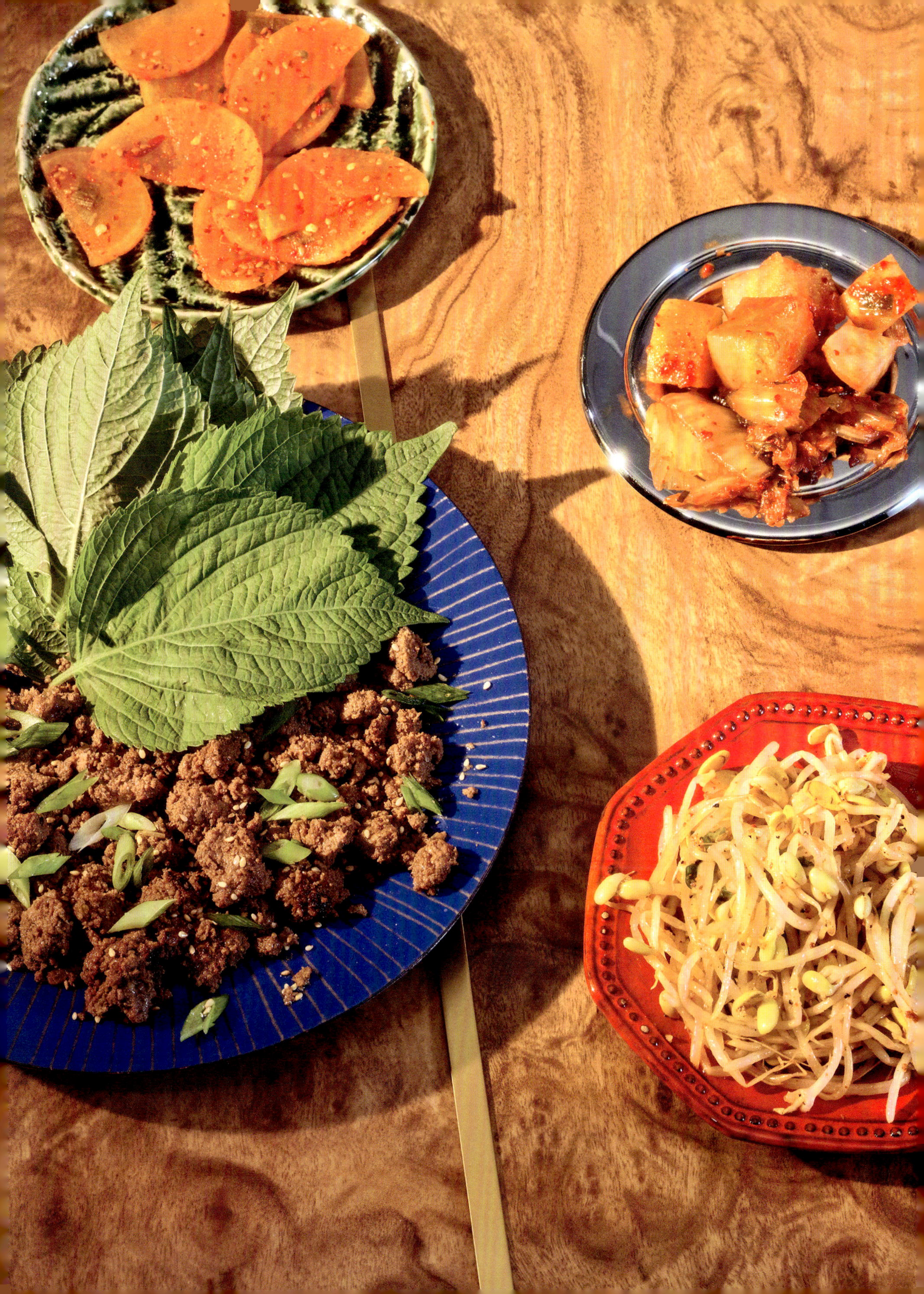

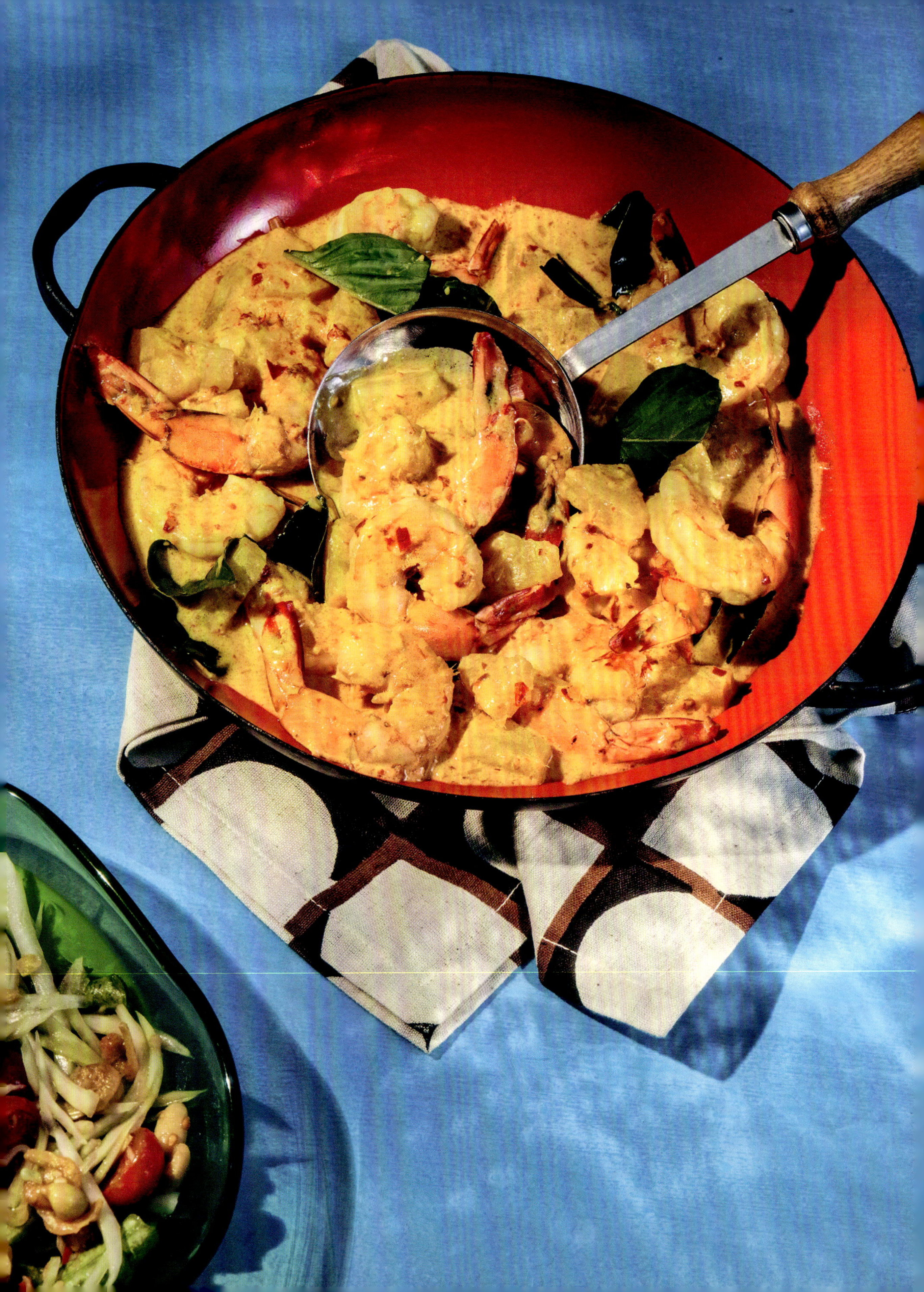

SHRIMP & PINEAPPLE THAI CURRY

SERVES 2 TO 4

2 fresh bird's-eye chilies, stems removed

2 fresh Fresno chilies, stems removed

1 lemongrass stalk, tough outer layers removed and roughly chopped

½ teaspoon kosher salt

1-inch knob of galangal, peeled and finely chopped

½-inch knob of fresh turmeric, peeled and roughly chopped

½-inch knob of ginger, peeled and roughly chopped

½ small shallot, roughly chopped

3 large garlic cloves, smashed

1½ teaspoons shrimp paste

½ teaspoon dried red pepper flakes

1 tablespoon neutral oil (I use avocado oil)

1 (13.5-ounce) can coconut milk

1 teaspoon palm sugar or light brown sugar (see page 16)

1 cup fresh or canned pineapple chunks, drained

6 fresh makrut lime leaves, torn in half

1 tablespoon fish sauce

1 pound jumbo shrimp (around 25/pound), peeled and deveined (page 46)

6 fresh Thai basil leaves, torn

FOR SERVING

The Perfect Steamed Rice (page 242)

There's no shame in using store-bought curry paste, but not until I traveled to Bangkok did I realize how easy it is to make your own. I specifically took a cooking class while I was in Thailand to learn how to make a curry that could stand up to the ones I ate there. The cooking class included the full experience of walking to the local market and picking out all of the spices. And yes, this recipe requires a trip to the Asian market for a few unique ingredients like fresh turmeric, lime leaves, and shrimp paste, but the outcome is so worth it. The addition of pineapple was something I never knew I needed, but my chef-instructor, Chef Nooror at the Blue Elephant, convinced me otherwise. It takes a couple of minutes to pound out the paste, but after that, this curry comes together in no time.

Prepare the curry paste: In a mortar and pestle or a food processor, pound or pulse together the bird's-eye chilies, Fresno chilies, lemongrass, and salt until they become a rough paste. (This may take a few minutes, but you'll know you're done when you're sneezing. If you ain't sneezing, you ain't seasoning!) Add the galangal, turmeric, ginger, shallot, and garlic, and continue pounding or pulsing until it's a smooth and cohesive paste, another few minutes. Remove to a clean bowl, then use a spoon to stir in the shrimp paste and red pepper flakes.

Make the curry: Heat a medium pot with the oil over medium heat. When the oil is hot and shimmering, add in the curry paste. Using a rubber spatula, fry the paste, stirring constantly, until the paste has dried out and thickened a little, about 2 minutes. Slowly pour in the coconut milk, ½ cup at a time while stirring constantly and allowing the curry to come up to a boil before adding in more (we're doing this so that we can boil and slowly thicken the coconut milk without overboiling and curdling). Stir in the palm sugar and boil until the sugar has dissolved, 1 to 2 minutes. Stir in the pineapple, lime leaves, and fish sauce, and reduce the heat to medium-low so the curry gently simmers.

Simmer, stirring frequently, until the curry has thickened slightly and everything is combined, 3 to 5 minutes. Stir in the shrimp and cook until they are tender and have just curled into a C shape—that's how you know they're cooked through—2 to 3 minutes. Mix in the Thai basil and stir until everything is combined before serving over the steamed white rice.

CHICKEN KATSU CURRY

SERVES 4

CURRY

2 tablespoons neutral oil (I use avocado oil)

1 large russet potato, peeled and cut into 1½-inch cubes

2 medium carrots, sliced thick

½ medium yellow onion, roughly chopped

3 large garlic cloves, minced

½ cup Shaoxing wine

3 cups store-bought low-sodium chicken broth or bone broth

1 Golden Curry block (see page 15)

CHICKEN CUTLETS

4 boneless, skinless chicken thighs, pounded into cutlets, or 8 chicken cutlets (see Notes)

¼ cup all-purpose flour

2 large eggs, lightly beaten

1 teaspoon light soy sauce

2 teaspoons ground white pepper

2 large garlic cloves

1-inch knob of ginger, peeled

2 cups panko breadcrumbs

1 teaspoon garlic powder

Neutral oil (I use avocado oil), for frying

FOR SERVING

The Perfect Steamed Rice (page 242)

The Jersey girl in me has the biggest appreciation for a good, crispy chicken cutlet. Chicken katsu curry is the Japanese equivalent of the Italian classic that might just be *even better* thanks to its extra-crispy panko-crumb crust. It's accompanied by a thick and creamy golden curry enhanced by tender potatoes and carrots swimming throughout. This combo alongside a fluffy bed of jasmine rice is unstoppable. Golden Curry cubes are one of my favorite pantry items to keep on hand so that I can whip up this comfort meal in thirty minutes.

Prepare the curry: Heat a medium pan with the oil over medium-high heat. When the oil is hot and shimmering, add in the potato cubes. Using a spatula, spread them into a flat layer and cook for 3 minutes, until they're golden on the bottom, before stirring. Cook for another 3 minutes, without stirring, before adding in the carrots and onion. Cook, stirring frequently now, until the carrots and onion start to soften, 3 to 5 minutes. Add garlic and cook, stirring frequently, until the garlic becomes fragrant, another 1 minute.

Pour in the Shaoxing wine to deglaze the pan—you're stirring and scrapping up all the browned goodness from the bottom of the pan—and cook for 1 minute until it's reduced by half. Pour in the chicken broth, stir, and bring it to a boil. Reduce the heat to low so the broth simmers, cover, and cook until the potatoes are fork tender, about 15 minutes. Cover and keep warm.

While the potatoes simmer, batter and fry the chicken cutlets: In a small bowl, combine the pounded chicken, flour, eggs, soy sauce, and 1 teaspoon white pepper. Now get out your grater and grate the garlic and ginger into the bowl (baddies, watch your nails) so the flavors really penetrate the chicken. Mix thoroughly until the chicken is coated in smooth batter with a consistency like pancake batter.

Line a sheet pan with aluminum foil. In a shallow dish, season the panko breadcrumbs with the garlic powder and the remaining 1 teaspoon white pepper. Working one piece of chicken at a time, let the excess batter drip off then coat it well in the breadcrumbs, making sure it is fully covered—use your knuckles to really press and stick the breadcrumbs to the chicken until there are no bald spots. Set aside on the lined sheet pan. Continue until each piece of chicken is coated.

Fill a large, deep skillet with 1 inch of neutral oil and heat to 350°F (if you don't have a thermometer, do the wooden chopstick test on page 47). Fit a cooling rack over a sheet pan or line a plate with paper towels.

(recipe continues)

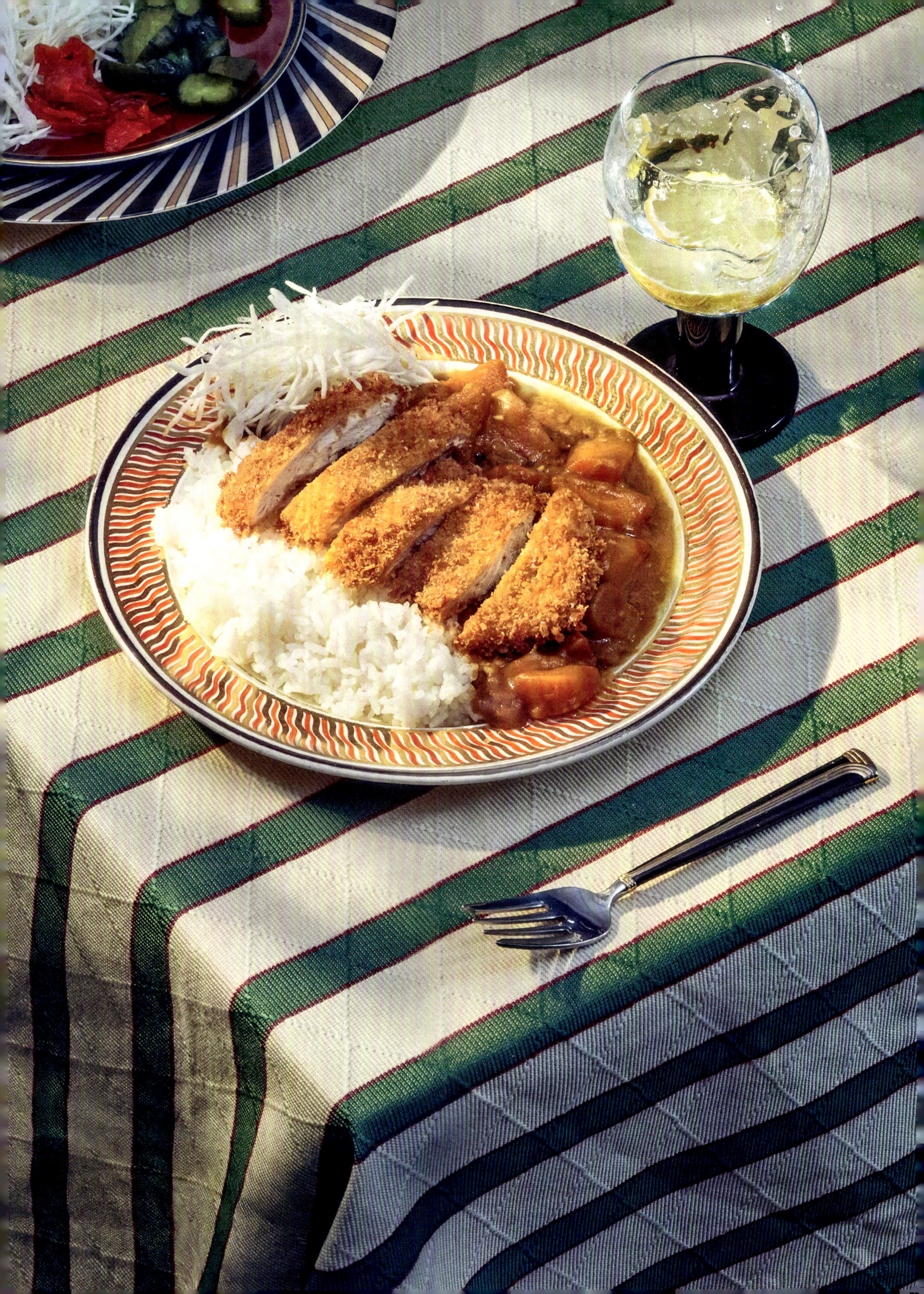

Add the chicken, frying in batches to avoid crowding the pan, until the chicken is deeply golden brown, about 4 minutes on each side. Remove with tongs to the cooling rack. Repeat with the remaining chicken and rest the chicken while you finish the curry.

Finish the curry: Once the potatoes are tender, break the curry block into pieces, drop into the mixture, and stir constantly until the curry block has completely dissolved, about 5 minutes.

To serve: Let the chicken rest for 5 minutes, then slice into ¼-inch-thick strips and serve beside a bed of white rice with the curry poured on top.

> **NOTES**
> - To turn **chicken breasts** into cutlets, use a sharp chef's knife to slice each breast into two halves by cutting parallel to the cutting board so you now have two same-size yet thinner cutlets. Make sure you're holding the chicken in place with your palm to keep your fingers away from the knife.
> - For **chicken thighs**, leave them whole since they're thinner already. Place one thigh on a sheet of plastic wrap, cover it with another sheet of plastic wrap, set on the cutting board, and pound with a meat mallet or something heavy like a rolling pin or small saucepan until they are an even ½-inch thickness. Repeat with the remaining pieces.

CANTONESE STEAMED FISH

SERVES 2

Ice water

4 green onions, white and green parts, cut into 2-inch-long thin matchsticks

2 (8-ounce) 1-inch-thick whitefish fillets, like cod or sea bass

2-inch knob of ginger, peeled and cut into thin matchsticks

¼ cup light soy sauce

½ teaspoon sugar

3 tablespoons neutral oil (I use avocado oil)

2 tablespoons toasted sesame oil

FOR SERVING

The Perfect Steamed Rice (page 242)

Leaves from ½ bunch of fresh cilantro, roughly chopped, for razzle-dazzle

Cantonese-style steamed fish always brings me right back to family dinners. My mom typically made this dish with a whole fish and served us all different parts of it. My parents were into the fish head, while my sister and I would eat the belly. Although this is traditionally made with an entire fish, I've adapted the recipe to use any boneless fillet to avoid my overwhelming fear of having to deal with fish bones—both in preparation and eating (when I was little I swallowed one—I'll spare you the details!). The fish is steamed with soy sauce and aromatics and gets topped with beautiful ribbons of green onions and fresh ginger, then sizzled and woken up with a splash of hot sesame oil. Fish is extremely symbolic in Chinese culture, so I often find this dish on the table at family celebrations. Here's to wealth, abundance, and a delicious dinner!

Fill a small bowl with ice water and add the sliced green onions so they curl up and create ribbons. Set aside to let it do its thing while you make the fish.

On a medium, heat-safe plate with high sides (if using a bamboo steamer, it needs to be small enough to fit inside), lay the fish fillets down with an inch of space in between and pat dry with paper towels. Top each fillet with half the ginger.

In a small bowl, whisk together the soy sauce and sugar. Pour the sauce onto the base of the plate so that it surrounds the fish fillets, but don't pour it onto the fish.

In a wok or large pot, add 1 to 2 inches of water and set up a bamboo steamer or round steamer rack (see page 27). Bring the water to a boil over medium-high heat, then reduce the heat to medium. Using a tea towel or oven mitts to avoid the steam, set the plate onto the bamboo steamer or steamer rack. Cover and steam for 7 to 10 minutes or until the fish easily flakes when poked with a fork. Use a pair of plate tongs or a tea towel to carefully remove the plate to a trivet.

Remove the green onions from the ice water and lay them on paper towels to soak up any excess water. Discard the ice water.

Heat the neutral oil and sesame oil in a small saucepan over medium heat to 325°F, or until you can stick a wooden chopstick in and it bubbles right away. Lay half the green onions on top of each fish fillet and pour the hot oil directly onto the green onions and watch them sizzle. Spoon the fish and sauce over the white rice, garnish with lots of the cilantro, and enjoy right away.

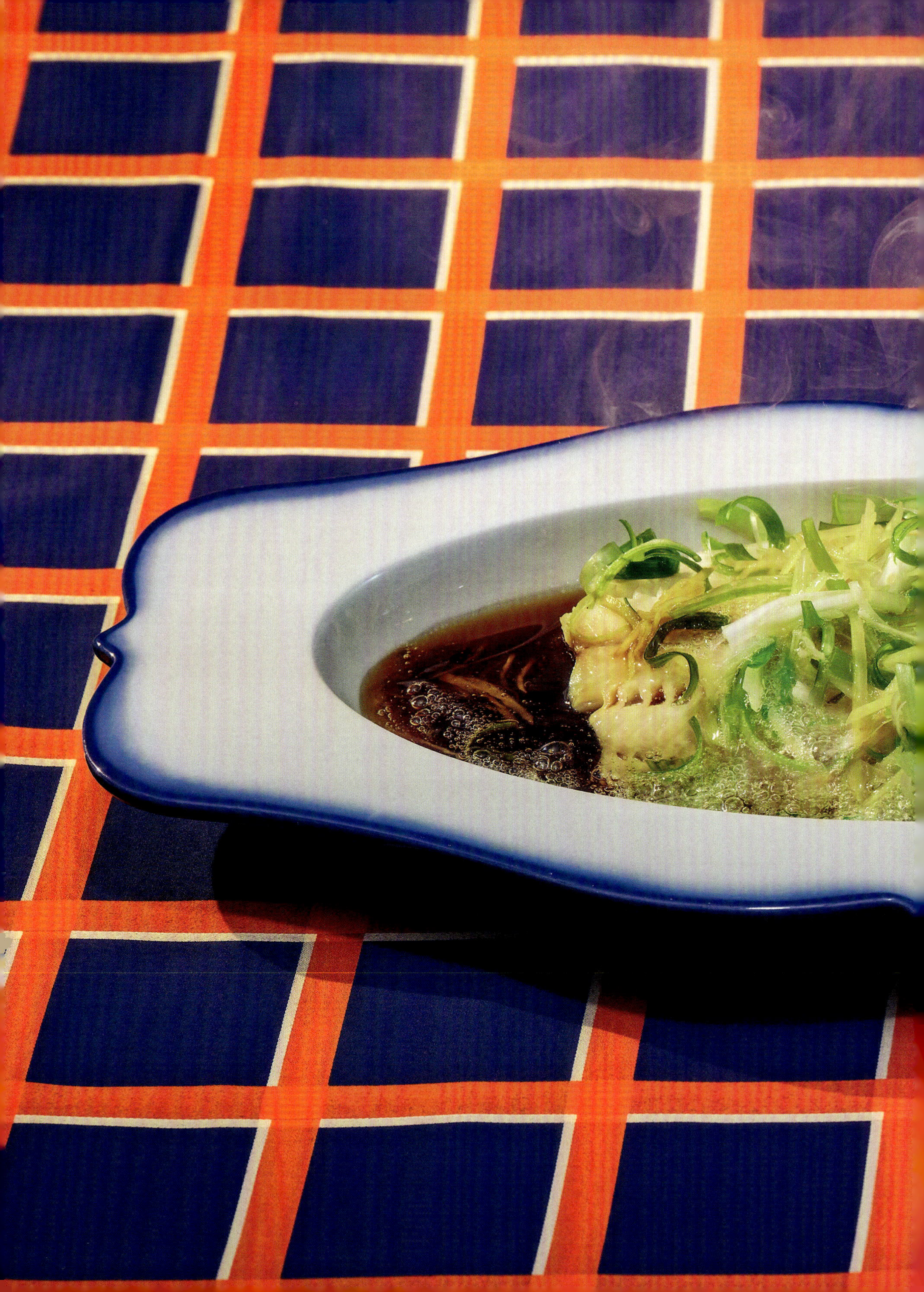

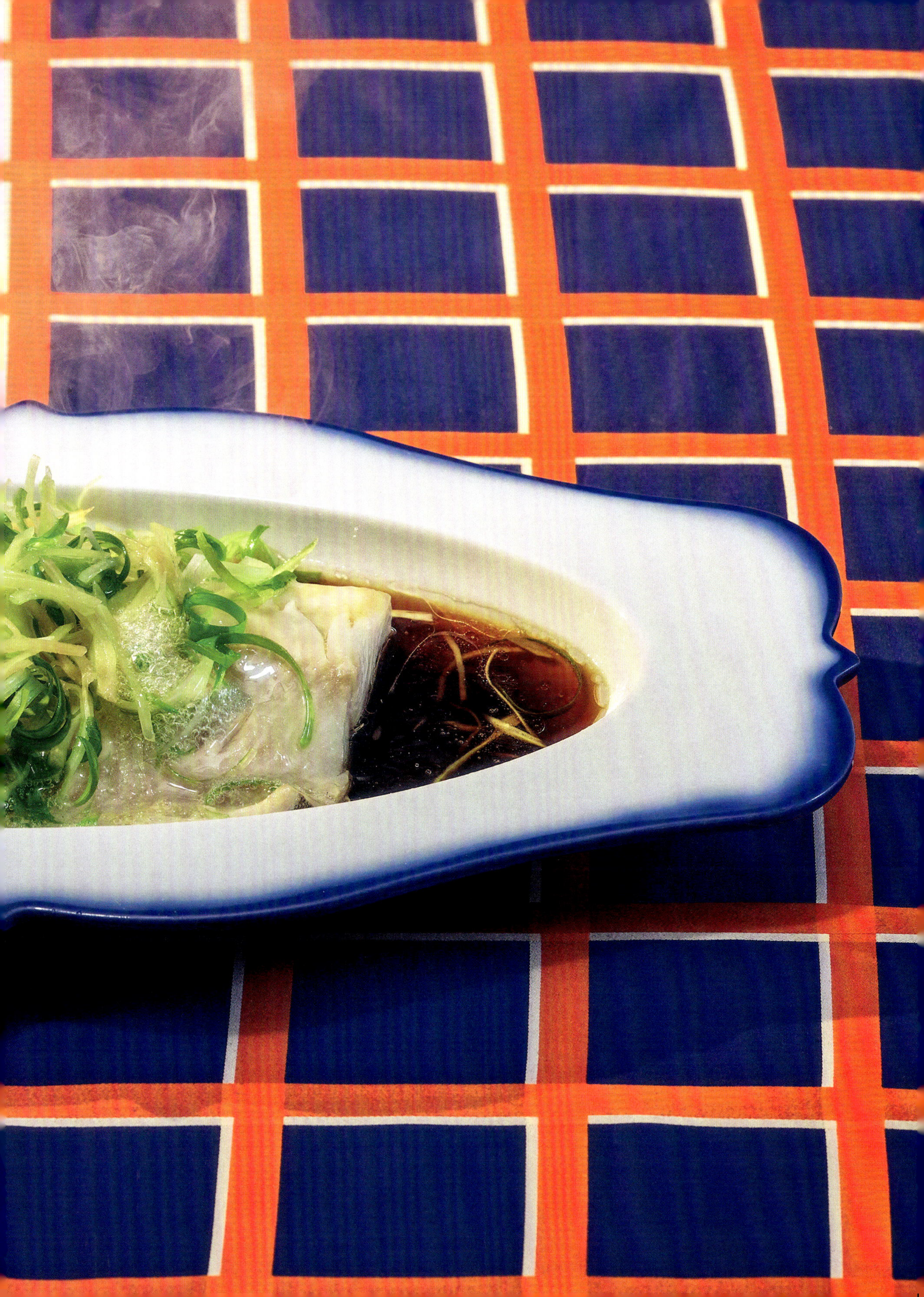

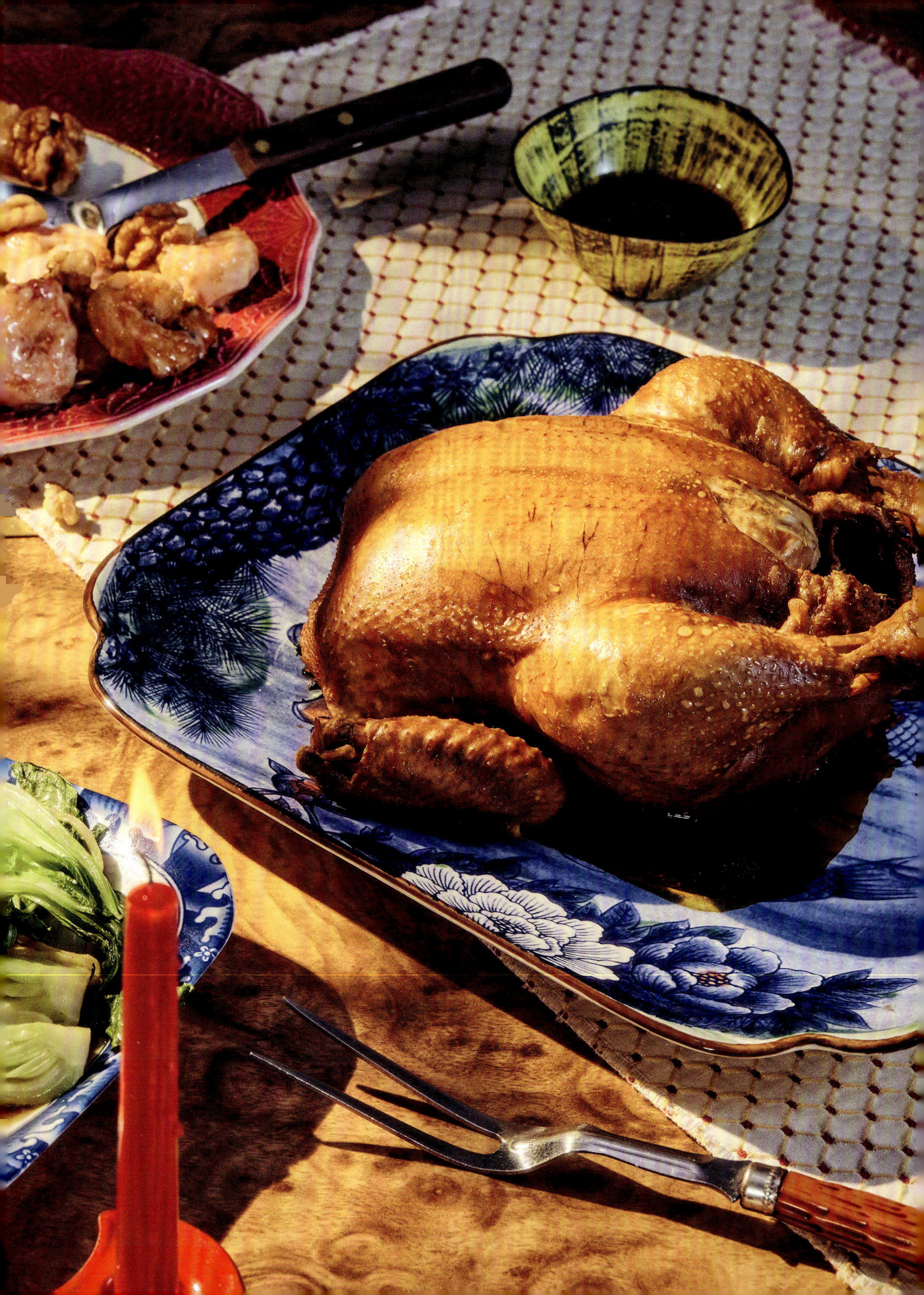

SOY SAUCE CHICKEN

SERVES 6 TO 8

1 (4- to 5-pound) whole chicken

2 tablespoons kosher salt

1 tablespoon neutral oil (I use avocado oil)

4 large garlic cloves, smashed

1-inch knob of fresh ginger, peeled and thinly sliced

4 green onions, white and green parts, cut into 2-inch pieces

2 cups light soy sauce

2 cups dark soy sauce

3 tablespoons toasted sesame oil

1-inch piece rock sugar or 2 teaspoons granulated sugar

3 star anise pods

FOR SERVING

The Perfect Steamed Rice (page 242)

One of my mom's dinners that I always get excited to visit home for is see yao gai, aka soy sauce chicken! When I moved out, I asked her how to make it and, like any Asian mother, she gave me the most generic instructions with no real measurements. This was definitely a *figure it out* moment, so I did just that. I took my mom's simple explanation and turned it into a foolproof recipe. It makes sense now why she didn't explain much because it really is *that* easy! I already love soy sauce so much that it practically runs through my veins, but we level up the flavor even more by infusing it with ginger, green onions, garlic, sesame oil, star anise, and rock sugar. The whole chicken then gets poached in the special soy sauce, which penetrates through the cavity and throughout the meat, leaving the skin a beautiful glossy brown. I love serving a whole chicken because everyone can choose their favorite pieces. Dark meat, white meat, breast, or drumstick—this satisfies everyone. You will have a lot of leftover poaching liquid, and it's perfect for drizzling over steamed white rice or even saving for other dishes like the base of Soy-Marinated Eggs (page 63), or as a sub for marinades that call for light soy sauce!

Prep the chicken: Bring the chicken to room temperature 30 minutes before cooking. Now, with your hands, give your chicken a spa day and massage and exfoliate the skin with the salt so that it's extra supple (how do I sign up next?). Rinse well and pat dry with paper towels. Set aside.

Prepare the sauce: Heat a large pot (big enough to fit the whole chicken) with the neutral oil over medium heat. When the oil is hot and shimmering, add the garlic, ginger, and green onions and cook, stirring frequently with a spatula, until the aromatics are lightly browned, 3 to 5 minutes. Pour in the light soy sauce, dark soy sauce, sesame oil, rock sugar, and star anise and add 8 cups of water. Bring to a boil, then cook, stirring occasionally, until the rock sugar dissolves, about 5 minutes.

Poach the chicken: Using a pair of tongs or a carving fork, slowly lower the chicken into the sauce breast side up, making sure the sauce also fills the cavity (the sauce will naturally fill the cavity if you hold it down—she may let out a few farts, don't embarrass her). Ladle the sauce onto any part of the chicken that is not submerged in it. Reduce the heat to low, cover, and simmer, basting the exposed parts every 5 minutes, until the skin is brown, about 20 minutes.

Use the tongs to carefully flip the chicken, cover, and continue simmering and basting every 5 minutes, until the skin is an even brown and fully saturated in soy sauce and the juices run clear, another 10 minutes. Carefully remove the chicken, allowing the sauce to drain from the cavity and drip off the chicken into the pot before moving it to a clean plate. Rest for 10 to 15 minutes before carving. Reserve the sauce for drizzling over the chicken and the steamed rice for serving.

SHAKING BEEF

SERVES 4

PICKLED ONIONS

½ medium red onion, thinly sliced into half moons

1 teaspoon sugar

1 cup boiling water

1 cup distilled white vinegar

SHAKING BEEF

1 pound boneless ribeye, cut into 1-inch cubes

1 tablespoon light soy sauce

1 tablespoon oyster sauce

1 teaspoon fish sauce

1 teaspoon sugar

1 teaspoon toasted sesame oil

1 teaspoon sambal oelek

½ teaspoon Maggi or Knorr brand liquid seasoning (optional; see Note)

½ teaspoon freshly ground black pepper

1 large garlic clove, minced

1 tablespoon neutral oil (I use avocado oil)

¾ cup whole cherry tomatoes

FOR SERVING

The Perfect Steamed Rice (page 242)

¼ pound fresh watercress

Persian cucumber, thinly sliced on a diagonal

A high-quality cut of meat can be pricey when you're feeding lots of people. Shaking beef to the rescue! Here, you can stretch one fillet to feed up to three people—and you can also easily scale up to serve a crowd. The name comes from the method of shaking the wok to toss and cook the beef. My favorite cut of steak to use is a ribeye because of its fat content. It's cubed and marinated with soy sauce, oyster sauce, fish sauce, Maggi, sugar, and sambal, which enhances the flavor of the steak even more. The steak is wok-fried with cherry tomatoes that blister and, along with the sweet pickled red onions, add a wonderful brightness. It's so good over steamed rice served with fresh watercress for its peppery taste, along with fresh cracked black pepper in lime juice (fresh, of course) for dipping.

Make the pickled onions: Add the thinly sliced onions to an airtight 1-quart heatproof glass jar. Sprinkle in the sugar, then pour in the boiling water and distilled white vinegar. Close the jar tight and shake lightly to mix. Set aside to pickle for 30 minutes at room temperature, then transfer to the fridge for 1 hour, or until you're ready to use them (they will keep for up to 2 weeks).

Marinate the beef: In a medium bowl, mix the steak cubes, soy sauce, oyster sauce, fish sauce, sugar, sesame oil, sambal oelek, Maggi, black pepper, and garlic. Marinate for at least 30 minutes or in the fridge, covered, for up to 8 hours.

Heat a wok or large skillet with the neutral oil over high heat. When the oil is hot and shimmering, add the beef and use a spatula to spread it into a flat layer. Let the beef cook without stirring until the pieces begin to char on the edges, 30 to 60 seconds. Shake the wok aggressively to flip the pieces and add in the cherry tomatoes. Cook, stirring occasionally, until the tomato skins begin to wilt, the beef is charred all over, and everything is combined, about another minute, before removing to a clean plate.

To serve: Spoon the beef over the steamed white rice and place the fresh watercress on the side. Finish with the charred tomatoes, fresh cucumber, and pickled onions.

> **NOTE**
>
> Liquid seasoning, similar to Worcestershire sauce, is a dark-colored flavor enhancer. As the name suggests, it's packed with seasoning so you only need a small amount. Although I highly recommend it, this can easily be omitted and substituted with more soy sauce.

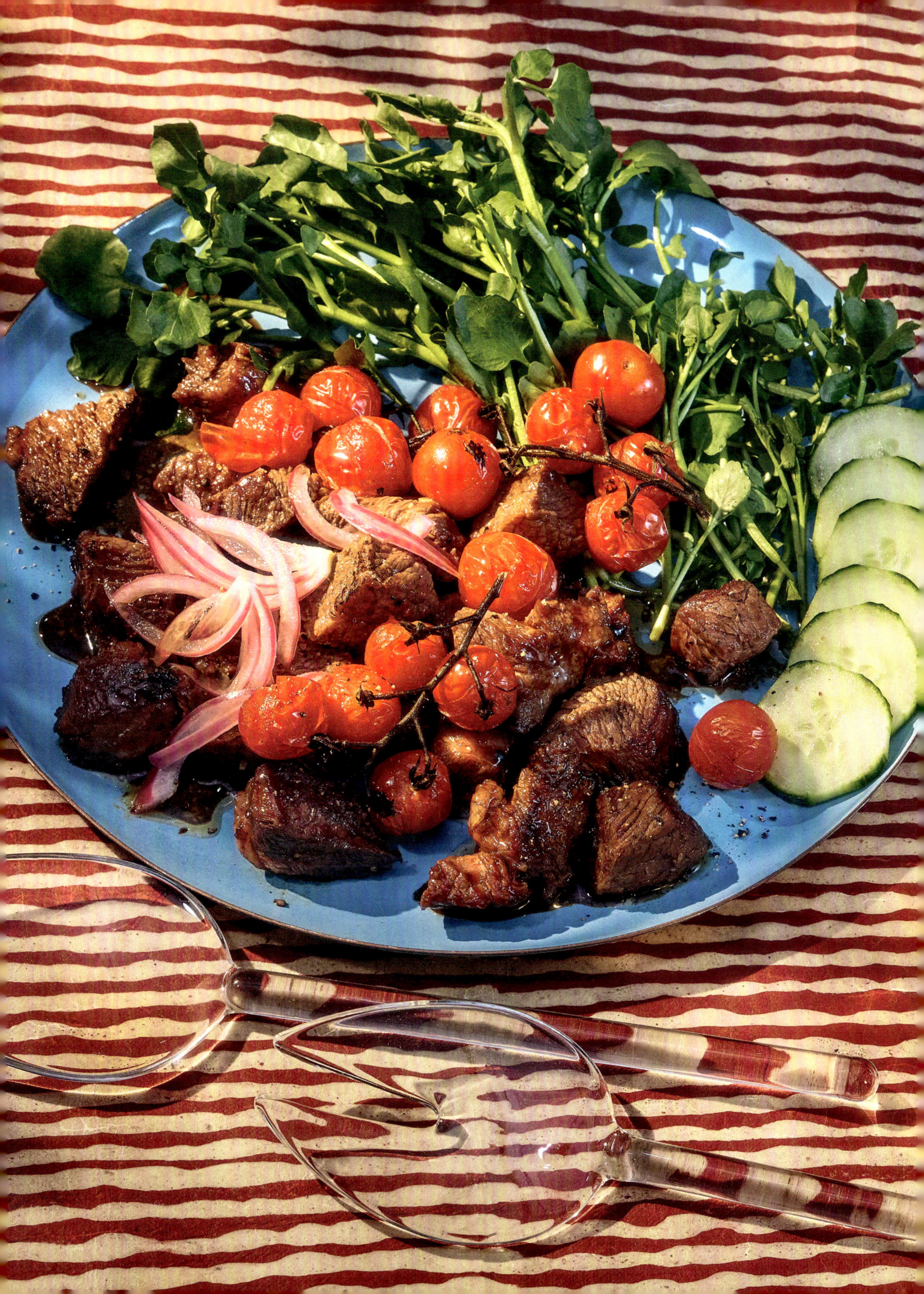

TASTE OF SINGAPORE

TASTE OF SINGAPORE

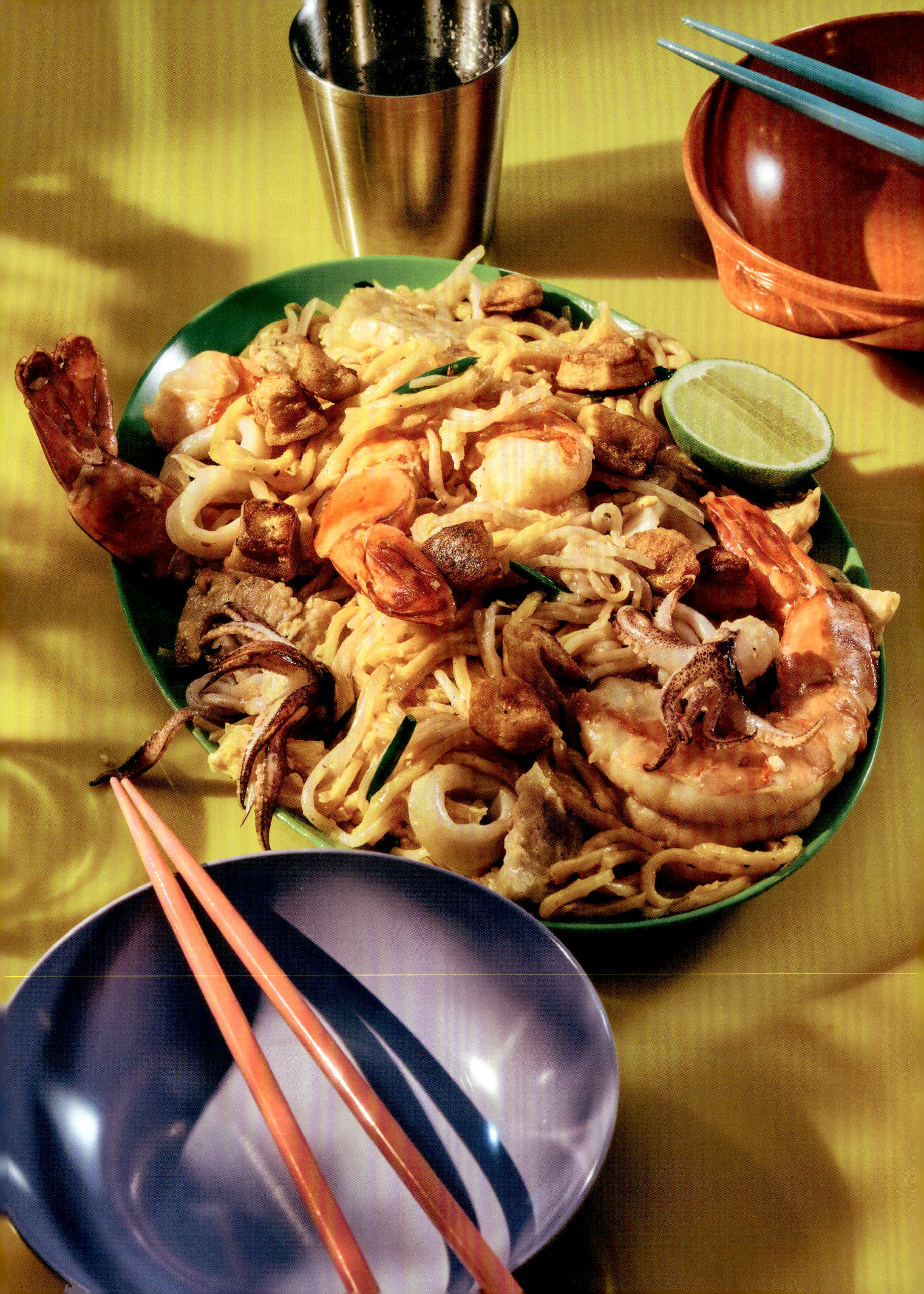

RECIPE LIST

Hainanese Chicken Rice
136

Hokkien Prawn Mee
140

Char Kway Teow
142

Curry Laksa
145

Singaporean Chili Crab
146

Bak Kut Teh
151

Auntie's Whole Braised Duck (Lor Ark)
152

Ah Ma's Mee Hoon Kueh
154

Claypot Rice
158

The most beautiful thing about food is that it's a universal language.

This sentimental chapter reminds me how I can bond with my family in Singapore without needing to translate. I come from a family of foodies, and recipes like Hokkien Prawn Mee, Auntie's Whole Braised Duck, and Ah Ma's Mee Hoon Kueh have been passed on from my Singaporean auntie who ultimately learned them from our ancestors. Food has always been an integral part of the country's culture and heritage that leaves a lasting impression. I'm constantly finding myself craving a taste of Singapore, so why not re-create it at home!

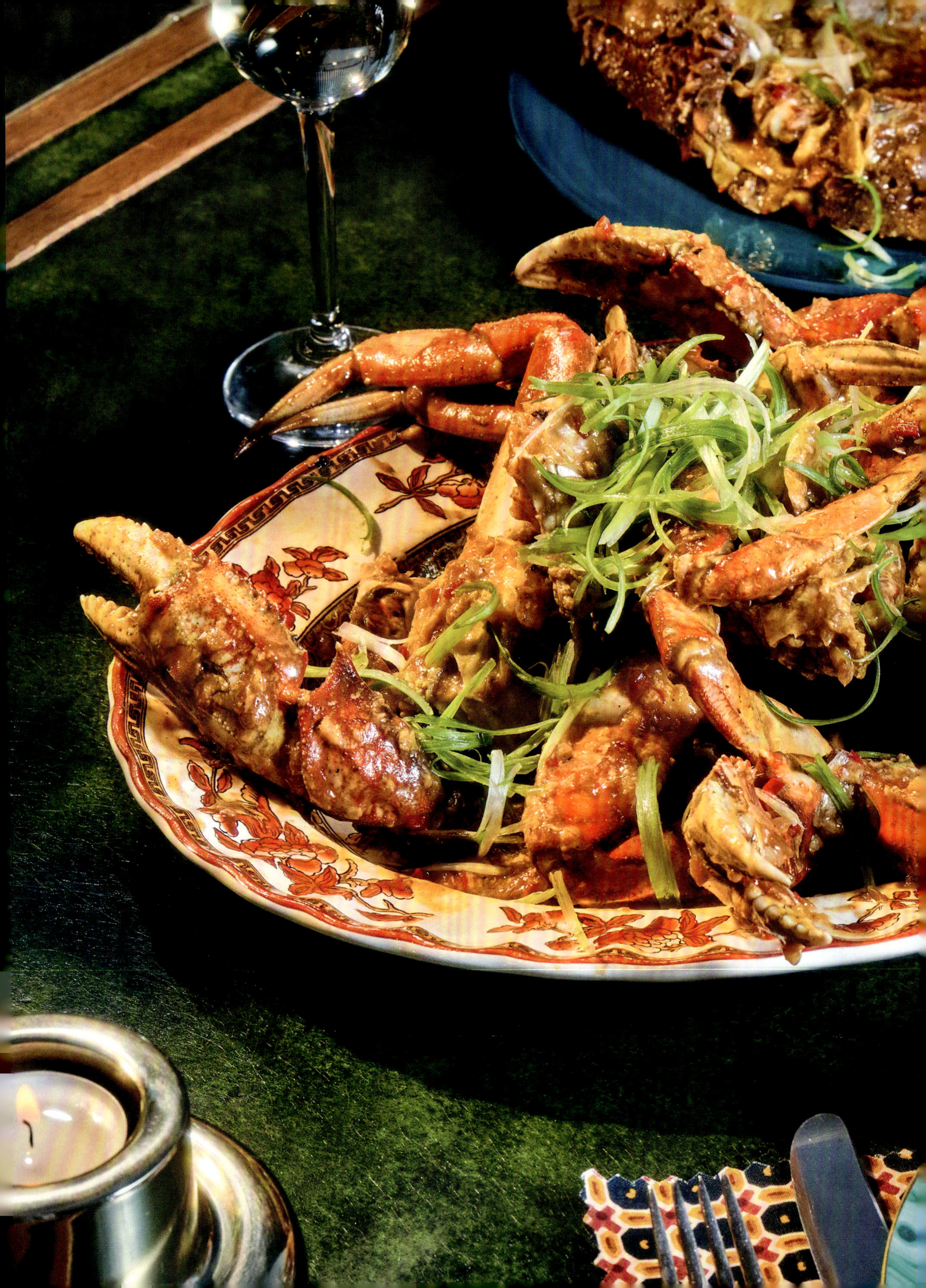

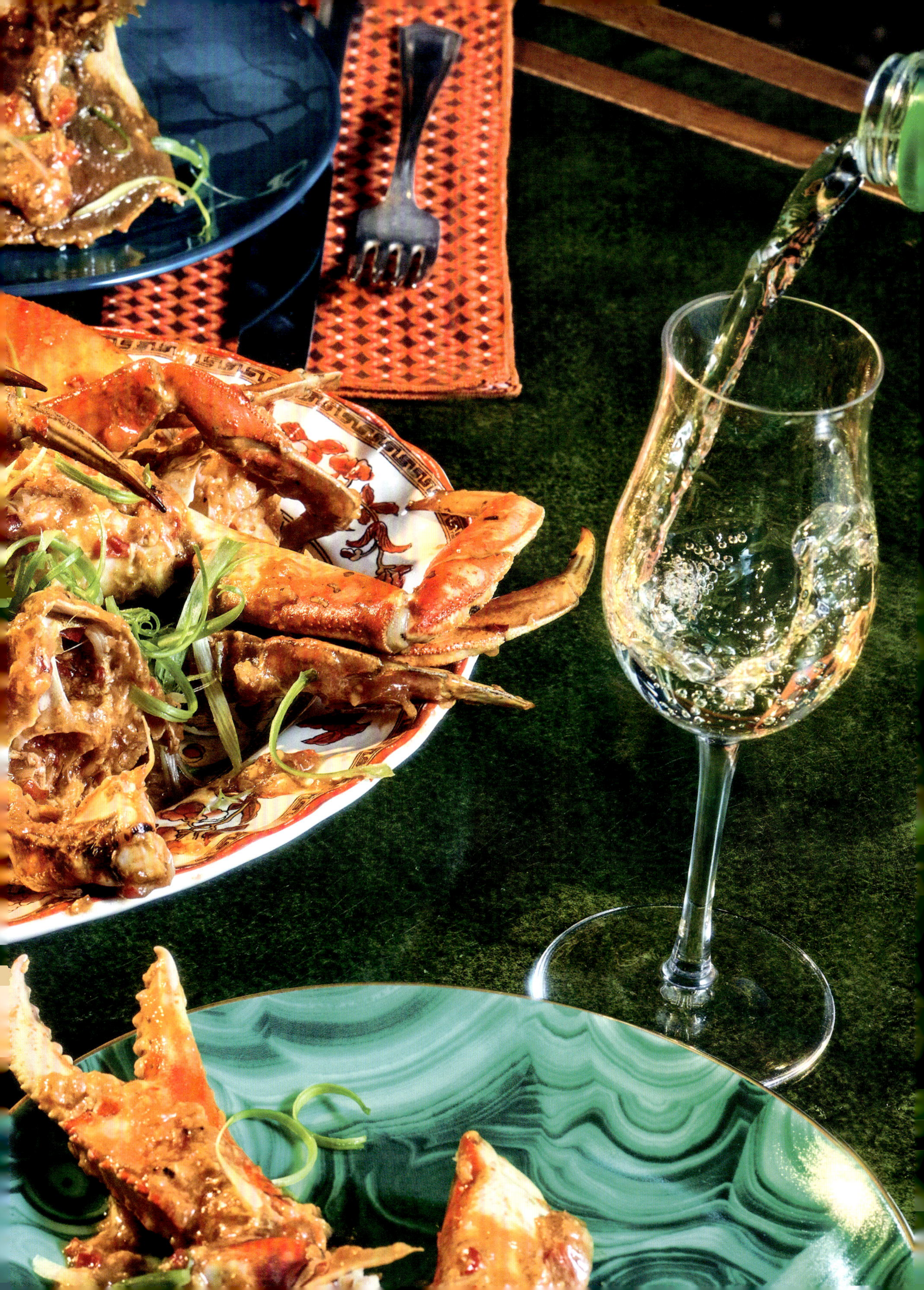

HAINANESE CHICKEN RICE

SERVES 4 TO 6

CHICKEN

1 (3-pound) whole chicken, neck reserved, giblets removed

3 tablespoons kosher salt

3 large garlic cloves

2-inch knob of ginger, peeled and thinly sliced

1 bunch green onions, white and green parts, cut into 2-inch pieces

3 tablespoons chicken bouillon powder

Ice water

1 tablespoon toasted sesame oil

RICE

2 cups long-grain white rice, rinsed

3 large garlic cloves, minced

1-inch knob of ginger, peeled and minced

FOR SERVING

Sweet soy sauce (kecap manis)

Ginger Scallion Sauce (page 256)

Sweet chili sauce, store-bought or homemade (see page 259)

Persian cucumber, thinly sliced on the diagonal (optional)

Roughly chopped fresh cilantro, for razzle-dazzle

I was only six when I first visited Singapore, and while memories from childhood can be selective, the one I'll never forget from that trip is the first time I tried and fell in love with Hainanese chicken rice. That first bite felt like it had stopped time. The dish was simple, yet flavor-packed: aromatic toasted rice served alongside tender and juicy poached chicken, with a soulful chicken broth that was like a warm hug. Every element of the dish enhances one another, and hints of garlic and ginger run throughout. My Singaporean relatives chuckled at the idea that I was so starstruck by a dish that was so *regular* to them. From that day on, I begged for chicken rice every day, and my mom started letting me go up to a hawker vendor to order for myself. Which I happily did.

Back at home, my mom started making the dish, and eventually taught me how simple it is.

What we're doing here is poaching the chicken with garlic, ginger, and green onions to make a hearty chicken broth. Extra fat reserved from the chicken is rendered and used to fry garlic and ginger to infuse the toasted rice, which is then steamed with the chicken broth to create a fluffy and flavor-packed rice. While you're waiting, you can make the ginger scallion oil and the sweet chili sauce. The chicken is massaged with sesame oil to give it its signature glossy skin and sliced for serving. The chicken and rice are best served with a bowl of the broth and sides of the ginger scallion and sweet chili dipping sauces!

Poach the chicken: Using kitchen shears or a paring knife, trim the fat and extra skin off the chicken from the neck and thigh area and reserve for the rice. Rub the salt all over the skin and inside the cavity of the chicken—you're exfoliating the skin—this will create a bouncy (in a good way, think about your own skin post-facial) texture once cooked. Rinse well under cold water and pat dry using paper towels.

To a large pot, add the whole chicken, garlic, ginger, green onions, chicken bouillon powder, and enough cool tap water to cover the chicken. Bring to a boil over high heat, then reduce the heat to medium-low, cover, and gently simmer until the broth is fragrant and lightly golden and the chicken juices run clear when pierced with a knife, occasionally skimming the top of the broth with a fat skimmer to remove any fat or scum, about 30 minutes.

Meanwhile, prepare the rice: To a medium, dry pot set over medium heat, add the chicken trimmings and cook, stirring occasionally, until the skin is crispy and the fat is rendered, 5 to 10 minutes. Using a slotted spoon, remove the pieces of crispy skin (chef's treat), then carefully add the rice, garlic, and ginger. Fry, stirring often, until the rice is lightly toasted, 1 to 2 minutes. Take 2 cups of the broth from the chicken and add to the rice and stir. Raise the heat to medium-high and cook for 5 to 10 minutes, uncovered, until there is visibly no more liquid on top. Reduce the heat to low, cover, and cook for 10 minutes more.

Finish the chicken: Fill a large bowl with ice water. Use a pair of tongs to remove the chicken from the pot and transfer to the ice bath for 30 seconds. Remove and transfer to a cutting board, letting any excess water drip off and lightly dab with paper towels. Rub the chicken all over with the sesame oil so that it's nice and glossy, and then carefully carve away the breasts and legs from the body. Separate the legs into thighs and drumsticks and slice each breast crosswise into ½-inch-thick pieces.

To serve: Divide the white meat and the dark meat on plates according to preference, drizzle with sweet soy sauce, and serve each portion with a scoop of rice, one small bowl of ginger scallion sauce and another of sweet chili sauce, a small bowl of broth, cucumbers if you like, and fresh cilantro.

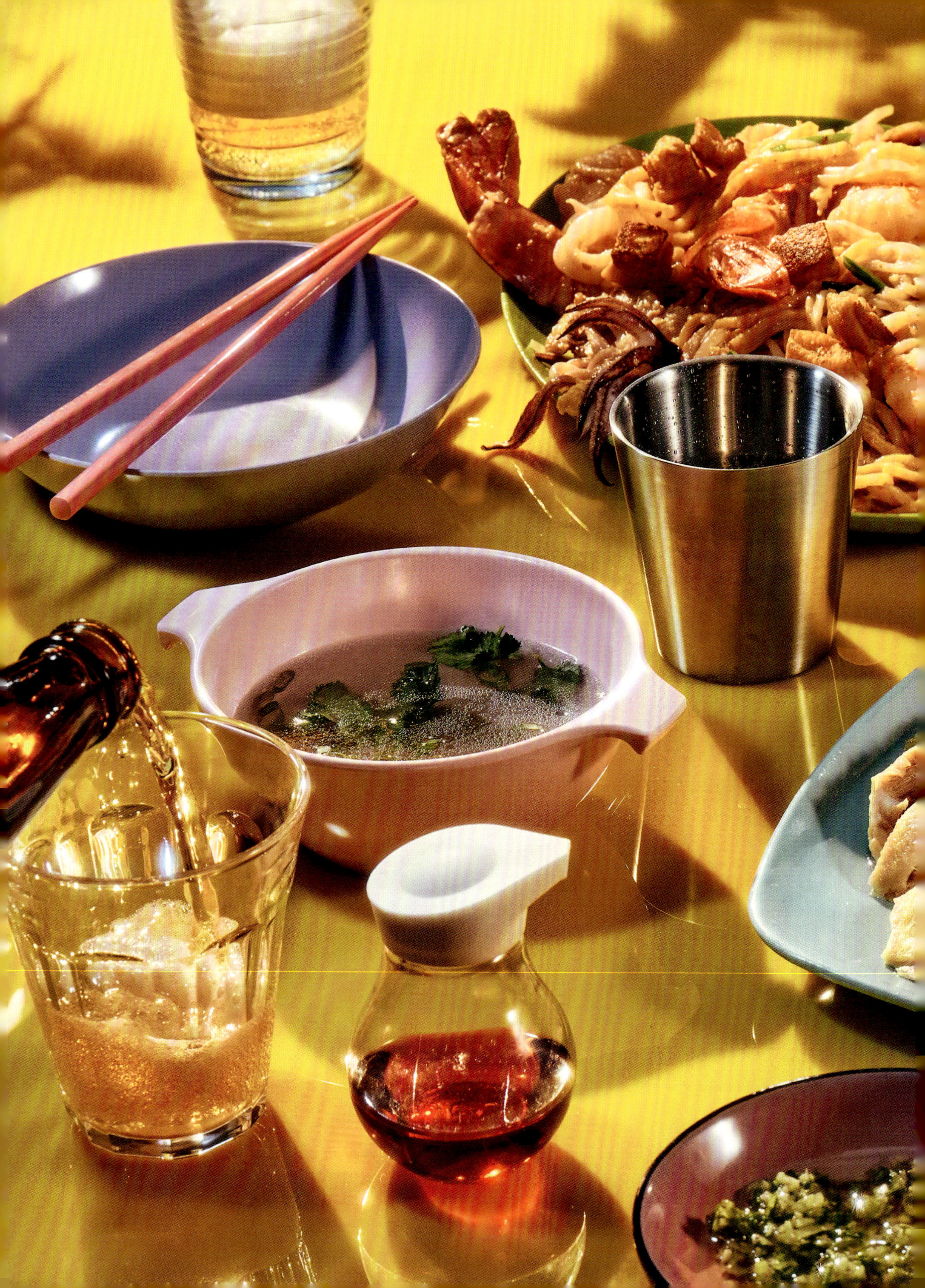

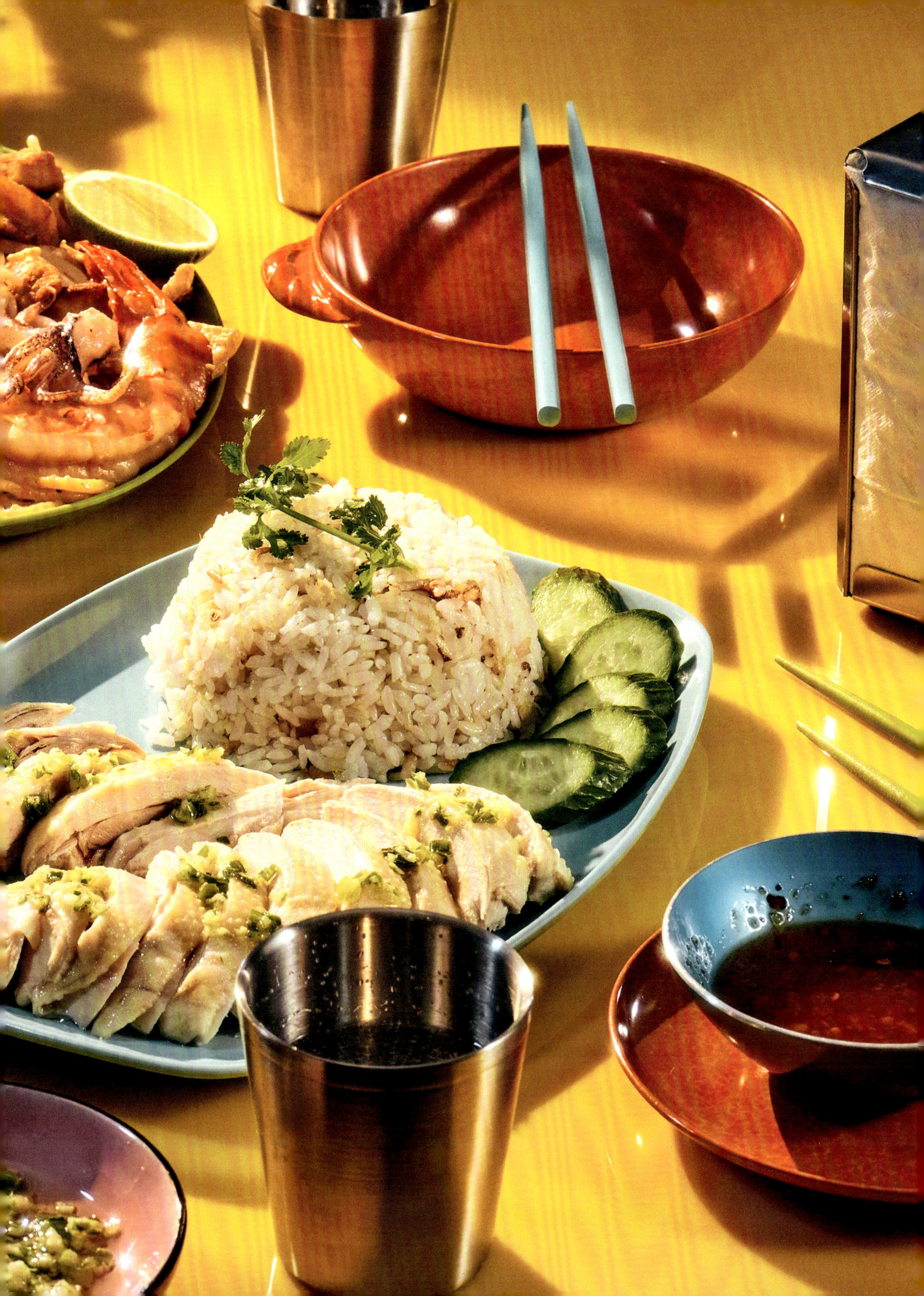

HOKKIEN PRAWN MEE

SERVES 6

1 pound tiger prawns, head-on with the shells (see Notes)

1 large whole squid (about 2 pounds), cleaned

Shells and heads from 2 pounds of prawns or shrimp

2 pounds skinless pork belly

2 pounds pork bones

1 tablespoon sugar

2 tablespoons neutral oil (I use avocado oil)

1 pound pork lard *or* pork fat, cut into 1-inch cubes (see Notes)

1 teaspoon kosher salt

6 large eggs

½ pound fresh bean sprouts

1 pound fresh mee hoon (yellow noodles; see page 21)

1 pound fresh bee hoon (white noodles; see page 21)

6 large garlic cloves, minced

1½ cups fresh Chinese chives, cut into 1-inch pieces (about ½ bunch; can sub with green onion greens)

Fish sauce

FOR SERVING

Sambal oelek or homemade chili paste (see page 142)

Lime wedges

There are so many stories to go with this dish, and I love seeing my mom's side of the family light up whenever they retell them. My uncle and auntie owned a famous stall at a hawker center and made this dish what it is today in Singapore. It's a fried noodle, but instead of being fried in sauce, a prawn and pork broth is patiently simmered and thickened to become a sauce that coats each noodle, giving it a silky texture.

My mom and her younger sister were required to finish their chores before leaving the house, and one of their jobs was to peel the prawn shells for the broth. They always laugh about how they would make it a competition and race to see whose pile would be bigger and who would ultimately finish first. This recipe will require a lot of shells, so start hoarding (anytime I cook with prawns or shrimp, I always reserve the shells and freeze them to use in this broth)!

This dish is very special to me because it's one of the recipes my auntie taught me how to make one plate at a time, just like the hawkers do, from her outdoor kitchen in Singapore, and since she said I can't disappoint with this recipe, I've kept it exactly the same. There are a few moving parts to this dish, but I promise you, your first bite will be worth it, bestie.

Make the broth: In a large pot, bring 1 gallon (16 cups) of water to a rolling boil over high heat. Drop in the prawns with the shells and heads still on, and cook until the water comes back up to a rolling boil, 3 minutes. Use a fine mesh sieve to remove the prawns to a medium bowl and set aside to cool. To the same pot of boiling water, add the squid and boil until it turns an opaque white color, 3 to 5 minutes. Remove to a clean plate to cool, about 15 minutes, before slicing into ¼-inch-thick rings. Add the additional shrimp shells and heads, pork belly, and pork bones to the boiling stock. Reduce the heat to low so the broth simmers and cook, covered, until the flavors are combined and the pork is tender, about 2 hours.

Meanwhile, peel the shells and heads from the boiled prawns when they're cool enough to handle and reserve. In a wok or large skillet set over medium heat, caramelize the sugar, stirring occasionally, until light brown, 3 to 5 minutes. Add in the oil followed by the reserved prawn shells and heads. Stir-fry (we're stirring and shaking the wok aggressively here) until the oil has an orange hue, 5 minutes. Pour the caramelized shells and heads into the broth to cook for the remaining time.

After 2 hours, remove the pot from the heat and use a spider to remove the shrimp shells and heads to a large bowl. Use a meat mallet to mash out any additional juices, then use the spider to discard the shells and pour the juices back into the broth. Remove and discard the bones from the broth using a spider, and remove the pork belly to a cutting board. Slice the pork belly lengthwise, then crosswise into ⅛-inch-thick bite-size slices. (You'll have some extra, save it for the summer rolls on page 50.)

Fry the pork lard: Line a plate with paper towels. In a clean wok or large skillet over medium heat, use a spatula to spread the cubes of pork lard into a flat layer and season with the salt. Cook the lard, stirring occasionally, until the fat begins to render out of the cubes, 10 to 15 minutes. When the oil starts to bubble and the lard is golden brown, reduce the heat to medium-low and cook, stirring frequently, until they are golden brown, just another 1 to 2 minutes. Use a fine mesh sieve to remove the fried lard to the lined plate immediately. Transfer the rendered oil to a heat-safe jar. You should have at least 1 cup of lard.

Assemble two portions at a time: Return the wok to high and heat 2 tablespoons of the rendered lard. When the lard is hot and shimmering, crack in 2 eggs. Cook, stirring constantly, until scrambled and just barely set, about 30 seconds, then add in 2 handfuls of bean sprouts followed by 2 healthy handfuls each of mee hoon and bee hoon noodles, breaking them apart as you do. Add in 2 ladles of broth and stir aggressively in a circular motion until most of the liquid has soaked into the noodles, about 2 minutes. Use the spatula to push the noodles to the side and add in another 2 tablespoons lard, 2 teaspoons garlic, 6 cooked prawns, 6 pieces of sliced pork belly, 6 pieces of squid, and 2 big pinches of chives. Stir and season with fish sauce to taste (starting with 1 tablespoon and add more if that's your vibe) and another 2 ladles of broth. Continue to stir aggressively until the sauce thickens and coats the noodles, about 5 minutes. If you need it, add another ladle of broth to help coat the noodles. Transfer to a serving bowl and repeat with the remaining ingredients in 2 more batches to make 6 servings total.

To serve: Top each bowl with a tablespoon of fried pork lard, a tablespoon of sambal oelek, and a lime wedge.

NOTES

- Prawns and shrimp have minor anatomical differences, but if I'm being honest, the difference in flavors are hardly noticeable when cooked. Prawns are generally larger than shrimp and don't curl up as much when cooked, but there's no harm in using jumbo shrimp if you can't get your hands on tiger prawns.

- Pork lard—don't skip this step! Crispy fried pork lard is the ultimate razzle-dazzle, and the rendered pork fat is also used to infuse the noodles and thicken the sauce. You can purchase pork fat in an Asian grocery store from the fresh or frozen meat section. For easier slicing, freeze for 30 minutes.

CHAR KWAY TEOW

SERVES 4

CHILI PASTE

1 ounce dried red chilies (about 30; see page 16), stems removed

Warm water, as needed

2 fresh mild red chilies, such as Fresno, stems removed and roughly chopped

3 small shallots, roughly chopped

1 teaspoon kosher salt

¼ cup neutral oil (I use avocado oil)

STIR-FRY SAUCE

3 tablespoons light soy sauce

1 tablespoon oyster sauce

2 teaspoons fish sauce

1 teaspoon sweet soy sauce (kecap manis)

1 teaspoon sugar

¼ teaspoon ground white pepper

NOODLES

1 teaspoon neutral oil

2 Chinese sausage links, thinly sliced diagonally (see page 158)

4 large garlic cloves, minced

½ pound jumbo shrimp (around 25/pound), peeled and deveined (see page 46)

¼ pound fish cakes, thinly sliced (see Note)

1 pound fresh wide rice noodles, store-bought or homemade (page 251)

2 large eggs, lightly beaten

1 small bunch Chinese chives (can sub with green onion greens), ends trimmed, cut into 2-inch pieces

¼ pound fresh bean sprouts

This is my mom's favorite noodle dish, and it's a must-have when we visit the motherland. The charred wide rice noodles are infused with spicy and aromatic chili paste, bites of sweet and salty Chinese sausage, fish cakes, and juicy shrimp. This dish is iconic on the streets of Singapore and Malaysia, and the vendors at the hawker stalls who make it are artists. They stir-fry the noodles in a wok over a large open flame, so we're going to try to emulate that and cook this over high heat and bring everything together quickly. I use a homemade chili paste as part of the stir-fry sauce, but it's also delicious for finishing the noodles (and just about everything else in this book).

Make the chili paste: In a medium bowl, add the dried chilies and pour in enough warm water to cover and make sure they stay submerged. Soak until they're soft and pliable, 10 to 20 minutes. In a food processor or blender, blend the soaked dried chilies (letting any water drip off and reserving the water if you need it for blending), fresh mild red chilies, shallots, and salt until it becomes a chunky paste, scraping down the sides a few times as you go.

Heat a wok or large skillet with the oil over medium heat. When the oil is hot and shimmering, stir-fry (we're stirring and shaking the wok aggressively here) the chili paste, stirring constantly, until the paste has thickened, about 5 minutes. Remove to a heat-safe, airtight jar and set aside. (This will make enough for leftovers and is delicious with Hokkien Prawn Mee, page 140, any proteins, and even eggs! Store in the fridge for up to 3 months.)

Prepare the stir-fry sauce: In a small bowl, whisk together the light soy sauce, oyster sauce, fish sauce, sweet soy sauce, sugar, and white pepper, and set aside.

Stir-fry the noodles: Heat a wok or large skillet with the oil over medium heat. When the oil is hot and shimmering, add the Chinese sausage and garlic and cook, stirring constantly, until the garlic is golden brown, about 1 minute. Add the shrimp and fish cakes, stir, and cook, continuing to stir frequently, until the shrimp is pink and slightly curled, 1 to 2 minutes. Add the noodles and pour the sauce directly over. Stir violently for 30 seconds, then add in 1 to 2 tablespoons chili paste, depending on your spice tolerance.

Raise the heat to high, then leave the noodles alone without stirring until the bottom gets a nice char, 1 to 2 minutes. Stir and leave alone again for an additional minute to char more. Push the noodles to the side and pour in the eggs in the empty space. Scramble, stirring constantly, until almost cooked, about 30 seconds, then stir to combine with the noodles. Add the chives and bean sprouts and give the noodles a final toss. Serve right away with additional chili paste if you desire!

> **NOTE**
>
> Asian fish cakes can be found in the fridge or freezer section at the Asian market. I like to look for the fried, square-type fish cakes and thinly slice them.

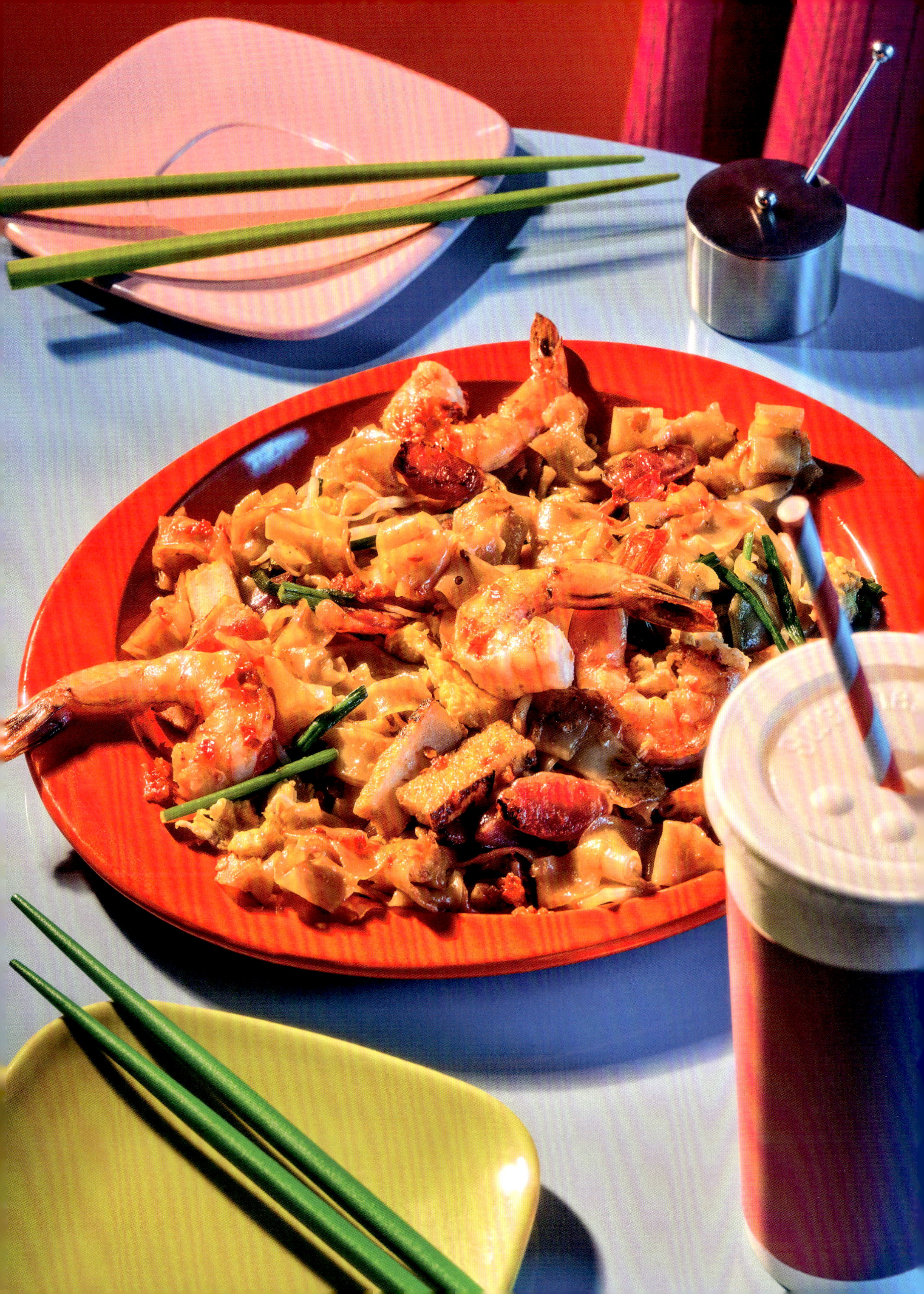

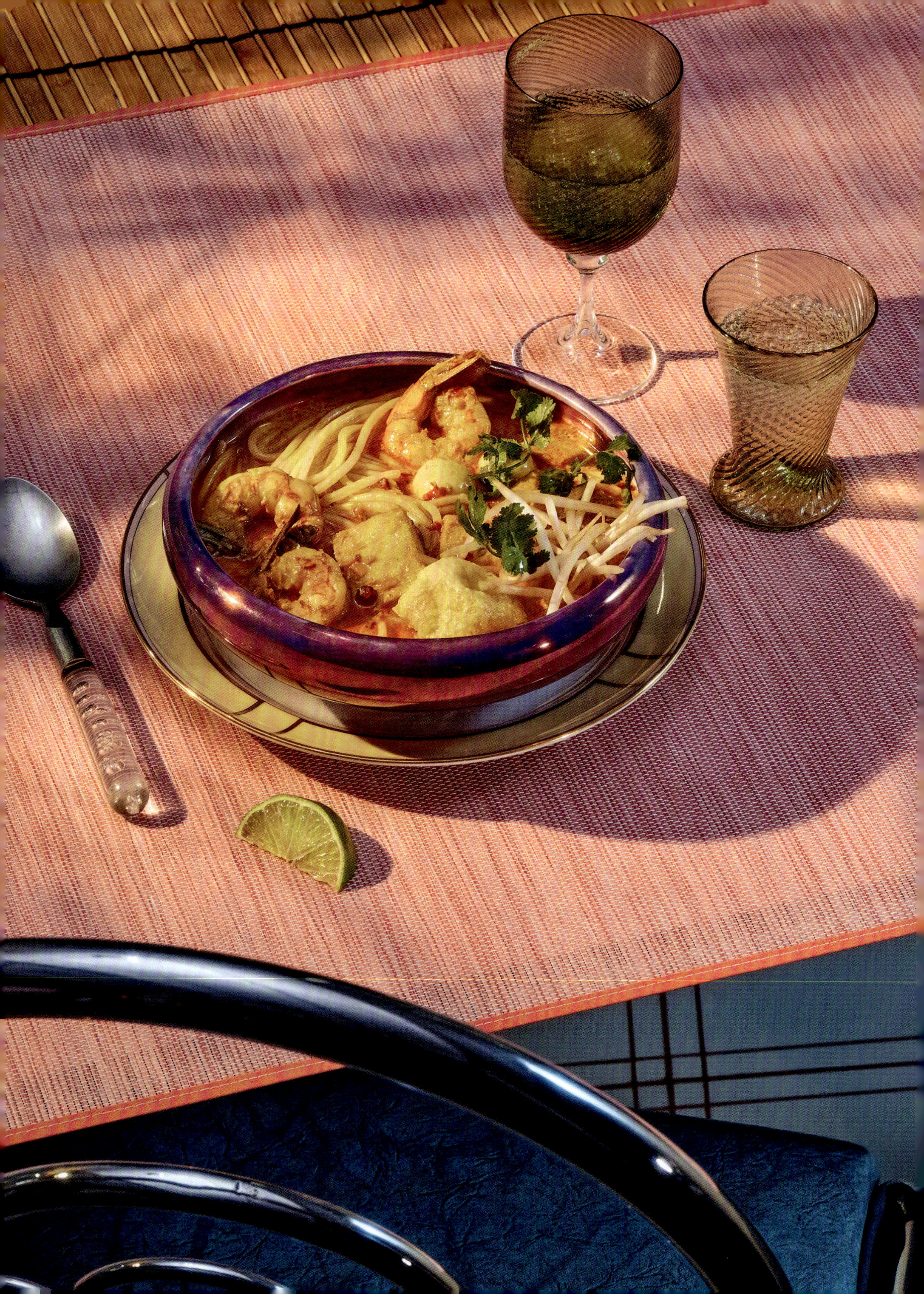

CURRY LAKSA

SERVES 6 TO 8

SOUP

3 tablespoons neutral oil (I use avocado oil)

2 pounds head-on jumbo shrimp (around 25/pound), peeled and deveined (see page 46), shells and heads reserved

2 pounds fresh rice vermicelli noodles or 1 pound dried rice vermicelli noodles

1 (13.5-ounce) can coconut milk

2 tablespoons fish sauce

1 tablespoon sugar

CURRY PASTE

6 large garlic cloves

2 lemongrass stalks, tough outer layers removed and finely chopped

2-inch knob of fresh turmeric, peeled and roughly chopped

1-inch knob of galangal, peeled and finely chopped

2 medium shallots, roughly chopped

15 dried chilies (see page 16), stems removed and roughly chopped

2 fresh bird's-eye chilies, stems removed and roughly chopped

8 fresh cilantro stems

2 tablespoons shrimp paste

1 tablespoon kosher salt

FOR SERVING

½ pound fish balls

½ pound medium tofu puffs

1 pound fresh bean sprouts

Fresh cilantro leaves

1 lime, cut into wedges

I am such a saucy curry fanatic—oftentimes I just want to pick up the bowl and drink it! Singapore laksa, a seafood curry and noodle soup, allowed this desire to come true without being shamed for it. We'll be making a shrimp stock as the base for our spicy coconut curry broth. Shrimp stocks are not only amazing for recipes that are seafood focused, but I also love the idea of using the shells and heads of shrimp, leaving nothing to go to waste. Homemade curry paste is also quite simple, and worth the extra flavor you get versus store-bought. In Singapore, most restaurants display copious amounts of noodles that you can choose to enjoy with your curry, but my personal fave are rice vermicelli noodles. Served with shrimp, fish balls, tofu puffs, and bean sprouts that all soak up those rich curry flavors and rounded out with a squeeze of fresh lime juice.

Make the shrimp stock for the soup: Heat a medium pot with 2 tablespoons neutral oil over medium-high heat. When the oil is hot and shimmering, cook the shrimp shells and heads, stirring constantly, until the oil is bright orange, 3 to 5 minutes. Add 8 cups water, stir, and bring to a boil. Reduce the heat to low, cover, and simmer the stock, stirring occasionally, until it is an orange-pink color and fragrant, about 45 minutes. Use a fine mesh sieve to remove the shrimp shells and heads and press out any remaining juices using a wooden spoon back into the stock, then discard the shells. Cover and keep warm.

Cook the noodles for the soup: If using dried noodles, first soak them in a large bowl in room temperature water for 30 minutes so that they cook evenly, then drain. Bring a medium pot of water to a boil. For fresh noodles, cook until tender, about 2 minutes. For dried, cook them according to the package directions. Strain and rinse under cool water. Set aside.

Make the curry paste: In a food processor or blender, blitz the garlic, lemongrass, turmeric, galangal, shallots, dried and fresh chilies, cilantro, shrimp paste, and salt until they form a smooth paste, stopping to scrape down the sides regularly. This should take 5 or so minutes to break everything down; be patient! Remove to a clean dish and set aside.

Finish the soup: Heat a large pot with the remaining 1 tablespoon neutral oil over medium heat. When the oil is hot and shimmering, stir-fry the curry paste using a wooden spoon (we're stirring and shaking the pot aggressively here) until the paste thickens, 2 to 3 minutes. Stir in the coconut milk and shrimp stock, bring to a boil, then reduce the heat to low and simmer uncovered, stirring occasionally, for 10 minutes to let the flavors mingle. Season with the fish sauce and sugar and cook, stirring occasionally, until the sugar has dissolved, another 2 minutes.

To serve: Add the fish balls and tofu puffs to the soup and cook until the fish balls and tofu puffs are heated through, about 2 minutes. Add the peeled shrimp and cook until the shrimp are pink and curled into a C shape, about 2 minutes. Remove from the heat and taste and season the soup with more salt if necessary.

Divide the cooked noodles and bean sprouts among individual bowls, then use a slotted spoon to divide the shrimp, fish balls, and tofu puffs into the bowls. Ladle the hot broth over the bowls and serve garnished with cilantro leaves and a lime wedge.

SINGAPOREAN CHILI CRAB

SERVES 4 TO 6

- 4 green onions, white and green parts, cut into 2-inch-long thin matchsticks
- Ice water
- 2 whole live crabs, such as Dungeness (3 to 4 pounds total)
- 1½ cups store-bought low-sodium chicken broth or bone broth
- ⅓ cup sweet chili sauce, store-bought or homemade (see page 259)
- ¼ cup light soy sauce
- ¼ cup ketchup
- 1 tablespoon sugar
- 2 teaspoons fish sauce
- ¼ cup neutral oil (I use avocado oil)
- 4 fresh mild red chilies, like Fresno, stems removed and finely chopped
- 3 fresh bird's-eye chilies, stems removed and finely chopped
- 2 medium shallots, finely chopped
- 2-inch knob of ginger, peeled and minced
- 6 large garlic cloves, minced
- 3 tablespoons cornstarch
- 2 large eggs

Getting down and dirty in a tray of chili crab is an absolute must when visiting Singapore—it's totally iconic. Chili crabs are cooked entirely in their shells, which are smashed to let in all the flavors of the signature bright red sauce. The sauce is a sweet, tangy, and spicy stew that's been thickened with ribbons of egg throughout. My auntie showed me how to make this in her outdoor kitchen, where she broke down and cleaned these crabs like a boss. I haven't come across any restaurants in the States that serve good Singaporean chili crab, so I made sure not to leave Singapore without learning how to make it. Crabs can also be expensive when going out to eat, so taking some time to make it at home is extra rewarding. This is typically made with mud crabs, but I use Dungeness crabs since they're easier to find. Don't be intimidated by live crabs—we'll be breaking these down like pros at home. I love how my auntie also tops this in what she calls "curly hair"—which is her own version of green onion razzle-dazzle—and we will do the same.

Make the razzle-dazzle: In a small bowl, cover the green onions with ice water and soak until they curl up, about 10 minutes. Pat dry with paper towels.

Prep the crabs: Place the crabs in the freezer until they are no longer active and moving, 30 minutes to 1 hour to immobilize them. Remove from the freezer and quickly and thoroughly wash and scrub them all over (don't worry, they won't spunk back up after freezing!). Flip one crab over so its underside is facing up on a cutting board. Using the tip of a chef's knife, "spike" the crab by piercing the stomach area (this is considered the most humane way to kill a crab—it destroys the crab's nervous system, so our friend won't feel the pain).

Using a butcher's knife or pair of sharp kitchen shears, cut an inch off the ends of the legs and discard (they don't have any meat and they can be sharp, so this will make the crabs easier to handle). Locate the top of the triangle shape on the underside of the crab, lift, and then tear the "belly flap" piece off. At the opposite end of where the crab's eyes are, use your thumbs to grasp in between the top and bottom of the crab shell. Tear away from each other, exposing the inside of the crab. Reserve the top half of the shell along with the yellow substance, which is called the crab "mustard" (this part is packed with flavor), and set aside. Remove and discard the soft brown gills that sit on top of the ribs from the bottom half of the crab by tearing them off with your fingers. Discard anything that's not shell, crab meat, or the yellow "mustard."

Use the butcher's knife to cut the claws off the base of the crab. Carefully use a meat mallet or the back of the knife to lightly smash the claws to allow all of the sauce to get into the shell, but don't fully cut it in half. Halve the body of the crab by cutting lengthwise down the spine, then cut each half between the two center legs to create quarters. Repeat with the remaining crab.

Make the sauce: In a medium bowl, mix the chicken broth, sweet chili sauce, soy sauce, ketchup, sugar, and fish sauce until smooth.

Heat a wok or large pot with the oil over medium heat. Let it get hot (and bothered) for a few minutes, and when it's shimmering, add both chilies, the shallots, ginger, and garlic and stir-fry (we're stirring constantly and shaking the wok aggressively here) until they're golden brown, 3 to 5 minutes. Add in all of the crab pieces and thoroughly mix until they're swimming in the aromatic oil. Reduce the heat to medium-low, cover, and cook until the shells begin to turn red, about 3 minutes. Pour in the sauce and mix until well combined with the crabs. Raise the heat to high to bring the sauce to a boil, then reduce to low, cover, and simmer until the meat is opaque and the shells are mostly bright red, about 5 minutes.

In a small bowl, prepare the cornstarch slurry by mixing the cornstarch and ¼ cup cold water until smooth—no lumps! Mix the cornstarch slurry in with the sauce. Simmer uncovered until the sauce has thickened slightly, 1 to 2 minutes. Meanwhile, in a small bowl, crack the eggs and whisk until there are no streaks of white. Pour the eggs over the crabs and mix in while stirring until the eggs have set, about 1 minute.

To serve, use tongs to transfer the crab pieces to serving plates and drizzle any remaining sauce in the wok over the tops. Garnish with the green onion razzle-dazzle, or "curly hair," and eat immediately.

> **NOTE**
>
> If you don't want to make your own sweet chili sauce, my favorite brands are ABC and Mae Ploy.

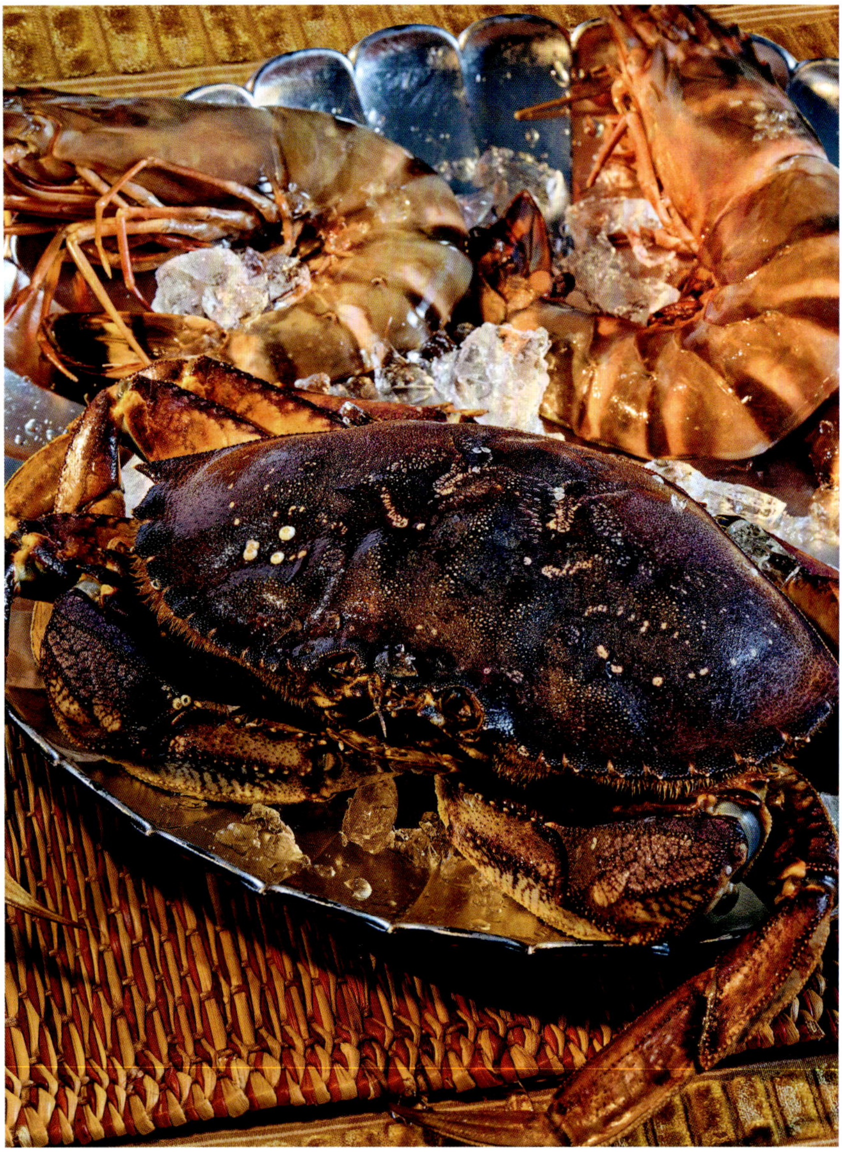

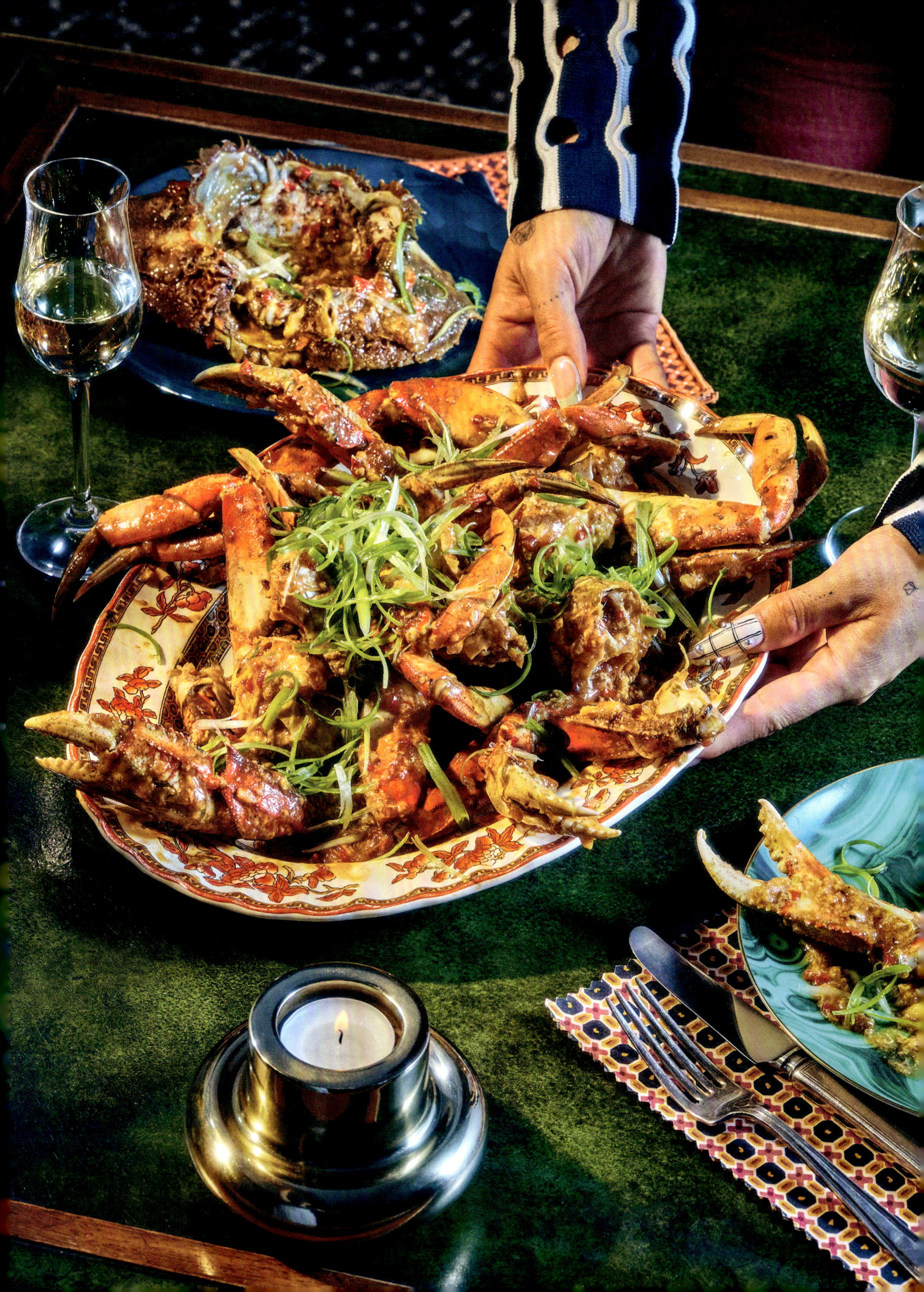

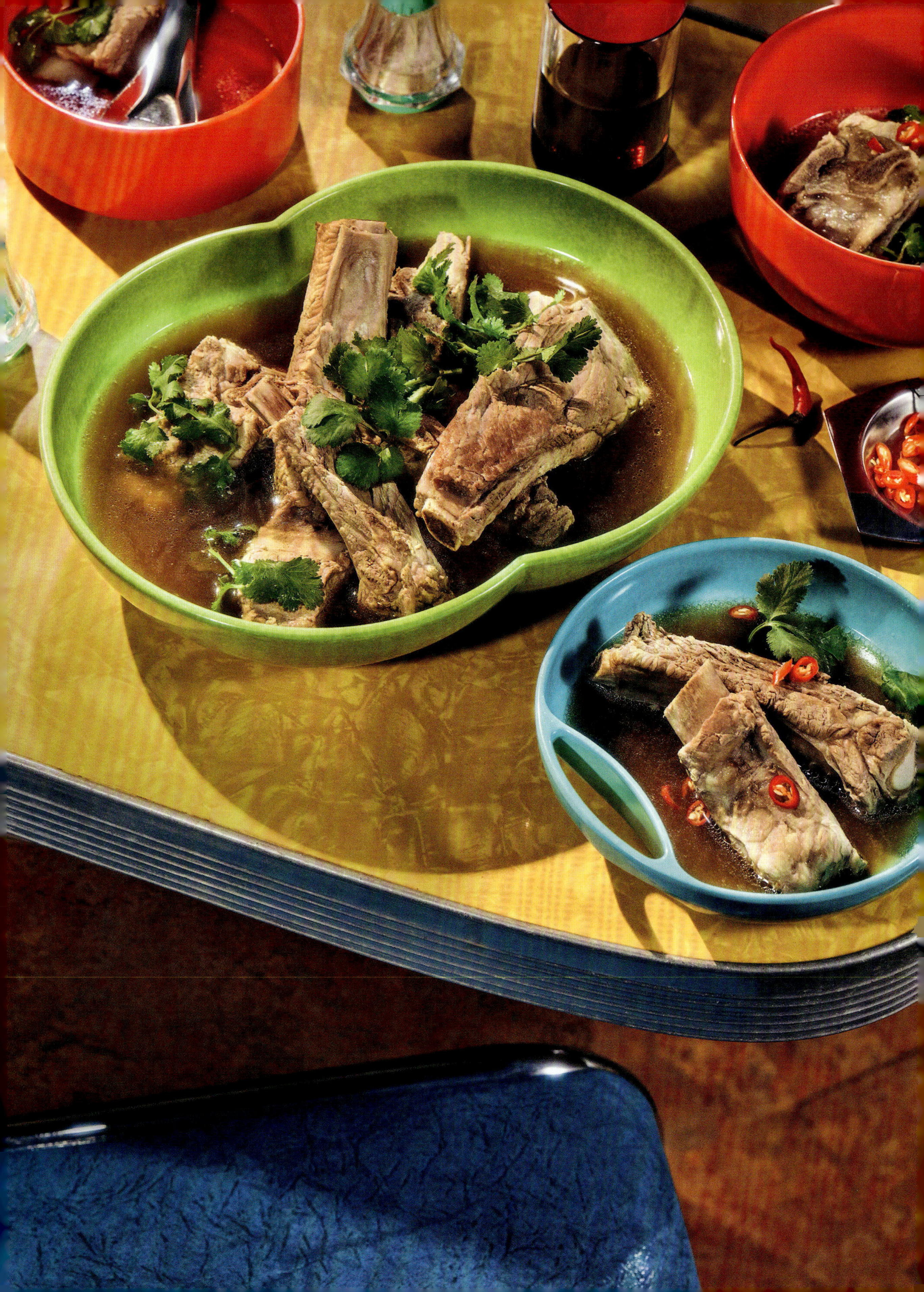

BAK KUT TEH

SERVES 5 TO 6

2½ pounds pork bones

2½ pounds pork ribs, individually sliced

3 tablespoons whole white peppercorns

1 teaspoon whole black peppercorns

2 star anise pods

8 cloves

1 small cinnamon stick

1 head of garlic

1 tablespoon dark soy sauce

Kosher salt

FOR SERVING

6 to 8 fresh bird's-eye chilies, stems removed and thinly sliced (1 per serving)

6 to 8 tablespoons light soy sauce (1 per serving)

Fresh cilantro leaves, for razzle-dazzle

If you know you know, I am addicted to white pepper, and it's the star of this soup, so I am obsessed with it, go figure. Bak kut teh is actually known to be a late-night soup offered after hours in restaurants in Singapore that people enjoy after a night out. I've always been in the habit of craving the broth after one too many glasses of wine or tequila sodas, and now it all makes sense. My favorite memory of this soup is that in Singapore, most restaurants will refill your bowl with broth as many times as you want. They walk around with it in an xx-large mug, which is fitting since the soup's name directly translates to *pork rib tea*. By the time I left Singapore, I swear bak kut teh was pumping through my veins. My auntie showed me how to make this over her old-school charcoal grill and I was in awe of how easy it is. There's no need to even peel the garlic (the worst job of them all)! It takes a few hours to simmer, but the longer you let it simmer, the stronger the flavor. I also prefer mine extra peppery, so I love to let the seasonings sit and steep into the broth.

Blanch the pork bones: Bring a large pot of water to a boil over high heat. Add in the pork bones and pork ribs and bring it back up to a rolling boil. Cook until a dingy foam rises to the surface, about 5 minutes. Strain the bones in a colander and rinse well with cool water. Clean the pot.

Meanwhile, gather the white and black peppercorns, star anise, cloves, and cinnamon stick in a small spice bag or cheesecloth and tie together and set aside. Lightly smash a head of garlic to separate the cloves, leaving the skins on.

Pour 9 cups of fresh water into the cleaned pot and bring to a boil over high heat. Add the cleaned pork ribs and pork bones, spice bag, and garlic cloves. If the bones aren't completely submerged, add just enough water to cover. Return to a boil, then cover and reduce the heat to low so the mixture simmers. Cook until the meat is tender, about 1½ hours. Stir in the dark soy sauce and taste for seasoning, adding salt if you think it needs it.

To serve: Prepare the dipping sauce for the pork rib by mixing the chopped chilies with the soy sauce and dividing among small dipping bowls for each person. Serve a bowl of broth with a pork rib, the dipping sauce for dipping or drizzling on the pork rib, and garnish with cilantro.

AUNTIE'S WHOLE BRAISED DUCK (Lor Ark)

SERVES 4 TO 6

1 (5-pound) whole duck, gizzards and neck removed and reserved

1 tablespoon Chinese five-spice powder

5 green onions, white and green parts, cut into 2-inch pieces

3-inch knob of fresh galangal, unpeeled and cut into 2-inch and 1-inch pieces

1 head of garlic, cloves separated and unpeeled (about 12)

¼ cup rock sugar, broken up if large, or ¼ cup granulated sugar

5 tablespoons sweet soy sauce (kecap manis)

1 whole bunch cilantro

1 small cinnamon stick

1 star anise pod

3 tablespoons fish sauce

I wasn't really sure my auntie knew what my job as a content creator meant, but I posted a video of her teaching me how to make her whole duck braised in a bath of soy sauce infused with spices like star anise and cinnamon in her outdoor kitchen in Singapore, and she still watches it with pride. She told my mom in Hokkien that she's glad I'm learning how to make it so that when she's gone someone will know. So I present to you the most succulent and love-filled whole duck. The skin is crispy, sweet, and salty, and the duck itself is so rich in flavor with the perfect amount of fat. This recipe is special to me because it was the first thing I learned how to cook in Singapore.

Prep and marinate the duck: Pat the duck dry with paper towels and massage the skin and inside the cavity generously with the Chinese five-spice powder. Put the duck on a plate, cover with plastic wrap, and marinate overnight in the fridge. The next day, an hour before cooking, rinse the duck well and dry with paper towels. Let it come to room temperature, about 1 hour.

Cook the duck: Shove the green onions, the 2-inch piece of galangal, and 6 garlic cloves into the cavity of the duck. In a wok or large pot over medium heat, melt the rock sugar and stir-fry (we're stirring constantly and shaking the wok aggressively here) until the sugar has caramelized to a dark brown color, about 10 minutes. Add in the remaining garlic and the 1-inch piece of galangal along with half of the sweet soy sauce and stir-fry until fragrant, 1 to 2 minutes. Add the entire duck into the wok, breast side down, and spread the soy sauce onto the duck (don't worry if it's not fully covered at this point). Reduce the heat to medium. Flip the duck so that it's breast side up and spread around the soy sauce on both sides. Add in the cilantro, cinnamon stick, and star anise. Pour the fish sauce over the duck and keep the duck moving in the wok by gently pushing it back and forth to avoid anything burning.

Pour in 4 cups of water around the duck, being careful to avoid pouring directly on top of the skin. Use a spoon to scoop some of the braising liquid into the cavity. Pour the remaining sweet soy sauce on top of the duck skin, then cover the wok and reduce the heat to medium-low so the braising liquid simmers. Cook, stirring occasionally, for 15 minutes. Add the gizzards and neck to the braising liquid and more water if needed to keep the duck halfway submerged. Cover and continue simmering, occasionally basting the exposed area of the duck, until the skin is an even brown and fully saturated in the sauce and the juices run clear when pierced with a knife, about 1 hour.

Remove the duck to a clean plate and rest for 10 minutes. Skim the layer of fat off the top of the braising liquid. Raise the heat to medium-high to bring the braising liquid back up to a boil and cook, stirring frequently, until the liquid is thickened enough to coat the back of a spoon, 10 to 15 minutes.

Carve the duck (just like a chicken or a turkey!) and serve family style with a drizzle of thickened braising liquid.

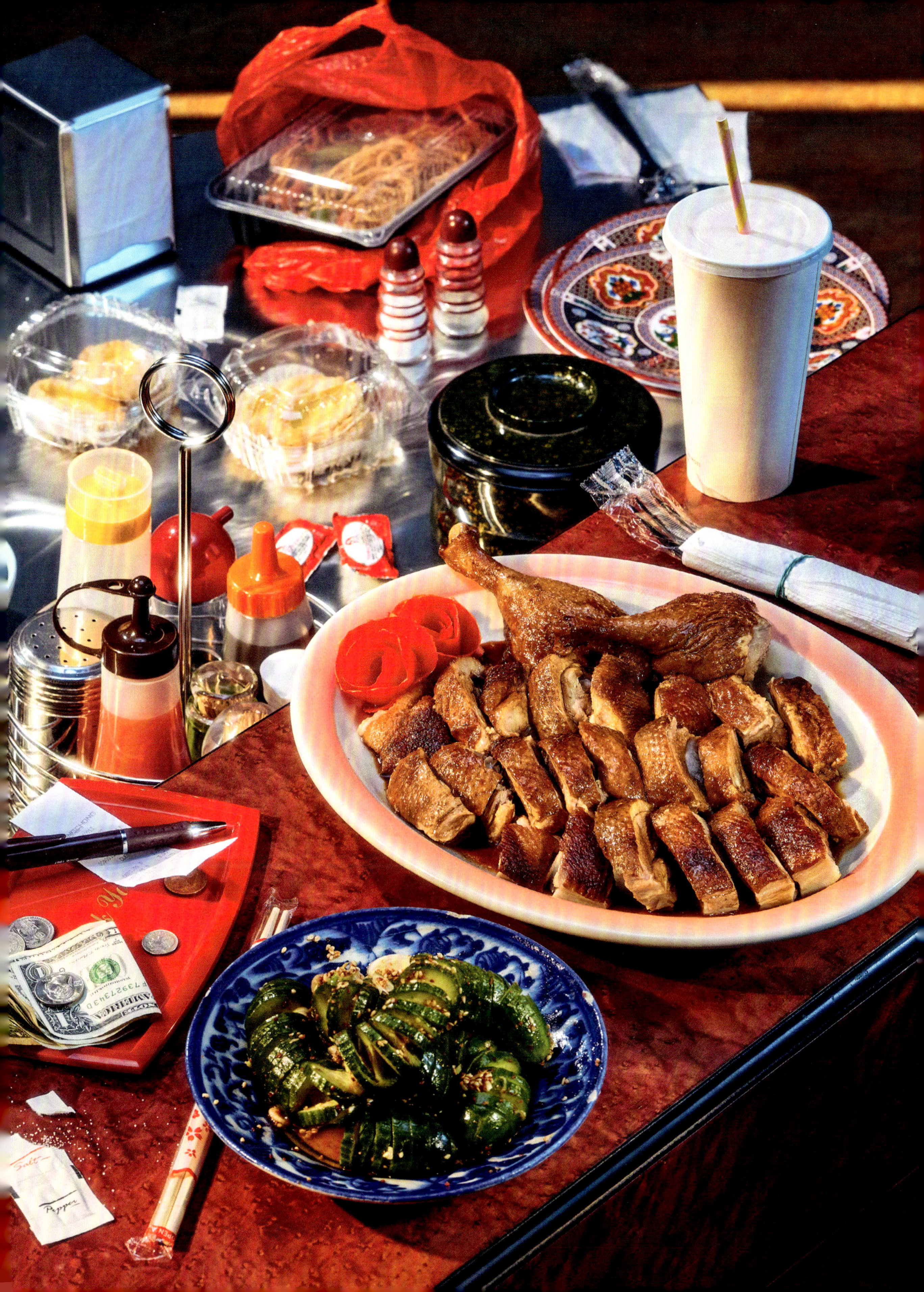
Salt
Pepper

AH MA'S MEE HOON KUEH

SERVES 4 TO 6

BROTH

1 teaspoon neutral oil (I use avocado oil)

1 head of garlic, cloves peeled

1 cup ikan bilis (dried anchovies)

1 whole chicken carcass (from a 4-pound rotisserie or roasted chicken)

1 tablespoon chicken bouillon powder

1 tablespoon fish sauce

Kosher salt

NOODLES

2½ cups all-purpose flour, plus more for dusting

1 large egg

1 teaspoon kosher salt, plus more for cooking

1 teaspoon neutral oil (I use avocado oil)

My mom has eight brothers and sisters, and being cost efficient was really important especially when it came to feeding the family. Mee hoon kueh is a humble soup and noodle dish that's loaded with complexity. It's made with hand-torn noodles and a chicken carcass and ikan bilis (Southeast Asian anchovy) broth. The noodles are a charming, curly-edged shape from being hand-torn and I think that's what gives this dish its character. You shouldn't need to break the bank to make a delicious dish! The handmade noodles are chewy, bouncy, and soft, and only require flour, egg, oil, and a little bit of salt to put together. This is something Ah Ma (my grandmother) used to make for her family, and my auntie adapted the recipe and taught me how to make it. The noodles are the star, but the broth is the heartwarming supporting character. She also adds mini pork meatballs and a poached egg to complete it. This dish is a wonderful intro into making homemade noodles, because the more imperfect they are, the more charming they are, too. The texture of a handmade noodle cannot be replicated by the store-bought kind, so it's worth the effort!

Prepare the broth: Heat a large pot with the oil over medium-high heat. When the oil is hot and shimmering, add the garlic and ikan bilis and cook, stirring frequently with a spatula, until everything is fragrant and the garlic is lightly golden, about 5 minutes. Add the chicken carcass and enough water to fully submerge it. Add in the chicken bouillon powder and fish sauce and stir to combine. Bring the broth to a boil, then immediately reduce the heat to low so the broth simmers. Cover and simmer until the carcass falls apart and the flavors are combined, at least 1 hour and sometimes up to 3 hours.

Meanwhile, make the noodle dough: In a large bowl, combine the flour, egg, salt, and oil, and pour in ½ cup water. Begin stirring with a wooden spatula until the dough becomes shaggy (meaning there's no more loose flour but it looks like the dough could use a little more TLC). Once the dough starts coming together, switch to your hands and knead in the bowl for 5 minutes or until the dough is smooth and bounces back when you poke it. If the dough is at all sticky, dust it lightly with flour and knead it in. Repeat just until the dough no longer sticks. Cover lightly with plastic wrap and rest for 45 minutes.

Prepare the meatballs: In a small bowl, mix together the ground pork, cornstarch, fish sauce, sesame oil, and 1 teaspoon water just until combined—don't overwork the mixture or you'll have tough meatballs. Cover with plastic wrap and set aside in the fridge.

MEATBALLS

½ pound fatty ground pork

1 tablespoon cornstarch

1 tablespoon fish sauce

1 teaspoon toasted sesame oil

FOR SERVING

1 (15-ounce) can abalone, drained (optional; see Note)

¼ pound Chinese spinach (can sub with regular spinach or another leafy green), roughly chopped

4 to 6 large eggs (1 per serving)

1 tablespoon chili oil, per serving (optional)

2 green onions, green tops only, thinly sliced, for razzle-dazzle

Stretch and boil the noodles: Bring a large pot of salted water to a boil over high heat—make sure it's salty like pasta water, or as salty as you are after stubbing your toe. Divide the dough into four equal pieces, working with one piece at a time and covering the other pieces with a tea towel or plastic wrap while you work. Lightly flour your work surface and a rolling pin. Roll the dough out into a rectangle until it's $1/8$-inch thick (no need to be too particular about the shape!). Use a sharp knife to cut the dough into 1-inch-wide pieces. Using your hands, gently stretch out the strips until they're $1/16$-inch thick, then starting at one end, begin to pinch and rip off the dough to create 1- to 2-inch-long noodles. Add the noodles immediately to the boiling water as you rip the dough. Boil the first batch until the noodles are tender, 3 to 5 minutes. Strain and rinse under cool water and set aside in a colander to drain. Repeat with the remaining dough portions.

To serve: Remove and discard all of the solids from the broth and taste for seasoning, adding salt if you think the broth needs it. Raise the heat to medium-high and allow the broth to come back up to a gentle boil. Using a teaspoon, scoop heaping teaspoon-size balls directly from the meatball mixture in the bowl and drop into the broth (they're tiny—there's no need to roll or shape them!). Add the drained abalone, if using, into the broth. Add in the Chinese spinach and cook until it has wilted, 1 to 2 minutes. Crack the eggs directly into the broth to poach. Stir and allow to boil until the whites are set, 2 to 3 minutes. By this time the meatballs will definitely be cooked through.

Divide the cooked noodles among the bowls, then pour over the broth and distribute the meatballs, abalone, spinach, and eggs. Enjoy with chili oil if that's your thing, and always garnished with green onions.

> **NOTE**
>
> Abalone has a unique buttery and salty, umami-packed flavor with a chewy texture similar to calamari. My auntie prepares this dish with added abalone, but it can easily be omitted if you can't find it or prefer to skip it!

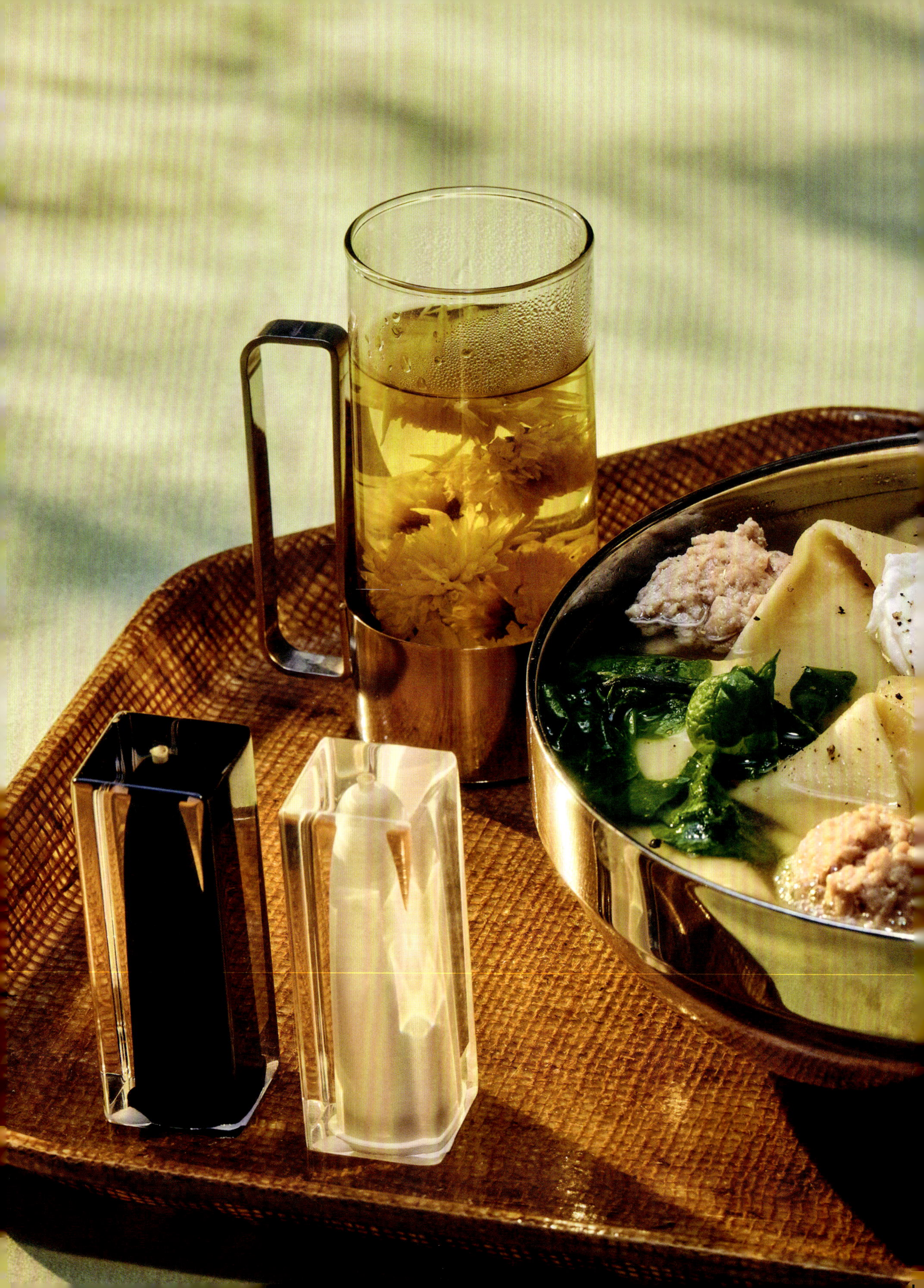

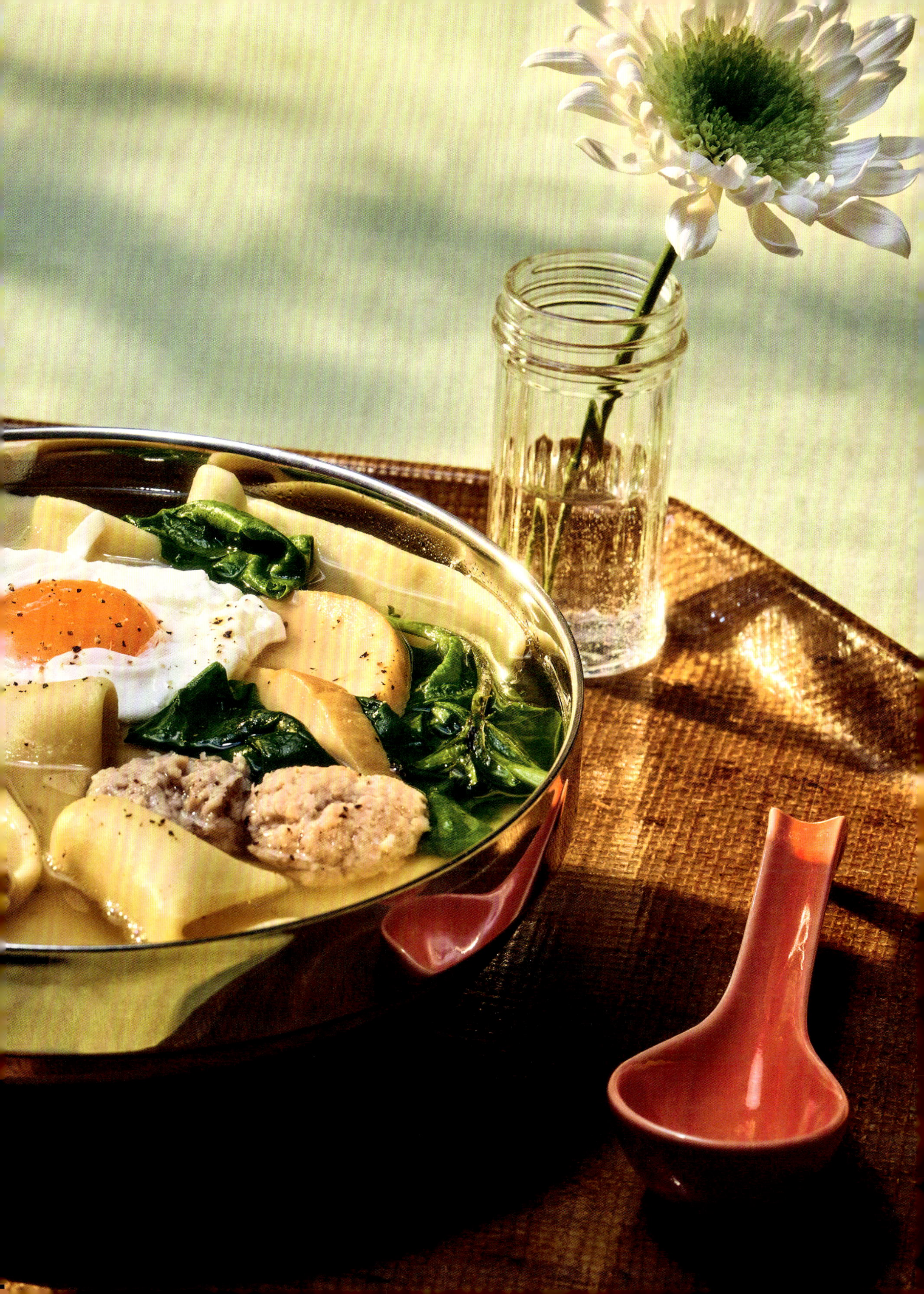

CLAYPOT RICE

SERVES 4 TO 6

½ cup dried shiitake mushrooms

2¼ cups warm water

1 pound boneless, skinless chicken thighs, cut into thin strips

1 tablespoon oyster sauce

1 tablespoon cornstarch

1 teaspoon light soy sauce

1 teaspoon toasted sesame oil

2 Chinese sausage links, diagonally sliced (see Note)

2 cups jasmine rice, rinsed

2 tablespoons sweet soy sauce (kecap manis)

¼ cup fresh cilantro leaves

2 green onions, green tops only, thinly sliced

Another *love her, leave her alone* dish that I absolutely adore and quite literally never get sick of. There was a time when my college boyfriend and I were living at my parents' house in between moves and my mom would always ask what we wanted for dinner. We both repetitively asked for this dish, and it got to the point where my dad said, "This rice AGAIN?" (but more dramatically and in Cantonese). I could eat this rice every day, and I don't think my mom was going to complain because it's one of the easiest one-pot meals to throw together in 20 minutes. Claypot rice is similar to Korean bibimbap in the way that the bottom gets nice and crispy, almost to the point of being burned, adding an entirely new semicharred and toasty flavor to the dish. The claypot itself is the key to getting that crispy bottom, but don't worry, you can still make it in a regular pot. I have followed my mom's recipe, most often using chicken thighs and Chinese sausage, but the protein can easily be switched out (or left out for vegetarians). I don't know of a better meal you can get on the table in under 30 minutes—and by the depth of the flavors, you'll think it required a lot more.

Soak the mushrooms: In a small bowl, cover the dried mushrooms with the warm water and soak until they begin to soften, 5 minutes. Strain and reserve the soaking liquid (you should have about 2 cups), and then remove the stems and thinly slice the mushrooms.

Marinate the chicken: In a medium bowl, mix the chicken thighs with the oyster sauce, cornstarch, light soy sauce, and sesame oil until evenly coated. Mix in the rehydrated, sliced mushrooms and sliced Chinese sausage, then marinate for 15 minutes, or covered in the fridge for up to 8 hours.

Cook the rice: In a traditional 2-quart Chinese claypot or a Dutch oven, add the rice and all of the mushroom-soaking liquid. Stir with a rice paddle, bring it to a boil over high heat, then cover and reduce the heat to low so the water simmers steadily. Cook until most of the liquid has evaporated (try not to peek too often, we don't want to let out the steam!), 10 to 15 minutes. Spread the chicken, mushrooms, and sausage evenly over the rice (don't stir!), then cover and steam for another 15 minutes or until the chicken is no longer pink (if it doesn't seem like your chicken is steaming, you can raise the heat to medium-low). Remove from the heat and drizzle the sweet soy sauce over the top and sprinkle with the cilantro and green onions. Mix well using a rice paddle or rubber spatula and serve right away.

> **NOTE**
>
> Chinese sausage, or lap cheong, is a cured meat and can be found in a vacuum-sealed pack in the refrigerated aisle of an Asian grocery store.

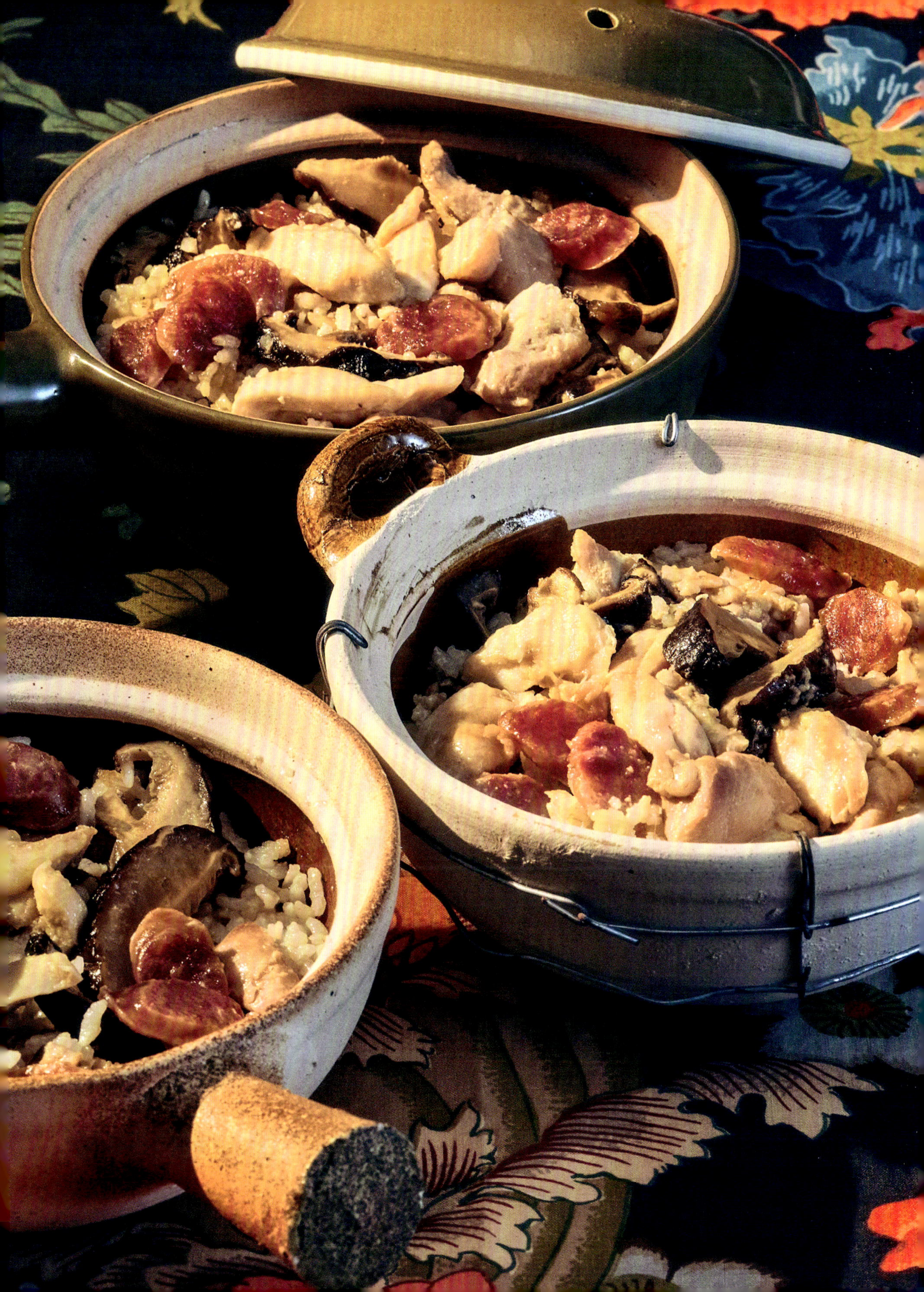

YUM TONG

TONG YUM
YUM TONG

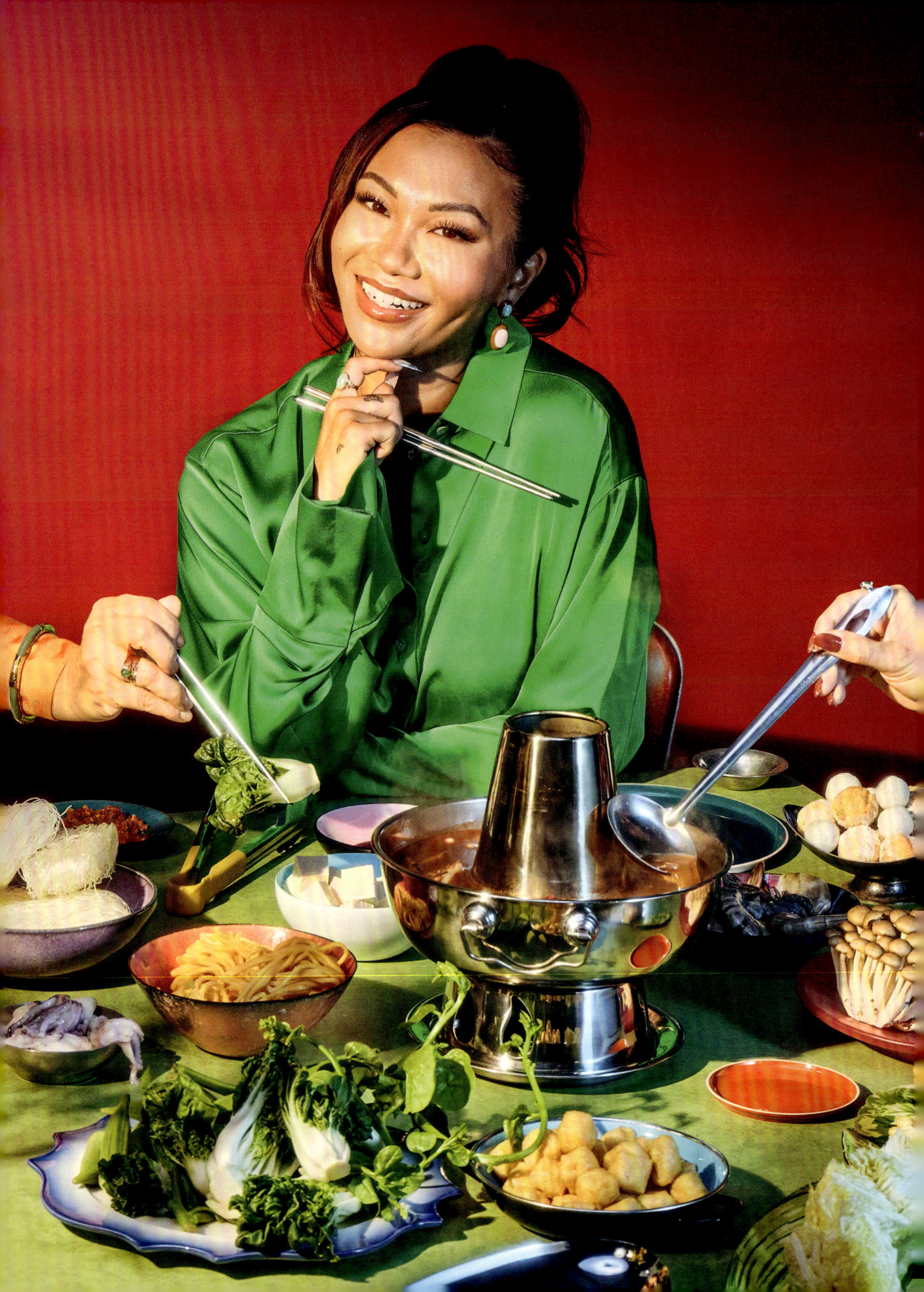

RECIPE LIST

Wonton Soup
166

Egg Drop Soup
169

Hot & Sour Soup
170

Congee (Chinese Jook)
173

Tom Yum Goong (Thai Hot & Sour Soup with Shrimp)
174

Japanese Clear Soup
177

Miso Soup
178

Chinese Watercress Soup
181

Every night, I'd hear from my parents "yum tong,"

which means *drink soup* in Chinese. Drinking soup before *and* after a meal is a huge part of Cantonese culture, so growing up, I knew there was always a big pot of soup on the stove. I've since become a huge broth girl and find myself constantly craving a piping-hot bowl no matter the time of day or the temperature outside. I have different soup moods—sometimes I want a light and simple clear broth and sometimes nothing will do but a rich and creamy one, sometimes spicy, sometimes sour. I love them all equally, and in this chapter, we're covering all of my favorites!

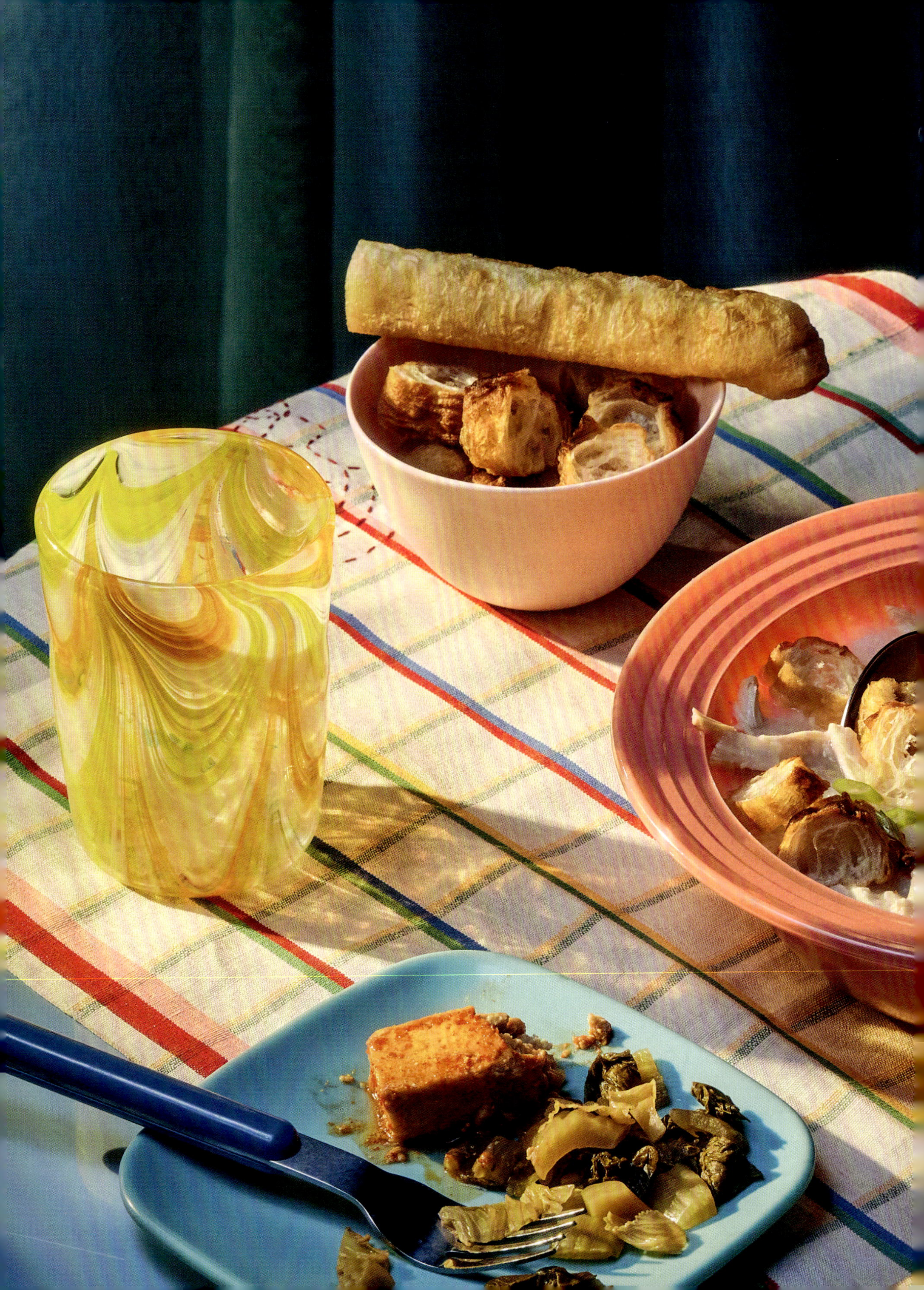

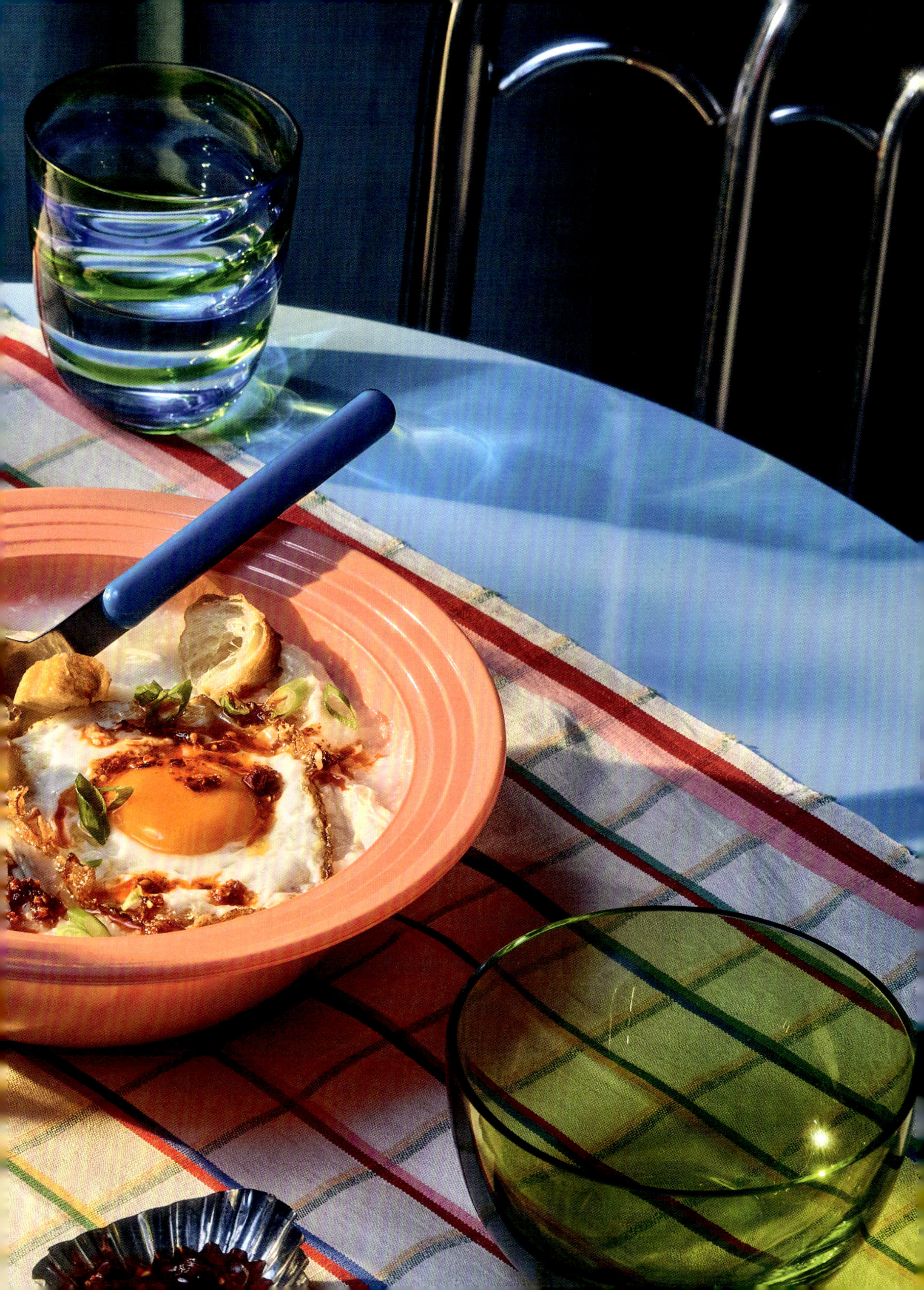

WONTON SOUP

SERVES 2

4 cups store-bought low-sodium chicken broth or bone broth

1-inch knob of ginger, peeled and sliced

6 garlic cloves, smashed

4 green onions, white and green parts, thinly sliced and separated

1 tablespoon light soy sauce

1 teaspoon fish sauce

1 teaspoon ground white pepper (or less if you don't want it to be too spicy)

½ teaspoon chicken bouillon powder

1 head of baby bok choy, root intact and quartered lengthwise

12 shrimp wontons, store-bought or homemade (see page 44)

1 teaspoon toasted sesame oil

This is the easiest, quickest soup—it's truly in my weekly rotation because I always have the ingredients on hand. I actually believe this is the video that got the attention of the producers that cast me for *Next Level Chef*. There was a day that I was experiencing nothing short of a violent hunger, and when I usually reach this point (a normal occurrence), I can barely think clearly enough to speak, let alone cook a meal. I decided to film myself making wonton soup with the addition of egg noodles, which you can easily do with this recipe as well, in thirty minutes. I guess people loved to see the chaos, so the video went viral . . . and the next day I received an email from the *Next Level Chef* producer. This is a hard recipe to mess up—if you get a little heavy-handed with the seasoning, it will only taste better because you cooked it with love.

In a medium pot, bring the chicken broth to a boil over medium-high heat. Stir in the ginger, garlic, green onion whites, soy sauce, fish sauce, white pepper, and chicken bouillon powder. Reduce the heat to low and simmer, covered and stirring occasionally, for 15 minutes to let the flavors mingle.

Bring a small pot of water to a boil over medium-high heat. Blanch the bok choy until they turn a bright green color and are tender, about 1 minute. Remove with a slotted spoon and add into the broth. To the same pot of boiling water, add the wontons, stir gently so they don't stick, and boil until they float, 3 to 5 minutes. Remove with the slotted spoon and combine with the broth. Remove the broth from the heat and stir in the sesame oil.

To serve, divide the soup between 2 bowls, leaving the aromatics in the pot, and garnish with the green onion greens.

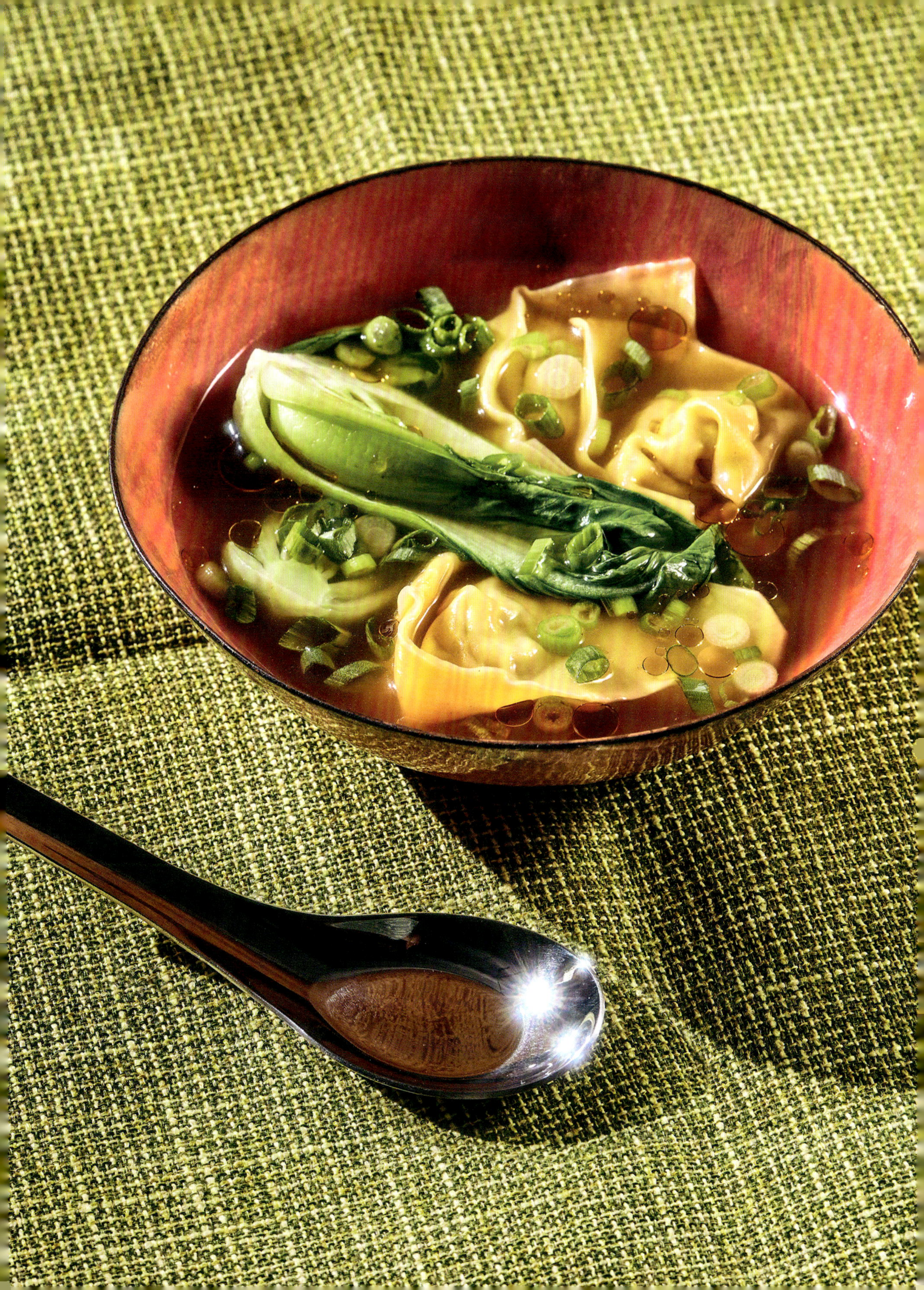

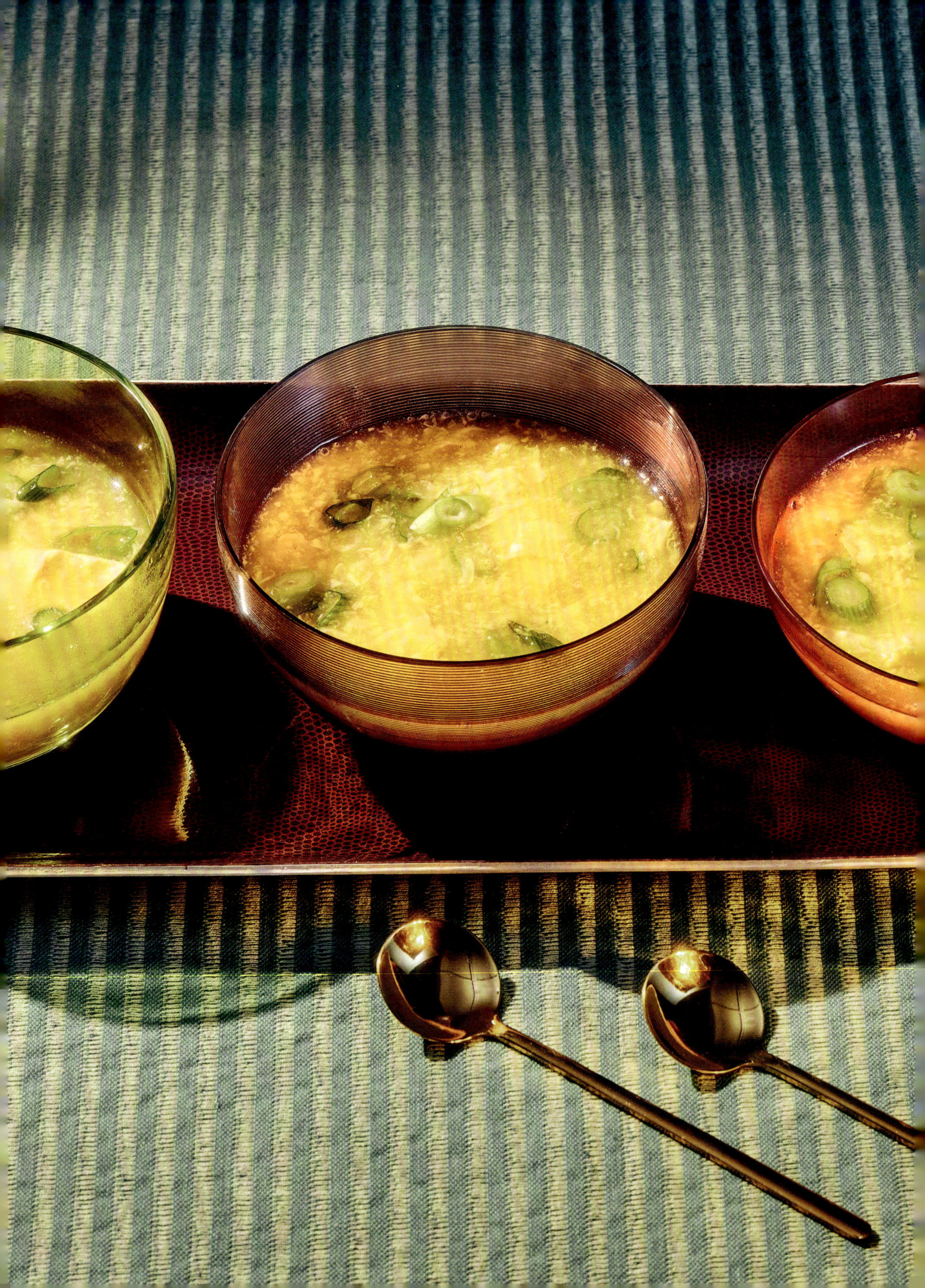

EGG DROP SOUP

SERVES 2

4 cups store-bought low-sodium chicken broth or bone broth

1 tablespoon light soy sauce

1 teaspoon ground white pepper

½ teaspoon garlic powder

½ teaspoon ground turmeric

½ teaspoon chicken bouillon powder

3 tablespoons cornstarch

3 large eggs

1 teaspoon toasted sesame oil

2 green onions, green tops only, thinly sliced, for razzle-dazzle

When I don't know what I'm craving and nothing sounds appetizing, I whip up a quick pot of egg drop soup. It's comforting, healthy, and filling, plus there's no chopping necessary—a lazy girl's best friend. My favorite trick is to use chicken bone broth as the base to sneak in extra protein and gut-health benefits. I also use turmeric for that signature bright yellow color but also for its anti-inflammatory properties. The broth is seasoned with soy sauce, garlic, and chicken bouillon powder and is thickened with a cornstarch slurry. The beaten eggs are streamed in slowly and stirred over low heat to create long and silky egg ribbons that make this soup feel hearty and filling. It's finished with a drizzle of sesame oil for that subtle nutty flavor and, of course, green onion razzle-dazzle.

In a medium pot, bring the chicken broth to a boil over medium-high heat. Stir in the soy sauce, white pepper, garlic powder, turmeric, and chicken bouillon powder. In a small bowl, prepare the cornstarch slurry by mixing the cornstarch and ¼ cup cold water until smooth—no lumps! Using a ladle, mix the cornstarch slurry in with the broth. Reduce the heat to medium-low and simmer until the broth has thickened slightly, 2 to 4 minutes. Meanwhile, in a small bowl, crack the eggs and whisk with 1 tablespoon of water until there are no streaks of white.

Reduce the heat to low and make sure the broth is not bubbling (remove it from the heat if you have to). With one hand, slowly mix the broth with a ladle as you slowly pour in the egg mixture with the other hand to create long egg ribbons. Continue to stir for 1 minute or until all of the egg ribbons have set. Remove from the heat and stir in the sesame oil. Garnish with green onion greens and serve right away.

HOT & SOUR SOUP

SERVES 2

- 4 cups store-bought low-sodium chicken broth or bone broth
- ¼ cup stemmed and thinly sliced fresh shiitake mushrooms (about 2)
- ¼ cup sliced fresh wood ear mushrooms (about 6)
- 2 tablespoons light soy sauce
- 1 teaspoon dark soy sauce
- 1 teaspoon ground white pepper
- ½ teaspoon dried red pepper flakes
- ½ teaspoon sugar
- ¼ teaspoon kosher salt
- 8 ounces firm tofu, cut into ¼-inch cubes
- ¼ cup canned bamboo shoot strips, drained
- 2 tablespoons cornstarch
- 2 large eggs
- 1 teaspoon toasted sesame oil
- 2 to 3 tablespoons white distilled vinegar, to taste
- 2 green onions, green tops only, thinly sliced, for razzle-dazzle

Hot and sour soup mimics the same texture of egg drop soup, but has a completely different flavor profile and extra razzle-dazzle. Along with the signature egg ribbons, hot 'n' sour boasts both shiitake and wood ear mushrooms, soft tofu, and bites of bamboo shoots. The soup is also thickened with a cornstarch slurry but has a deeper savory flavor with a bright tanginess. If you're like me and you're a fan of anything vinegary, you have to give this soup a try.

In a medium pot, bring the chicken broth to a boil over medium-high heat. Stir in the shiitake and wood ear mushrooms, light and dark soy sauces, white pepper, red pepper flakes, sugar, and salt until well incorporated. Reduce the heat to medium-low, stir in the tofu and bamboo shoots, and cook, uncovered, for 5 minutes to heat everything through. In a small bowl, prepare the cornstarch slurry by mixing the cornstarch and ¼ cup cold water until smooth—no lumps! Mix the cornstarch slurry into the soup and cook, stirring with a ladle occasionally, until the broth thickens and appears glossy, 3 to 5 minutes.

In a small bowl, beat the eggs with 1 tablespoon water until there are no streaks of white. Reduce the heat to low and make sure the broth is not bubbling (remove it from the heat if you have to). Stir slowly with a ladle in one hand as you slowly pour in the eggs with the other hand to create long egg ribbons. Continue to stir until all of the egg ribbons have set, 1 to 2 minutes. Remove from the heat and add in the sesame oil and then the vinegar 1 tablespoon at a time to your taste (I personally like the punch of 3 tablespoons). Divide the soup between two bowls and garnish with the green onion greens.

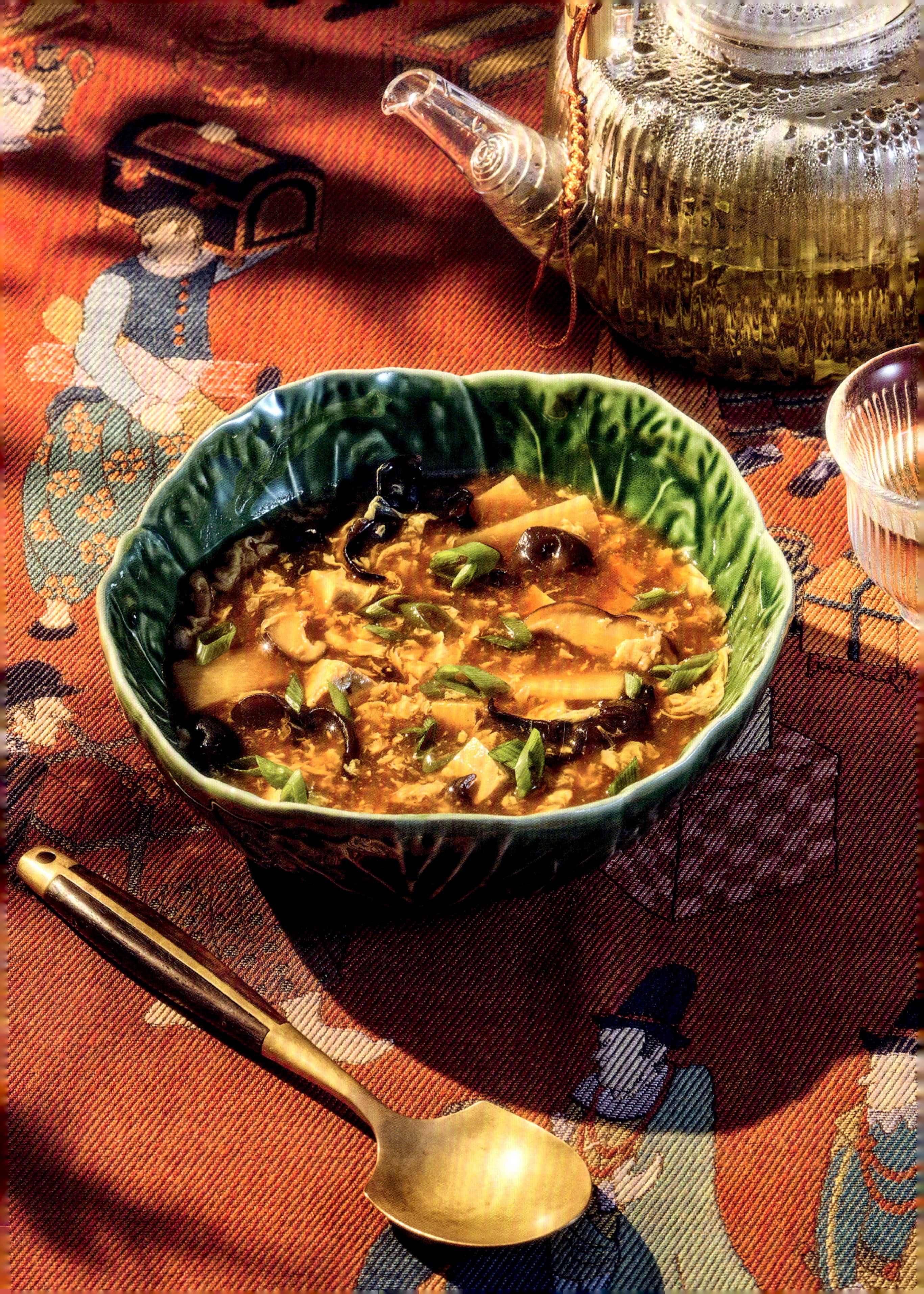

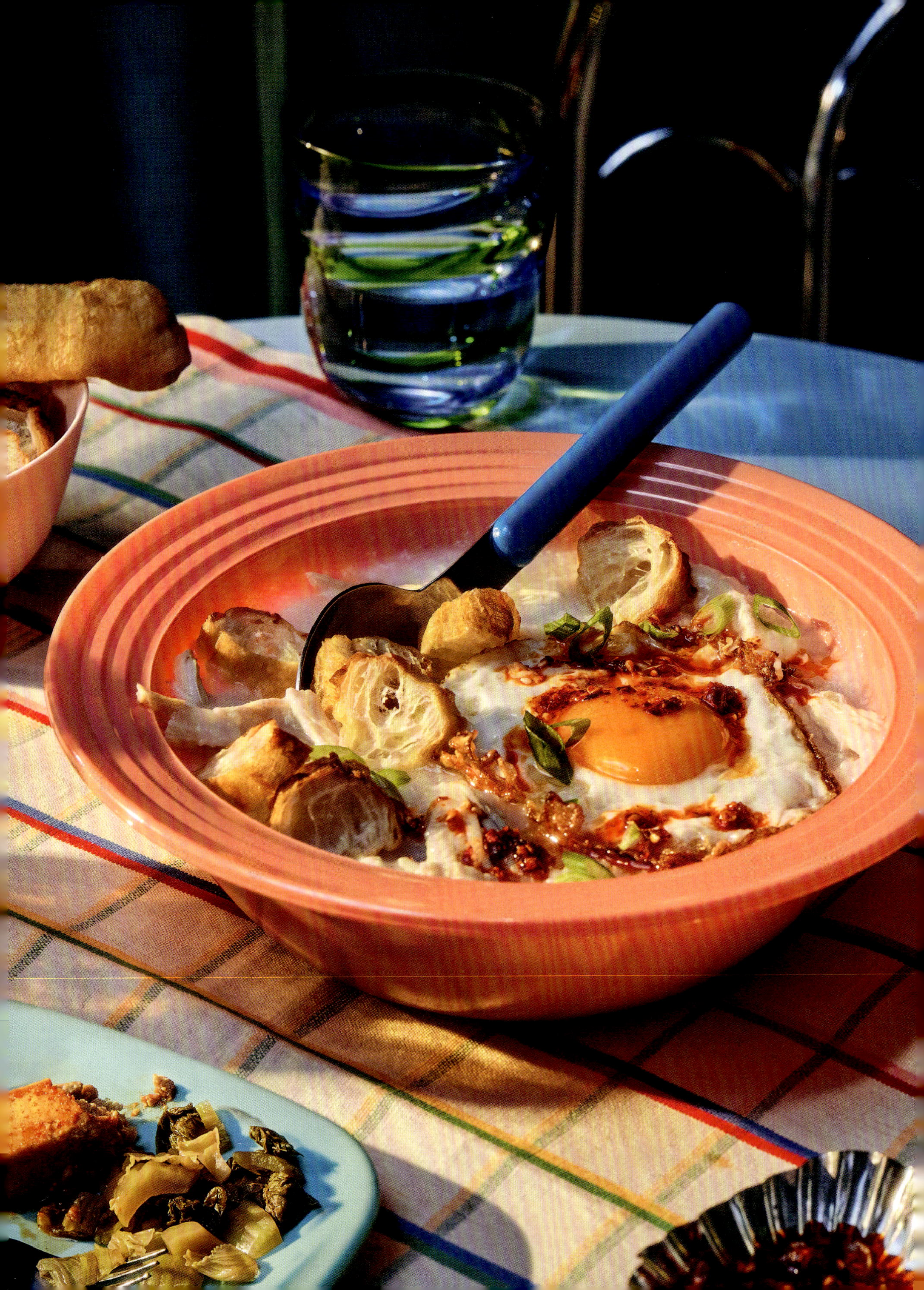

CONGEE (Chinese Jook)

SERVES 4 TO 6

1 cup jasmine rice

1 (3-pound) rotisserie chicken, meat removed and shredded and carcass reserved

2-inch knob of ginger, peeled and thinly sliced

1 teaspoon chicken bouillon powder

½ teaspoon kosher salt

FOR SERVING

(choose a few or all of them!)

Ground white pepper

Toasted sesame oil

2 green onions, green tops only, thinly sliced, for razzle-dazzle

Chinese donut, sliced (see Note)

1 fried egg, per person

Chili oil

Chinese people believe in healing foods, and jook (congee rice porridge) is what my family believes is the cure to any sickness or blues you might have. This was the first thing my mother made the minute I showed any sign of sickness, and now it's the first thing on the stove when I visit home. It's extremely quick and affordable, and always delivers big on comfort. Jook calls for the carcass of a cooked chicken, but my mother will make a congee out of essentially any leftover protein we have around, from Thanksgiving turkey to lobster shells. Rotisserie chickens are easily accessible so that's what I use here—but don't be afraid to switch it out for anything from lobster shells to your leftover Thanksgiving turkey bones, or even dried shiitake mushrooms if you don't eat meat!

In a fine mesh strainer, rinse the rice 2 to 3 times under cool water until the water runs clear. Let any excess water drip off, then add the rice to a small resealable bag. Spread the rice into a flat layer on a plate, then freeze for at least 30 minutes and up to overnight. (Freezing your rice before adding it to the boiling water will help the starches break down faster, decreasing the cook time. We love efficiency.)

In a large pot, bring 8 cups of water to a boil over high heat. Add the frozen rice, chicken carcass, ginger, chicken bouillon powder, and salt. Stir once and reduce the heat to medium. Partially cover the pot and then love her and leave her alone or else the rice can stick to the bottom of the pot! Cook for 30 minutes, until the water looks cloudy from the rice breaking down.

Remove the carcass and discard (or set aside to pick off any extra meat if you were lazy the first time around—chef's treat). Now whisk the congee aggressively to break up the rice. Add in 1 cup of the reserved shredded chicken (or more depending on how meaty you like it—save any leftover chicken in the fridge to make the Spicy Miso Instant Ramen on page 91).

Now it's time to serve, and the beauty of congee is the fixings: I like mine with white pepper, a drizzle of sesame oil, and green onion razzle-dazzle, or occasionally with Chinese donuts for dunking, a fried egg, and a final drizzle of chili oil. But you do you.

> **NOTE**
> Chinese donuts, or youtiao, are light and crispy crullers that are *so* good for dipping. They go hand in hand with jook the same way bread does soup. I stash them in the freezer and heat in the air fryer on 350°F for about 4 minutes until they're crisp again.

TOM YUM GOONG (Thai Hot & Sour Soup with Shrimp)

SERVES 8

- 2 tablespoons neutral oil (I use avocado oil)
- 2 pounds head-on jumbo shrimp (around 25/pound), peeled and deveined (page 46), shells and heads reserved
- 2 lemongrass stalks, tough outer layers removed, halved crosswise and lightly smashed
- 2-inch knob of fresh galangal, roughly sliced
- 1 bunch fresh cilantro, stems and leaves separated
- 6 fresh makrut lime leaves, torn in half
- 4 to 6 fresh bird's-eye chilies, stems removed and lightly smashed, to taste
- 4 plum tomatoes, roughly chopped
- 3 tablespoons nam prik pao (Thai chili paste)
- 1 (3½-ounce) package fresh oyster mushrooms, torn into bite-size pieces
- 1 (3½-ounce) package fresh beech mushrooms, stemmed and torn into bite-size pieces
- 3 tablespoons fish sauce
- 1 lime, halved

The first time I had tom yum soup, I was so amazed at how one sip took me on a total flavor journey. First you get the perfectly sour taste with notes of lemongrass and lime leaves that's then backed by a luxurious seafood broth infused with galangal and chilies. This is easily my favorite Thai soup, and I had it with practically every meal when I was in Bangkok. Although *goong* translates to "shrimp," various types of seafood can be added to this soup (always save your prawn shells and heads to add to the broth). In my family, it has become tradition that I host Christmas day with a tom yum hot pot—an experience similar to fondue. My family loves to gather around this aromatic pot of tom yum, individually cooking thin slices of meat, seafood, vegetables, and more in the soup. As if the soup wasn't good enough on its own, it becomes even better after everything has been cooked in it.

Heat a large pot with the oil over medium-high heat. When the oil is hot and shimmering, add in the shrimp shells and heads. Using a wooden spoon, cook while mashing the shells and heads until the oil has a red hue, about 5 minutes. Pour in 1 gallon (16 cups) of water. Bring to a boil, then cover and reduce the heat to low so the broth maintains a simmer for at least 1 hour (and up to 3 hours) to extract all the flavor from the shrimp. Using a fine mesh sieve, remove the shrimp shells and heads and press and squeeze them in the sieve over the pot to remove any remaining juices before discarding.

To the shrimp stock, add the lemongrass, galangal, cilantro stems, lime leaves, chilies, tomatoes, and nam prik pao. Stir well and simmer, partially covered and stirring occasionally, until the flavors are combined, 1 hour. Stir in the mushrooms and fish sauce and simmer, covered, until the mushrooms are soft and infused with the broth, 30 more minutes. In the last 2 minutes of simmering, add the shrimp and cook until they're pink and curled into a C shape.

To serve, ladle the soup into bowls (avoid serving the lemongrass, galangal, cilantro stems, or lime leaves), add a squeeze of fresh lime juice, and garnish with the cilantro leaves.

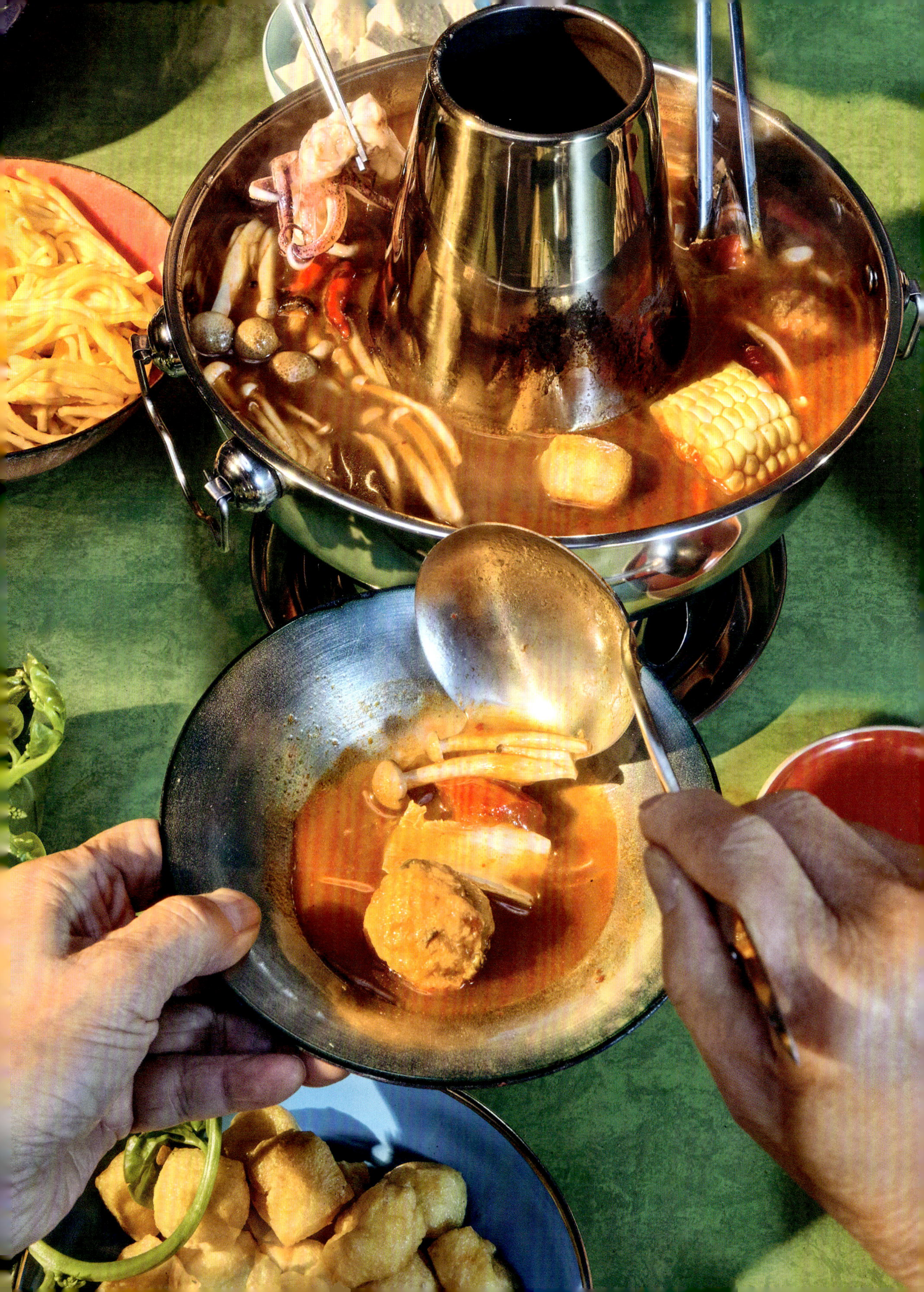

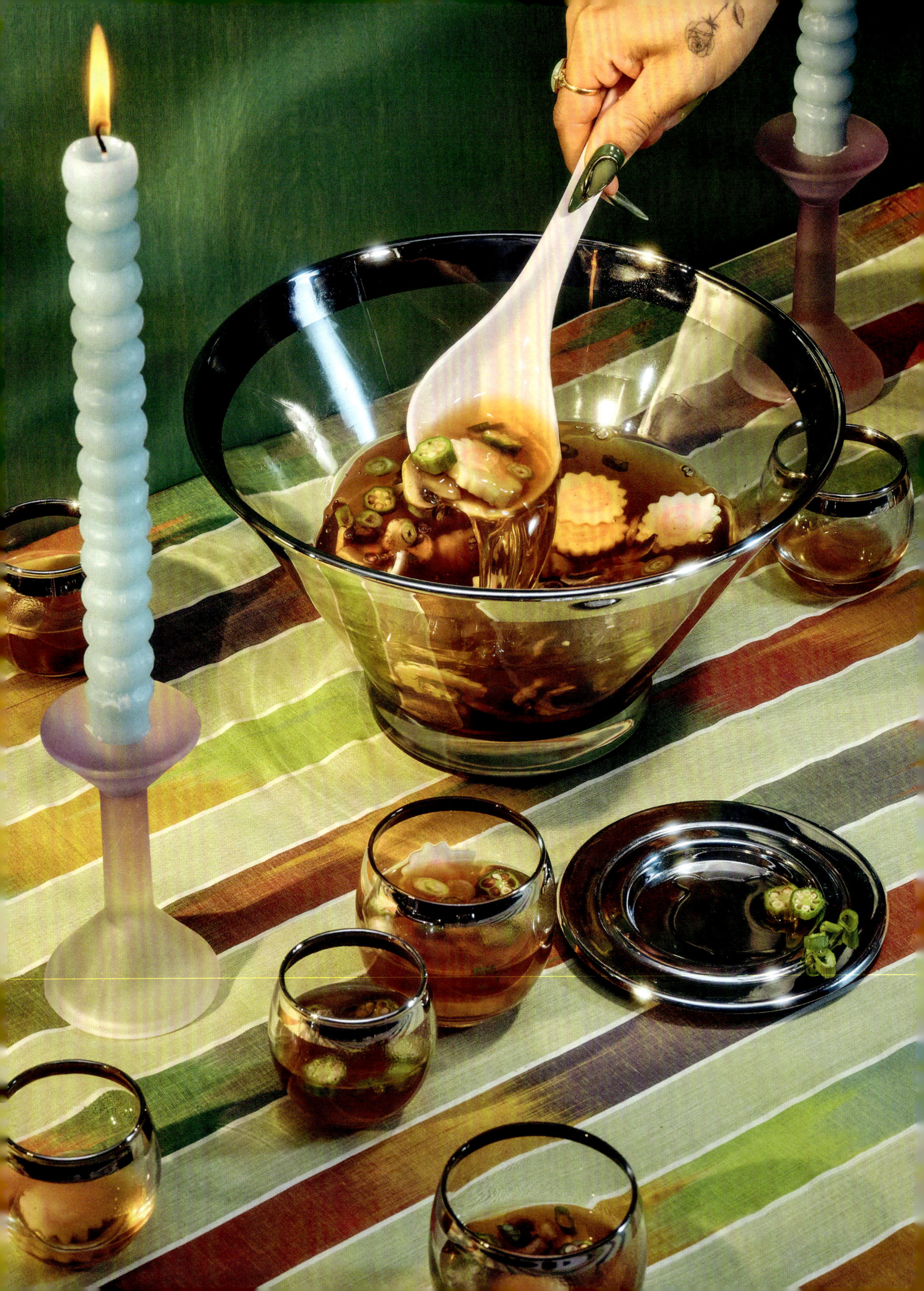

JAPANESE CLEAR SOUP

SERVES 4 TO 6

1 tablespoon neutral oil (I use avocado oil)

1 large sweet onion, roughly chopped

1 medium carrot, roughly chopped

6 green onions, white and green parts, thinly sliced and separated

1 teaspoon kosher salt, plus more to taste

2-inch knob of ginger, peeled and thinly sliced

6 large garlic cloves, smashed

8 cups store-bought low-sodium beef broth or bone broth

¾ cup stemmed and thinly sliced white mushrooms (about 3)

2 teaspoons toasted sesame oil

Hibachi is an experience from the moment you sit down, from the zucchini toss-and-catch in your mouth to the onion volcano. While it can be easy to be distracted by these dinnertime theatrics, I urge you not to neglect the clear soup! Clear soup is a light and healthy yet deep, layered beefy broth that is provided as a starter at most hibachi restaurants. It's infused with onions, carrots, green onions, ginger, and garlic (I like to roughly chop it all, making prep nice and easy). I use store-bought beef broth to make this even simpler, but of course you can use homemade! Regardless of the beef broth route you choose, the broth is slowly simmered for 1 hour to marry with the vegetables before straining out for smooth sipping. This soup is easy to make, but hard to forget!

Heat a large pot with the neutral oil over medium-high heat. When the oil is hot and bothered (okay, shimmering), add the sweet onion, carrot, the green onion whites, and salt. Cook, stirring frequently, until they've cooked down and the sweet onion is starting to turn translucent, about 5 minutes. Add the ginger and garlic, continuing to stir often, until golden brown, 2 minutes.

Pour in the beef broth and raise the heat to high to bring to a boil. Cover, reduce the heat to low, and simmer until the vegetables are soft and the broth is flavorful, about 1 hour. Use a fine mesh sieve to remove and discard the vegetables and season the broth with more salt to taste—no measurements, just vibes for the salt.

Add the mushrooms and simmer, stirring occasionally, until the mushrooms have softened, about 2 minutes. Remove from the heat and add the green onion greens and sesame oil. Divide among the bowls and serve immediately.

MISO SOUP

SERVES 2 ON ITS OWN OR 4 AS PART OF A SPREAD

2 tablespoons wakame dried seaweed

Warm water, as needed

2 teaspoons HonDashi stock powder

2 tablespoons white miso paste

8 ounces silken tofu, cut into ¼-inch cubes

3 green onions, white and green parts, thinly sliced

½ cup fresh white beech mushrooms, torn from the base and into bite-size pieces (about 1 ounce)

We all know and love miso soup at the start of a good sushi dinner, but are you aware how simple it is to make at home? This Japanese soup is such a classic and truly is the benchmark to a great meal. It will require a trip to your local Asian market for a few particular ingredients, but that homemade taste is always worth it. Miso soup is simply a dashi stock (a rich umami stock made from kombu seaweed and dried bonito flakes) flavored with miso paste. I like to add silky sheets of rehydrated wakame seaweed and tiny cubes of silken tofu, too—and since the beauty of making everything at home is customizing to your liking, I love adding white beech mushrooms to my miso soup as well. Once you acquire the few ingredients needed, this classic will only take 15 minutes to make.

In a small bowl, add the dried seaweed and cover with warm water by an inch. Soak until soft and flexible, about 5 minutes. Drain and set aside.

In a small pot, bring 4 cups water to a boil over medium-high heat. Reduce the heat to low so the water is just steaming, then stir in the dashi stock powder (don't boil—you'll lose the nutritional value of the dashi and miso!). In a small bowl, whisk the miso paste with a ladle of the hot broth until there are no lumps. Pour the miso into the broth and stir.

Add the tofu, green onions, mushrooms, and wakame. Cook for 10 minutes, adjusting the heat as necessary to make sure the soup only steams, never bubbles, to heat the ingredients through and combine the flavors. To serve, split evenly into bowls and enjoy immediately.

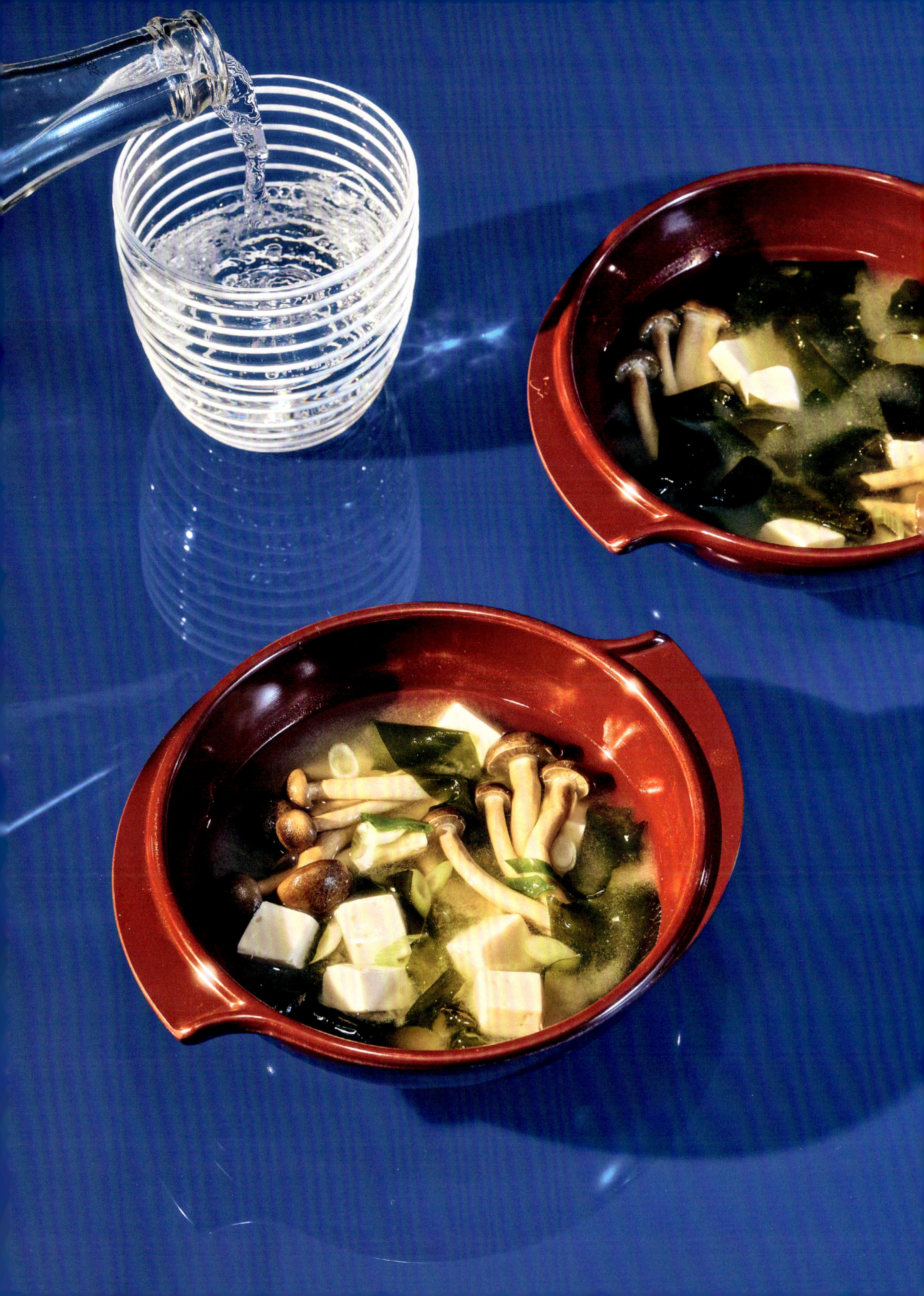

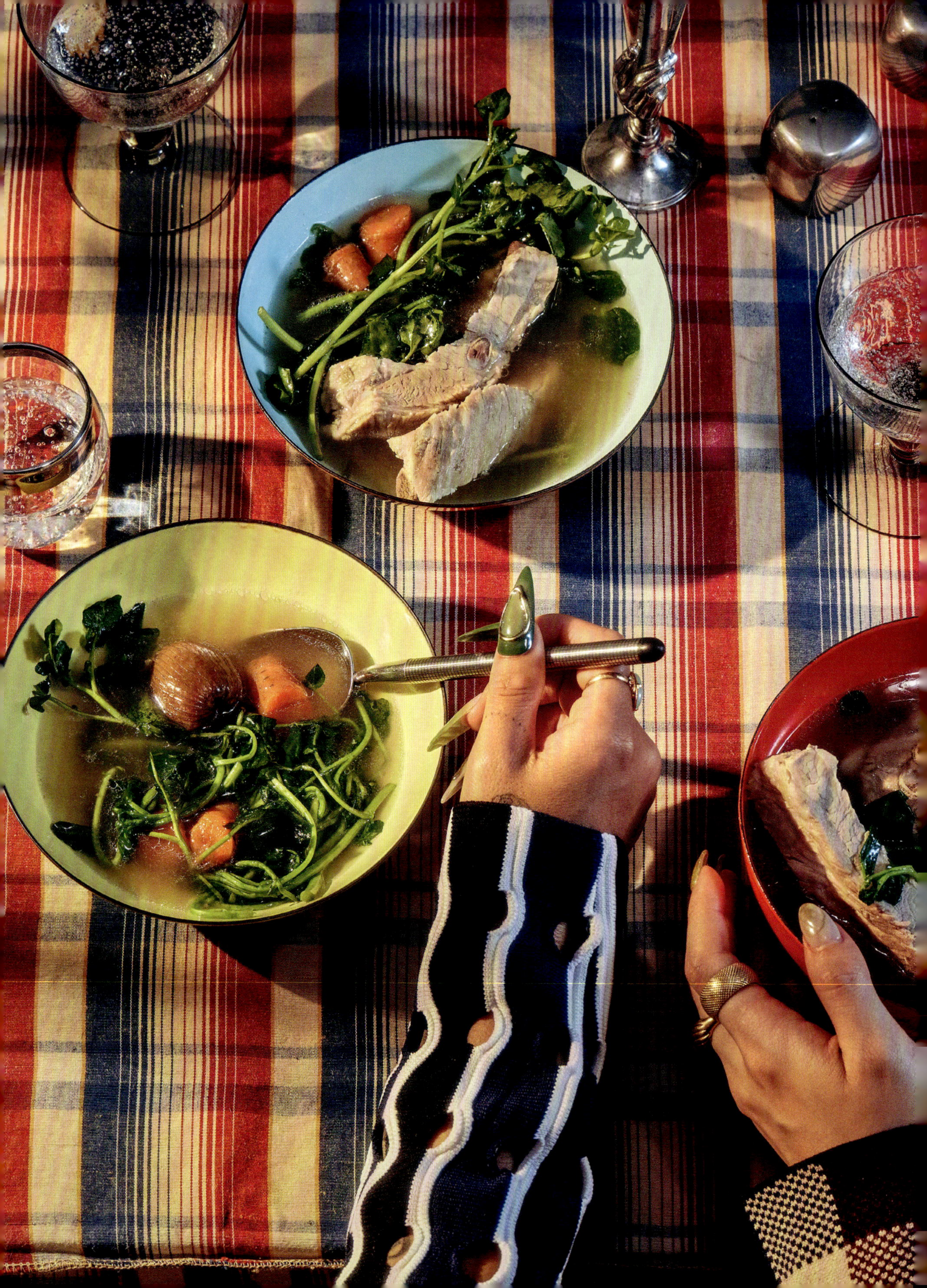

CHINESE WATERCRESS SOUP

SERVES 6 TO 8

2 pounds pork bones or pork ribs

2 large carrots, roughly chopped

¼ cup dried Chinese scallops

3 dried Chinese figs

1 teaspoon kosher salt

½ pound fresh watercress (about 1 bunch)

Ground white pepper

If you've grown up in a Cantonese household, you're probably familiar with this staple soup. Watercress soup, or sai yeung choy tong, is something from my childhood that I've really taken for granted. My parents *always* have a pot of soup on the stovetop to end a meal with, and this simple soup was by far my favorite. Watercress is a bright, leafy green with a naturally peppery flavor, which is probably why I'm so obsessed with it. The broth is made with pork rib bones that usually come with some meat still on them, or pork ribs if you can't find them, which really complement the watercress. Simmering will make the bright green color begin to fade, but the leaves become very delicate and extremely comforting to enjoy. This will require a trip to the Asian market for Chinese dried scallops and figs, but they both add another layer of flavor to the broth—I think they're musts—no subs allowed. The dried scallops add so much umami flavor while the dried figs add a subtle sweetness. My dad has never been the one to usually cook, but he was often in charge of making the soup and that's your sign that this is extremely doable.

Bring a large pot of water to a boil over high heat and add the pork bones. Bring the water back to a boil and cook for 5 minutes, using a slotted spoon to remove any foam that rises to the top, then strain and rinse the bones well under cool water to remove the impurities. Clean the pot.

Bring 8 cups water to a boil in the cleaned pot over high heat and add the pork bones back in. Add the carrots, scallops, and figs and season with the salt. Reduce the heat to low so the broth simmers and cook, covered and stirring occasionally, until the flavors are combined and the meat is tender, about 1½ hours (same if using pork ribs).

Meanwhile, wash the watercress twice (I like to soak them in a bowl of water for 10 minutes, then drain using a salad spinner) to remove all the grit. Add the watercress to the broth and stir until wilted. Let the soup simmer, covered, for 30 more minutes until the watercress has softened and mixed in with the soup (the color won't be as vibrant but the flavors will pop, don't worry).

To serve, ladle the soup into bowls along with whatever each person likes in their broth: a few carrots, watercress to your liking, a fig if that's your thing, and top each bowl with white pepper to taste—no measurements, just vibes for the pepper—and a piece of pork bone or a pork rib.

EAT Y
VEGGIES
OUR

EAT YOUR VEGGIES

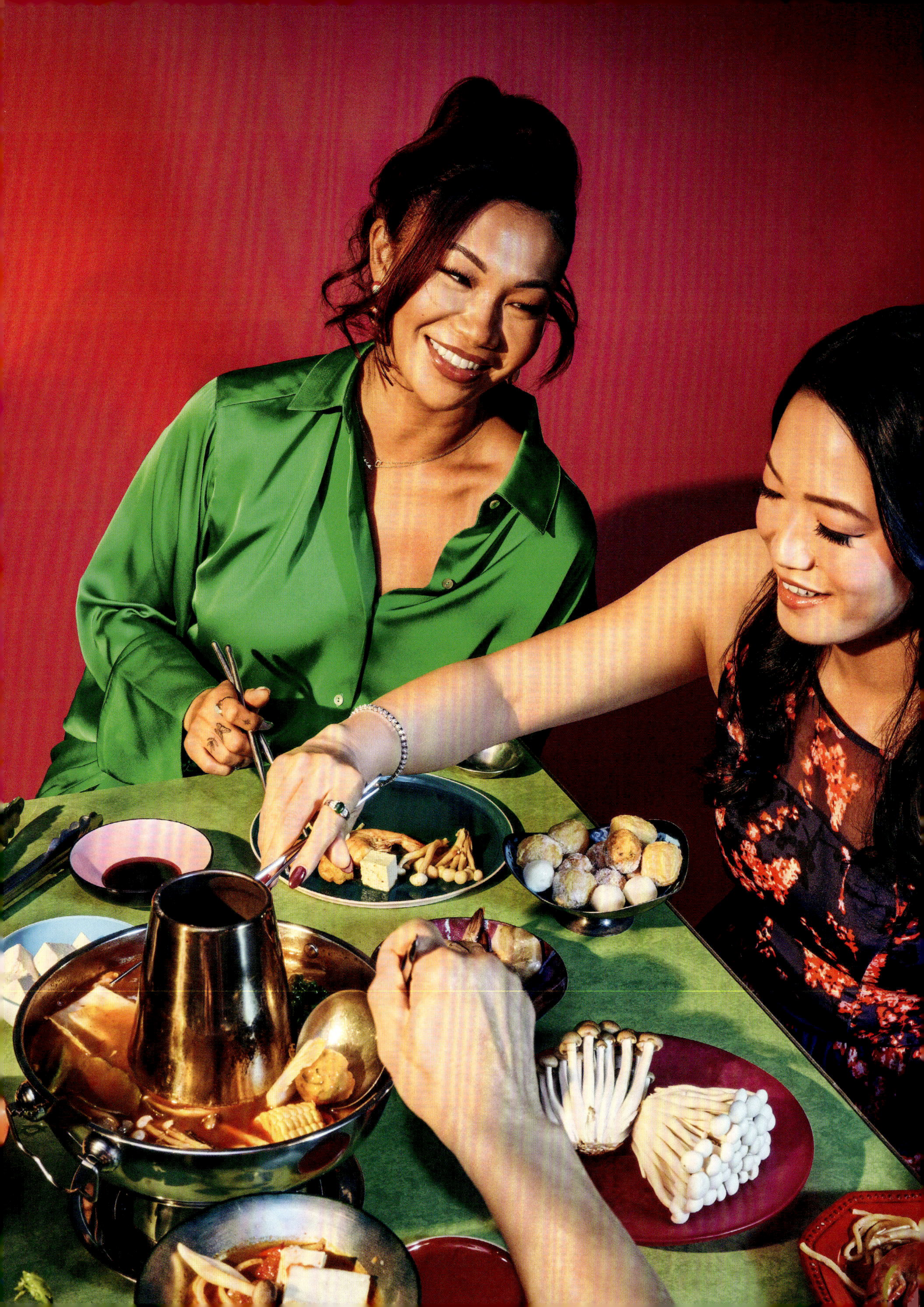

RECIPE LIST

Copycat Din Tai Fung Green Beans
188

10-Minute Bok Choy
191

Tomato Egg
192

Banchan-Style Korean Bean Sprouts
195

Easy Kimchi
196

Not Boring Vegetarian Dumplings
198

Quick Chili-Vinegar Onions
202

Rainbow Carrot Ribbon Salad
205

Accordion Cucumber Salad
206

Som Tum (Papaya Salad)
209

These are the vegetables I actually crave—

the ones that make me forget I'm eating something healthy. I like my vegetables pickled, immersed in sauce, and bright and crispy. I guarantee you'll be revisiting a lot of these humble veggies, either as snacks or sides.

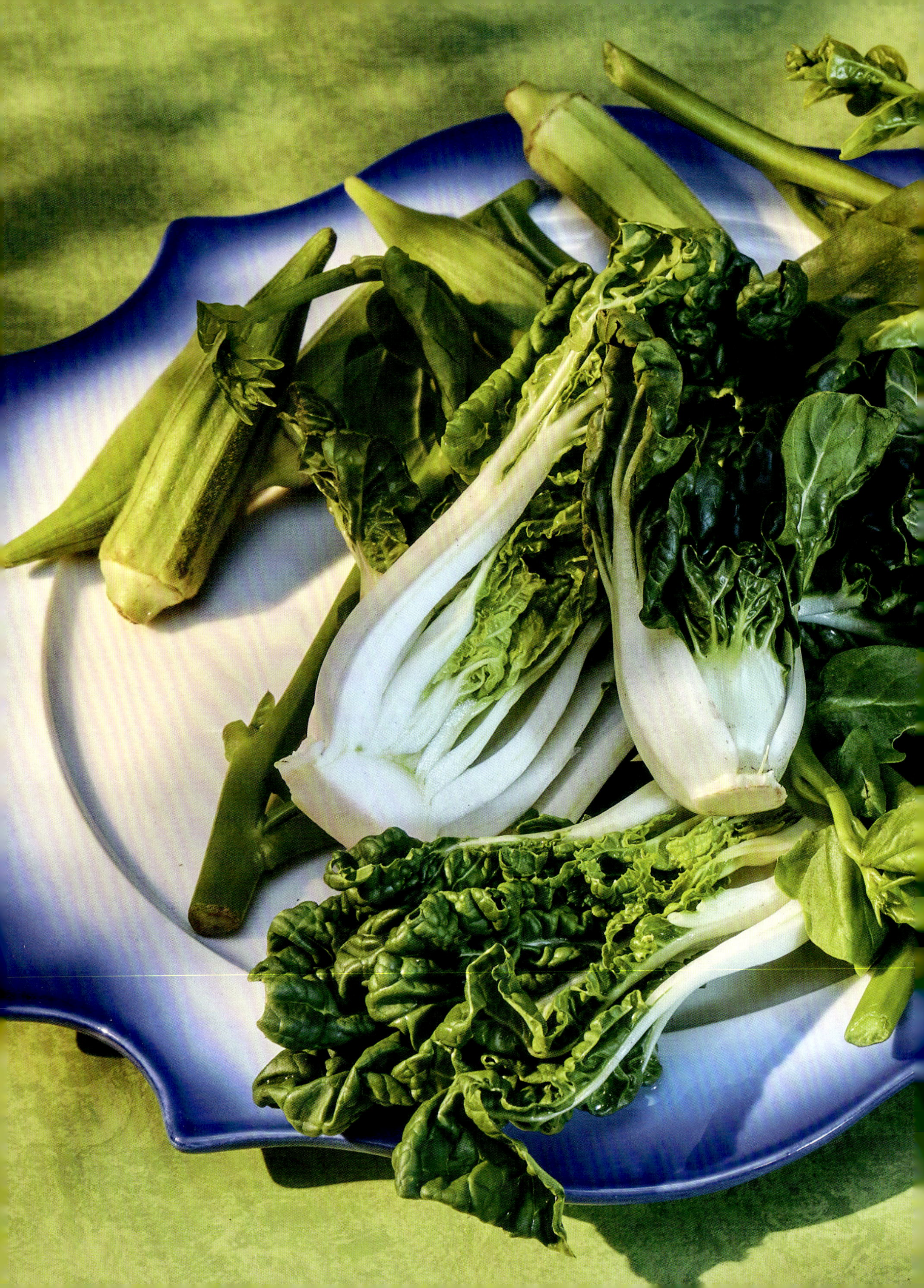

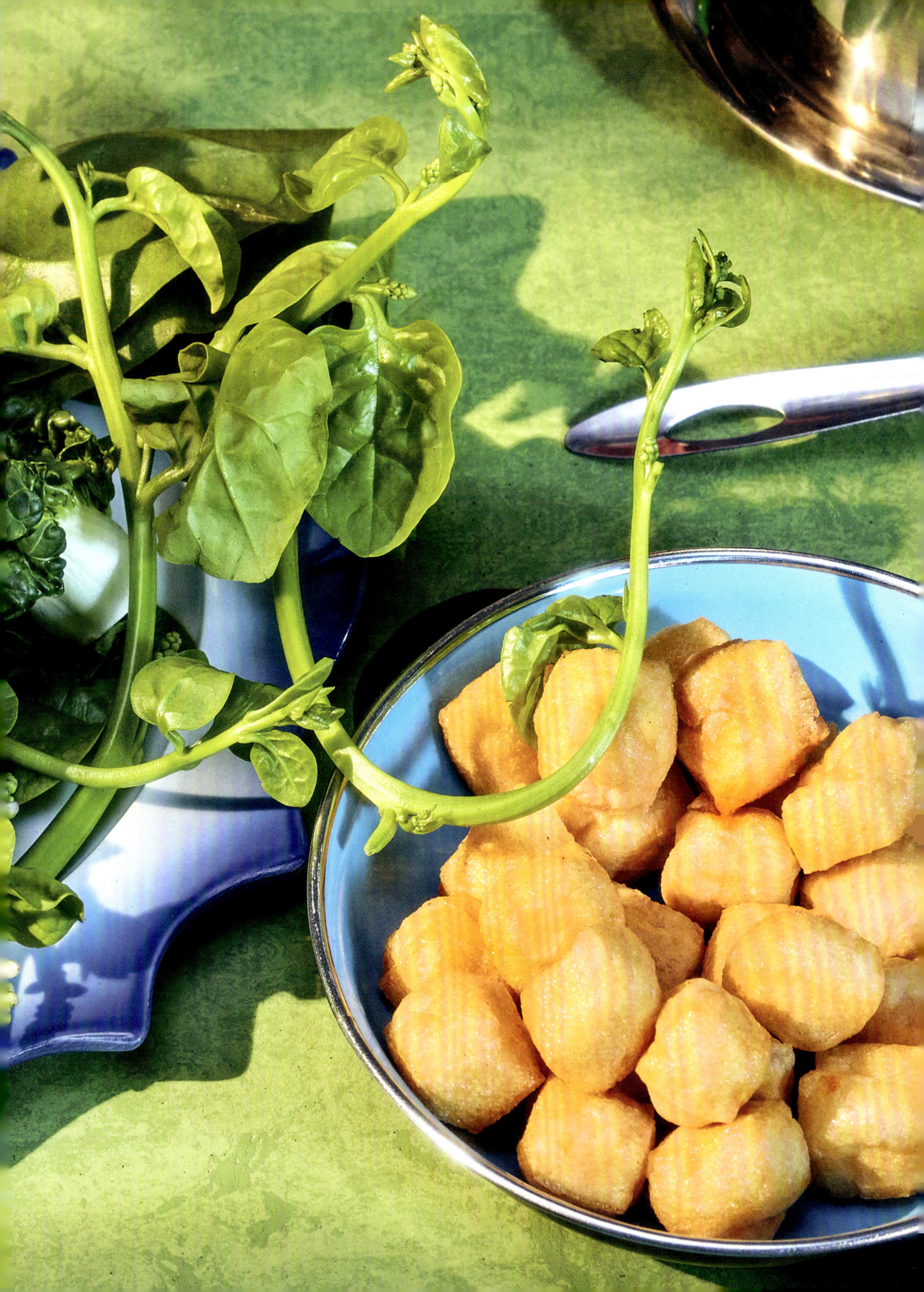

COPYCAT DIN TAI FUNG GREEN BEANS

SERVES 2 TO 4

Neutral oil (I use avocado oil), for frying

1 pound green beans, ends trimmed

1 head of garlic (12 to 15 cloves), minced

½ teaspoon kosher salt

¼ teaspoon chicken bouillon powder or mushroom bouillon powder

Din Tai Fung, a world-renowned restaurant chain from Taiwan known for its iconic soup dumplings and noodles, has so many memorable dishes, so the vegetables can sometimes be overlooked—which is a huge error! Because then you'd be missing their green beans, which are flash-fried and loaded with garlic and are *far* from basic. I remember having a conversation with a friend in college, and they told me they don't eat vegetables unless they're from a Chinese restaurant. As shocking as it was to find out they were completely against veggies, I wasn't too surprised knowing that garlic, oil, and high heat are magic and can transform just about anything. We'll be using an entire head of garlic for this, so you may want to hold off on any kissing (unless they're having some, too, of course).

Fill a wok or medium pot with 1 inch of neutral oil and heat to 325°F (if you don't have a thermometer, do the wooden chopstick test on page 47). Line a plate with paper towels. Dry the green beans completely with paper towels.

Drop the green beans in the oil to flash-fry, stirring frequently, for 1 minute or just until the skin begins to blister. Use a spider to remove them to the paper towel–lined plate, then discard all but 1 tablespoon of the oil.

Put the wok over medium-high and fry the garlic, stirring constantly, until golden brown, 30 seconds to 1 minute. Add the green beans back to the wok and season with the salt and chicken bouillon powder. Stir for another 30 seconds to 1 minute until the green beans are fully coated, then transfer to a serving dish immediately.

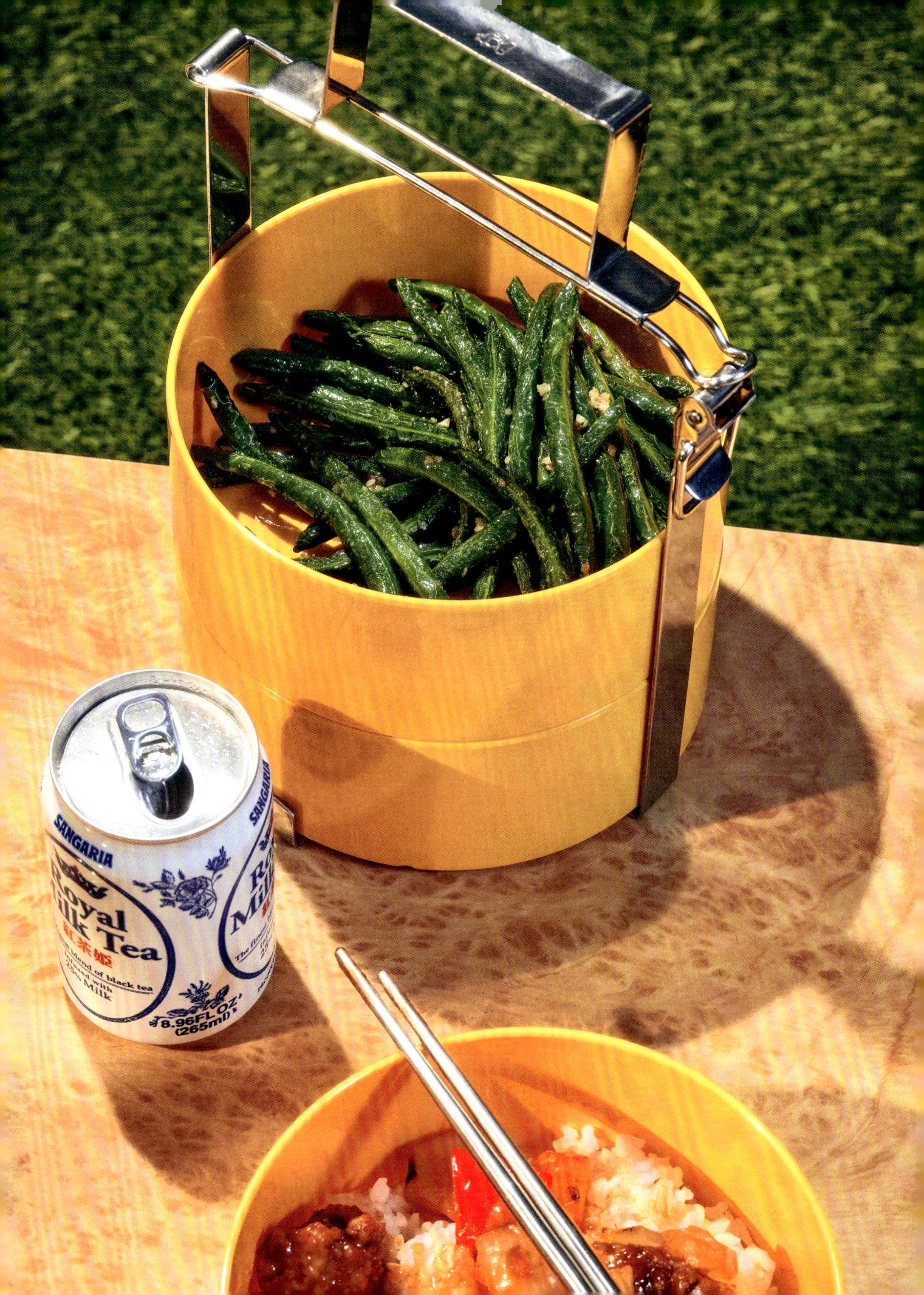
SANGARIA
Royal Milk Tea
8.96FL OZ
(265ml)

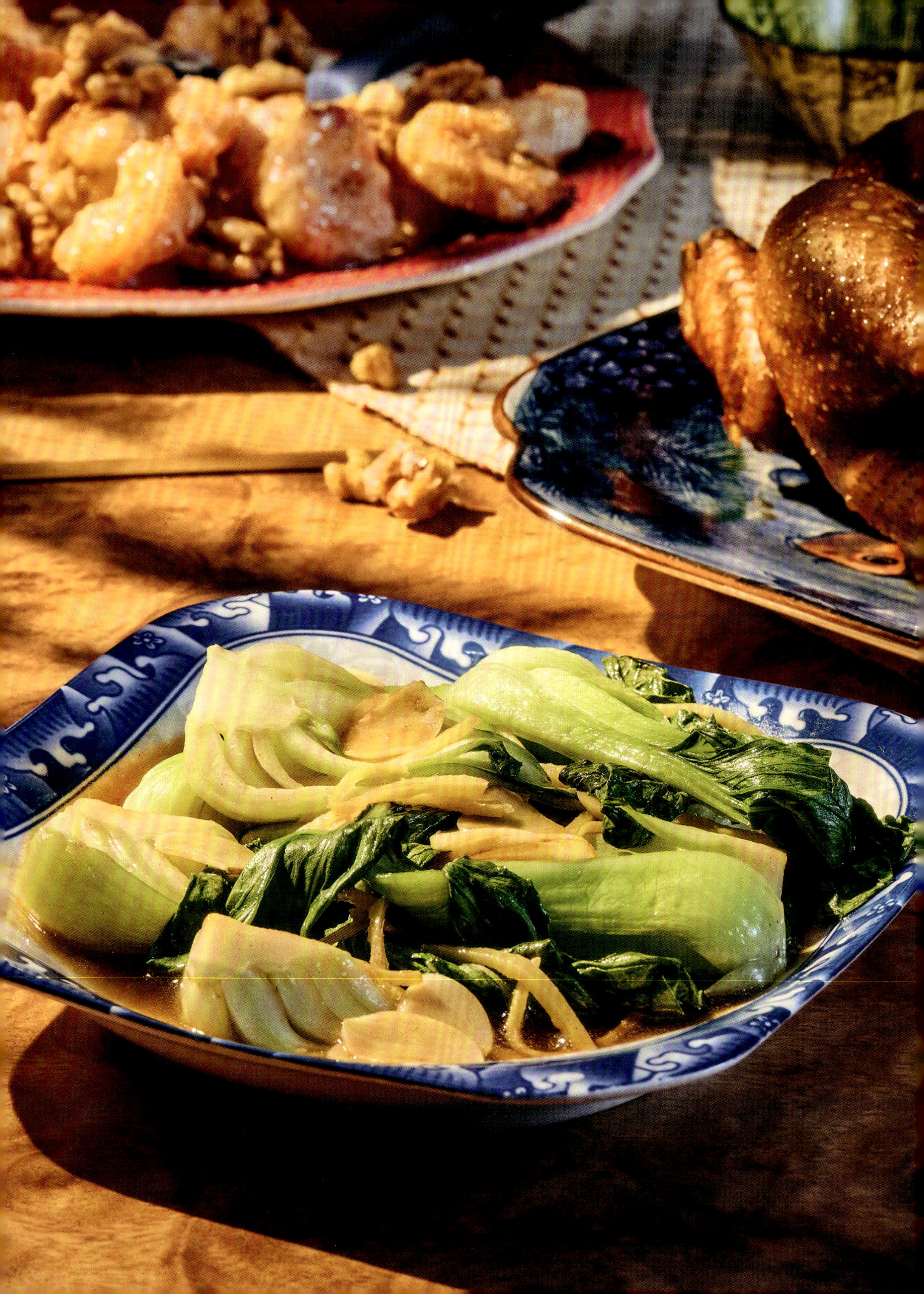

10-MINUTE BOK CHOY

SERVES 2 TO 4

1 tablespoon oyster sauce

2 teaspoons light soy sauce

1 teaspoon chicken bouillon powder or mushroom bouillon powder

½ teaspoon ground white pepper

1 tablespoon neutral oil (I use avocado oil)

3 large garlic cloves, thinly sliced

1-inch knob of ginger, peeled and cut into thin matchsticks

2 tablespoons Shaoxing wine

1 pound baby bok choy (about 6 heads), core intact and quartered lengthwise

Sometimes less is more, and bok choy is the perfect example of that. My mom has always cooked choy, or vegetables, in a simple combo of oyster sauce, soy sauce, Shaoxing wine, garlic, and ginger that enables the pure flavor of the greens to shine through. The stem of the bok choy is tender yet snappy, the leaves are earthy, and the flavors of the sauce enhance them without masking their delicacy. This takes ten minutes and is the best sidekick to any meal.

In a small bowl, mix the oyster sauce, soy sauce, chicken bouillon powder, and white pepper until smooth. Set aside.

In a wok or large skillet, heat the neutral oil over medium-high heat. When the oil is hot and shimmering, add the garlic and ginger and stir-fry (we're stirring and shaking the wok aggressively here) until golden brown, about 1 minute. Pour the Shaoxing wine around the sides of the wok and stir constantly for 1 minute until reduced by half. Add the bok choy and stir constantly to combine for 30 seconds, then pour in ¼ cup water and cover and steam until the bok choy is tender, 1 to 2 minutes. Pour in the sauce and stir-fry for 1 minute to coat the bok choy.

Transfer to a serving plate, drizzling any remaining sauce in the wok over the top, and serve.

TOMATO EGG

SERVES 2

- 1 teaspoon neutral oil (I use avocado oil)
- 2 green onions, white and green parts, thinly sliced and separated, plus extra greens for razzle-dazzle
- 1 large garlic clove, minced
- 1 teaspoon red pepper flakes
- 3 Roma tomatoes, cut into 1-inch cubes
- 1 tablespoon oyster sauce or vegan oyster flavored sauce
- ½ teaspoon ground white pepper
- ¼ teaspoon kosher salt
- 4 large eggs
- 1 teaspoon toasted sesame oil
- The Perfect Steamed Rice (page 242), for serving

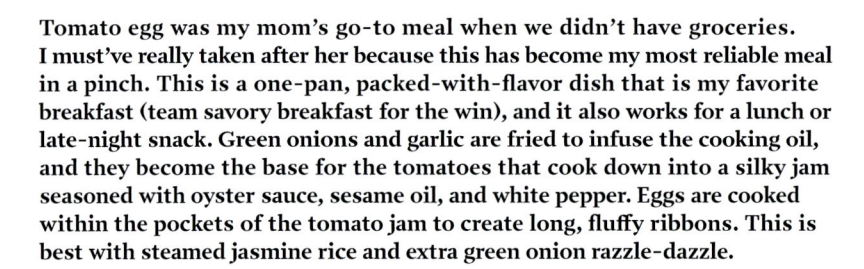

Tomato egg was my mom's go-to meal when we didn't have groceries. I must've really taken after her because this has become my most reliable meal in a pinch. This is a one-pan, packed-with-flavor dish that is my favorite breakfast (team savory breakfast for the win), and it also works for a lunch or late-night snack. Green onions and garlic are fried to infuse the cooking oil, and they become the base for the tomatoes that cook down into a silky jam seasoned with oyster sauce, sesame oil, and white pepper. Eggs are cooked within the pockets of the tomato jam to create long, fluffy ribbons. This is best with steamed jasmine rice and extra green onion razzle-dazzle.

In a medium skillet, heat the neutral oil over medium heat. When the oil is hot and shimmering, add the green onion whites, the garlic, and red pepper flakes. Cook, stirring occasionally with a spatula, until the garlic is slightly browned, about 2 minutes. Add the tomatoes, oyster sauce, white pepper, and salt and mix. Reduce the heat to medium-low and cook, stirring occasionally, until the tomatoes have cooked down into a jammy consistency, about 5 minutes.

In a separate small bowl, lightly beat the eggs until no streaks of white remain and pour over the tomatoes. Cover the pan and cook until the eggs begin to set, 1 minute. Uncover and drag the eggs from the outside toward the center using a spatula. Mix in the sesame oil and the green onion greens and cook, stirring constantly, until the eggs are set, another minute. Serve hot over the rice and garnish with green onion greens.

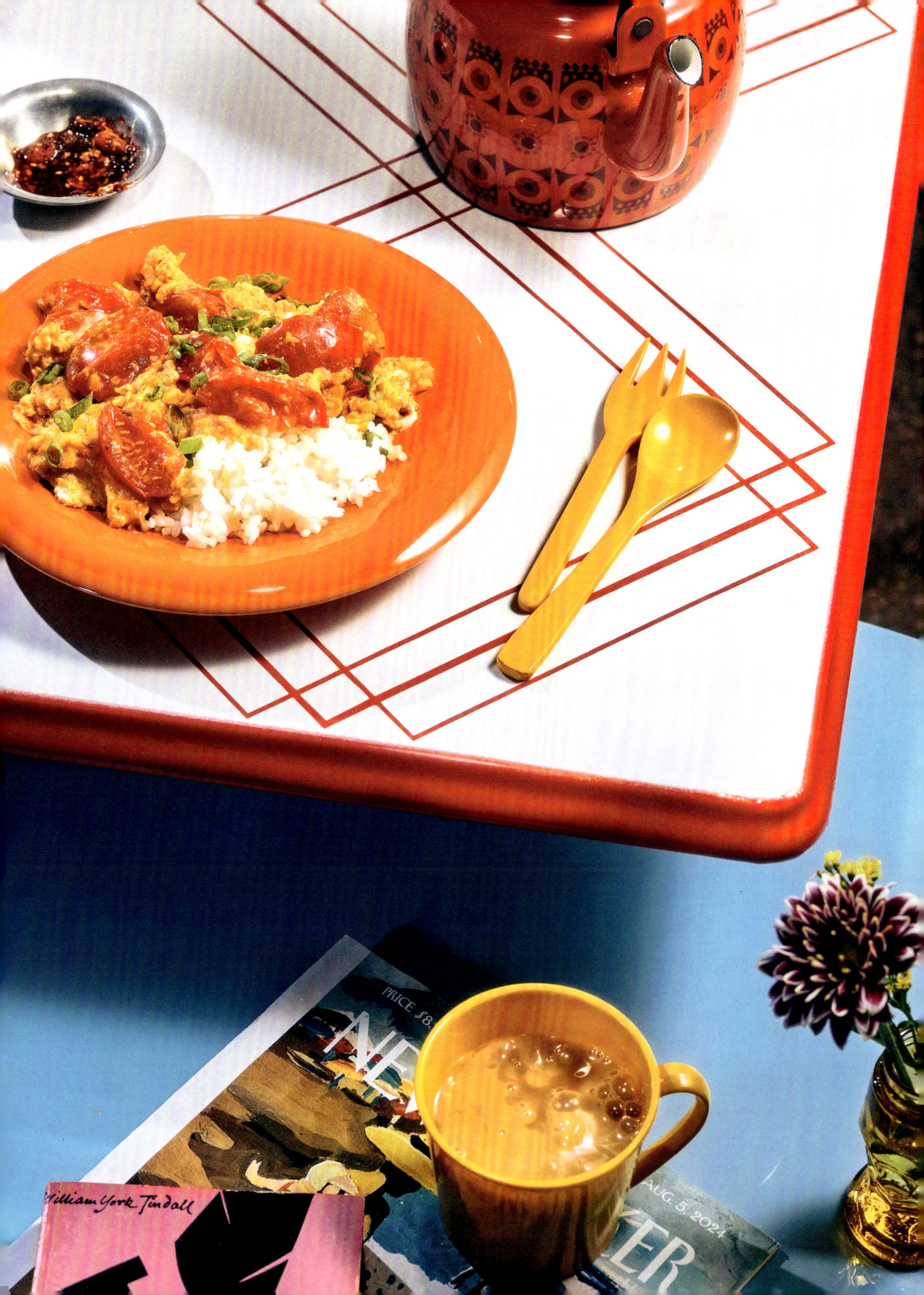
PRICE $8.
AUG. 5, 2024
William York Tindall

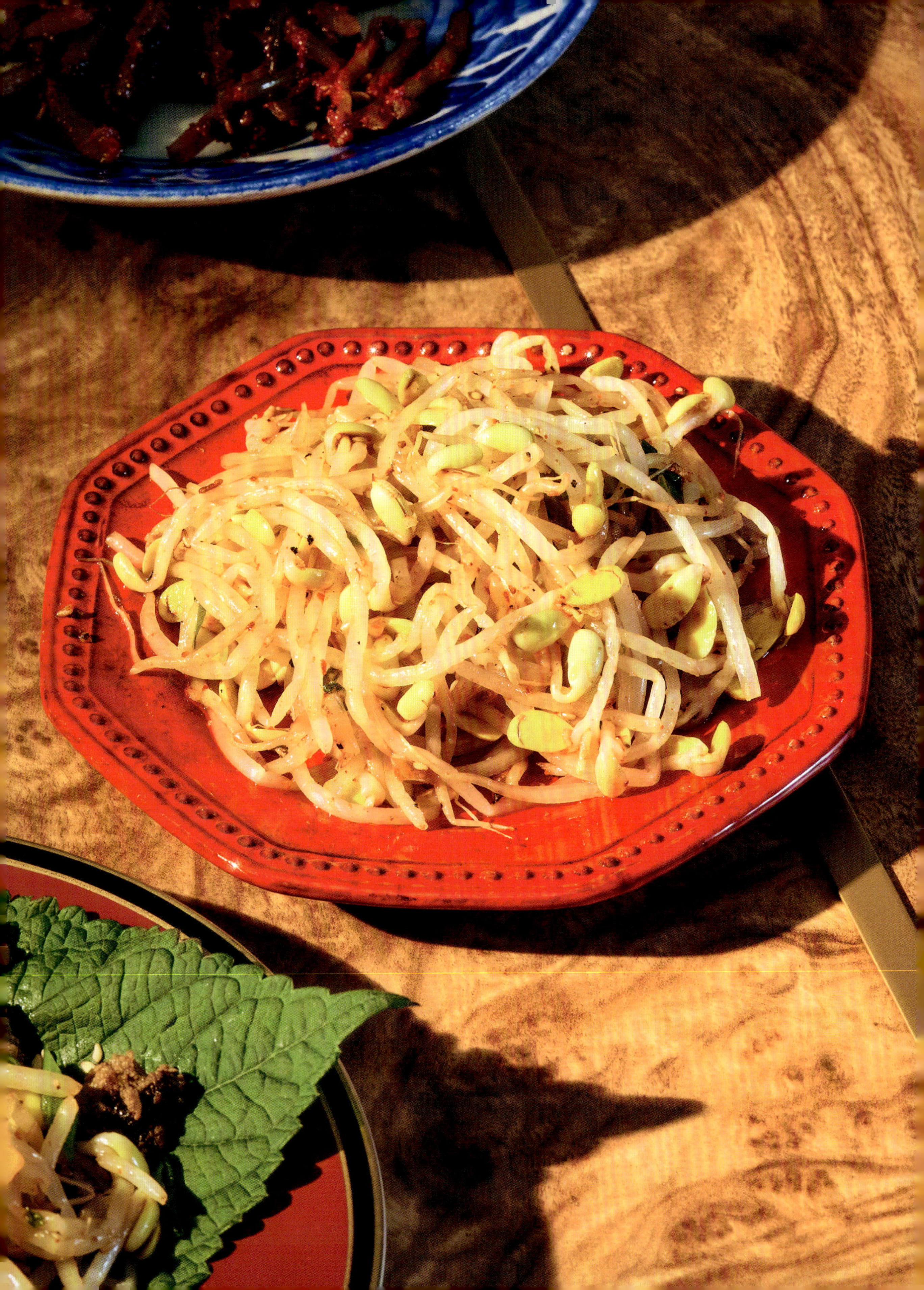

BANCHAN-STYLE KOREAN BEAN SPROUTS

SERVES 2 TO 4

Kosher salt

1 pound fresh mung bean sprouts

2 tablespoons light soy sauce

1 tablespoon toasted sesame oil

1 teaspoon gochugaru (Korean chili flakes)

1 teaspoon toasted sesame seeds

2 green onions, white and green parts, thinly sliced

2 large garlic cloves, minced

¼ teaspoon kosher salt

¼ teaspoon freshly ground black pepper

What really completes a Korean barbecue experience or even a bowl of bulgogi (page 116) is the unlimited supply of banchan, or side dishes. Anytime I have KBBQ, I tell the waiter to keep them coming because I'm basically a bottomless pit when it comes to banchan. Bean sprout salad is one of my personal favorites, and I wish I was exaggerating when I say I could eat an entire pound in one sitting. This only takes fifteen minutes to make and is a great way to sneak in extra veggies. I love any dish that feels naughty but is actually healthy.

Bring a medium pot of salted water to a boil over medium-high heat—make sure it's salty like pasta water, or as salty as you are when you think your waiter is bringing out your food but they walk right past you. Add the bean sprouts and boil them until they are tender, about 3 minutes, then drain and rinse under cool water.

In a medium bowl, whisk together the soy sauce, sesame oil, gochugaru, sesame seeds, green onions, garlic, salt, and pepper. Add the bean sprouts, toss to coat, and chill, covered, in the fridge for 30 minutes or up to 3 days. Serve chilled, straight from the fridge.

EASY KIMCHI

MAKES 12 CUPS

- ¼ cup kosher salt, plus more for boiling potatoes
- 1 medium russet potato, peeled and roughly chopped
- 1 large head napa cabbage (about 4 pounds)
- ½ medium Asian pear (or sub with apple), cored and roughly chopped
- ½ medium yellow onion, roughly chopped
- 8 large garlic cloves
- 1-inch knob of ginger, peeled
- ¼ cup fish sauce
- ⅔ cup gochugaru (Korean chili flakes)
- 1 small daikon radish (about 8 ounces), peeled and cut into thin matchsticks
- 2 medium carrots, cut into thin matchsticks
- 8 green onions, white and green parts, cut into 2-inch pieces

Not a day goes by that I don't enjoy a little kimchi—it's my favorite pickled snack that doubles as my skincare secret. I read that when Margot Robbie was preparing for *Barbie*, her team created a specific skincare regimen that included kimchi to help promote healing and reduce the stress in the body. I'm not an expert on all the science, but fermented foods contain probiotics that hold so many health benefits. The flavor of kimchi is unique and remains difficult to explain, but I would describe it as a spicy, umami, subtly sweet version of sauerkraut. Asian pear adds a natural sweetness and also helps tenderize the cabbage during fermentation. A rice flour paste is traditionally used as a binder for the ingredients, but I like to use mashed potato for a richer flavor! Similarly to sauerkraut, kimchi is packed down and left at room temperature to ferment and become a bubbly, gut-friendly side with the addition of Asian seasonings, aromatics, and vegetables that hold their crunch.

Bring a medium pot of salted water to a boil over medium-high heat—make sure it's salty like pasta water. Add the potato and cook until fork tender, 12 to 15 minutes. Thoroughly drain and return the potato to the pot. Mash with a potato masher until there are no lumps. Set aside to cool.

Make a 2-inch cut through the base of the napa cabbage, then tear it in half using your hands. Repeat on each half of the cabbage to create quarters (go on and work out that anger, bestie; this is how the Korean aunties do it). Cut out the core from each quarter, then chop the cabbage crosswise (and again if they're long) into 2-inch square pieces. Add the cabbage pieces to an extra-large bowl in four layers, sprinkling generously with one-quarter of the salt as you build each layer. Using your hands, massage the cabbage well until it wilts, about 5 minutes. Now love her and leave her alone: Set the cabbage aside until it shrinks by half, about 30 minutes. Rinse the salt off in a colander, then squeeze out all of the excess moisture with your hands. Clean the bowl and return the cabbage to it.

Add the Asian pear, onion, garlic, ginger, and fish sauce to a blender and puree until smooth. Transfer to a medium bowl and use a silicone spatula to mix in the gochugaru and cooled mashed potato. Wearing kitchen gloves, add the daikon, carrots, and green onions to the chili mixture and combine, then slowly work this mixture in with the cabbage until fully incorporated. Use your hands to get the chili mixture into each crevice and ruffle of the leaves.

Now let's ferment her: Add the kimchi to a 5.2L fermentation storage container or a glass container that holds 12 cups a handful at a time, leaving at least 1 inch of space at the top. When filling the container, make sure to press the cabbage down after each addition to compact it and eliminate air pockets. If using a fermentation storage container, insert the inner pressing plate and seal the burping spout, then lock the outer lid. If using a glass container, make sure the kimchi is submerged in liquid by pressing down and the lid is airtight. Leave the container out at room temperature for 2 days, burping the container twice a day (meaning you open the burping spout and reseal it if using a fermentation container, or open the lid just enough to let out any pressure then reseal it—there's no need to open the container completely, and you're doing this so it doesn't explode!), or until bubbles begin to form in the liquid. After 2 days, transfer the container to the fridge and ferment for another 2 to 3 days, tasting it daily, until the kimchi is sour and bubbly to your liking. The cooler temperature will slow down the fermentation, so you can cut down the burping to once a day (aw, they grow up so fast).

Kimchi technically does not go bad, but it will continue to ferment and taste more sour the longer you keep it. I recommend transferring it to smaller glass containers (to free up fridge space) and keeping it in the fridge for up to 6 months, but it's best enjoyed in the first month (although I doubt you won't finish it by then!).

NOT BORING VEGETARIAN DUMPLINGS

MAKES ABOUT 75 DUMPLINGS

- 3 ounces mung bean or rice vermicelli noodles
- Warm water, as needed
- 2 cups finely chopped napa cabbage (from about ¼ small cabbage)
- 2 tablespoons kosher salt
- 2 tablespoons light soy sauce
- 1 tablespoon rice vinegar
- 1 tablespoon vegan oyster flavored sauce
- 1 teaspoon toasted sesame oil
- 1 tablespoon neutral oil (I use avocado oil), plus more for frying
- 1 medium carrot, shredded (about 1 cup)
- 1 cup stemmed and finely chopped fresh shiitake mushrooms (4 to 6)
- 1 green onion, white and green parts, finely chopped
- 6 medium garlic cloves, minced
- 2-inch knob of ginger, peeled and minced
- 1 tablespoon cornstarch
- 1 teaspoon mushroom bouillon powder
- 1 teaspoon ground white pepper
- 1 teaspoon sugar
- ¼ cup finely chopped fresh cilantro
- 2 (14-ounce) packages Twin Marquis Dumpling Wrappers

My pork dumpling recipe is probably one of my most popular, and I think I've come up with the vegetarian equivalent. Just because we're opting for vegetables doesn't mean we're holding back on flavor! I love to pack these dumplings with stir-fried vegetables and let all of the excess sauce soak up in vermicelli noodles. These are filled with texture from cabbage, carrots, mushrooms, and bouncy bites of noodles. You can pan-fry or deep-fry these babies, so pick your pleasure!

Prepare the filling: In a medium bowl, soak the vermicelli noodles in enough warm water to cover and set aside until pliable, 15 to 30 minutes. Drain, return to the bowl, and use kitchen shears to cut them into very small pieces.

In a large bowl, mix the cabbage and salt and massage well with your hands to help release its moisture. Set aside until the cabbage has shrunken down, 10 minutes. Rinse twice to remove the salt and use your hands to squeeze out any extra moisture. Return to the bowl and set aside for now.

In a small bowl, mix the soy sauce, rice vinegar, vegan oyster sauce, and sesame oil and set aside.

In a wok or a large skillet, heat 1 tablespoon neutral oil over medium-high heat. When the oil is hot and shimmering, stir-fry the carrot—we're stirring frequently and aggressively here—until they are tender and have shrunk in size just a bit, 2 to 3 minutes. Add the mushrooms, green onion, garlic, and ginger and stir-fry until everything is fragrant and the veggies have softened, about 2 minutes. Sprinkle with the cornstarch, mushroom bouillon powder, white pepper, and sugar. Pour in the sauce and stir constantly for another minute to combine everything and heat through.

Pour the vegetable mixture into the large bowl of cabbage along with the chopped vermicelli noodles and cilantro and stir well using a large spoon. The filling should cool down as it mixes with the cabbage and noodles, but be sure it's cool to the touch before filling the dumpling wrappers.

Assemble the dumplings: Fill a small bowl with water and keep it close by. Place a dumpling wrapper in the palm of your hand and spoon in 1 level teaspoon of the filling. Don't be tempted to add more (you'll want to add more . . . don't do it!), or it will make folding difficult. Using your finger and some water, wet the edge of half of the dumpling wrapper. Fold the wet edge of the dumpling wrapper over and pinch just the center of the halves together. Starting on one side of the pinched area, grab the front half of the wrapper and pleat it toward the center using your pointer finger and thumb. Repeat two more times until you are left with a gap at the end. Push the gap inward to create a heart shape on the end and pinch it shut. Repeat on the other side, pleating toward the center. Set the dumpling aside, cover lightly with a tea towel, and repeat with the remaining wrappers and filling. (See the photos on page 56 for a step-by-step breakdown. If you have any extra wrappers, you can freeze them.)

To pan-fry the dumplings: In a large skillet, add 3 tablespoons of water and heat over medium-high heat. When the water starts to bubble and steam, add as many dumplings as you like, without crowding the pan, pleat side up. Cover and steam until the water has evaporated, 3 to 5 minutes. Remove the lid and drizzle in 2 tablespoons neutral oil and cook until the dumplings easily slide off the pan and are crisp on the bottom, 3 to 5 minutes. Remove to a clean plate and serve. Repeat with as many more dumplings as you like.

To deep-fry: In a wok or large pot, heat 2 inches of neutral oil to 350°F (if you don't have a thermometer, do the wooden chopstick test on page 47). Fit a wire rack into a sheet pan or line a plate or sheet pan with paper towels. Carefully drop in a few of the dumplings, taking care not to crowd the pan and cool the oil, and fry, stirring occasionally, until the skin is golden brown, about 3 minutes. Use a spider or slotted spoon to remove the dumplings to the rack to drain and cool a bit. Repeat with more dumplings, if desired. Transfer to a serving dish and serve.

To freeze: Line a sheet pan with parchment paper. Lay the dumplings flat side down on the pan, without touching, and transfer to the freezer. Once completely frozen, about 8 hours, transfer the dumplings to a resealable bag or container and freeze for up to 6 months. Cook from frozen following the same instructions as if you were to enjoy them immediately, adding another minute or two if needed.

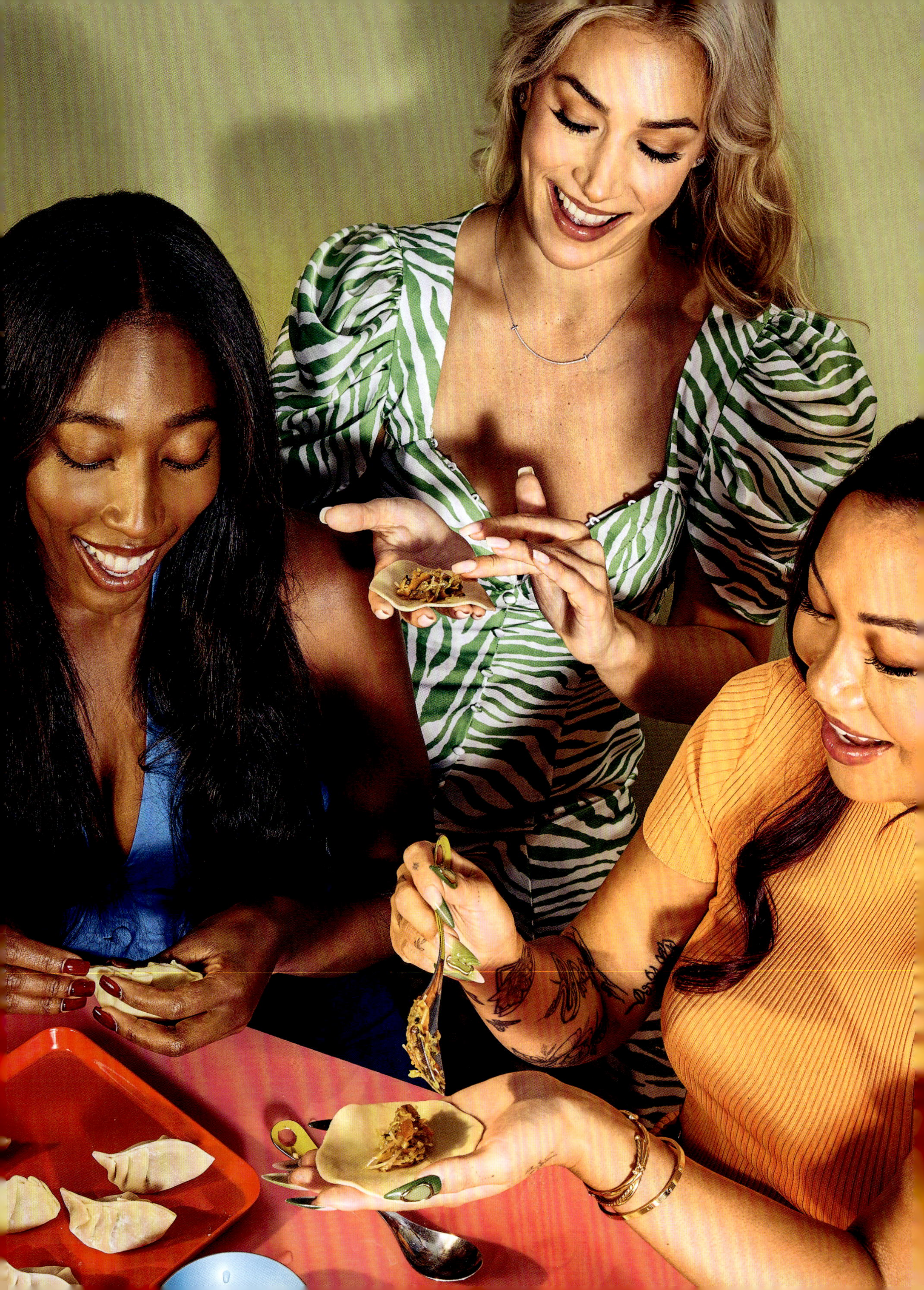

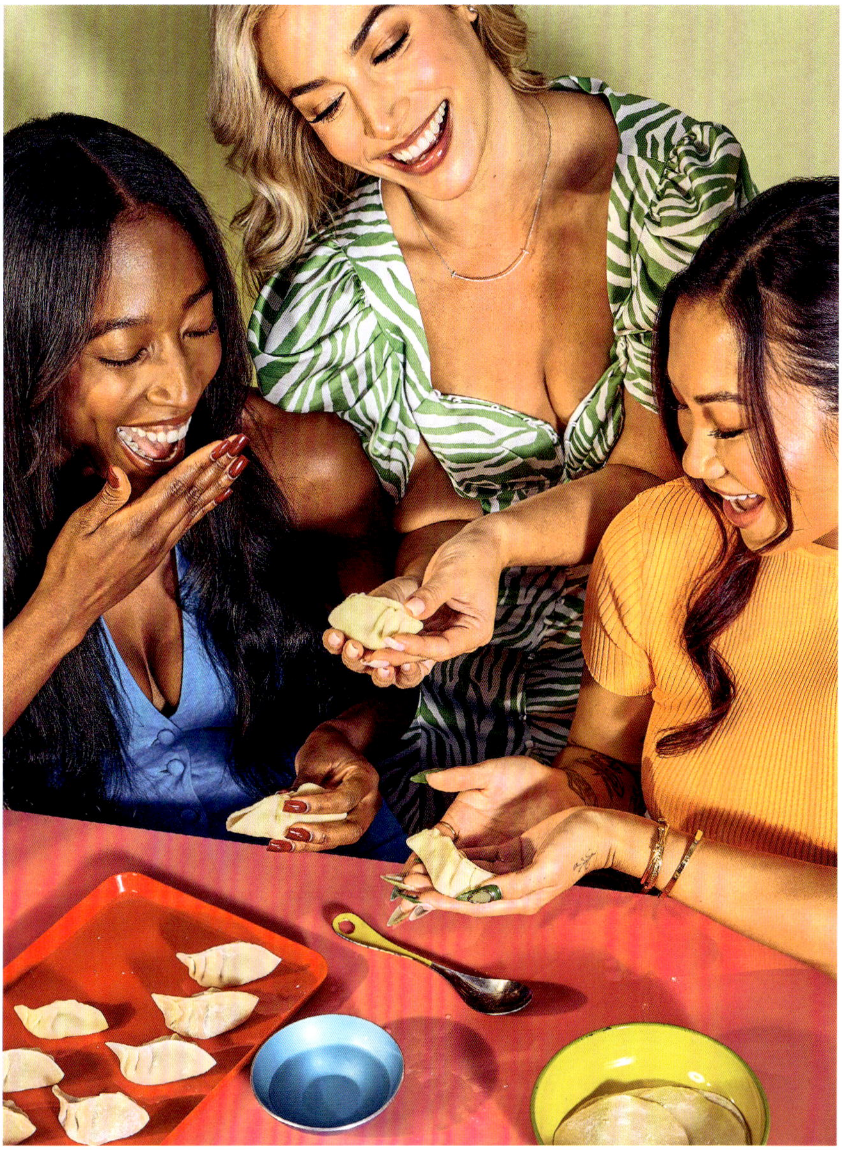

QUICK CHILI-VINEGAR ONIONS

MAKES ABOUT 4 CUPS

1 large yellow onion, thinly sliced

8 fresh bird's-eye chilies, stems removed and thinly sliced

4 teaspoons granulated sugar

1 cup boiling water, or as needed

1 cup distilled white vinegar

While these are technically an optional side, I consider them the necessary component to complete a bowl of hot, steaming pho. These tangy and slightly spicy pickled onions add a bright contrast to the rich, savory broth in 45-Minute Phở Gà (page 92) and Oxtail Phở (page 96). There's a controversial take on adding condiments like sriracha and hoisin sauce directly to pho broth, with some arguing that it can overpower the delicate flavors, so I like to enjoy a plate of chili-vinegar onions smothered in the sauces so that I can enjoy a bit with every bite of noodles. Of course, besides pho, they're a great addition to salads, rice bowls, or just about anything that needs a little extra something.

Using a mandoline, thinly (and safely!) slice the onion. If you don't have a mandoline, use a chef's knife to slice the onion as thin as possible.

In a medium heat-proof 1-quart or larger jar, add the onion, bird's-eye chilies, and sugar. Pour enough boiling water over them to cover the onion halfway (you may not need all of it). Then add the vinegar so that everything is completely covered. Set aside for 30 minutes or let them cool to room temperature, about 1 hour. Close the jar, shake gently, and transfer to the fridge for at least 1 hour or up to overnight to pickle. They'll keep in an airtight container in the fridge for about 2 weeks.

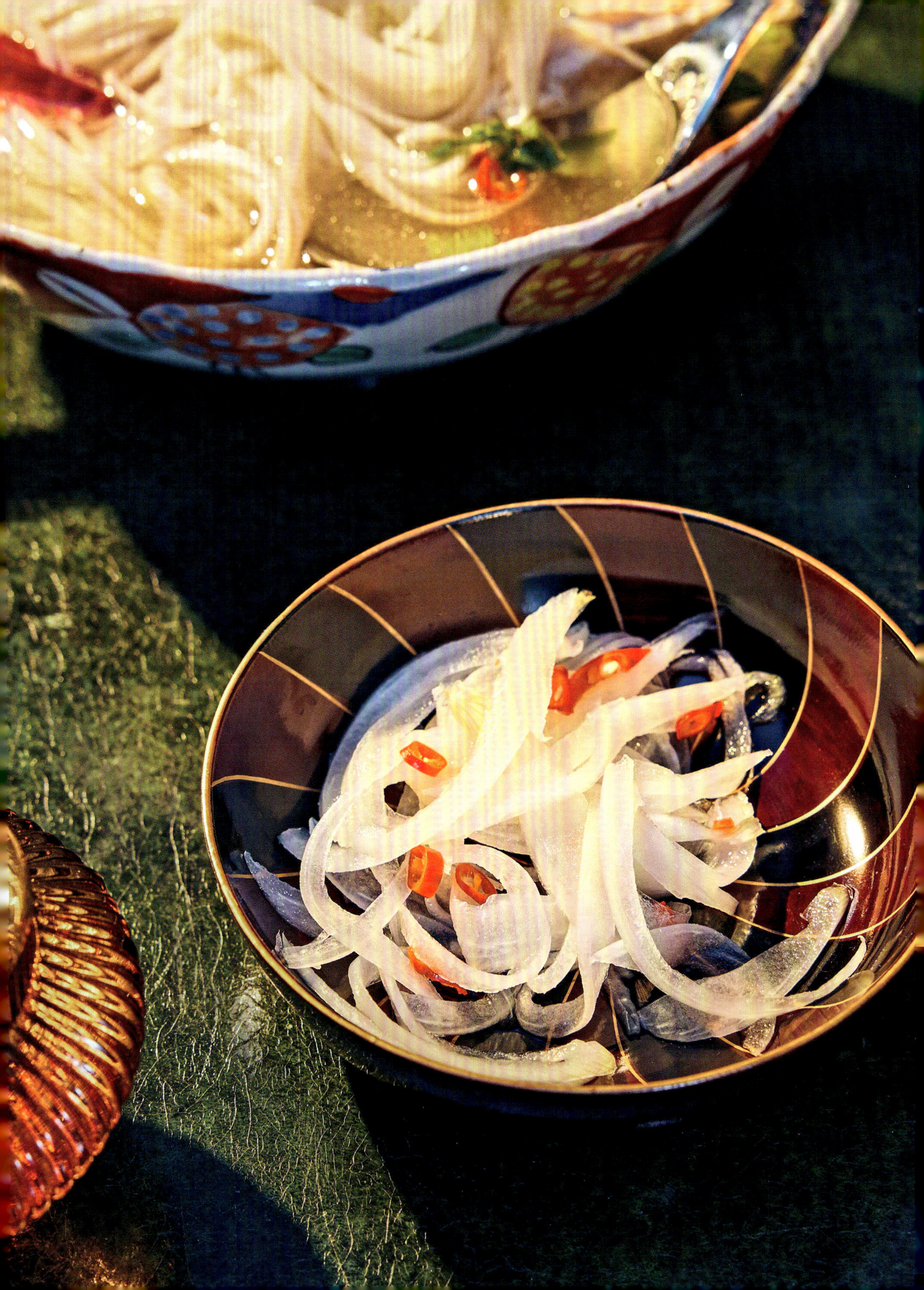

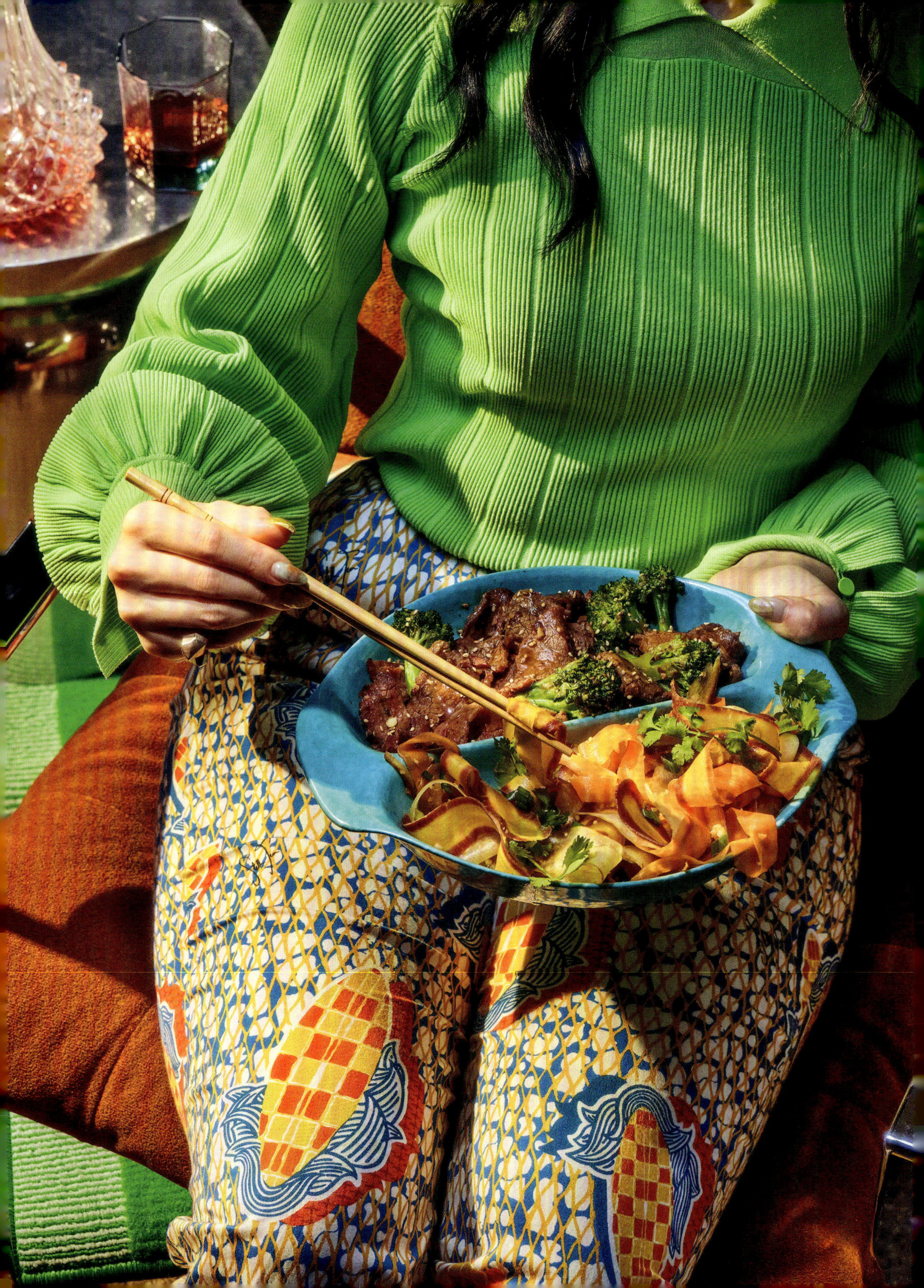

RAINBOW CARROT RIBBON SALAD

SERVES 2

1 pound rainbow carrots (about 6 medium carrots), ends trimmed

½ teaspoon kosher salt

1 large garlic clove, minced

2 green onions, white and green parts, thinly sliced

3 tablespoons rice vinegar

1 tablespoon light soy sauce

2 teaspoons toasted sesame oil

1 teaspoon chili crunch sauce

1 teaspoon toasted sesame seeds, for razzle-dazzle

Fresh cilantro, leaves roughly chopped

One of my favorite activities is visiting the farmers' market and admiring all of the beautiful produce on offer. This recipe was born when I was drawn to the most stunning heirloom carrots, radiating a variety of purple, orange, and yellow colors that I knew needed to be showcased for all their beauty. Raw carrots are known to have several health benefits because of their high fiber content, so this salad tastes even better knowing it's good for you. I love eating them with chopsticks because the ribbons mimic a noodle shape, making this dish feel even more posh. The dressing is made up of garlic, rice vinegar, soy sauce, chili crunch, and sesame oil, soaking into each bite of crispy-crunchy carrot.

Using a vegetable peeler, shave the carrots lengthwise to create long ribbons. In a medium bowl, salt the carrots and massage well. Mix in the garlic, green onions, rice vinegar, soy sauce, sesame oil, and chili crunch sauce. Transfer to a serving dish and garnish with the sesame seeds and as much cilantro as you like.

ACCORDION CUCUMBER SALAD

SERVES 2 TO 4

6 Persian cucumbers

2 tablespoons kosher salt

1 green onion, white and green parts, thinly sliced

2 large garlic cloves, minced

¼ cup rice vinegar

2 tablespoons gochugaru (Korean chili flakes)

2 tablespoons light soy sauce

1 tablespoon toasted sesame oil

1 teaspoon toasted sesame seeds

½ teaspoon sugar

Spiralized cucumber salad is a big step forward in making eating vegetables playful and fun. I promise you this recipe will have you eating an entire pack of cucumbers at a time. These accordion cucumbers are so easy to create, but they are all the more satisfying to eat. All of the seasonings get into every crevice, and each crunchy bite is spicy, garlicky, and fresh. These are amazing year round, but during the summer I always have a batch made to munch on all week. They're the perfect refreshing snack, and all you need are a pair of wooden chopsticks or skewers to help guide where you're slicing the cucumber.

Slice off the ends of one cucumber and discard. Place two wooden chopsticks or skewers along each side of the cucumber. Using a sharp chef's knife, make thin diagonal slits about $1/8$ inch apart from end to end on the cucumber, cutting down until you hit the chopsticks. Flip the cucumber over 180 degrees and repeat the process except make the slits straight across the cucumber. Now when you pick up the cucumber, it should open up like an accordion. Magic! Repeat with the remaining cucumbers.

In a large bowl, combine the cucumbers and salt and gently massage before setting aside for 10 minutes to soften. Rinse the salt off and strain the cucumbers, pat dry with paper towels, and return to the bowl. Gently mix in the green onion, garlic, rice vinegar, chili flakes, soy sauce, sesame oil, sesame seeds, and sugar. Transfer to an airtight container and marinate for at least 30 minutes—but they're best left in the fridge overnight. Enjoy chilled and be sure to spoon extra dressing on top!

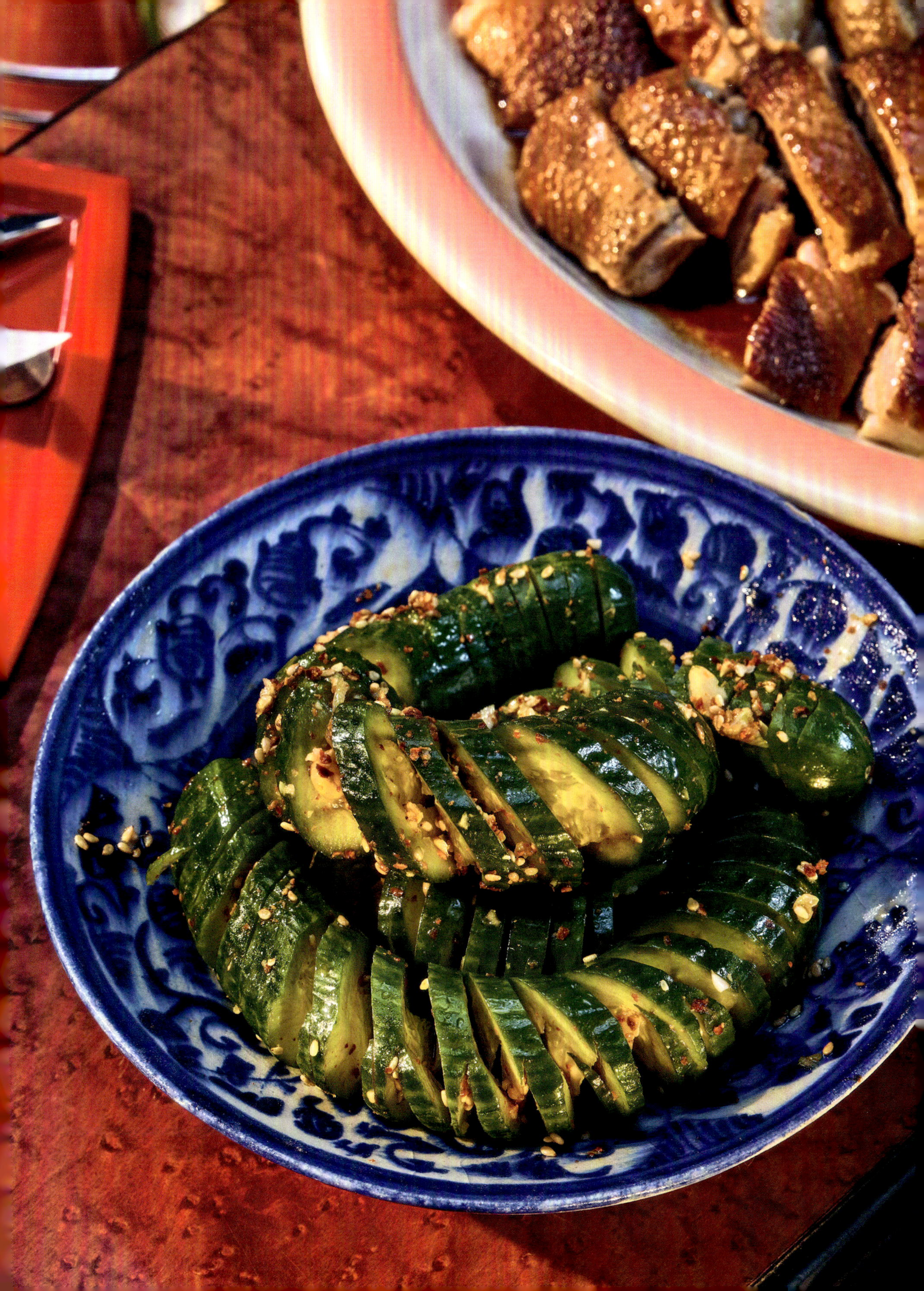

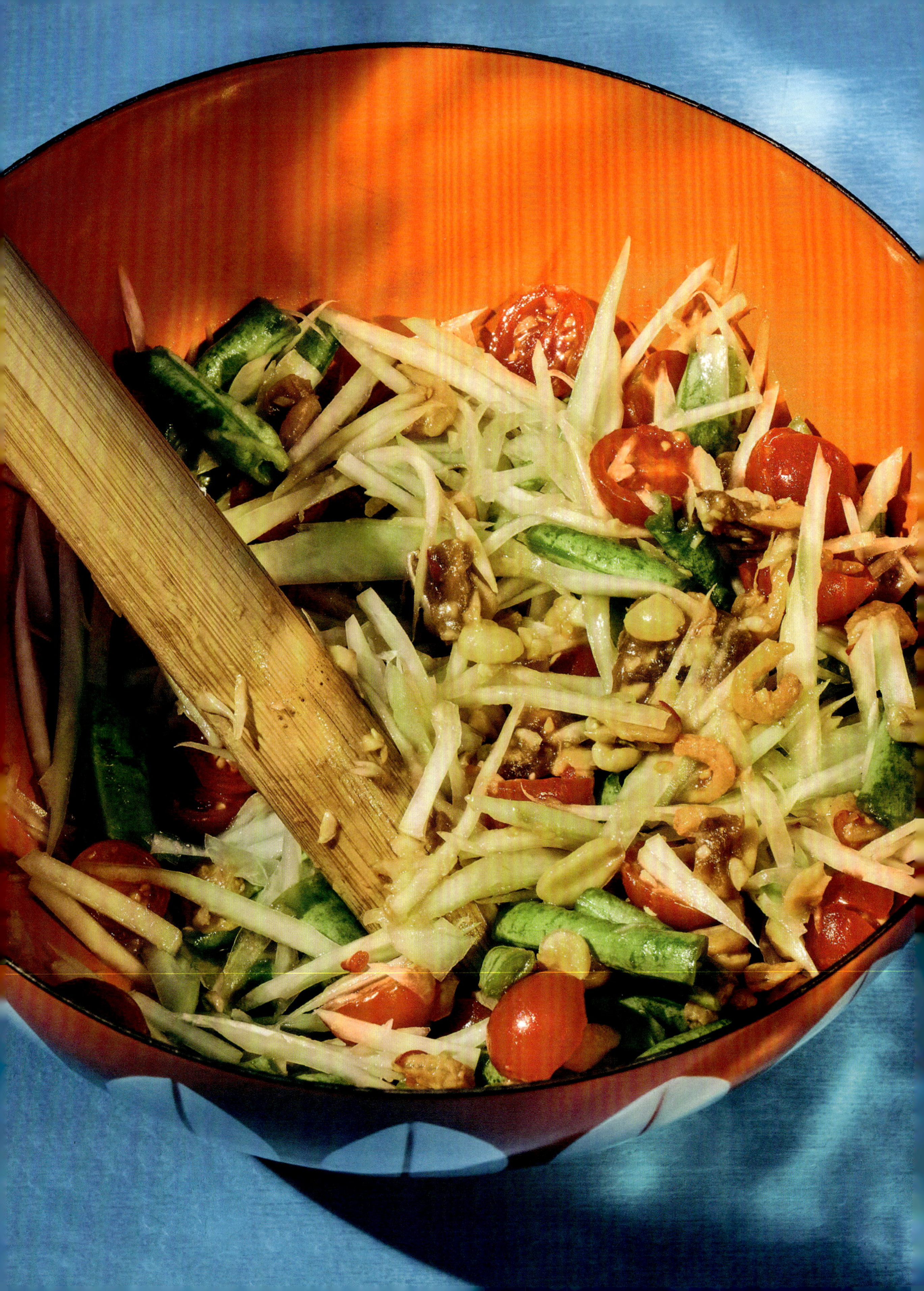

SOM TUM (Papaya Salad)

SERVES 4

12 ounces green papaya, peeled (about ½ medium papaya)

Ice water

4 large garlic cloves

4 fresh bird's-eye chilies, stems removed

4 long beans, torn into 2-inch pieces (see Note)

1 cup halved cherry tomatoes

¼ cup roasted unsalted peanuts

2 tablespoons dried shrimp

3 tablespoons palm sugar or light brown sugar (see page 16)

3 tablespoons fish sauce

2 tablespoons tamarind paste

Juice of 1 lime (about 2 tablespoons)

An order of Thai food is *never* complete without some papaya salad. It's the perfect prelude to warm up the taste buds with its signature pungent, sour, and bright flavors. I always assumed this was difficult to make, and something I could enjoy only when I went out to eat. But when I was in Bangkok, I learned how to make it—and my life changed! I really get into making this with a large mortar and pestle, but if you don't have one, no stress, bestie—you can use a julienne peeler, mandoline, or a good ol' chef's knife, and mash everything in a large bowl.

Cut the papaya into thin matchsticks by hand or using a julienne peeler or mandoline slicer (that's how I do it—easy and fast!). In a medium bowl, soak the papaya matchsticks in ice water for 10 minutes so that they're extra crunchy and any extra starches are removed. Strain and pat dry with paper towels. Set aside.

In a large mortar and pestle, pound the garlic and chilies into a lumpy paste. Add the beans, tomatoes, roasted peanuts, and dried shrimp and roughly pound until everything is broken down but still a chunky mix. Add the palm sugar, fish sauce, tamarind paste, and lime juice and stir together. Mix in the papaya until everything is well combined. Transfer to a serving dish and eat right away.

> **NOTE**
>
> Long beans can be found in Asian markets, but you can always substitute with French beans (a skinnier, lengthier green bean) and increase the quantity to 12 beans.

NOT SWEET TOO

TOO SWEET NOT

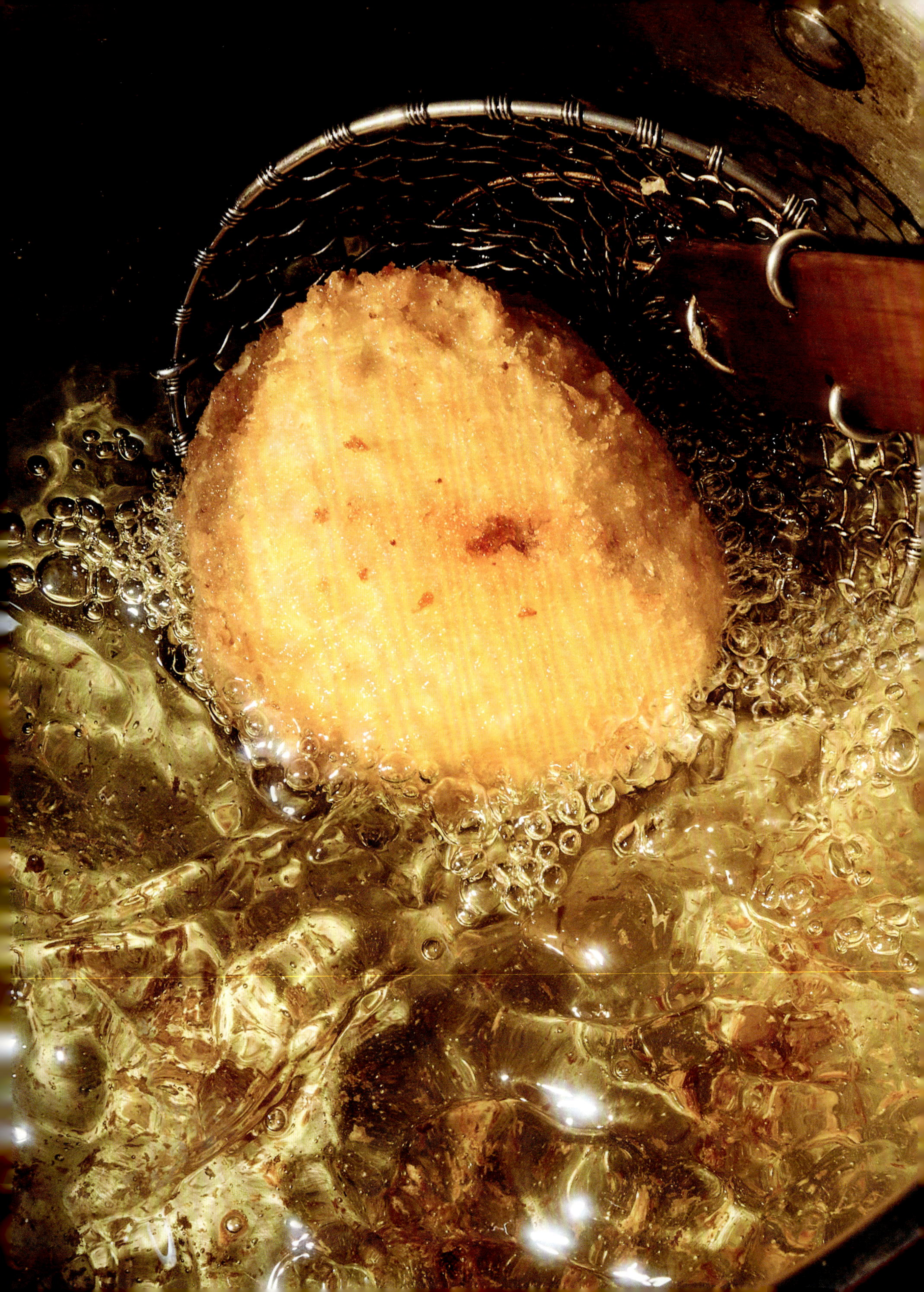

RECIPE LIST

Lazy Girl Mango Sticky Rice
216

Ice Cream Mochi
219

Mom's Apple Cake
223

Ice Cream Tempura
224

Brown Butter Matcha Cheesecake with Cookie Butter Crust
227

No-Churn Pandan Coconut Ice Cream
228

Vietnamese Coffee Tiramisu
231

Thai Tea Tres Leches
232

If you know you know—"not too sweet" is the *ultimate* compliment.

I am the first to admit that I don't have the biggest sweet tooth and I very well could survive without dessert, but I know I'm in the minority, so I've put together the desserts that I turn to when the sweet tooth strikes. They're both the desserts I've eaten as a kid and haven't grown out of, plus some of my all-time faves with bonus Asian flair.

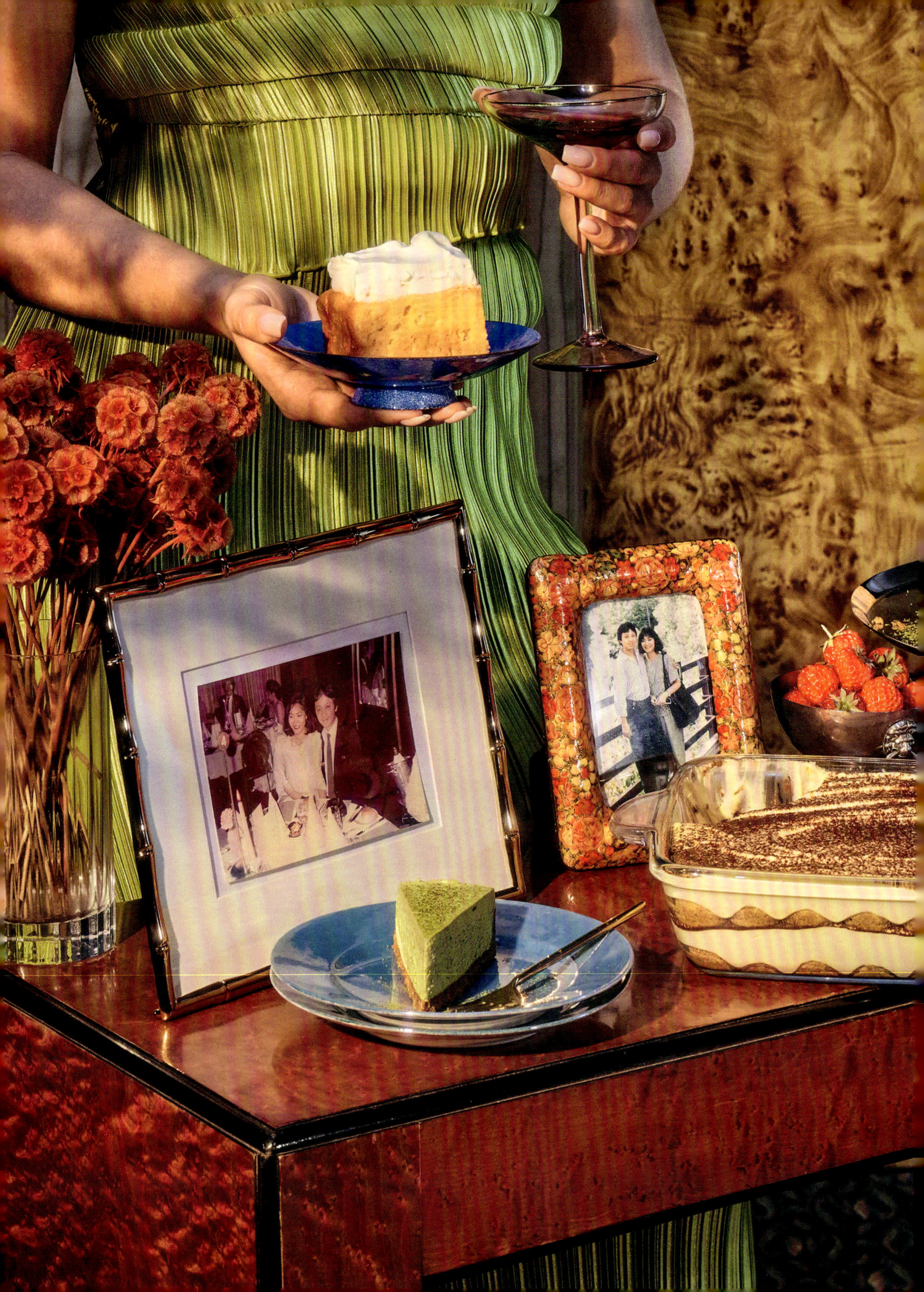

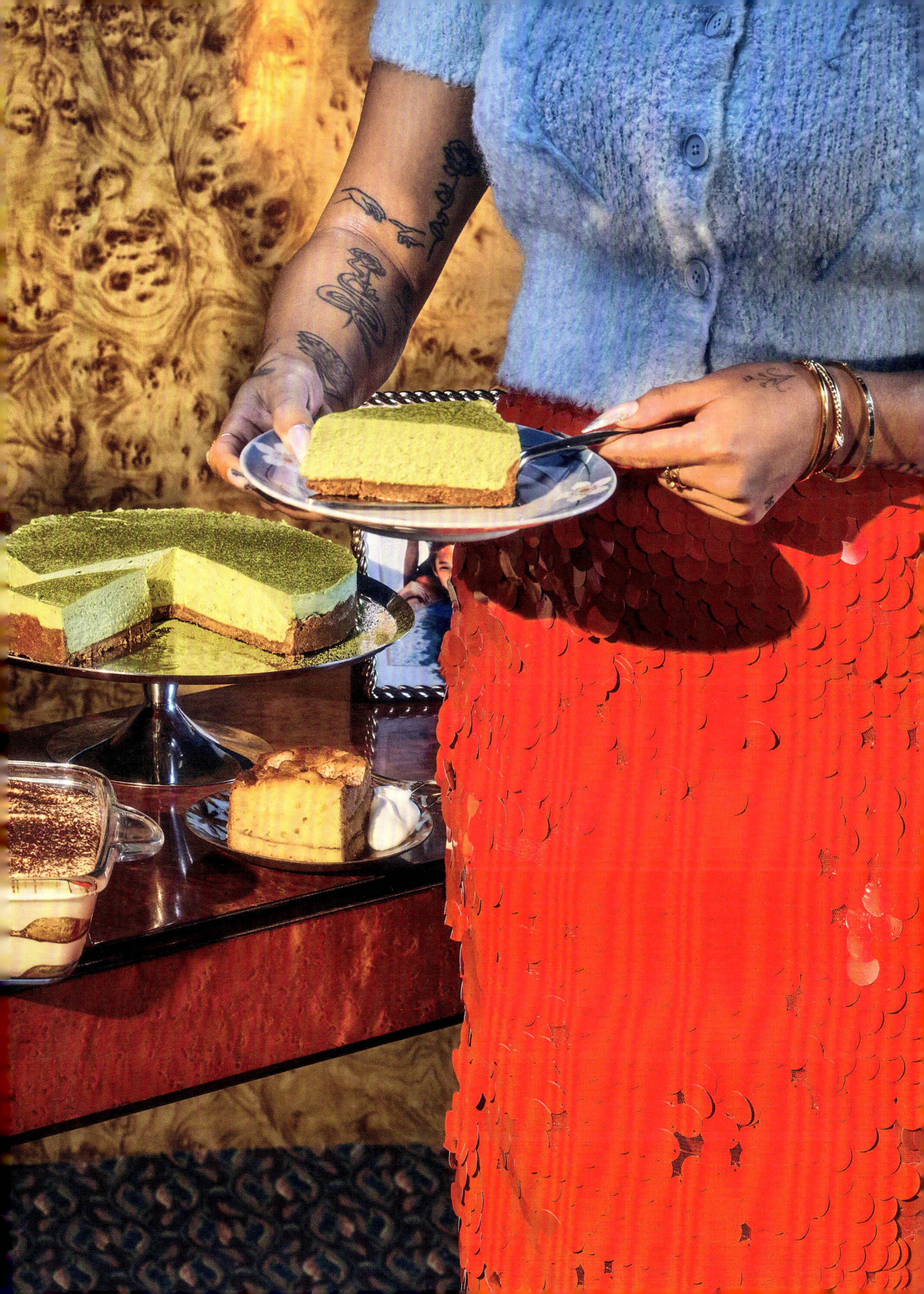

LAZY GIRL MANGO STICKY RICE

SERVES 4 TO 6

1½ cups sweet rice or glutinous white rice

1 (13.5-ounce) can full-fat coconut milk

½ cup sugar

¼ teaspoon kosher salt

2 teaspoons cornstarch

FOR SERVING

4 ripe mangos, sliced

1 teaspoon toasted sesame seeds, for razzle-dazzle

Fresh mint leaves, for razzle-dazzle

This sticky rice is "not too sweet" at its finest. The slightly sweetened coconut milk paired with the buttery mango is truly an ideal combo that satisfies even those who say they don't do dessert. Traditionally in Thailand, where this dish was born, the sweet rice is steamed, but for the sake of laziness, you can easily make it in a rice cooker or on the stove with just a little more water than the usual 1:1 water-to-rice ratio. I could have this dessert every single night. Once you have your first bite, I'm almost positive you'll feel the same.

In the bowl of the rice cooker or in a small pot, rinse the rice 2 to 3 times under cool water until the water runs clear. Add enough cold water to cover the rice and soak for at least 1 hour or up to overnight at room temperature.

Strain, rinse again, then add 2 cups water. If using a rice cooker, cook according to the machine instructions. If cooking over the stovetop, bring the water to a boil over medium-high heat, stir the rice once with a fork, then cover and reduce the heat to low. Simmer for 15 minutes, remove from the heat, and allow it to steam—still covered—for an additional 5 minutes.

In a small pot, whisk the coconut milk, sugar, and salt together and heat over medium-low heat, stirring frequently, until the sugar has dissolved, about 5 minutes.

Using a rice paddle or fork, gently mix ¾ cup of the coconut sauce in with the rice. In a small bowl, mix together the cornstarch and 2 teaspoons cold water until smooth—no lumps!—then stir the cornstarch slurry into the remaining coconut mixture. Warm over medium heat, stirring constantly, to thicken it until it coats the back of a spoon, about 2 minutes.

Serve 1 cup of the cooked sweet sticky rice per person, drizzled with 1 to 2 tablespoons of the coconut sauce. Arrange the mango slices on both sides of the rice and sprinkle with toasted sesame seeds. Garnish with a few mint leaves and enjoy!

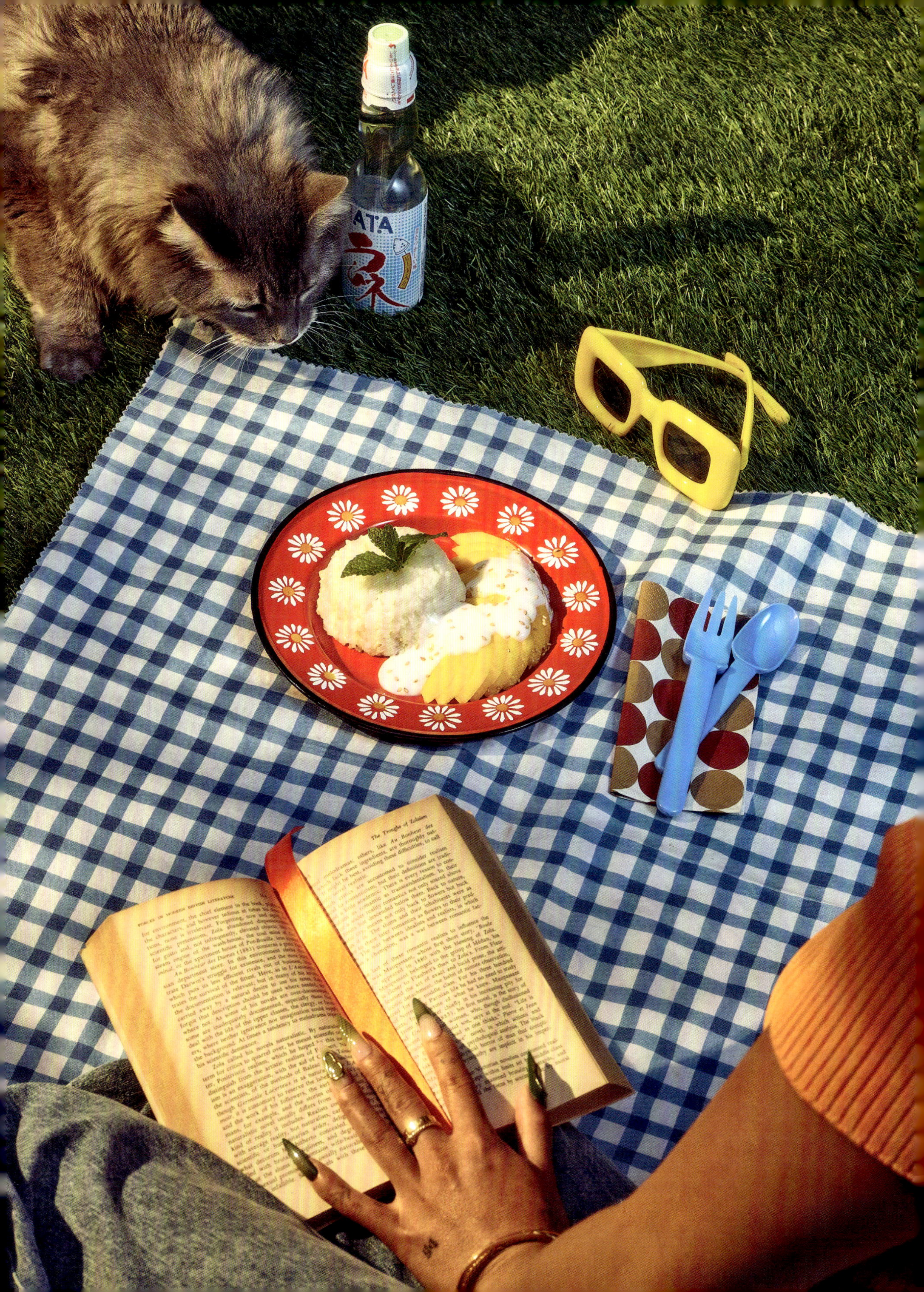

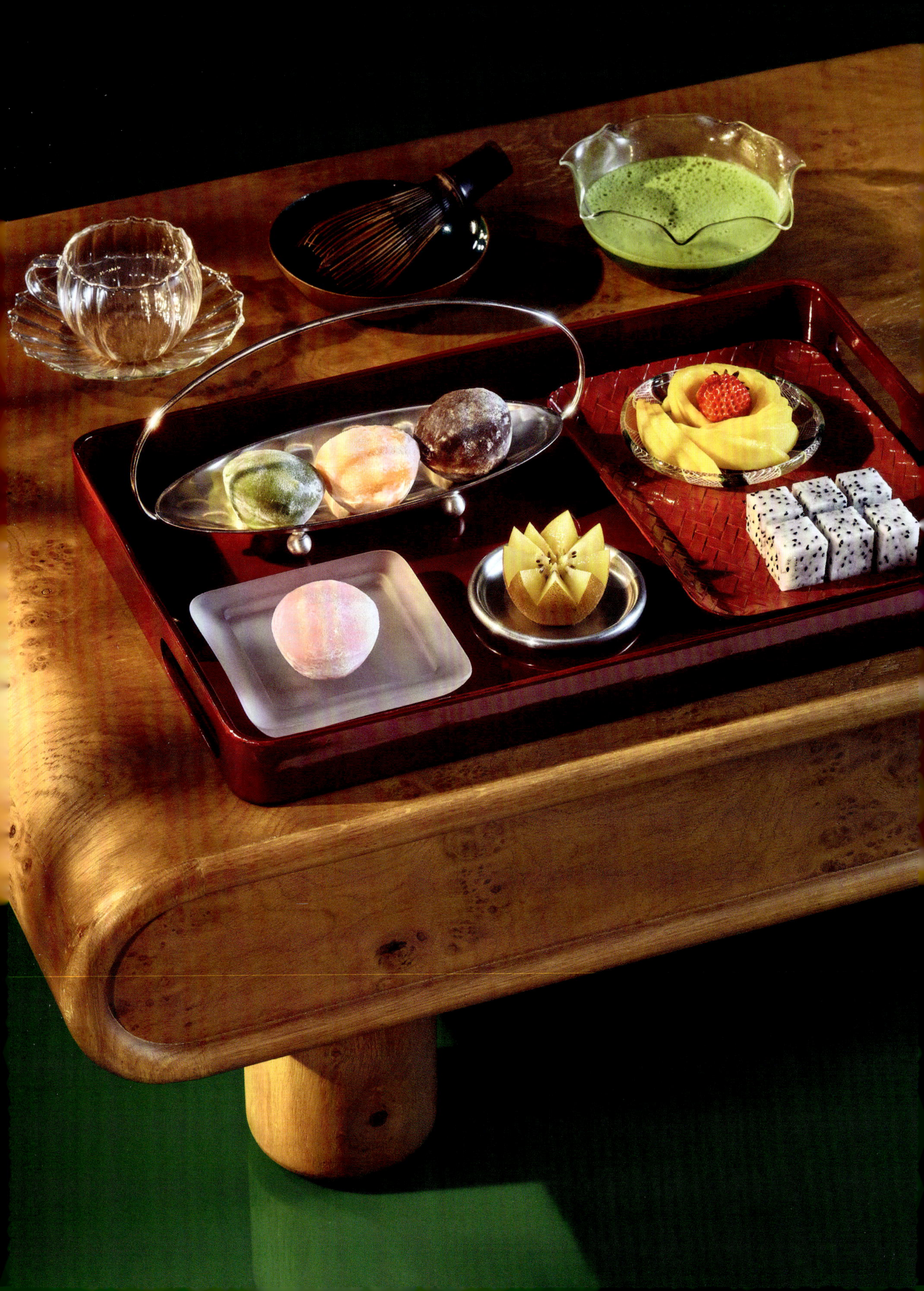

ICE CREAM MOCHI

MAKES 12 INDIVIDUAL MOCHI

Nonstick spray

1 pint ice cream of choice, softened slightly

1 cup glutinous rice flour

¼ cup granulated sugar

2 tablespoons powdered sugar

1 teaspoon flavoring of choice (optional; see page 221), such as matcha powder, cocoa powder, strawberry extract, mango extract, etc.

1 teaspoon hot water (optional)

¼ cup potato starch or cornstarch, for dusting

I've been obsessed with ice cream mochi since I was just a kid—how can anyone resist these bite-size, ice-cream-filled chewy desserts? I love anything that is portioned individually and hand-to-mouth poppable, plus these are the best small-but-mighty-sweet end to a meal. They may *appear* to be daunting, but they're actually so simple to make! I started playing around with the idea when giant mango mochi started trending on TikTok. I realized how easy mochi is to make, so I decided to freeze ice cream in a mini cupcake mold and wrap them with the mochi—and just like that, I had homemade ice cream mochi! The mochi is made with glutinous rice flour, powdered sugar, granulated sugar, and water—and in the *microwave*. (Yes, in the microwave!) After a few minutes, a sticky mochi dough is born. Making mochi at home means you can be creative with flavors and ice cream–mochi combos.

Prepare the ice cream: Spray a mini cupcake or muffin pan with nonstick spray (or get crafty with an ice cube tray!). Pack the ice cream into the molds to the top and freeze until solid, at least 4 hours or up to overnight.

Make the dough: In a microwave-safe medium bowl, whisk the glutinous rice flour, granulated sugar, powdered sugar, and 1 cup warm water until there are no lumps. Cover with a microwave-safe plate and microwave for 1 minute. Use a rubber spatula to knead the mochi, then cover and microwave for another minute. Knead again, then microwave for 30 seconds to 1 minute at a time, until the dough comes together and is smooth, milky-white, and still very sticky, 3 to 5 minutes total, depending on your microwave. If you're flavoring the dough with a liquid flavoring, knead it in now with a spatula until there is an even color. If you're using a powdered flavoring, put it in a small bowl and add 1 teaspoon hot water. Whisk until the powder is dissolved, then knead the mixture into the dough with a spatula until the color is even.

Dust a clean work surface generously with the potato starch and knead the dough to gather into a ball. Dust a rolling pin generously with the starch and roll the dough out to ¼-inch thick or slightly thinner. Use a 4-inch biscuit cutter to cut the mochi. Knead any scraps back into a ball and repeat the process so you get 12 rounds of mochi.

Assemble the mochi: Line a sheet pan with parchment paper. Remove the ice cream from the freezer. (Hot tip: Either set the pan over a tray of ice or leave the tray in the freezer and only take a few ice cream balls at a time out so the rest don't melt.) Take one mochi skin at a time and dust as much of the potato starch off as you can. Wrap the skin over one piece of the ice cream, pinching the ends at the bottom to seal. If you're having trouble, make sure the side of the skin facing you is sticky so the edges will seal. If the mochi skins are sticking to your hands, try cutting a square of plastic wrap and putting the skin, then the ice cream, on top. It will help you shape the mochi without it sticking to your fingers! Transfer to a lined pan and transfer it to the freezer, and repeat with the remaining mochi skins. Freeze until the mochi has solidified, about 1 hour. Thaw slightly before enjoying, or store in the freezer for up to 3 months.

ICE CREAM MOCHI GONE WILD

You can use just about anything to flavor mochi, from powders to extracts, and add food coloring to the dough for a more vibrant color, too. Here are some ideas to start with.

Matcha mochi: Dissolve 1 teaspoon of ceremonial matcha powder in 1 teaspoon hot water and knead with the dough after microwaving. Pair with vanilla or strawberry ice cream, or mango sorbet!

Chocolate mochi: Dissolve 1 teaspoon of unsweetened cocoa powder in 1 teaspoon hot water and knead with the dough after microwaving. Be a true chocolate lover and fill this with chocolate ice cream or get a little crazy and use peanut butter, coffee, or caramel ice cream.

Strawberry mochi: Knead 1 teaspoon of strawberry extract with the dough after microwaving plus 2 drops of red food coloring. Pair with classic vanilla ice cream or maybe get fancy with a lychee sorbet.

Mango mochi: Knead 1 teaspoon of mango extract with the dough after microwaving plus 2 drops of orange food coloring. This is the perfect place to use No-Churn Pandan Coconut Ice Cream (page 228) or go straight-up mango-ho with mango sorbet.

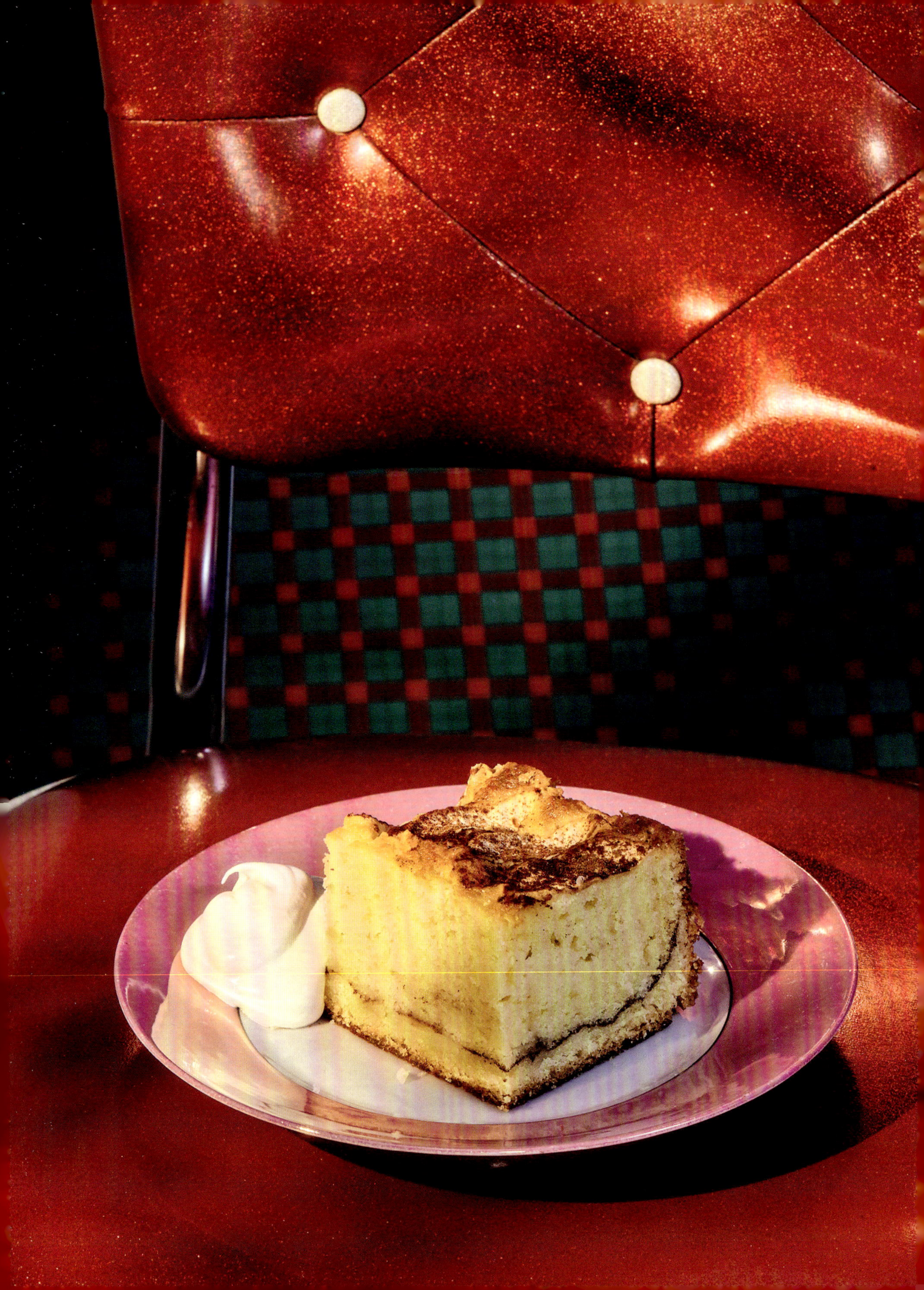

MOM'S APPLE CAKE

MAKES ONE 8-INCH CAKE

Nonstick spray

2 cups all-purpose flour

1 teaspoon baking powder

½ teaspoon baking soda

¼ teaspoon kosher salt

1 cup (2 sticks) unsalted butter, softened

1½ cups granulated sugar

2 large eggs

1 cup sour cream

1 teaspoon vanilla extract

3 small to medium sweet and crisp apples (like Honeycrisp), peeled, cored, and thinly sliced

3 tablespoons ground cinnamon

2 tablespoons powdered sugar

This cake is one of the first things my mom let me help her with in the kitchen. She taught me how to make it from her original recipe written on a beat-up old notecard. We made it for family gatherings and holidays, and truly for as long as I can remember, everyone always went crazy for it. We thought my sister was allergic to apples for the longest time, but one year, she just couldn't hold out any longer and she had to try a few bites . . . thank goodness, she had no reaction, and since then, my mom's apple cake became an essential dessert! The texture resembles a pound cake but is extra moist from the secret ingredient—sour cream. The batter is layered three times with sweet apple slices and a sprinkle of cinnamon. The cake looks as good as it tastes when it's pulled out of the cake pan and dusted with powdered sugar.

Preheat the oven to 350°F. Grease an 8-inch square metal baking dish, then line it with parchment paper, making sure to leave some overhang on the sides.

In a small bowl, whisk together the flour, baking powder, baking soda, and salt and set aside.

In the bowl of a standing mixer fitted with a paddle attachment or in a large bowl if using a hand mixer, cream the butter and granulated sugar on medium-high speed until it turns a pale white, 3 to 5 minutes. Stop the machine and add the eggs 1 at a time, beating on medium speed until completely incorporated in between, just a few seconds. Use a rubber spatula to scrape down the sides and bottom of the bowl, then add the sour cream and vanilla extract and mix on medium-low speed for 1 minute or just until combined.

Add half of the dry ingredients and mix on low speed until incorporated, which only takes a few seconds, then add the remaining dry ingredients just until combined. Scrape down the bottom and sides of the bowl to make sure there's no loose flour.

Spoon one-third of the batter into the pan and use a rubber spatula to spread it into all of the corners and in an even layer. Arrange one-third of the apples nicely, facing in one direction, so they're touching but not overlapping and taking up the entire layer of batter. Evenly sprinkle with 1 tablespoon cinnamon. Repeat the process two more times to create three layers, dolloping the batter in small spoonfuls on top of the cinnamon to help spread it out without disturbing the layer underneath, and being sure to arrange the apples on the top layer the nicest, since this will be the presentation side. You may have some apples left over (chef's treat).

Bake until a toothpick stuck into the center of the cake comes out clean, 50 to 60 minutes. Transfer the pan to a cooling rack and cool until just warm to the touch, 1 to 2 hours. Use the parchment paper to remove the cake from the pan and transfer to a serving dish. Sprinkle with powdered sugar, slice, and serve. Cover any leftovers with plastic wrap and refrigerate for up to 1 week.

ICE CREAM TEMPURA

SERVES 4

1 pint ice cream of choice

Eight 1-inch-thick slices of store-bought pound cake

Neutral oil (I use avocado oil), for frying

1 cup all-purpose flour

1 cup ice-cold water

1 large egg

2 cups panko breadcrumbs

1 tablespoon powdered sugar, for serving

Fried ice cream was a huge, excuse my language, mind f*ck the first time I had it as a kid. I kept wondering, how is the outside fried and crispy but the ice cream still ice cold and hard in the center? The answer is to pack scoops of ice cream into a ball, shape it with plastic wrap, and freeze it long enough to be rock hard. The ice cream is then wrapped in a layer of pound cake that's been rolled out and flattened, frozen again before being dipped in a tempura batter, followed by extra-flakey panko breadcrumbs and flash-fried to a crispy brown delight. Fried ice cream is already magnificent, but add tempura batter for an extra-light and crispy shell and an already stunning dish gets even better.

Cut four 8-inch-square sheets of plastic wrap and lay them on a work surface. Use an ice cream scoop to scoop a ½ cup ball of ice cream onto each sheet of plastic. Wrap each tightly and form the ice cream into a ball. Freeze on a plate for 1 hour (or longer) to harden.

Cut four new 8-inch squares of plastic wrap, then place 2 slices of pound cake next to each other on each square and use a rolling pin to gently roll the slices out to a 6-inch square that's about ⅛-inch thick. Remove the ice cream from the freezer, unwrap them, and place each in the center of the pound cake, on the seam where the two pieces meet. Use the plastic wrap to wrap the pound cake around the ice cream, twist the ends to seal, and shape into a ball, trying to seal any gaps. Place back in the freezer for another 2 hours to harden.

Fill a medium pot with 4 inches of oil or halfway (but don't fill it more than halfway) and heat to 375°F (if you don't have a thermometer, do the wooden chopstick test on page 47). Set a cooling rack over a sheet pan or line a plate with paper towels.

In a medium bowl, whisk the flour, ice-cold water, and egg until there are no lumps. In a separate shallow bowl, add the breadcrumbs. Remove one pound-cake ball from the freezer at a time and dip it into the tempura batter to coat, letting any excess drip off, then dip it directly into the breadcrumbs and roll it around to evenly coat. Immediately (and carefully) drop the ball into the oil, turning to help encourage even browning, until golden brown, about 1 minute. Use a spider to remove to a wire cooling rack and repeat with the remaining ice cream. Dust the powdered sugar over the top and enjoy.

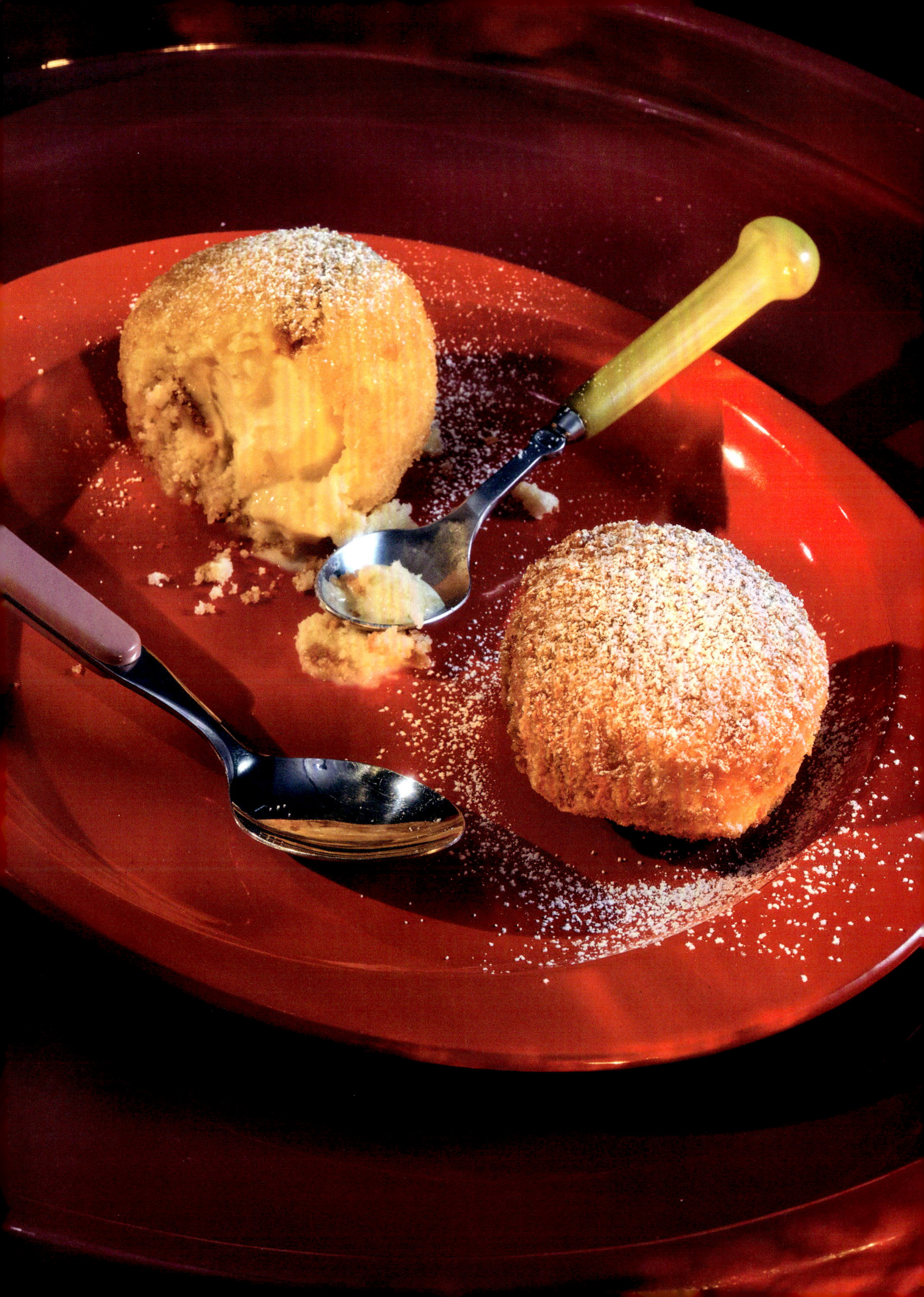

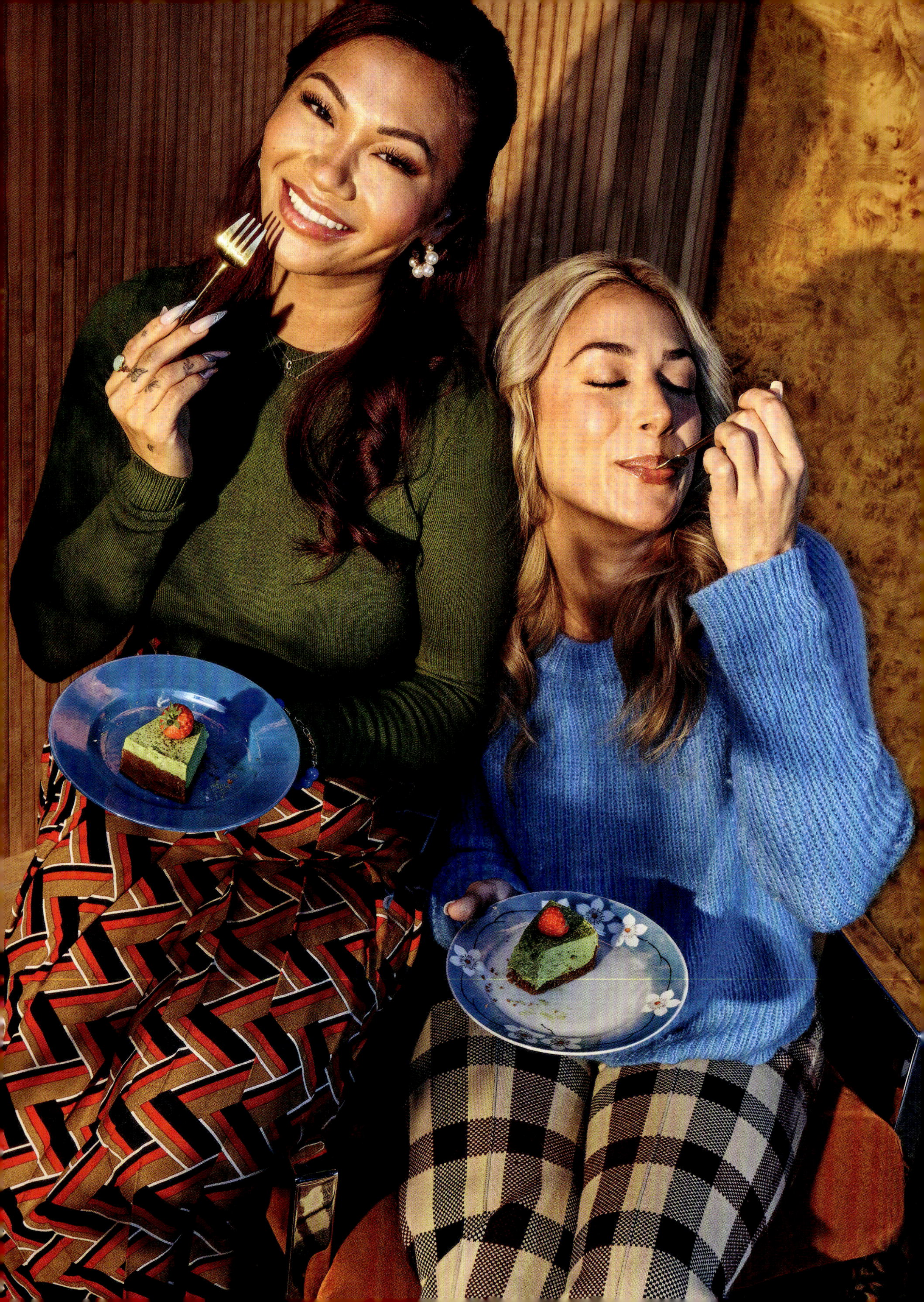

BROWN BUTTER MATCHA CHEESECAKE with Cookie Butter Crust

SERVES 12

8 tablespoons (1 stick) unsalted butter, sliced

1 (8.8-ounce) sleeve of Biscoff cookies

Nonstick spray or softened unsalted butter, for the pan

1 cup heavy cream

24 ounces cream cheese, softened

1 cup powdered sugar

1 teaspoon vanilla extract

3 tablespoons ceremonial-grade matcha powder, plus 1 teaspoon, for razzle-dazzle (Ceremonial grade is the highest quality of matcha and will yield a smoother and sweeter flavor. Look for a deep shade of green!)

I had a cookie butter–matcha latte once that absolutely rocked my world, and it inspired me to pour that into a no-bake cheesecake. And to mimic that cookie butter flavor, I swapped graham crackers for Biscoff and then took it even *further* by browning the butter. The brown butter adds a deep and nutty flavor, and when combined with the cookies, it's irresistibly sexy. We'll be whipping the heavy cream separately before folding it into the whipped, sweetened cream cheese for an extra fluffy cream cheese. Matcha powder is mixed in as well as sprinkled on top for that razzle-dazzle. This combo is incredibly impressive given how little effort it requires.

In a small pot, melt the butter over medium heat stirring frequently with a rubber spatula. Once the butter is melted, continue stirring constantly, and the butter will start to foam. Once the foam subsides, the butter will sizzle and turn golden brown. Keep cooking and stirring until the butter is a deep golden brown and the aroma is nutty, about 8 minutes total. Remove immediately to a spouted bowl or measuring cup and set aside to cool to room temperature, about 30 minutes.

In a food processor, pulse the Biscoff cookies until there are no big chunks. Slowly pour in the butter and pulse until the texture resembles wet sand.

Prepare an 8-inch springform pan with nonstick spray or softened unsalted butter. Pour the cookie mixture into the base of the pan and use the back of a spoon or measuring cup to spread and pack the cookies down evenly across the bottom and 1½ inches up the sides. Set aside.

In the bowl of a standing mixer fitted with the whisk attachment or a large bowl if using a handheld mixer, start to whip the heavy cream on medium speed until it's no longer runny, 1 to 2 minutes, then raise the speed to high and whip until stiff peaks form (if you pull out the whisk, the cream should hold its shape), about 1 minute. Transfer to a large bowl and set aside.

Return to the bowl of the standing mixer (no need to clean it!) and whip the cream cheese, powdered sugar, and vanilla extract on medium speed until the mixture is light like a mousse, about 3 minutes. Scrape the sides of the bowl with a rubber spatula, then sift in the matcha powder. Whip on low to incorporate and then increase the speed to medium and beat until the matcha is fully combined, about 30 seconds. Use a rubber spatula to spread the mixture over the cookie crust in an even layer, flattening the top. Cover the cheesecake with plastic wrap and refrigerate to set for at least 8 hours, or up to overnight.

When you're ready to serve, sift the remaining 1 teaspoon of matcha over the top of the cheesecake, run a knife around the sides to make sure it's not sticking to the pan, and remove the side of the springform pan. Use a wet knife to slice into wedges, and enjoy!

NO-CHURN PANDAN COCONUT ICE CREAM

SERVES 6 TO 8

½ cup full-fat coconut milk

6 whole pandan leaves, thawed (see Note)

1 cup heavy cream

1 (14-ounce) can sweetened condensed milk

Pandan and coconut go together like two peas in a pod. Pandan leaves have a fragrant floral flavor resembling jasmine with notes of coconut and vanilla, which, when combined with coconut, is simply beautiful. I recently traveled to the stunning Maldive Islands where the sun was so powerful it was unlike any heat I've ever experienced. One of the chef's treats that were handed out on the beach were pandan coladas, and it was the most refreshing, creamy drink that I couldn't stop thinking about it. I decided to play around and turn it into a frozen dessert since I'm a sucker for ice cream. Contrary to belief, you don't need an ice cream churner to make ice cream at home. Ice cream can always be made with heavy cream and sweetened condensed milk with any added flavors. Instead of churning, we'll whip the heavy cream until stiff peaks form to create that fluffy texture. Then whisk in the sweetened condensed milk and the pandan-infused coconut milk and freeze overnight. Done.

In a blender, blend the coconut milk and pandan leaves until the leaves are broken down and you have a chunky paste. Pass the mixture through a fine mesh sieve to strain, using a rubber spatula to press any extra juice out. Discard the solids.

In the bowl of a standing mixer fitted with the whisk attachment or a large bowl if using a handheld mixer, whisk the heavy cream on medium-high speed until stiff peaks form (if you pull out the whisk, the cream should hold its shape), about 2 minutes. Reduce to medium speed and whisk in the sweetened condensed milk and pandan-infused coconut milk, mixing just until combined and it's a smooth light-green color, 1 to 2 minutes. Transfer the mixture to a loaf pan and freeze until firm, at least 8 hours or up to overnight. To serve, scoop and enjoy immediately!

> **NOTE**
>
> Pandan leaves can be found at most Asian markets in the frozen section, but you can also substitute with 2 to 3 tablespoons of pandan extract and skip the blending step. Sometimes the leaves are sold in pre-cut sections, so if you have trimmed pieces, use eighteen 6-inch or so pieces.

精記蛋卷王

CHINESE COOKIE ROLLS

NET WT .500 g.

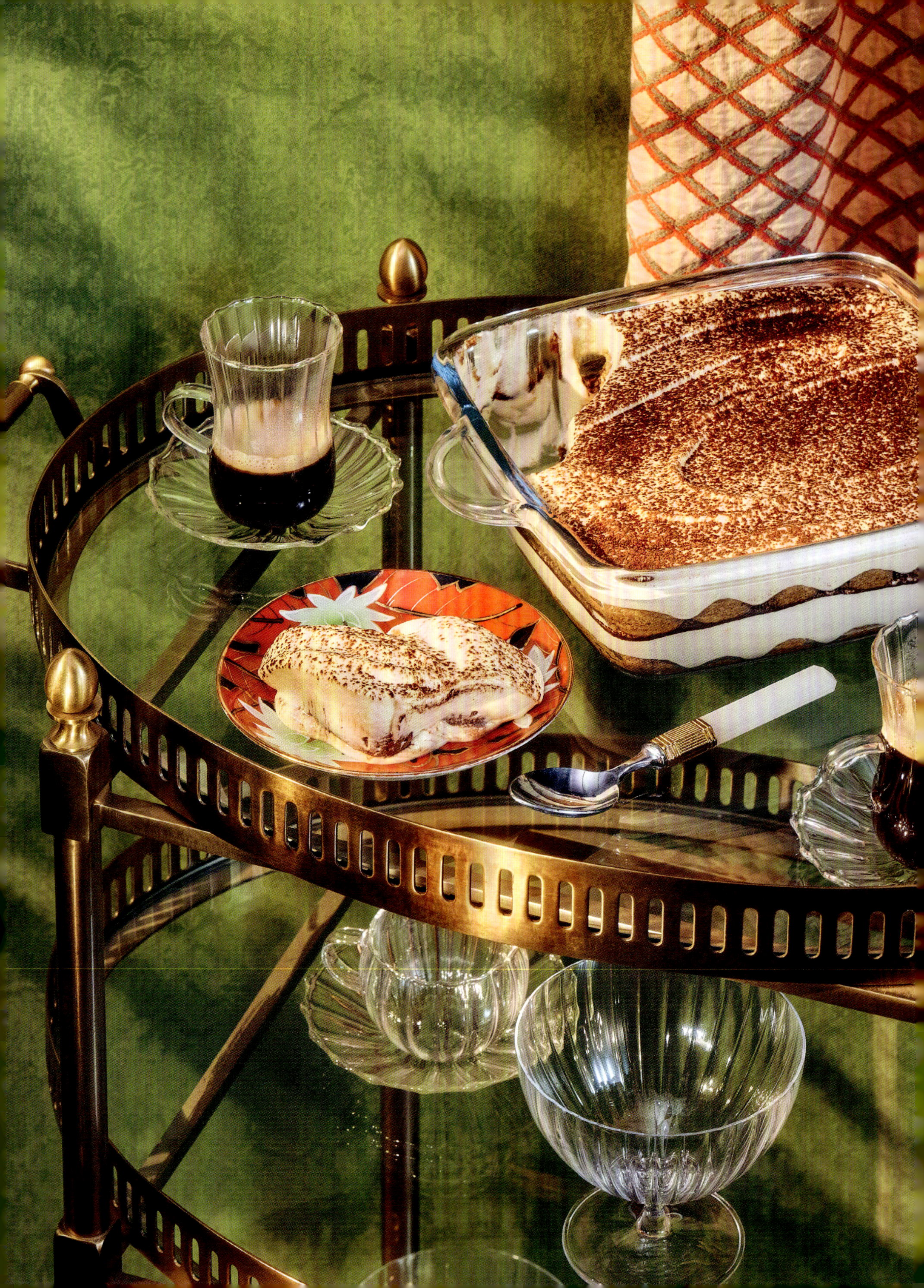

VIETNAMESE COFFEE TIRAMISU

SERVES 8

3 tablespoons ground Vietnamese coffee (preferably Trung Nguyen brand)

Boiling water, as needed

1 cup heavy cream

4 large egg yolks

½ cup sugar

1 pound mascarpone cheese, softened

¼ cup Frangelico (optional)

1 tablespoon vanilla extract

30 Savoiardi ladyfingers

3 tablespoons unsweetened cocoa powder

Over the years, I've kind of become a coffee snob—and am totally obsessed with different techniques of brewing and making coffee an *experience*. My morning grind begins with a literal grind of my own coffee beans and my gooseneck tea kettle set at the perfect temperature to brew. Vietnamese coffee is undoubtedly one of the strongest, richest cups of coffee on the market. It comes from Robusta beans, which have a higher caffeine content than Arabica; that plus the slow pour-over drip technique concentrates the coffee even more. You can make the coffee using a French press, but I highly recommend using a Vietnamese coffee filter, or phin, for brewing the best cup of drip coffee. You can find them on Amazon. Tiramisu is already amazing, so adding a good strong cup of Vietnamese coffee makes this even more out of this world.

If using a Vietnamese coffee filter: Place the phin over a mug followed by the chamber. Pour the coffee grounds into the chamber, then insert the press, gently pressing the coffee grounds to flatten. Bring a kettle or small pot of water to a boil (205°F if you want to be obsessive about it), then pour enough water to cover the press and wait 1 minute for the coffee to drip down. Once it is done dripping, fill the chamber up completely with the hot water again and wait for the coffee to stop dripping. Discard the coffee grounds and leave the coffee to cool. This should yield 1 to 1½ cups of coffee.

If using a French press: Add the coffee grounds into the French press and pour just enough boiling water to cover the coffee grounds to bloom, about 30 seconds. Pour in 1 cup boiling water, stir, and steep until the coffee is saturated, 4 minutes. Press, strain, and cool.

In the bowl of a standing mixer fitted with the whisk attachment or a medium bowl if using a handheld mixer, whisk the heavy cream on medium-high speed until stiff peaks form (if you pull out the whisk, the cream should hold its shape), about 2 minutes. Set aside.

In a separate large bowl, whisk the egg yolks with the sugar by hand or with a handheld mixer (no need to clean the attachment!) on medium speed until the mixture becomes a pale yellow, about 2 minutes. Mix in the mascarpone cheese, Frangelico (if using), and vanilla extract until combined, about 30 seconds. Using a rubber spatula, gently fold in the whipped cream just to combine, being careful not to deflate the cream.

Pour the cooled coffee into a shallow dish that can fit a ladyfinger flat. One at a time, quickly dip (we're not soaking here, besties, so when I say quickly, I mean move *fast*) both sides of the ladyfinger into the coffee and place it in a 9-inch square baking dish. Repeat until the entire bottom of the baking dish is filled—you may need to cut some of the ladyfingers to fill the space evenly.

Spread half of the mascarpone mixture evenly over the ladyfingers, then sift half the cocoa powder to cover the layer completely. Repeat the process with another layer of dipped ladyfingers, mascarpone, and cocoa powder. Cover and refrigerate for at least 8 hours or up to overnight to set and let the flavors mingle before enjoying.

THAI TEA TRES LECHES

MAKES ONE 8-INCH CAKE

Nonstick spray or butter, for the pan

CAKE BATTER

4 large eggs, whites and yolks separated

2 cups cake flour

1 teaspoon baking powder

½ teaspoon kosher salt

8 tablespoons (1 stick) unsalted butter, softened

⅔ cup granulated sugar

¾ cup whole milk

THAI TEA MILK SOAK

1 (14-ounce) can sweetened condensed milk

1 (12-ounce) can evaporated milk

¼ cup whole milk

⅓ cup unsweetened Thai tea mix

WHIPPED CREAM

2 cups heavy cream

½ cup granulated sugar

1 teaspoon vanilla extract

Sorry, lactose-intolerant friends, I know it may be hard to resist, but you might need to sit this one out—the name of this Latin American dessert comes from the blend of three milks (sweetened condensed, evaporated, and whole milk) soaked into a light sponge cake to make the best and most moist cake there is. We're kicking this classic up a notch with the simple addition of Thai tea mix, which is a black tea blend with notes of warm spices like cardamom, cloves, and star anise. The milk mixture is soaked into the cake, which is poked aggressively with a fork to create tiny drinking pockets. The ingredients for the batter are simple, but we'll whip the egg whites separately to make the cake extra fluffy so it doesn't become dense watering cake gets topped with homemade whipped cream.

Preheat the oven to 350°F. Grease an 8-inch baking dish and line it with parchment paper, making sure to leave some overhang on the sides.

Whisk the egg whites for the cake batter: In a standing mixer fitted with the whisk attachment or a large bowl if using a handheld mixer, whisk the egg whites on medium speed until medium peaks form (if you pull out the whisk, the egg should almost hold its shape, but still fall over), about 3 minutes. Transfer to a medium bowl.

Mix the dry ingredients: In a separate medium bowl, whisk together the cake flour, baking powder, and salt and set aside.

Make the cake batter: No need to clean the bowl of the standing mixer, but do switch to the paddle attachment. Cream the butter and sugar on low to combine, then increase to medium-high until it turns a pale white, 3 to 5 minutes, stopping occasionally to scrape the sides and bottom of the bowl with a rubber spatula. Add the egg yolks all at once and mix on medium speed until well combined, about 30 seconds.

Stop the mixer, add one-third of the dry ingredients, and mix on low just until combined, a few seconds, then pour in half the milk and beat just until combined. Repeat adding the dry, the remaining milk, and then the remaining dry ingredients for another few seconds—don't overmix here! Remove the bowl from the mixer and use a rubber spatula make sure there's no flour hiding on the bottom, then gently fold the egg whites into the cake batter just until combined but no more, we're not losing all that hard work and fluffiness we (the mixer) did.

Bake the cake: Use a silicone spatula to gently scrape the batter into the prepared baking dish and spread it evenly. Bake until a toothpick comes out clean when you poke it into the center of the cake, 25 to 30 minutes. Remove from the oven and cool to room temperature in the pan, 1 to 2 hours.

(recipe continues)

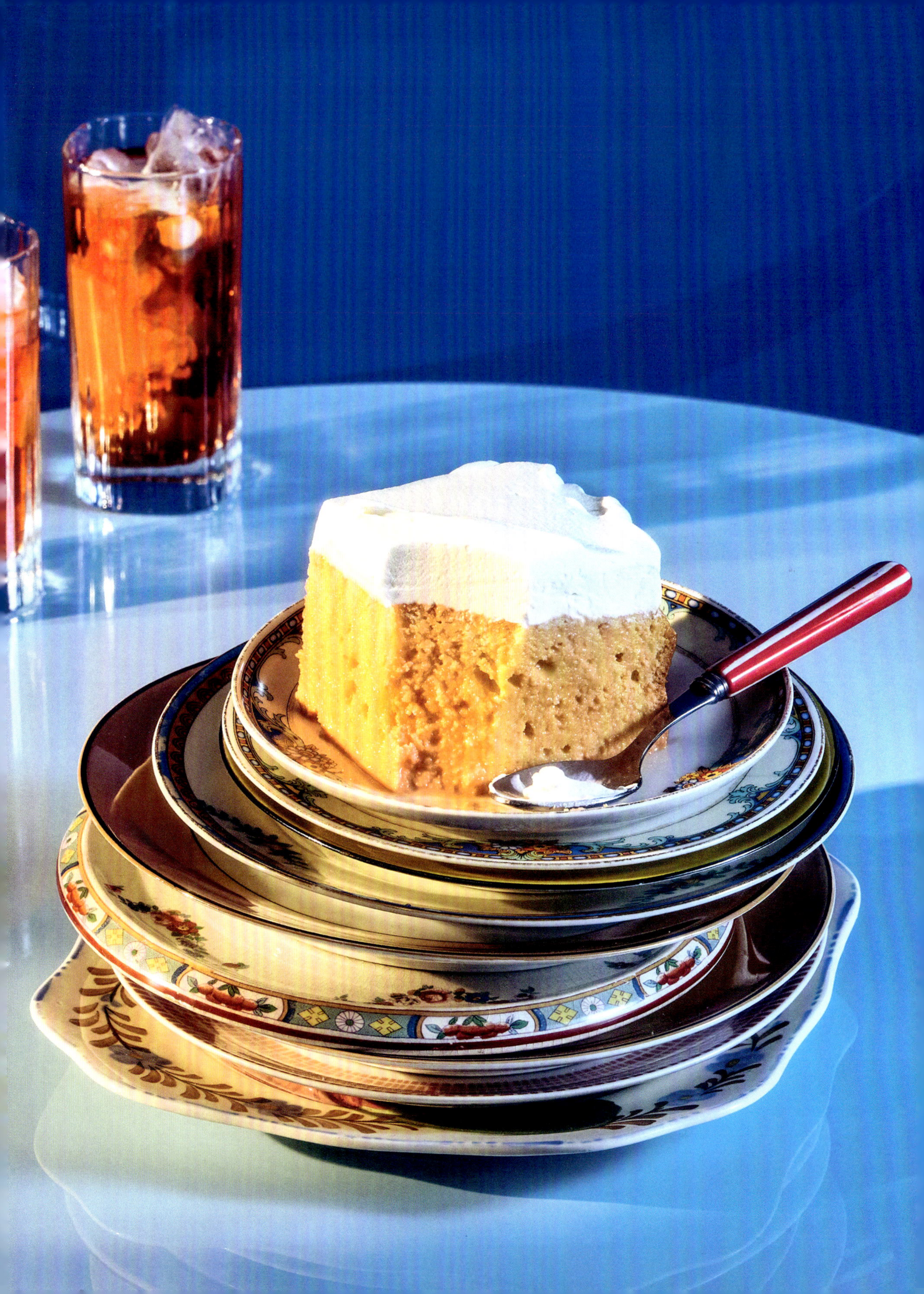

Prepare the Thai tea milk soak: In a small saucepan over medium heat, whisk the sweetened condensed milk, evaporated milk, and whole milk until well combined and heat until simmering, about 5 minutes. Whisk in the Thai tea mix, then remove from the heat, cover, and steep until it's a burnt-orange color and the flavors are married, about 10 minutes. Strain through a fine mesh sieve to remove the solids and don't press them. Transfer to a heat-safe dish and cool for about 15 minutes.

Pour the milk over the cake: Keeping the cake in the baking dish, use a fork to poke the surface of the cake (don't be shy, poke violently and copiously). Slowly pour the milk soak over the entire cake. Cover with plastic wrap and refrigerate for at least 1 hour or up to overnight.

Make the whipped cream: In a standing mixer fitted with a whisk attachment or a large bowl if using a handheld mixer, whisk the heavy cream, sugar, and vanilla extract on medium speed just until combined and starting to thicken, about 2 minutes. Increase to high speed until stiff peaks form (if you pull out the whisk, the cream should hold its shape), another 1 to 2 minutes.

Spread the whipped cream over the entire surface of the cake. Use the parchment paper to help remove the cake to a cutting board. Slice and serve!

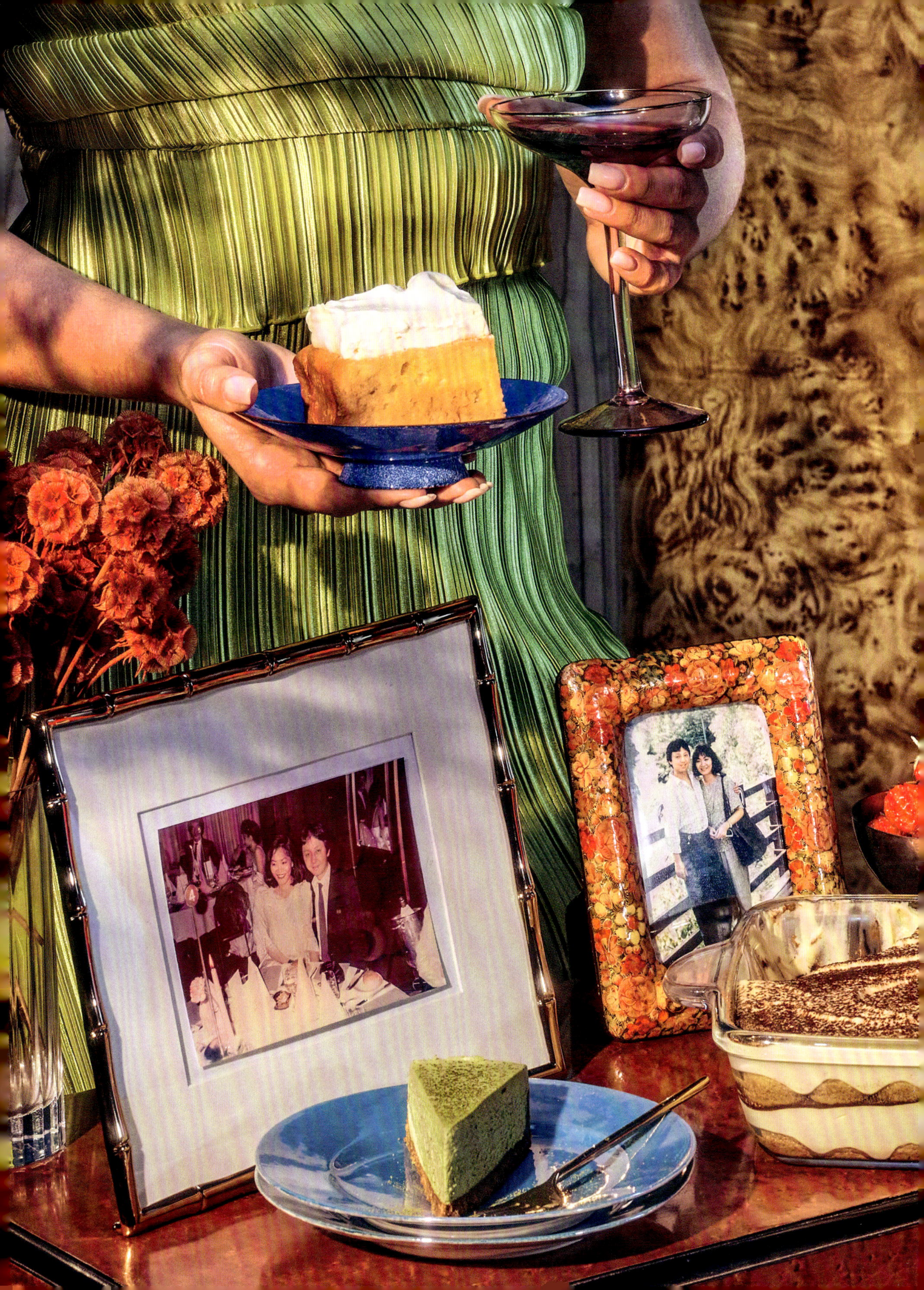

WHOLE LOTTA BASICS

WHOLE LOTTA BASICS

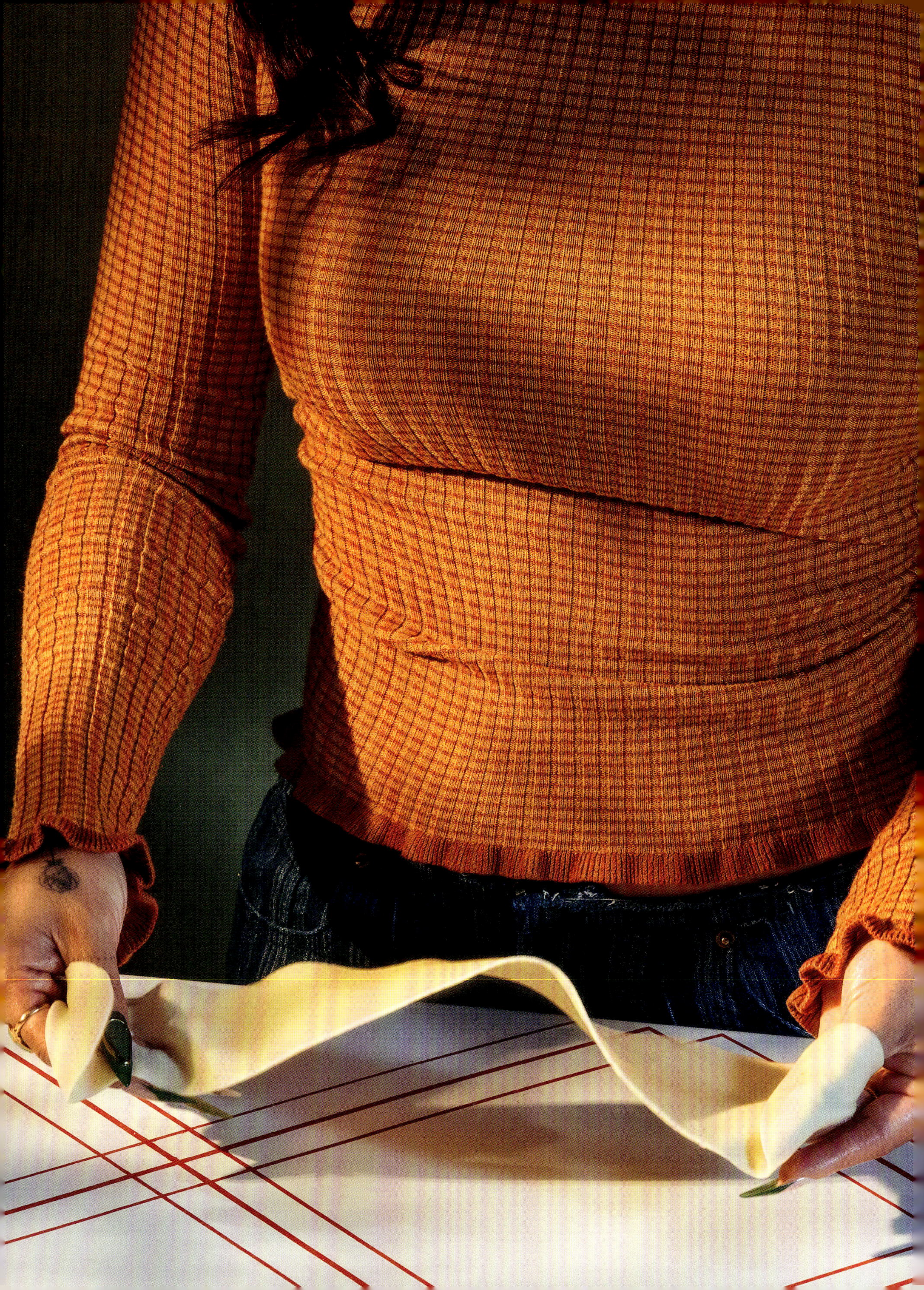

RECIPE LIST

The Perfect Steamed Rice
242

Hand-Pulled Noodles
243

Homemade Dumpling Wrappers
247

Homemade Wonton Skins
248

Homemade Flat Rice Noodles
251

Wet-Wet Sauce
255

Ginger Scallion Sauce
256

Sweet Chili Sauce
259

Nước Chấm
260

Peanut Dipping Sauce
263

We're covering a bunch of basics

from homemade dumpling wrappers to my favorite sauces. These are great to integrate into other recipes or keep in mind when you can't make that trip to the Asian market. Making an *entire* meal from scratch is a flex, and this chapter will help you achieve that.

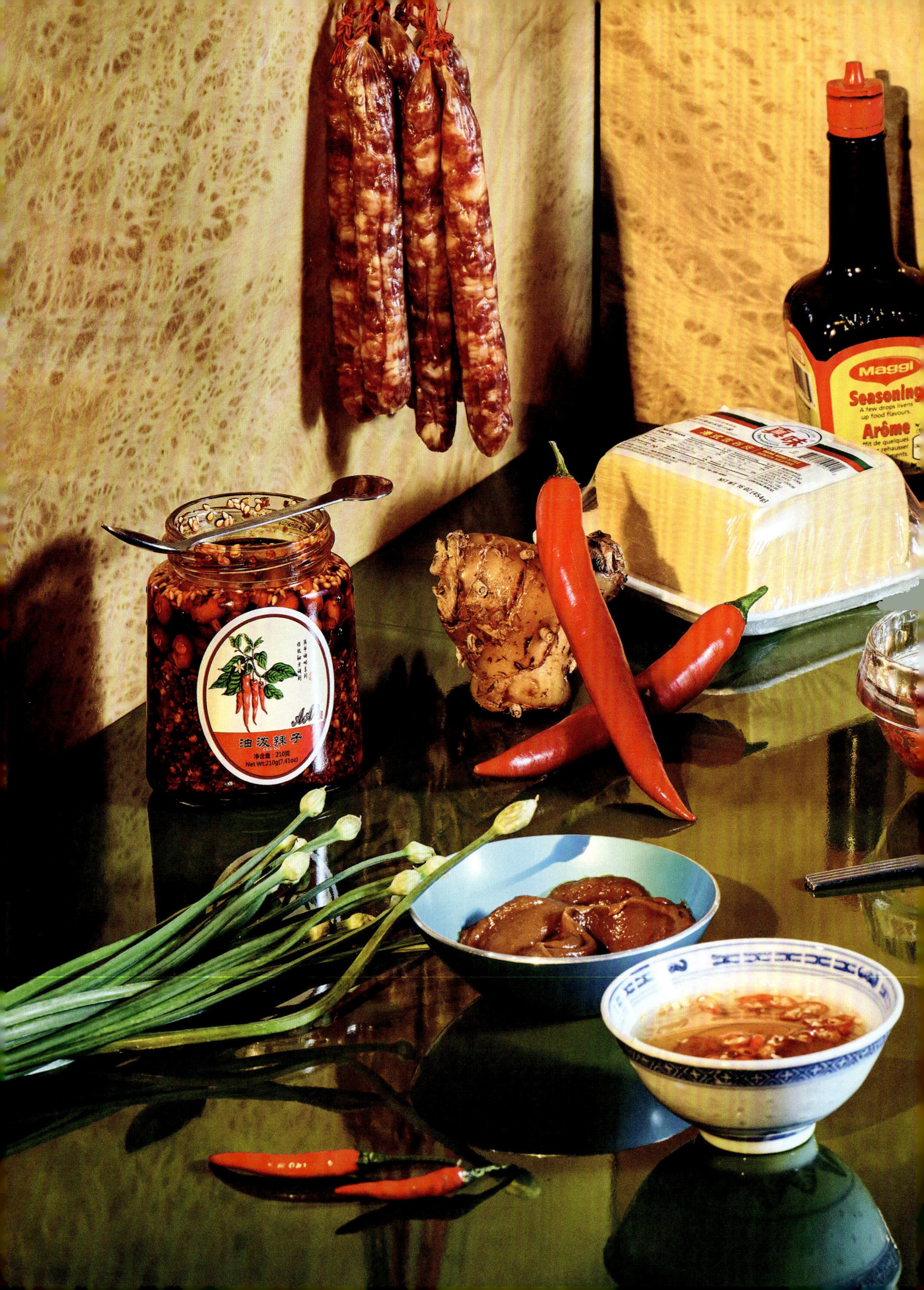
Maggi
Seasoning
Arôme
油泼辣子

李錦記
LEE KUM KEE
特級
鮮味生抽
REMIUM SOY SAU
First Draw Naturally
NET 16.9 fl oz (1.05 pt)
KADOYA
純淨上等
麻油
ASTED SESAME OIL
PRODUCT OF JAPAN
5.5 FL.OZ.
(163ml)

THE PERFECT STEAMED RICE

MAKES 3 CUPS

1 cup jasmine rice

When I was growing up, my family had steamed rice with every meal. Like every good Asian kid, I was in charge of making it while my mom cooked, so I'd like to consider myself a pro now. Having a rice cooker is an absolute game changer and I do recommend investing in one—I've had the same rice cooker for 10 years (it was actually passed down to me from my parents). If you don't have one, don't panic; you can definitely make the perfect steamed rice over the stovetop.

Jasmine rice has always been my favorite—it makes for the fluffiest, takeout-like rice. First things first, I always rinse my rice of any extra starchiness, which could be the reason your rice isn't turning out fluffy. As for the water, I've grown up using the finger trick, where you place the tip of your index finger at the top of the rice, and add enough water to reach your first knuckle. No one really knows how this works, especially since everyone's fingers vary in size, but it's how many Asian households prepare their rice. Have no fear if you're unfamiliar, you want a 1:1 rice-to-water ratio (easy for doubling!). This will result in the perfect side chick to your main piece. Bonus: Make extra so you can make Shrimp Fried Rice (page 112) the next day!

Add the rice to the pot and cover with water, using your hand to swish the rice. Use a fine mesh sieve to drain, then repeat the process two more times or until the water is just slightly cloudy. Set the rice aside to drain.

Boil 1 cup water in a medium pot over medium-high heat, then stir in the rice with a fork. Cover the pot, reduce the heat to medium-low, and cook until all of the water has evaporated, about 15 minutes (if the lid of your pot starts to wobble or any liquid starts to come out, turn the heat down to low). Without removing the lid (no peeking, bestie!), turn off the heat and allow to steam for another 5 minutes. Remove the lid and then fluff with a fork or a rice paddle and serve immediately, or store in an airtight container in the fridge for up to 2 days.

> **HOT (GIRL) TIP**
>
> If you want to get fancy and serve a perfect restaurant-style rice dome, gently press the rice into a small bowl and carefully flip the bowl onto a plate.

HAND-PULLED NOODLES

SERVES 2 (MAKES ABOUT 12 OUNCES)

2 cups all-purpose flour

¼ teaspoon kosher salt, plus more for cooking

½ cup boiling water

Neutral oil (I use avocado oil), for brushing

One of my proudest moments was successfully making hand-pulled noodles in forty-five minutes during the Chinese Challenge on *Next Level Chef* and Gordon Ramsay actually *loving* them. Everyone, including the contestants and judges, was so impressed that I made them in the short amount of time, but to tell you the truth, they're actually quite simple. The trick to making them under a time constraint was to use boiling water to make the dough to speed up the gluten development. Then add the noodles to a broth or stir-fry in any sauce (like Wet-Wet Sauce, page 255).

In a medium bowl, whisk together the flour and salt until well incorporated, then create a well in the center using your hands. Pour the boiling water into the center then use a wooden spoon to begin to mix it in with the dry ingredients. Stir until a shaggy dough forms (meaning there's no more loose flour but it looks like the dough *kneads* a little more TLC), then switch to your hands. Begin kneading in the bowl to gather the dough together, then turn the dough out onto a clean work surface and continue kneading until the dough is smooth, just slightly tacky, and bounces back when you poke it with your finger, about 10 minutes. If the dough is at all sticky, dust it lightly with more flour and knead it in. Repeat just until the dough no longer sticks. If the dough is dry, sprinkle on a few drops of water and knead in. Repeat until the dough is just slightly tacky.

Cover the dough with plastic wrap and rest at room temperature for 15 to 20 minutes. Cut the dough into 8 equal portions, then shape and flatten each piece into a small rectangle about 2 by 4 inches using your hands. Generously brush each piece with the oil on both sides and transfer to a clean plate. Cover with plastic wrap and rest at room temperature for 1 hour.

Working with one piece at a time and keeping the rest covered, use a rolling pin to roll out the dough into a long, thin rectangle to begin to flatten; just 2 to 3 inches longer than it was just to get the process started. Use the back of a knife or a chopstick to make an indented line down the center of the entire length of the dough. Gently but firmly, grab each end of the dough using your thumb and index finger so you're clamping down rather than just pinching with your fingertips. Begin shaking the noodle in an up-and-down motion and slap the dough onto the counter as you continue to stretch. Each slap should stretch out the noodle more. Keep slapping until the noodle is about $\frac{1}{16}$-inch thick (meaning it's thin but not so thin you can see through it) and 18 to 20 inches long. Grab the center of the noodle and tear through the dent to create two long noodles. Cover with a tea towel while you repeat with the rest of the dough.

Bring a large pot of salted water to a boil over high heat—make sure it's salty like pasta water, or as salty as your boss when they see yet another request for PTO. Drop the noodles into the boiling water and cook, stirring constantly, until they are tender, 3 to 4 minutes. Drain and prepare as desired.

WHOLE LOTTA BASICS • 243

razzle

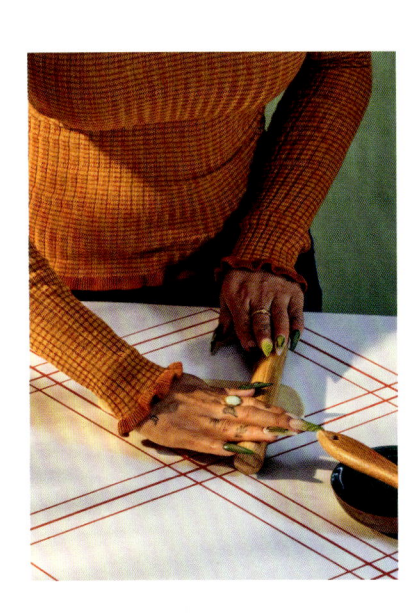

dazzle

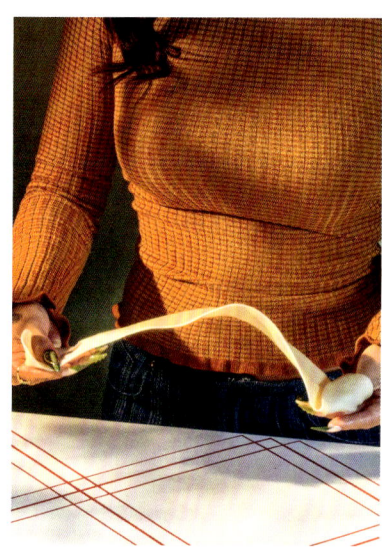

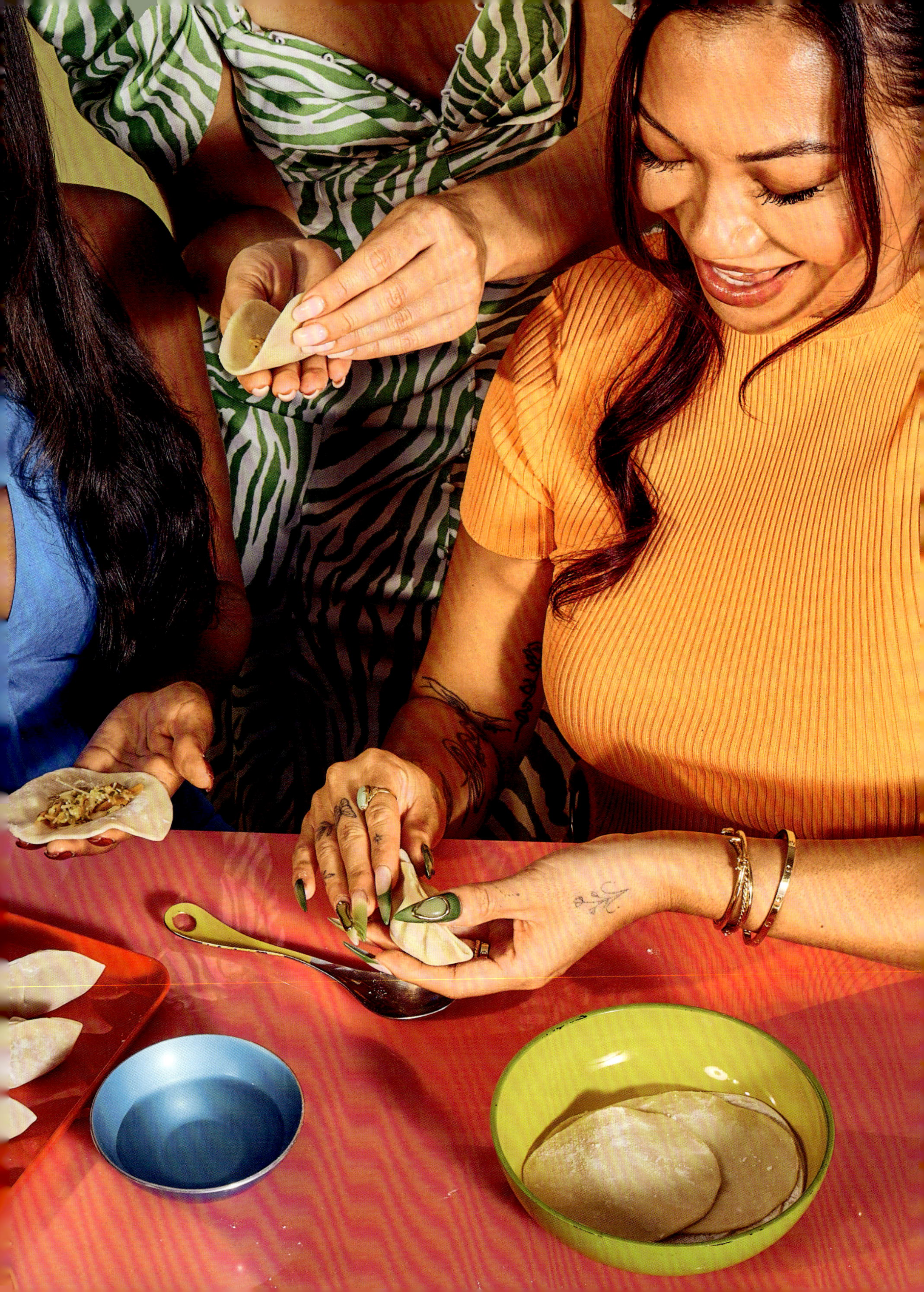

HOMEMADE DUMPLING WRAPPERS

MAKES 32 WRAPPERS

2 cups all-purpose flour, plus more for dusting

½ teaspoon kosher salt

½ cup hot water

I admittingly love using store-bought dumpling wrappers as a shortcut, but homemade dumpling wrappers have a bouncy texture that is so worth the labor and love you put into them. I find myself making dumpling wrappers from scratch when I'm preparing a smaller batch. All you need are flour, salt, and hot water—this simple recipe came in handy during my time on *Next Level Chef*, which if you've seen any episodes while I was competing, I almost always forgot to grab an important ingredient from the platform like a starch, protein, or veggie. Straight away in episode 1, I forgot to grab a carb to make my dish so I was left to find my way with just pantry ingredients. I grabbed the flour and salt, and made a complete and stunning (might I add) plate of dumplings.

In a large bowl, whisk the flour and salt until well incorporated. Pour the hot water in, then use a pair of chopsticks or a wooden spoon to mix the dough until it is shaggy (meaning there's no more loose flour or water but it looks like the dough *kneads* a little more TLC). Switch to your hands and knead the dough in the bowl until it's smooth and just slightly tacky, about 10 minutes. If the dough is at all sticky, dust it lightly with more flour and knead it in. Repeat just until the dough no longer sticks. If the dough is dry, sprinkle on a few drops of water and knead in. Repeat until the dough is just slightly tacky. Transfer to a clean work surface and continue to knead until the dough is smooth and bounces back when you poke it with your finger, about 10 minutes more. Cover the dough with plastic wrap or a tea towel and rest at room temperature for 30 minutes to 1 hour.

Split the dough into 4 equal portions, working with 1 piece at a time and keeping the rest covered with plastic wrap or a tea towel so they don't dry out. Roll the piece into a long, even rope about ¾-inch thick and split the rope into 8 equal portions (the dough shouldn't be sticking, but lightly flour your surface if it is). Take each piece and press it down with the palm of your hand to flatten. Then use the rolling pin to roll it out as thin as possible. It should be 3 inches wide. As you finish each piece, lightly dust it with flour so it doesn't stick and stack it under a tea towel to prevent it from drying out. Repeat the process with all the remaining dough.

Use the wrappers to prepare dumplings immediately, or dust the tops with more flour, then stack and store in a resealable bag and freeze for up to 6 months. To thaw, transfer to the fridge 24 hours before using (they will separate when they thaw).

HOMEMADE WONTON SKINS

MAKES 32 WONTON SKINS

1 large egg

2 cups all-purpose flour, plus more for dusting

¾ teaspoon kosher salt

My favorite reason to make homemade wonton skins is because you can control the size of the wrapper. I *love* giant wontons, just like those you get in wonton soup at Chinese takeout restaurants, with those extra bites of the tender noodle hanging off the ends. Unlike dumpling wrappers, you don't need to individually roll out each wrapper but rather roll the dough out to a pasta sheet, then slice the squares to your desired size. Although it takes a little patience, using these paper-thin wonton skins do level up your homemade wontons. This is also a great hack to keep in your back pocket if you don't have any Asian markets nearby!

In a small bowl, whisk the egg with 5 tablespoons water until smooth.

In a large bowl, mix the flour and salt until well incorporated and create a well in the center. Pour the egg mixture in the center of the well, then use a fork to whisk, slowly bringing in the dry ingredients from the sides and mix until a shaggy dough forms (meaning there's no more loose flour or water but it looks like the dough could use more love and attention). Transfer the dough to a lightly floured work surface and knead until smooth and just slightly tacky, about 10 minutes. If the dough is at all sticky, dust it lightly with more flour and knead it in. Repeat just until the dough no longer sticks. If the dough is dry, sprinkle on a few drops of water and knead in. Repeat until the dough is just slightly tacky. Cover with a tea towel and let rest at room temperature for 1 hour.

Split the dough into 8 equal portions. Roll out one at a time and keep the rest covered so they don't dry out. Use a floured rolling pin to roll it as thin as possible—it should be about 12 inches long and 3 or 4 inches wide, and very thin, but not so thin you can see through it. Try to get the dough into as precise of a rectangle as you can, so the skins are an even shape. Keep flouring and flipping the dough as you roll to prevent it from sticking. If the dough is shrinking back when you roll it, let her rest for 10 minutes and try again. Use a knife to cut the sheet into four 3- to 4-inch squares, and if some have rounded edges, that's okay. (Rolling out perfect squares is a skill that takes some practice, but we still love our wonky wontons.)

You can use the skins immediately to make wontons or dust with flour and stack them before storing in a resealable bag in the freezer for up to 6 months. To thaw, transfer to the fridge 24 hours before using.

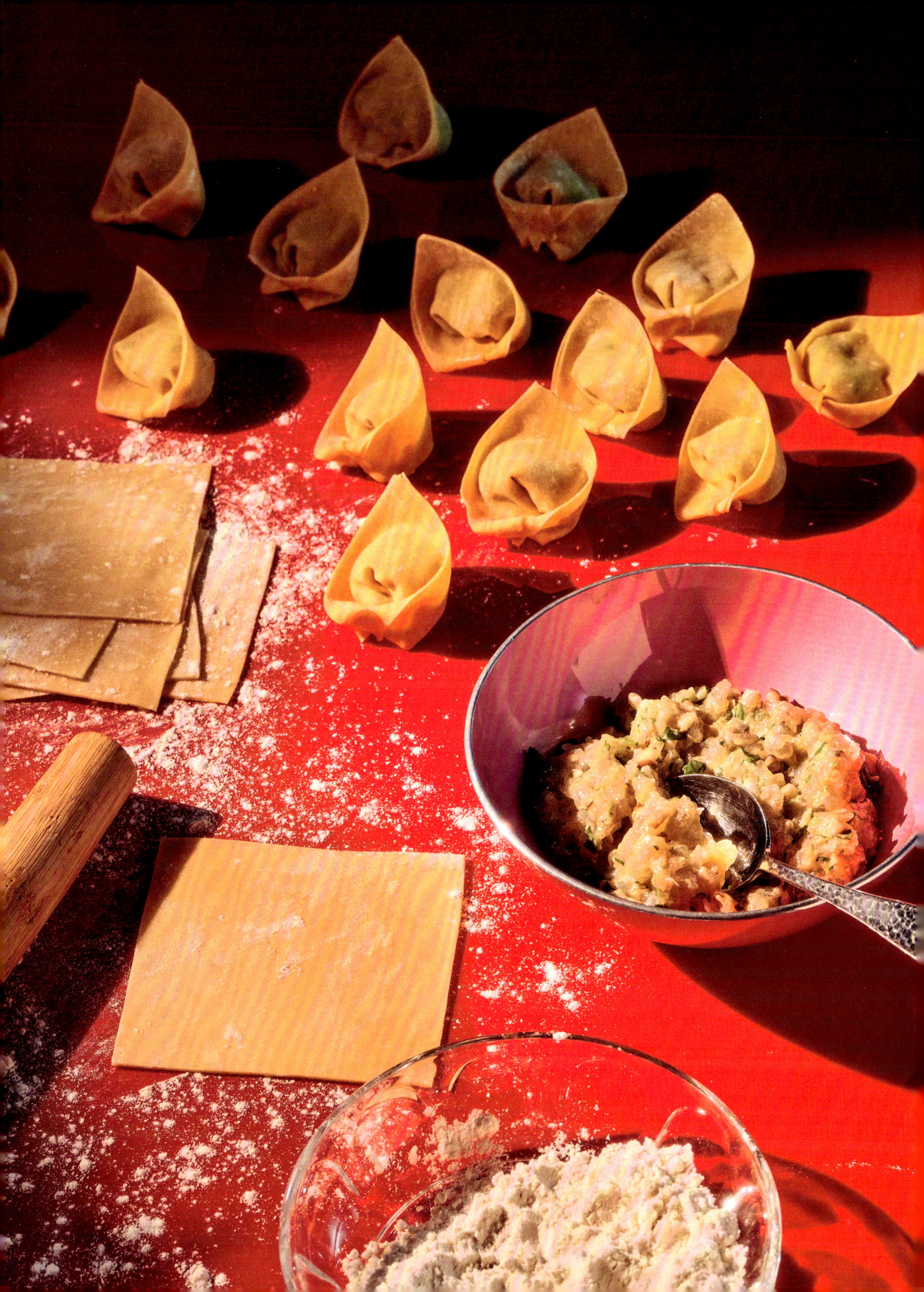

STEPS TO STEAMING

If using a steamer basket...
Add 2 to 3 inches of water to the pan and bring it to a boil over medium-high heat. Meanwhile, line the basket with pieces of lettuce, cabbage, or a perforated sheet of parchment paper (you can get these specifically made for steamer baskets, or DIY—fold a square piece of parchment paper in half and use a pair of scissors to round the corners to create a circle, then use a chopstick or skewer to poke holes) to prevent the food from sticking. When the water boils and starts steaming, reduce the heat to medium-low and put the basket on top of the pan. Add whatever you're cooking to the steamer basket, cover, and steam!

If using a wire steaming rack...
Add 2 to 3 inches of water to the pot, but you can eyeball the amount as long as the water doesn't touch the top of the steaming rack. It's important that you use a pot tall enough that a plate of food can sit on top of the steaming rack and not touch the lid. The lid also needs to fit snugly so that none of the steam can escape. I love opting for a wire steaming rack because you can steam the food in a heat-safe dish and serve immediately, and also the wire steaming rack folds nicely to save storage space.

If using a DIY steamer...
If you don't have a steamer basket or steaming rack, have no fear—you can make a DIY version. The idea here is to lift the food enough so that the plate is not touching the water. Rip off a long sheet of aluminum foil and roll it up into a long rope. Starting at one end of the rope, begin rolling it up to create a coil. It doesn't need to be perfect, just enough to elevate a dish. Add this coil to a pot with enough water to reach just shy of the top of the coil. Set the dish on top of the foil (which will weigh it down—be sure the water is still below the plate) and steam!

HOMEMADE FLAT RICE NOODLES

SERVES 4 (MAKES 1 POUND)

1 cup white rice flour

½ cup tapioca starch or cornstarch

¼ teaspoon kosher salt

Neutral oil (I use avocado oil), for brushing

A number of my recipes call for fresh, wide rice noodles, but you may find they are difficult to get your hands on. Many Asian markets carry them, but I find they are often out of stock due to their high demand (I may or may not be the one buying them all). Have no fear, they're actually easy to make, and it's quite rewarding when you do. The key is finding the right tools and getting comfortable with a system. The actual batter is quite simple—rice flour, tapioca starch, salt, water, and oil. The tapioca starch is what gives the noodles that bouncy texture, but it can still be substituted with cornstarch if that's easier to find. These noodles will be steamed, so you'll need a wire steaming rack and it's very important to have a wok or pot big enough to fit and still have a tight seal with the lid. I find it best to use two 9 × 7-inch baking dishes so that by the time you're removing one pan, you'll have another pan of batter ready to be steamed. Fresh rice noodles can be the difference to level up your noodle dish, so don't be afraid to take the extra step!

Mix the batter: In a small bowl, whisk the rice flour, tapioca starch, and salt until thoroughly combined. Slowly pour in 1½ cups room temperature water as you continue to whisk, until all the water is added and the batter is well combined and smooth. Make sure the flour is completely incorporated for even steaming.

Steam the noodles: Fill a wok or large pot with 2 cups of water and fit a wire steaming rack in the center (see page 250) and make sure it's got a tight-fitting lid. Bring to a boil over medium heat. Meanwhile, brush a 9 × 7-inch baking dish with just enough oil to coat the bottom and sides (too much oil will create bubbles in the noodles, which we do not want). Pour in ⅓ cup of batter, or just enough to cover the bottom of the pan.

When the water starts steaming, carefully put the baking dish on the wire steaming rack, ensuring it's level. Cover the wok, reduce the heat to medium-low, and steam until the noodle sheet has solidified and turned milky-white and opaque and the edges start to pull away from the sides of the pan, 5 to 10 minutes. Carefully remove the pan using plate tongs (see page 27) or a towel, and brush the top of the noodle sheet with more oil. Use a rubber spatula to remove it from the pan (it should come off easily in one piece; if the bottom is sticking that means it's not done yet and it needs to keep steaming) and place on a cutting board. Repeat the process with the remaining batter, stirring the batter vigorously between each batch because it will separate as it sits. Cut the noodles to desired width by batch, or stack the sheets on top of each other and cut them all once you've steamed all of the batter.

Use immediately, or store the noodles in an airtight container in the fridge for up to 3 days. You can freeze as sheets for up to 3 months. To thaw, transfer to the fridge 24 hours before using and slice before preparing.

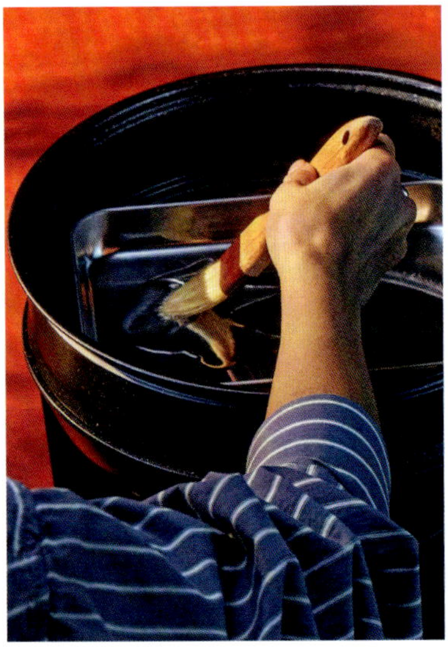
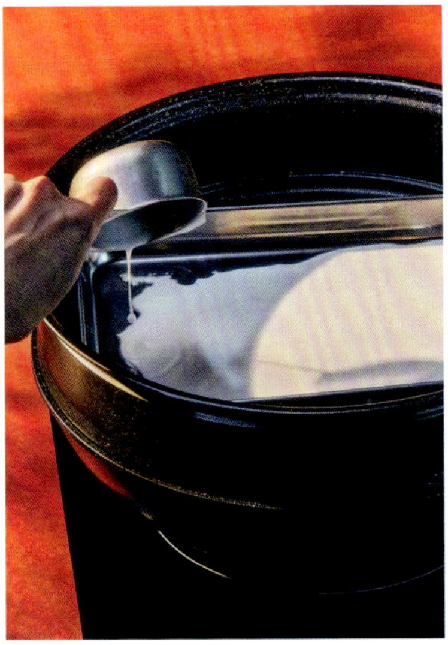
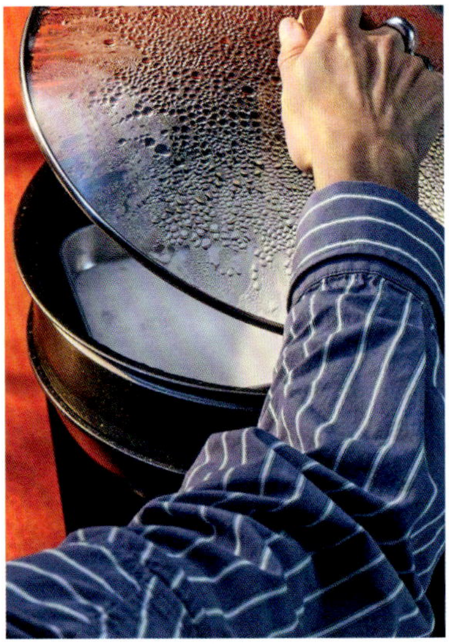

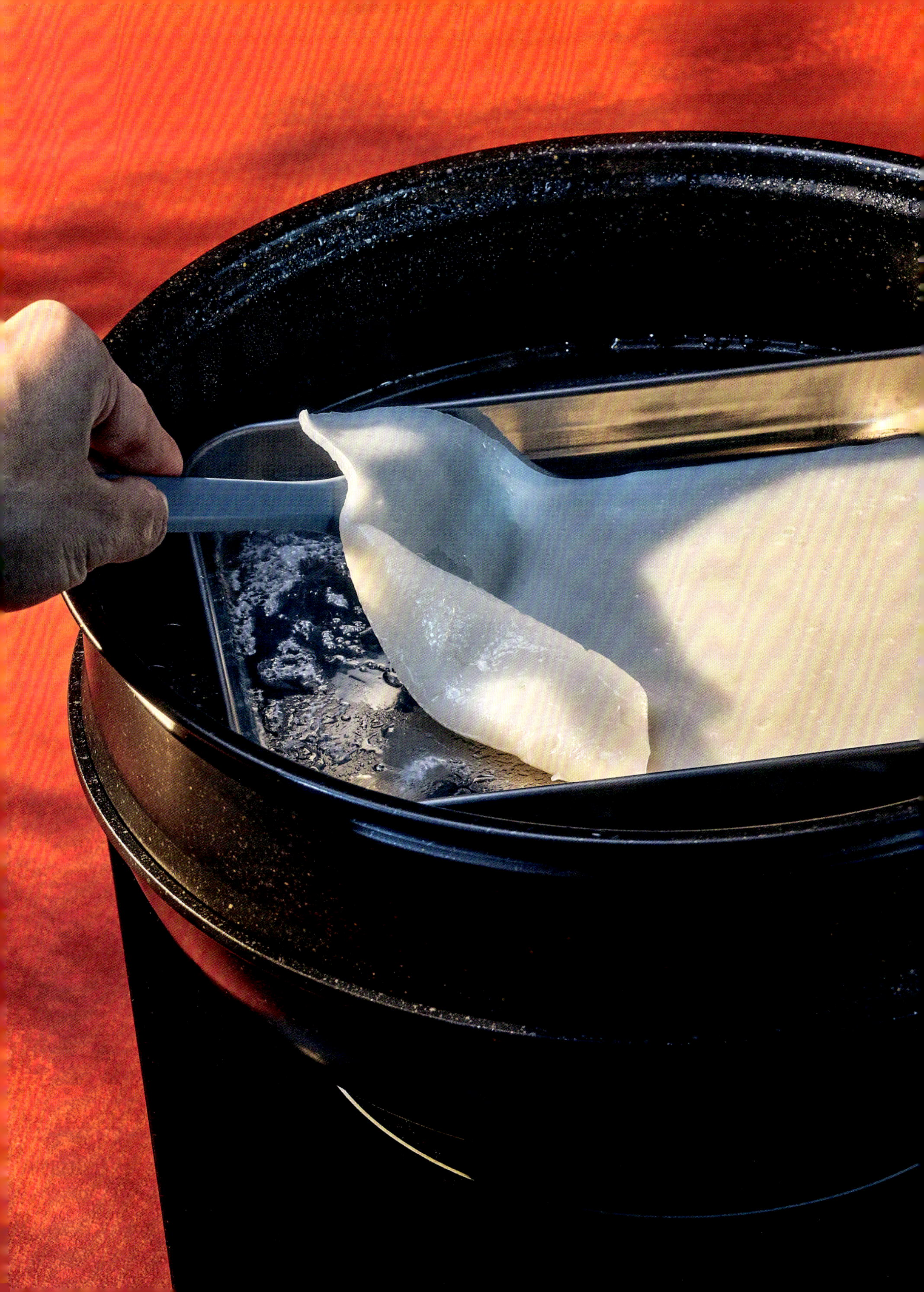

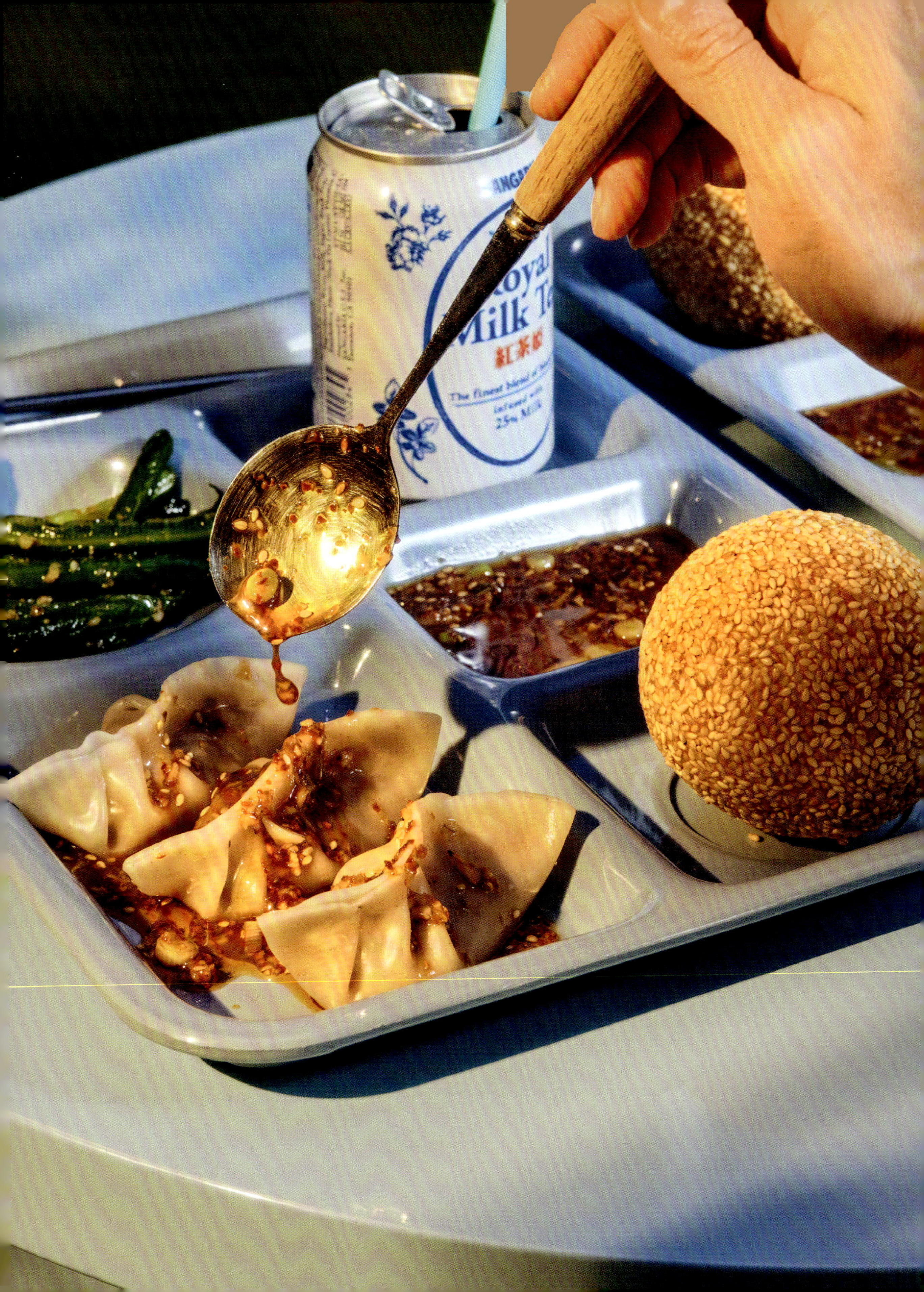
infused with
25% Milk

WET-WET SAUCE

MAKES ABOUT 1 CUP

4 green onions, white tops only, finely chopped

6 large garlic cloves, minced

2-inch knob of ginger, peeled and minced

3 tablespoons coarse gochugaru (Korean chili flakes)

1 teaspoon toasted sesame seeds

½ cup neutral oil (I use avocado oil)

3 tablespoons light soy sauce

2 tablespoons rice vinegar

1 tablespoon oyster sauce

1 tablespoon toasted sesame oil

If you are at all familiar with my videos, then you are already well aware of the infamous Wet-Wet Sauce—which is really the best chili sauce, I think, ever. This all started when I first began posting videos and cooking for my friends on TikTok live and celebrated hitting 500k followers. With my followers I made homemade dumplings, bok choy, and beef udon noodles with (unnamed at the time) wet-wet sauce. It was the first time my friends were trying these noodles, and their reactions were priceless. My followers said I had to name the sauce, and without any deep discussion, we all came up with "Wet-Wet Sauce." Since then, it's become my signature sauce that I use for dipping, stir-frying, and basically drowning in. The holy trinity of aromatics—green onions, garlic, and ginger—are mixed in a bowl with Korean chili flakes for spice and toasted sesame seeds for a nutty flavor. A hot oil is poured all over the aromatics and spices to wake up the flavors, and then it is finished off with sesame oil, soy sauce, oyster sauce, and rice vinegar for *the best* version of a chili oil. There are no limits with this sauce, and it can level up any dish that's in need of some extra razzle-dazzle. Use this sauce to stir-fry noodles, toss fried chicken in, or as a simply addictive dipping sauce.

In a medium heat-safe bowl, mix the green onion whites, garlic, ginger, gochugaru, and sesame seeds and spread in an even layer.

In a small saucepan, heat the neutral oil over medium-high heat to 325°F (if you don't have a thermometer, do the wooden chopstick test on page 47). Carefully pour the oil over the aromatics and wait for the oil to stop bubbling. Use a rubber spatula to stir and coat the aromatics with the oil, then mix in the soy sauce, rice vinegar, oyster sauce, and sesame oil. Enjoy immediately or store in a glass jar for up to 3 months in the fridge.

GINGER SCALLION SAUCE

MAKES ½ CUP

- 3 green onions, white and green parts, finely chopped
- 2-inch knob of ginger, peeled and minced
- 1 teaspoon kosher salt
- ½ cup neutral oil (I use avocado oil)
- 1 tablespoon toasted sesame oil

I'm a big condiment girl, and ginger scallion is my favorite dipping sauce for proteins. My mom first taught me how to make this sauce as a side for Hainanese Chicken Rice (page 136), but I now douse *everything* with it for extra flavor. Whenever Mom's green onions are about to go bad, she makes this sauce, which has become my favorite way to prevent waste, too. Ginger and green onions are salted and sizzled beneath a river of hot oil to bring out all of their flavors. It's completed with a nutty toasted sesame oil for the final touch.

In a medium heat-safe bowl, arrange the green onions and ginger in an even, flat layer. Season with the salt.

In a small saucepan, heat the neutral oil over medium-high heat to 325°F (if you don't have a thermometer, do the wooden chopstick test on page 47). Carefully pour the oil over the aromatics and wait for the oil to stop bubbling. Use a rubber spatula to stir in the sesame oil until well combined. Enjoy immediately or store in an airtight container in the fridge for up to 2 months.

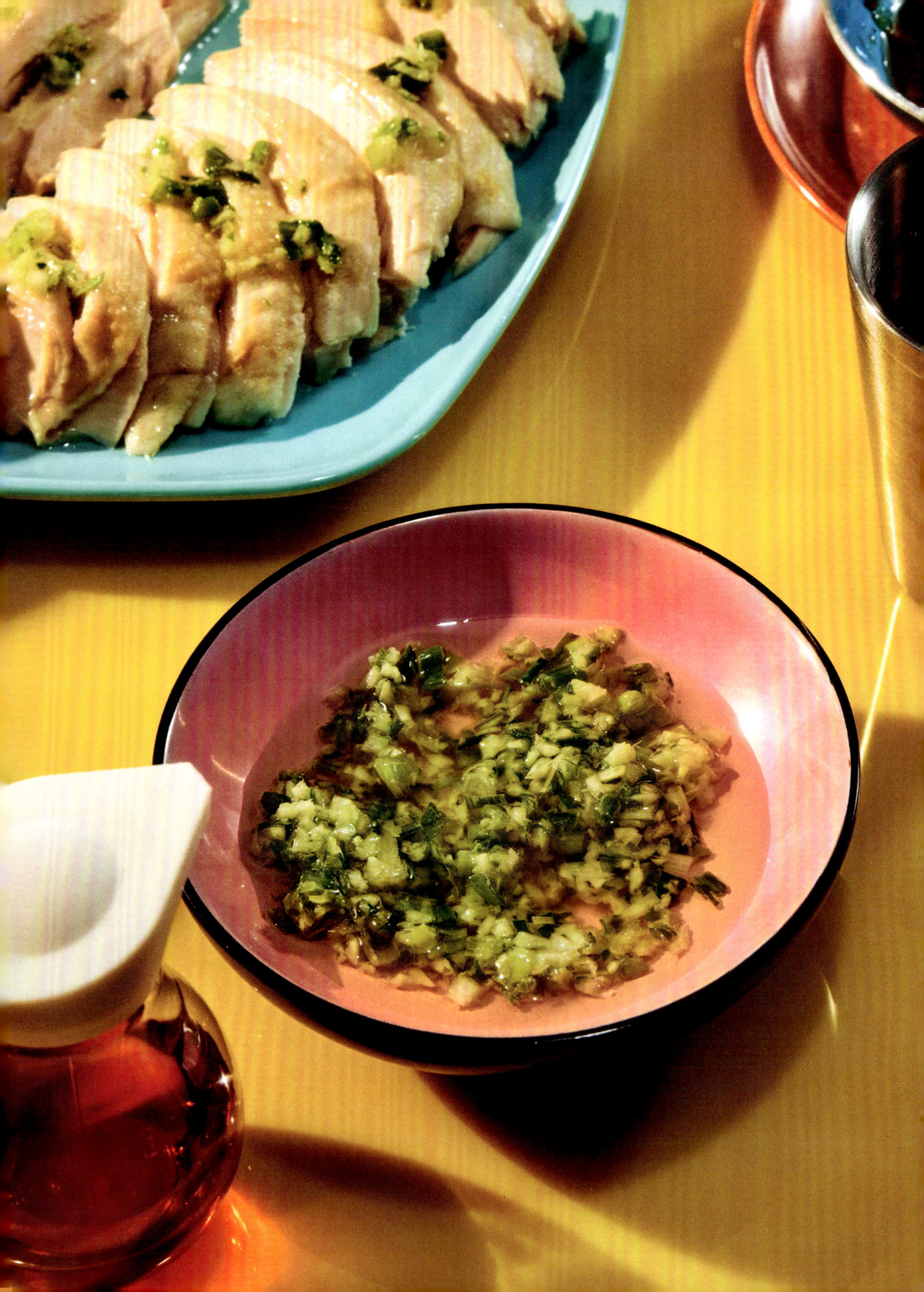

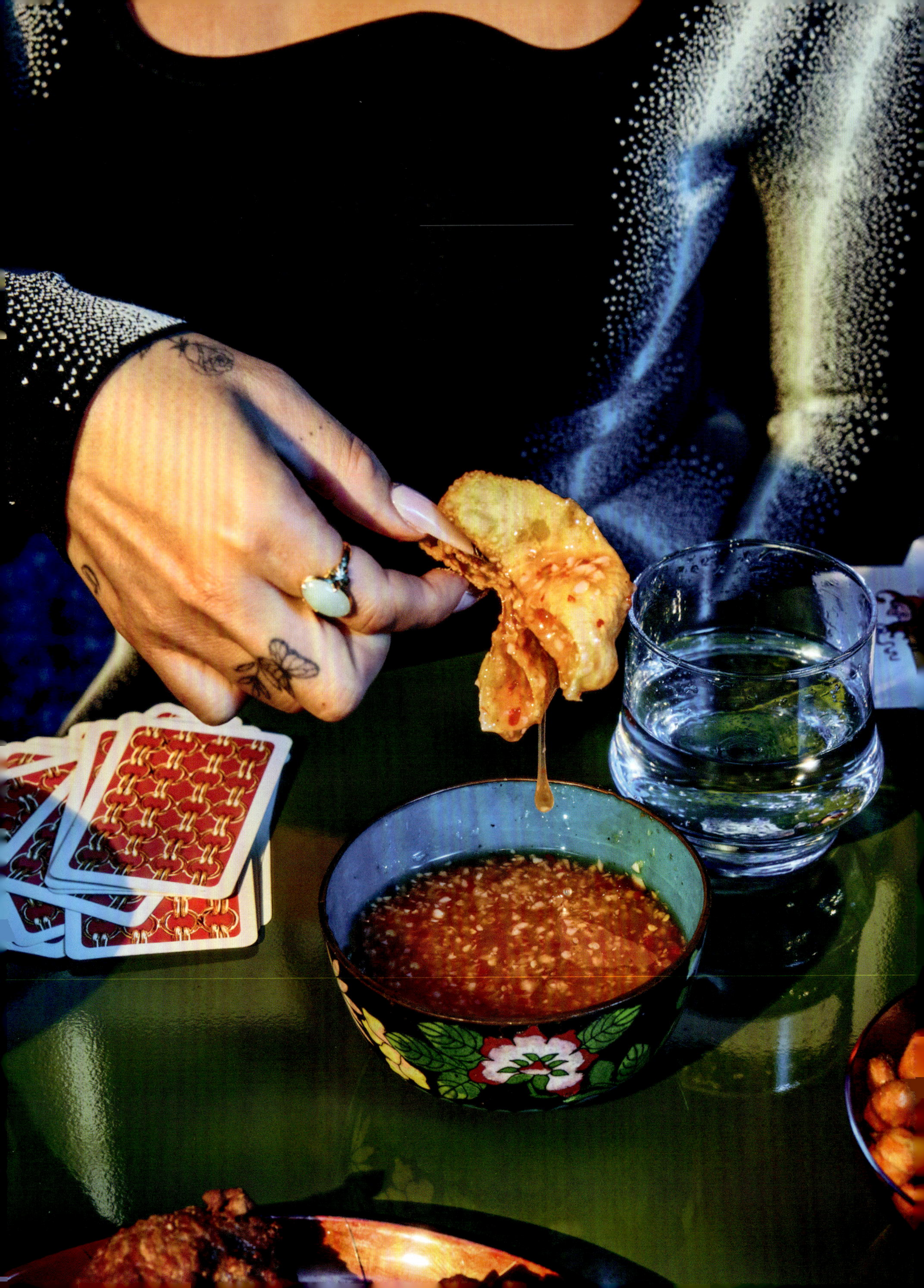

SWEET CHILI SAUCE

MAKES ABOUT ½ CUP

1 teaspoon cornstarch

5 fresh bird's-eye chilies, stems removed and finely chopped

5 large garlic cloves, minced

1-inch knob ginger, peeled and minced

¼ cup sugar

¼ cup rice vinegar

Sweet chili sauce is exactly what it sounds like, and how I imagine every baddie likes to describe themselves—sweet, spicy, and a little bit thick. Bird's-eye chilies pack a spicy punch, but they're balanced out with the acidity of rice vinegar and sweetness from sugar. Of course, there's a healthy amount of garlic and ginger to set the tone, and the whole deal is thickened with a cornstarch slurry to make the best dipping sauce for proteins, spring rolls, and more.

In a small bowl, prepare the cornstarch slurry by mixing the cornstarch and 1 tablespoon cold water until smooth—no lumps!

Heat a small saucepan over medium-high heat. When the pan is hot, stir-fry—we're stirring rapidly and aggressively here, really putting that wrist in action—the chilies, garlic, and ginger for 30 seconds until fragrant (if you're sneezing, you're doing it right). Stir in ¼ cup water, the sugar, and rice vinegar and heat while continuing to stir until the sugar has dissolved, about 1 minute.

Pour the cornstarch slurry into the chili sauce and stir, then cook until the sauce has thickened, 1 to 2 minutes. Remove from the heat and cool to room temperature, about 30 minutes, before enjoying, or transfer to an airtight container. Store in the fridge for up to 2 months.

NƯỚC CHẤM

MAKES 1 CUP

½ cup warm water

3 tablespoons sugar

2 large garlic cloves, minced

2 fresh bird's-eye chilies, stems removed and thinly sliced

¼ cup rice vinegar

¼ cup fish sauce

2 tablespoons fresh lime juice (from about 1 lime)

Nước chấm is *the* sauce, and the main character of so many Vietnamese dishes. This enhanced fish sauce is amazing for fried spring rolls, fresh summer rolls, grilled pork chops, and so much more. The method is simple, so there are no excuses for not having a serving ready to go in the fridge. Fish sauce is pungent and salty, but with the addition of sugar, garlic, chilies, rice vinegar, and lime juice, it's hard to resist the urge to just drink it. Nước chấm is *thật girl*, and you'll find yourself using your imagination to decide what else you can drown in it.

In a small bowl, combine the water and sugar and whisk until the sugar dissolves. Mix in the garlic, chilies, rice vinegar, fish sauce, and lime juice. Enjoy immediately or store in an airtight container in the fridge for up to 2 months.

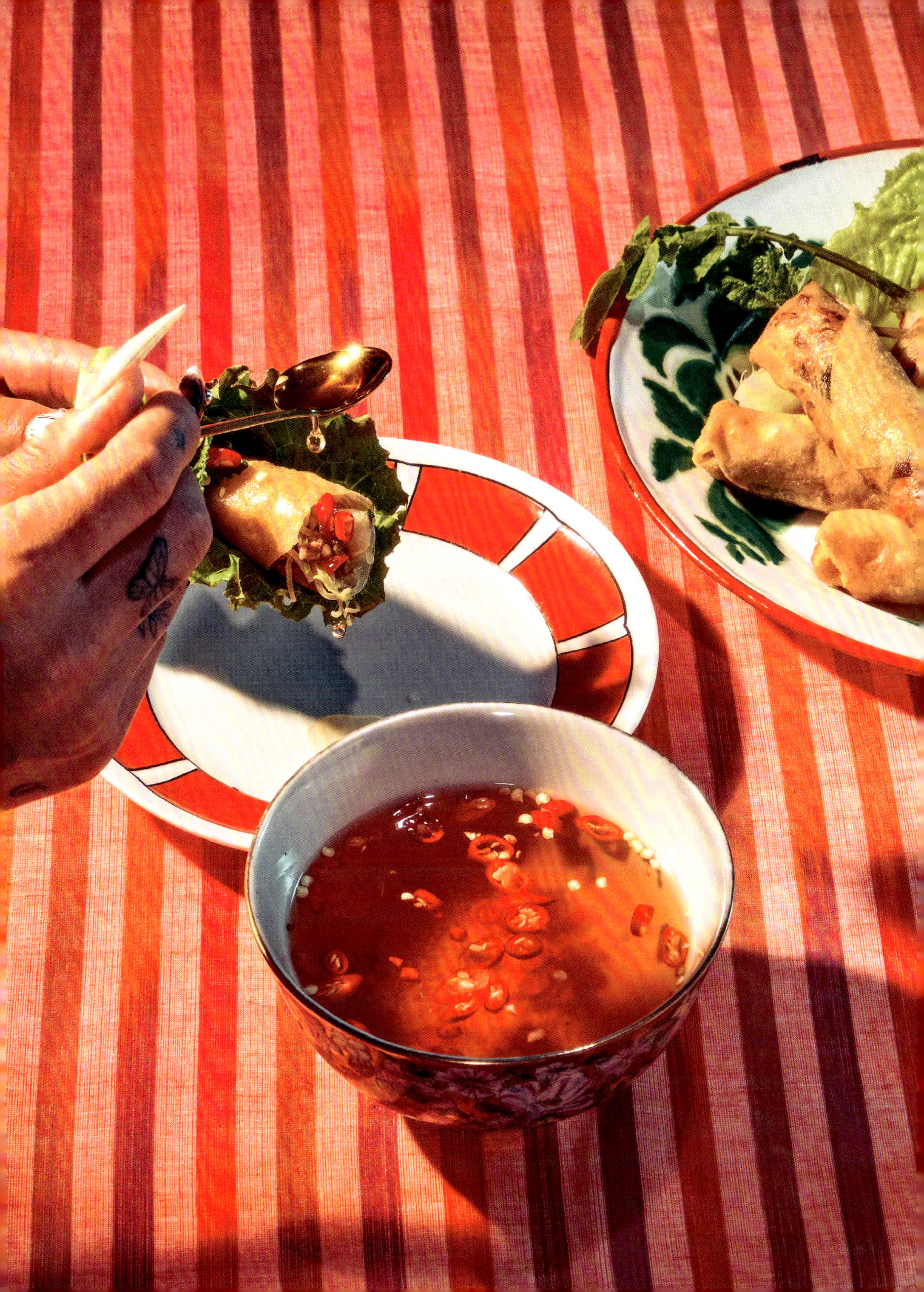

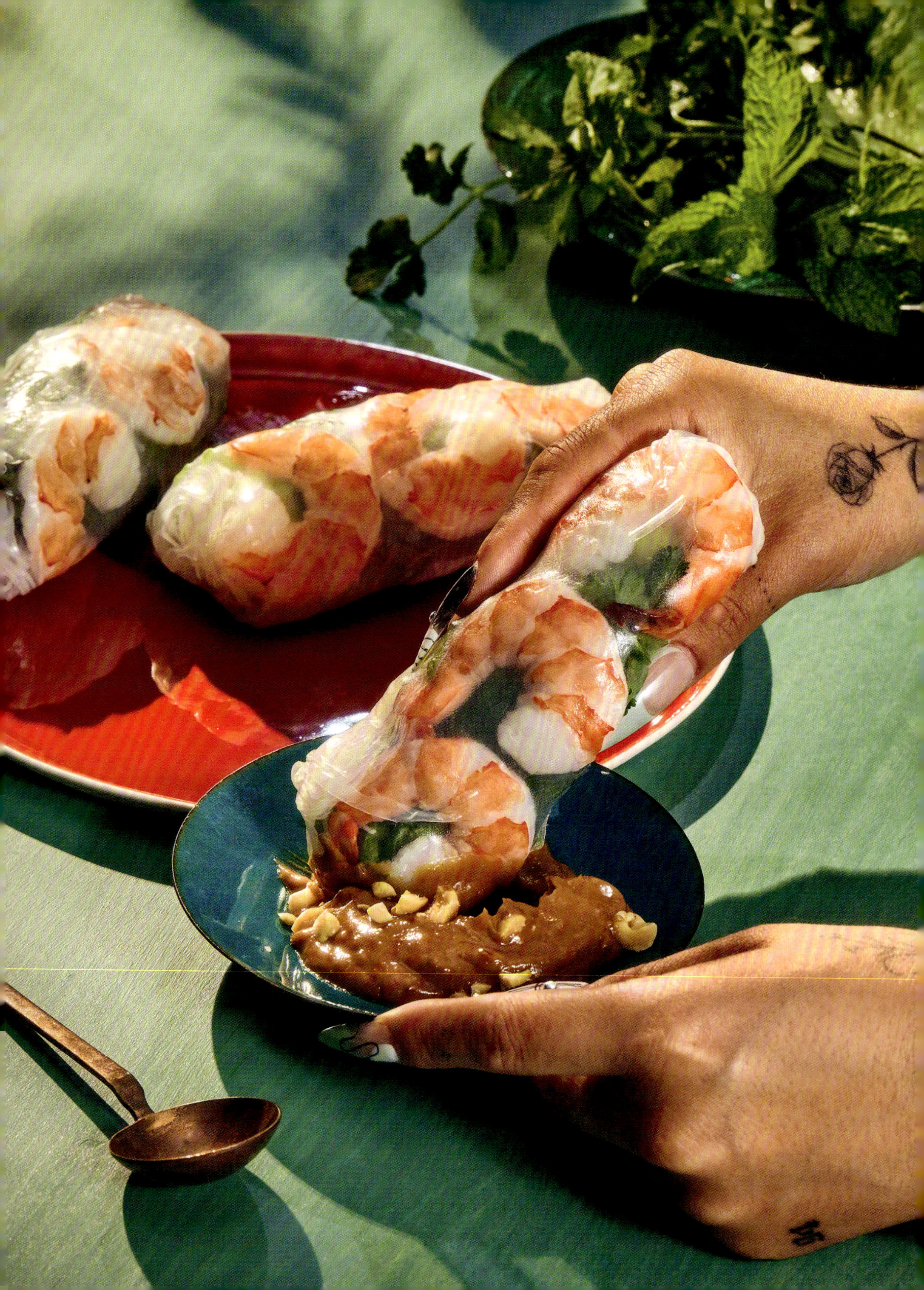

PEANUT DIPPING SAUCE

MAKES ABOUT ¾ CUP

⅓ cup creamy peanut butter

¼ cup hoisin sauce

2 tablespoons rice vinegar

1 tablespoon fresh lime juice (from about ½ lime)

1 teaspoon sriracha or sambal oelek

1 teaspoon toasted sesame oil

1 medium garlic clove, grated

2 teaspoons unsalted roasted peanuts, roughly chopped, for serving

Summer rolls just aren't complete without peanut dipping sauce. Beyond that, this sauce is amazing for dipping vegetables (raw or blanched) or serving alongside a quick vermicelli noodle bowl with the leftovers from your summer rolls. There's no cooking necessary for this sauce—it's a five-minute, one-bowl sauce situation.

In a small bowl, add the peanut butter, hoisin sauce, rice vinegar, lime juice, sriracha, and sesame oil. Now get out your grater and grate the garlic into the bowl (baddies, watch your nails). Mix everything together until thoroughly combined and smooth. If you prefer a thinner dipping sauce, add 2 to 4 tablespoons of hot water, 1 tablespoon at a time.

Transfer to a serving dish, top with roasted peanuts, and enjoy immediately, or refrigerate in an airtight container for up to 1 week. Take it out of the fridge to come back to room temperature and stir well before using.

ACKNOWLEDGMENTS

I owe many thanks to the people who have graciously stood by my side in one of the most challenging yet rewarding projects of bringing this book to life. I never imagined myself producing a cookbook and becoming an author, and I'm forever grateful to everyone who has been a part of the journey.

I'd first like to thank my mom, dad, and sister who have undoubtedly been there from the very beginning. Not only were they there to physically support me when I uprooted my life and began my journey as a content creator, but they were also there for me in every moment of distress to offer encouragement and support.

An extra thanks to my mom for being my first source of inspiration in the kitchen. For teaching me all of the flavors rooted in my culture and the tips and tricks she learned growing up.

My publishing agents, Tia Ikemoto and Kari Stuart, who believed in my ability to produce a cookbook. They have had my back and made sure I was comfortable throughout this process.

My editors, Susan Roxborough and Raquel Pelzel, and the entire team at Clarkson Potter for making this all possible. I'm truly honored to have such a supportive and reputable publishing group backing me.

My coeditor and recipe tester, Emily Stephenson, who held my hand and instilled so much confidence in me throughout this process. Her hard work and efforts played a huge role in bringing this together.

My agent, L Davis, for being one of the first people to see my potential and supporting me through every project. He has been a huge support and has made me feel like no idea or dream is too big to achieve.

My entire photography team including photographer Jenny Huang, food stylist Tyna Hoang, prop stylist Maggie DiMarco, and the assisting team. They seamlessly brought my vision to life and made the experience so memorable.

I would be nowhere without my friends, who have provided the emotional support, around the clock, necessary to make it through every wave of emotions that has come with this new territory of creating.

My therapist, who has helped me work through my anxieties and imposter syndrome as a new author.

Saving the best for last: I would never be anywhere without my followers. Every single person who has become one of my internet besties has been part of the journey in some way, shape, or form. Words will never be able to explain how grateful I am for the platform that I have been given.

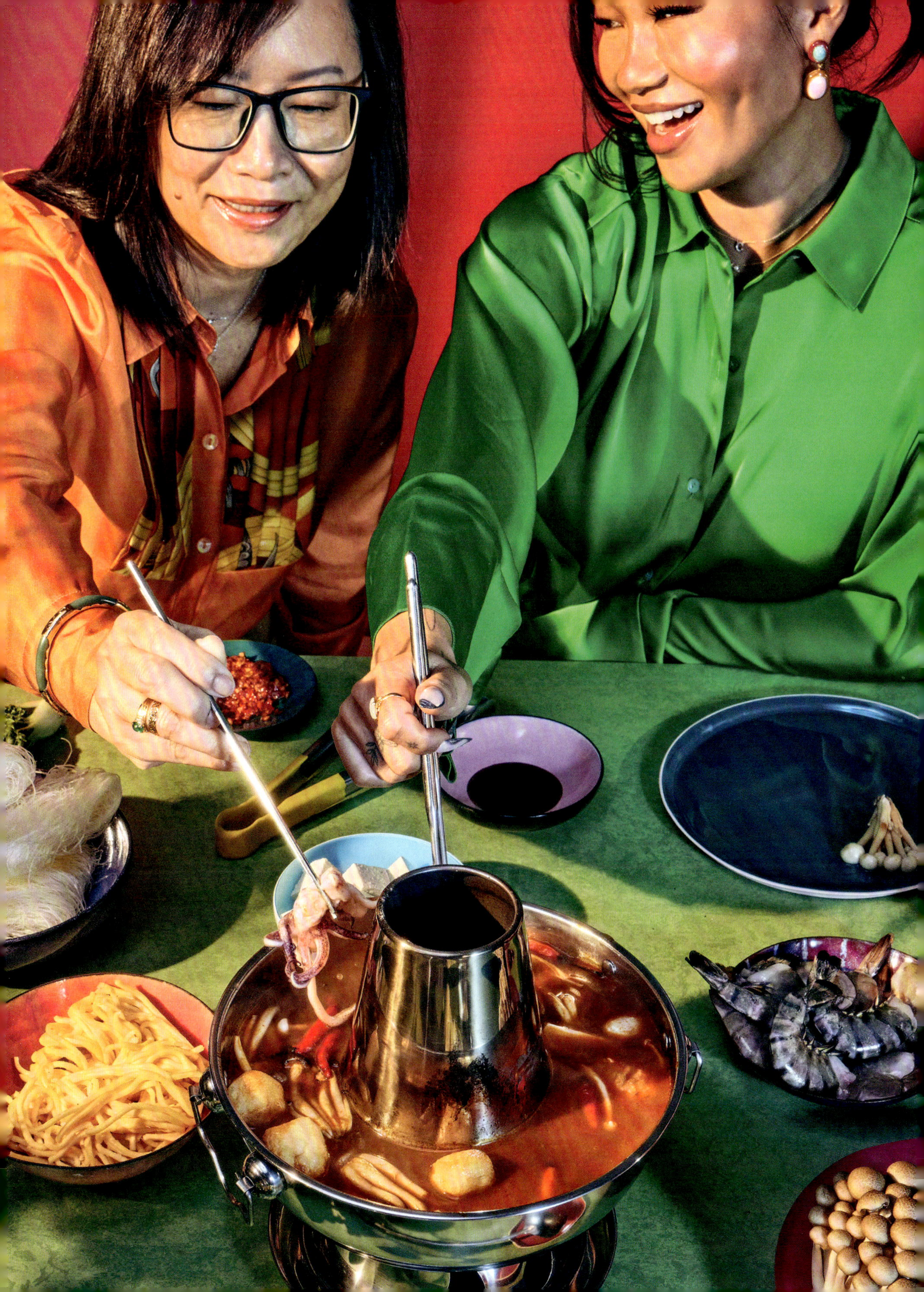

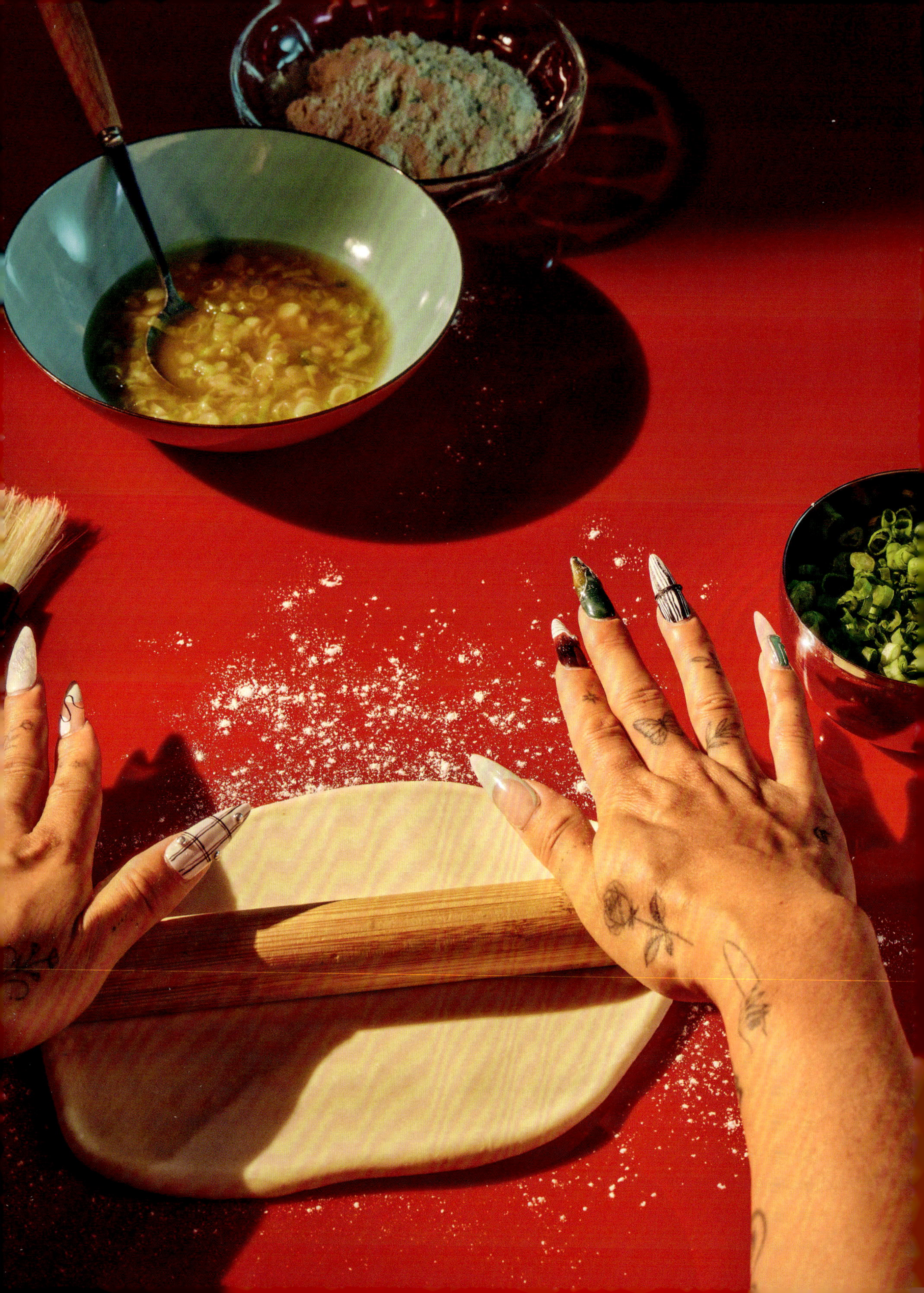

INDEX

Note: Page references in *italics* indicate photographs.

A
abalone
    Ah Ma's Mee Hoon Kueh, 154–55, *156–57*
Accordion Cucumber Salad, 206, *207*
Air Fryer Char Siu (Chinese BBQ Pork), 68, *69*
appetizers. *See* small plates
Apple Cake, Mom's, 222, *223*
avocado oil, 16

B
Bak Kut Teh, *150*, 151
Banchan-Style Korean Bean Sprouts, *194*, 195
basic recipes, 239–63
    Ginger Scallion Sauce, 256, *257*
    Hand-Pulled Noodles, 243, *244–45*
    Homemade Dumpling Wrappers, 246, *247*
    Homemade Flat Rice Noodles, 251, *252–53*
    Homemade Wonton Skins, 248, *249*
    Nước Chấm, 260, *261*
    Peanut Dipping Sauce, 262, *263*
    The Perfect Steamed Rice, 242
    Sweet Chili Sauce, 258, *259*
    Wet-Wet Sauce, *254*, 255
BBQ Pork, Chinese (Air Fryer Char Siu), 68, *69*
beans
    Copycat Din Tai Fung Green Beans, 188, *189*
bean sprouts
    Banchan-Style Korean Bean Sprouts, *194*, 195
    Hokkien Prawn Mee, *132*, 140–41
    Pad Thai, 82, *83*
beef
    Beef Chow Fun (Ho Fun), 78, *79*
    Ground Beef Bulgogi, 116, *117*
    Oxtail Phở, 96, *97*
    Shaking Beef, 128, *129*
    Taiwanese Beef Noodles, 94, *95*
    30-Minute Beef and Broccoli, 108, *109*
bee hoon. *See* white noodles
bok choy
    Taiwanese Beef Noodles, 94, *95*
    10-Minute Bok Choy, *190*, 191
    Wonton Soup, 166, *167*
bouillon powder, 16
broccoli
    Drunken Noodles (Pad Kee Mao), 86, *87*
    Pad See Ew, 84, *85*
    30-Minute Beef and Broccoli, 108, *109*
Brown Butter Matcha Cheesecake with Cookie Butter Crust, 214–15, *226*, 227
Bulgogi, Ground Beef, 116, *117*

C
cabbage
    Easy Kimchi, 196–97, *197*
    Fried Pork Spring Rolls, *48*, 49
    Pork Dumplings, 40–41, *42–43*
cake
    Brown Butter Matcha Cheesecake with Cookie Butter Crust, 214–15, *226*, 227
    Mom's Apple Cake, 222, *223*
    Thai Tea Tres Leches, 232–34, *233*
candied walnuts, 115
Cantonese Steamed Fish, 123, *124–25*
carrots
    Chicken Katsu Curry, 120–22, *121*
    Easy Kimchi, 196–97, *197*
    Rainbow Carrot Ribbon Salad, *204*, 205
Char Kway Teow, 142, *143*
Char Siu, Air Fryer (Chinese BBQ Pork), 68, *69*
Cheesecake, Brown Butter Matcha, with Cookie Butter Crust, 214–15, *226*, 227
chicken
    Chicken Katsu Curry, 120–22, *121*
    Chicken Lo Mein, 80, *81*
    Claypot Rice, 158, *159*
    Congee (Chinese Jook), 172, *173*
    Drunken Noodles (Pad Kee Mao), 86, *87*
    45-Minute Phở Gà (Chicken Pho), 92, *93*
    General Tso's Chicken, 106, *107*
    Hainanese Chicken Rice, 136–37, *138–39*
    Orange Chicken, 104, *105*
    Soy Sauce Chicken, 126, *127*
    Takeout-Style Chicken Wings, 64, *65*
chicken bouillon powder, 16
chili and chili sauces, 16
    Nước Chấm, 260, *261*
    Quick Chili-Vinegar Onions, 202, *203*
    Sweet Chili Sauce, 258, *259*
    Wet-Wet Sauce, *254*, 255
Chinese BBQ Pork (Air Fryer Char Siu), 68, *69*

Chinese broccoli
    Drunken Noodles (Pad Kee Mao), *86*, 87
    Pad See Ew, 84, *85*
Chinese sausage, 158
    Char Kway Teow, 142, *143*
    Claypot Rice, 158, *159*
Chinese Watercress Soup, *180*, 181
Chocolate Mochi, *218*, 219, 221
Chow Fun, Beef (Ho Fun), *78*, 79
Claypot Rice, 158, *159*
Clear Soup, Japanese, *176*, 177
coconut
    No-Churn Pandan Coconut Ice Cream, *228*, 229
coffee
    Vietnamese Coffee Tiramisu, *230*, 231
Congee (Chinese Jook), *172*, 173
cooking techniques
    deep-frying, 16, 47
    steaming, 27, 250
crab
    Crab Rangoons, *52*, 53
    Singaporean Chili Crab, 146–47, *149*
Crystal Shrimp Dumplings (Har Gow), 34–35, 36–39
cucumbers
    Accordion Cucumber Salad, *206*, 207
curry
    Chicken Katsu Curry, 120–22, *121*
    Curry Laksa, *144*, 145
    Shrimp and Pineapple Thai Curry, *118*, 119
curry blocks, 15

D

deep-frying, 16, 47
dim sum. *See* small plates
Din Tai Fung Green Beans, Copycat, *188*, 189
Drunken Noodles (Pad Kee Mao), *86*, 87
duck
    Auntie's Whole Braised Duck (Lor Ark), *152*, 153
dumplings
    Har Gow (Crystal Shrimp Dumplings), 34–35, 36–39
    Not Boring Vegetarian Dumplings, 198–99, *200–201*
    Pork Dumplings, 40–41, *42–43*
    Siu Mai (Steamed Pork and Shrimp Dumplings), 54, *55–57*
dumpling wrappers, 22
    Homemade Dumpling Wrappers, *246*, 247

E

egg noodles, 21
    Chicken Lo Mein, 80, *81*
    Hokkien Prawn Mee, *132*, 140–41
    Taiwanese Beef Noodles, 94, *95*
eggs
    Ah Ma's Mee Hoon Kueh with, 154–55, *156–57*
    Egg Drop Soup, *168*, 169
    Hokkien Prawn Mee, *132*, 140–41
    Hot and Sour Soup, 170, *171*
    Shrimp Fried Rice, 112, *113*
    Soy-Marinated Eggs, *62*, 63
    Tomato Egg, *192*, 193
equipment, 27, 250

F

fish cakes, 88, 142
    Basic Udon Noodle Soup, 88, *89*
    Char Kway Teow, 142, *143*
fish sauce, 15
    Nước Chấm, *260*, 261
Fish, Steamed, Cantonese, 123, *124–25*
Fried Rice, Shrimp, 112, *113*

G

General Tso's Chicken, *106*, 107
Ginger Scallion Sauce, *256*, 257
gochugaru, 16
    See also chili and chili sauces
green beans
    Copycat Din Tai Fung Green Beans, *188*, 189
Ground Beef Bulgogi, *116*, 117

H

Hainanese Chicken Rice, 136–37, *138–39*
Har Gow (Crystal Shrimp Dumplings), 34–35, 36–39
ho fun, 21
    Char Kway Teow, 142, *143*
    Ho Fun (Beef Chow Fun), *78*, 79
    Pad See Ew, 84, *85*
Hokkien Prawn Mee, *132*, 140–41
Hot and Sour Soup, 170, *171*

I

ice cream
    Ice Cream Mochi, *218*, 219, 221
    Ice Cream Tempura, 224, *225*
    No-Churn Pandan Coconut Ice Cream, *228*, 229
ingredients, 15–17, 21–22
Instant Ramen, Spicy Miso, 90, *91*

J

Japanese Clear Soup, *176*, 177
Jook, Chinese (Congee), *172*, 173

K

kecap manis, 15
Kimchi, Easy, 196–97, *197*
knives, 27
Korean Bean Sprouts, Banchan-Style, *194*, 195

L

Laksa, Curry, *144*, 145
lard, 35
lo mein noodles, 21
    Chicken Lo Mein, 80, *81*
Lor Ark (Auntie's Whole Braised Duck), 152, *153*

M

mango
    Lazy Girl Mango Sticky Rice, 216, *217*
    Mango Mochi, *218*, 219, 221
matcha
    Brown Butter Matcha Cheesecake with Cookie Butter Crust, *214–15*, 226, *227*
    Matcha Mochi, *218*, 219, 221
mee hoon
    Ah Ma's Mee Hoon Kueh, 154–55, *156–57*
    See also yellow noodles
mirin, 15
miso
    Miso Soup, 178, *179*
    Spicy Miso Instant Ramen, 90, *91*
Mochi, Ice Cream, *218,* 219, 221
mung bean vermicelli noodles, 22
    Fried Pork Spring Rolls, 48, *49*
    Not Boring Vegetarian Dumplings, 198–99, *200–201*
mushrooms
    Chicken Lo Mein, 80, *81*
    Fried Pork Spring Rolls, 48, *49*
    Hot and Sour Soup, 170, *171*
    Japanese Clear Soup, 176, *177*
    Miso Soup, 178, *179*
    Not Boring Vegetarian Dumplings, 198–99, *200–201*
    Siu Mai (Steamed Pork and Shrimp Dumplings), 54, *55–57*
    Spicy Miso Instant Ramen, 90, *91*
    Tom Yum Goong (Thai Hot and Sour Soup with Shrimp), 174

N

noodles, 21–22, 73–97
    Ah Ma's Mee Hoon Kueh, 154–55, *156–57*
    Basic Udon Noodle Soup, 88, *89*
    Beef Chow Fun (Ho Fun), 78, *79*
    Char Kway Teow, 142, *143*
    Chicken Lo Mein, 80, *81*
    Curry Laksa, *144*, 145
    Drunken Noodles (Pad Kee Mao), *86*, 87
    45-Minute Phở Gà (Chicken Pho), 92, *93*
    Hand-Pulled Noodles, 243, *244–45*
    Hokkien Prawn Mee, *132*, 140–41
    Homemade Flat Rice Noodles, 251, *252–53*
    Oxtail Phở, 96, *97*
    Pad See Ew, 84, *85*
    Pad Thai, *82*, 83
    Scallion Oil Noodles, 76, *77*
    Spicy Miso Instant Ramen, 90, *91*
    Taiwanese Beef Noodles, *94*, 95
Not Boring Vegetarian Dumplings, 198–99, *200–201*
Nước Chấm, 260, *261*

O

oil, 16
onions
    pickled onions, 128
    Quick Chili-Vinegar Onions, 202, *203*
onions, green. *See* scallions
Orange Chicken, 104, *105*
Oxtail Phở, 96, *97*
oyster sauce, 15

P

Pad Kee Mao (Drunken Noodles), *86*, 87
Pad See Ew, 84, *85*
pad Thai noodles, 21
    Pad Thai, *82*, 83
palm sugar, 16
Pancakes, Scallion, *58*, 59, *60–61*
Pandan Coconut Ice Cream, No-Churn, 228, *229*
pantry staples, 15–17, 21–22
Papaya Salad (Som Tum), *208*, 209
Peanut Dipping Sauce, 262, *263*
Perfect Steamed Rice, 242
pho
    45-Minute Phở Gà (Chicken Pho), 92, *93*
    Oxtail Phở, 96, *97*
pho noodles, 21
pickled onions, 128
pineapple
    Shrimp and Pineapple Thai Curry, *118*, 119
    Sweet and Sour Pork, *110*, 111
pork
    Air Fryer Char Siu (Chinese BBQ Pork), 68, *69*
    Bak Kut Teh, *150*, 151
    Chinese Watercress Soup, *180*, 181
    Crispy Pork Belly, 66, *67*
    Fried Pork Spring Rolls, 48, *49*
    Hokkien Prawn Mee, *132*, 140–41
    meatballs, Ah Ma's Mee Hoon Kueh with, 154–55, *156–57*

pork (continued)
- Pork Dumplings, 40–41, 42–43
- Shrimp and Pork Summer Rolls, 50, *51*
- Siu Mai (Steamed Pork and Shrimp Dumplings), 54, *55–57*
- Sweet and Sour Pork, *110*, 111

potatoes
- Chicken Katsu Curry, 120–22, *121*
- Easy Kimchi, 196–97, *197*

pots and pans, 27

prawns
- Hokkien Prawn Mee, *132*, 140–41

R

Rainbow Carrot Ribbon Salad, 204, *205*

ramen
- Spicy Miso Instant Ramen, 90, *91*

Rangoons, Crab, 52, *53*

rice
- Claypot Rice, 158, *159*
- Congee (Chinese Jook), *172*, 173
- Hainanese Chicken Rice, 136–37, *138–39*
- Lazy Girl Mango Sticky Rice, 216, *217*
- The Perfect Steamed Rice, 242
- Shrimp Fried Rice, 112, *113*
- *See also* takeout-style dishes

rice noodles, 21, 22
- Beef Chow Fun (Ho Fun), *78*, 79
- Char Kway Teow, *142*, 143
- Curry Laksa, *144*, 145
- Drunken Noodles (Pad Kee Mao), *86*, 87
- 45-Minute Phở Gà (Chicken Pho), 92, *93*
- Homemade Flat Rice Noodles, 251, *252–53*
- Not Boring Vegetarian Dumplings, 198–99, *200–201*
- Oxtail Phở, 96, *97*
- Pad See Ew, 84, *85*
- Pad Thai, *82*, 83
- Shrimp and Pork Summer Rolls with, 50, *51*

rice vinegar, 15

rice wine, 15

rock sugar, 16

S

salads
- Accordion Cucumber Salad, 206, *207*
- Rainbow Carrot Ribbon Salad, 204, *205*
- Som Tum (Papaya Salad), *208*, 209

salt, 16

sauces
- Ginger Scallion Sauce, 256, *257*
- Nước Chấm, 260, *261*
- pantry staple sauces, 15, 16
- Peanut Dipping Sauce, 262, *263*
- Sweet Chili Sauce, 258, *259*
- Wet-Wet Sauce, 254, *255*

sausage. *See* Chinese sausage

scallions
- Ginger Scallion Sauce, 256, *257*
- Scallion Oil Noodles, 76, *77*
- Scallion Pancakes, *58*, 59, *60–61*

sesame oil, 16

Shaking Beef, *128*, 129

shaoxing wine, 15

shrimp
- Char Kway Teow, *142*, 143
- Curry Laksa, *144*, 145
- deveining, 46
- Har Gow (Crystal Shrimp Dumplings), 34–35, *36–39*
- Pad See Ew, 84, *85*
- Pad Thai, *82*, 83
- Shrimp and Pineapple Thai Curry, *118*, 119
- Shrimp and Pork Summer Rolls, 50, *51*
- Shrimp Fried Rice, 112, *113*
- Shrimp Wontons, 44–46
- shrimp Wonton Soup, *166*, 167
- Siu Mai (Steamed Pork and Shrimp Dumplings), 54, *55–57*
- Tom Yum Goong (Thai Hot and Sour Soup with Shrimp), 174
- Walnut Shrimp, *114*, 115

Singaporean dishes, 133–59
- Ah Ma's Mee Hoon Kueh, 154–55, *156–57*
- Auntie's Whole Braised Duck (Lor Ark), *152*, 153
- Bak Kut Teh, *150*, 151
- Char Kway Teow, *142*, 143
- Claypot Rice, 158, *159*
- Curry Laksa, *144*, 145
- Hainanese Chicken Rice, 136–37, *138–39*
- Hokkien Prawn Mee, *132*, 140–41
- Singaporean Chili Crab, 146–47, *149*

Siu Mai (Steamed Pork and Shrimp Dumplings), 54, *55–57*

small plates, 31–69
- Air Fryer Char Siu (Chinese BBQ Pork), 68, *69*
- Crab Rangoons, 52, *53*
- Crispy Pork Belly, 66, *67*
- Fried Pork Spring Rolls, *48*, 49
- Har Gow (Crystal Shrimp Dumplings), 34–35, *36–39*
- Pork Dumplings, 40–41, *42–43*
- Scallion Pancakes, *58*, 59, *60–61*
- Shrimp and Pork Summer Rolls, 50, *51*
- Shrimp Wontons, 44–46
- Siu Mai (Steamed Pork and Shrimp Dumplings), 54, *55–57*
- Soy-Marinated Eggs, 62, *63*
- Takeout-Style Chicken Wings, 64, *65*

Som Tum (Papaya Salad), *208*, 209

soups, 163–81
- Ah Ma's Mee Hoon Kueh, 154–55, *156–57*
- Bak Kut Teh, *150*, 151
- Basic Udon Noodle Soup, 88, *89*
- Chinese Watercress Soup, *180*, 181
- Congee (Chinese Jook), *172*, 173
- Curry Laksa, *144*, 145
- Egg Drop Soup, *168*, 169

270 • INDEX

45-Minute Phở Gà (Chicken Pho), 92, 93
Hot and Sour Soup, 170, 171
Japanese Clear Soup, 176, 177
Miso Soup, 178, 179
Oxtail Phở, 96, 97
Spicy Miso Instant Ramen, 90, 91
Tom Yum Goong (Thai Hot and Sour Soup with Shrimp), 174
Wonton Soup, 166, 167
soy sauce, 15
Soy-Marinated Eggs, 62, 63
Soy Sauce Chicken, 126, 127
Spring Rolls, Pork, Fried, 48, 49
spring roll wrappers, 22
squid
Hokkien Prawn Mee, 132, 140–41
sriracha, 16
Steamed Rice, Perfect, 242
steaming equipment and technique, 27, 250
Strawberry Mochi, 218, 219, 221
sugar, 16
Summer Rolls, Shrimp and Pork, 50, 51
summer roll wrappers, 22
Sweet and Sour Pork, 110, 111
sweets, 213–35
Brown Butter Matcha Cheesecake with Cookie Butter Crust, 214–15, 226, 227
Ice Cream Mochi, 218, 219, 221
Ice Cream Tempura, 224, 225
Lazy Girl Mango Sticky Rice, 216, 217
Mom's Apple Cake, 222, 223
No-Churn Pandan Coconut Ice Cream, 228, 229
Thai Tea Tres Leches, 232–34, 233
Vietnamese Coffee Tiramisu, 230, 231

T

Taiwanese Beef Noodles, 94, 95
takeout-style dishes, 101–29
Cantonese Steamed Fish, 123, 124–25
Chicken Katsu Curry, 120–22, 121
General Tso's Chicken, 106, 107
Ground Beef Bulgogi, 116, 117
Orange Chicken, 104, 105
Shaking Beef, 128, 129
Shrimp and Pineapple Thai Curry, 118, 119
Shrimp Fried Rice, 112, 113
Soy Sauce Chicken, 126, 127
Sweet and Sour Pork, 110, 111
Takeout-Style Chicken Wings, 64, 65
30-Minute Beef and Broccoli, 108, 109
Walnut Shrimp, 114, 115
tea
Thai Tea Tres Leches, 232–34, 233
Tempura, Ice Cream, 224, 225
Thai Curry, Shrimp and Pineapple, 118, 119
Thai Tea Tres Leches, 232–34, 233
Tiramisu, Vietnamese Coffee, 230, 231

toasted sesame oil, 16
tofu
Hot and Sour Soup, 170, 171
Miso Soup, 178, 179
Pad Thai, 82, 83
tomatoes
Shaking Beef, 128, 129
Tomato Egg, 192, 193
Tres Leches, Thai Tea, 232–34, 233

U

udon noodles, 22
Basic Udon Noodle Soup, 88, 89

V

vegetables and vegetarian dishes, 185–209
Accordion Cucumber Salad, 206, 207
Banchan-Style Korean Bean Sprouts, 194, 195
Copycat Din Tai Fung Green Beans, 188, 189
Easy Kimchi, 196–97, 197
Not Boring Vegetarian Dumplings, 198–99, 200–201
Quick Chili-Vinegar Onions, 202, 203
Rainbow Carrot Ribbon Salad, 204, 205
Som Tum (Papaya Salad), 208, 209
10-Minute Bok Choy, 190, 191
Tomato Egg, 192, 193
vermicelli noodles, 22
Curry Laksa, 144, 145
Fried Pork Spring Rolls, 48, 49
Not Boring Vegetarian Dumplings, 198–99, 200–201
Shrimp and Pork Summer Rolls, 50, 51
Vietnamese Coffee Tiramisu, 230, 231

W

Walnut Shrimp, 114, 115
Watercress Soup, Chinese, 180, 181
Wet-Wet Sauce, 254, 255
white noodles, 21
Hokkien Prawn Mee, 132, 140–41
Scallion Oil Noodles, 76, 77
woks, 27
Wontons, Shrimp, 44–46
Wonton Soup, 166, 167
wonton wrappers, 22
Homemade Wonton Skins, 248, 249

Y

yellow noodles, 21
Hokkien Prawn Mee, 132, 140–41
See also egg noodles

INDEX • 271

Clarkson Potter/Publishers
An imprint of the Crown Publishing Group
A division of Penguin Random House LLC
1745 Broadway, New York, NY 10019
clarksonpotter.com
penguinrandomhouse.com

Copyright © 2025 by Cassie Yeung
Photographs copyright © 2025 by Jenny Huang
Penguin Random House values and supports copyright. Copyright fuels creativity, encourages diverse voices, promotes free speech, and creates a vibrant culture. Thank you for buying an authorized edition of this book and for complying with copyright laws by not reproducing, scanning, or distributing any part of it in any form without permission. You are supporting writers and allowing Penguin Random House to continue to publish books for every reader. Please note that no part of this book may be used or reproduced in any manner for the purpose of training artificial intelligence technologies or systems.

Clarkson Potter is a trademark and Potter with colophon is a registered trademark of Penguin Random House LLC.

Library of Congress Cataloging-in-Publication Data
Names: Yeung, Cassie author | Huang, Jenny (Photographer) photographer. Title: Bad b*tch in the kitch : craveable Asian recipes to ditch the takeout / Cassie Yeung ; photographs by Jenny Huang. Other titles: Bad bitch in the kitchen. Identifiers: LCCN 2025003311 (print) | LCCN 2025003312 (ebook) | ISBN 9780593797853 (hardcover) | ISBN 9780593797860 (ebook) Subjects: LCSH: Cooking, Asian | LCGFT: Cookbooks.
Classification: LCC TX724.5.A1 Y486 2025 (print) | LCC TX724.5.A1 (ebook) |
DDC 641.595—dc23/eng/20250227
LC record available at
https://lccn.loc.gov/2025003311
LC ebook record available at
https://lccn.loc.gov/2025003312

ISBN 978-0-593-79785-3
Ebook ISBN 978-0-593-79786-0

Editor: Susan Roxborough
Editorial assistant: Elaine Hennig
Designer: Robert Diaz
Art director: Ian Dingman
Production editor: Natalie Blachere
Production: Kim Tyner
Production designer: Christina Self
Compositors: Merri Ann Morrell and Nick Patton
Assistant photography: Thomas Kuczynski
Food stylist: Tyna Hoang
Assistant food stylists: Alyssa Kondracki and Scotty Fletcher
Prop stylist: Maggie DiMarco
Assistant prop stylist: Loz Mcinnes
Recipe tester: Emily Stephenson
Copyeditor: Eldes Tran
Proofreaders: L. J. Young, Mike Richards, and Ann Roberts
Indexer: Thérèse Shere
Publicist: Felix Cruz
Marketer: Stephanie Davis

Manufactured in China

10 9 8 7 6 5 4 3 2 1

First Edition

The authorized representative in the EU for product safety and compliance is Penguin Random House Ireland, Morrison Chambers, 32 Nassau Street, Dublin D02 YH68, Ireland, https://eu-contact.penguin.ie.